W9-BWP-116

AN
AMERICAN DILEMMA
REVISITED

AN AMERICAN DILEMMA REVISITED

Race Relations in a Changing World

Obie Clayton, Jr.
Editor

RUSSELL SAGE FOUNDATION · NEW YORK

The Russell Sage Foundation

The Russell Sage Foundation, one of the oldest of America's general purpose foundations, was established in 1907 by Mrs. Margaret Olivia Sage for "the improvement of social and living conditions in the United States." The Foundation seeks to fulfill this mandate by fostering the development and dissemination of knowledge about the country's political, social, and economic problems. While the Foundation endeavors to assure the accuracy and objectivity of each book it publishes, the conclusions and interpretations in Russell Sage Foundation publications are those of the authors and not of the Foundation, its Trustees, or its staff. Publication by Russell Sage, therefore, does not imply Foundation endorsement.

BOARD OF TRUSTEES
William Julius Wilson, Chair

Anne Pitts Carter	Ira Katznelson	Eugene Smolensky
Joel E. Cohen	Ellen Condliffe Lagemann	Harold Tanner
Peggy C. Davis	James G. March	Marta Tienda
Pheobe C. Ellsworth	Howard Raiffa	Eric Wanner
Timothy A. Hulquist	Neil J. Smelser	

Library of Congress Cataloging-in-Publication Data

An American dilemma revisited: race relations in a changing world / Obie Clayton, editor.
    p. cm.
Includes bibliographical references and index.
ISBN 0-87154-156-4 (hb : alk. paper). – ISBN 0-87154-157-2 (pb : alk. paper)
1. United States–Race relations–Congresses. 2. Afro-Americans–Social conditions–1975-
–Congresses. 3. Afro-Americans–Economic dilemma–Congresses. 4. Myrdal, Gunnar,
1898- American dilemma–Congresses. I. Clayton, Obie, 1954-
E185.615.A6718   1996
305.896'073–dc20   95-47475
                                                    CIP

Copyright © 1996 by Russell Sage Foundation. All rights reserved. Printed in the United States of America. No part of this publication may be reproduced, stored in a retrieval system, or transmitted in any form or by any means, electronic, mechanical, photocopying, recording, or otherwise, without the prior written permission of the publisher.

Reproduction by the United States Government in whole or in part is permitted for any purpose.

The paper used in this publication meets the minimum requirements of American National Standard for Information Sciences–Permanence of Paper for Printed Library Materials. ANSI Z39.48-1992.

Text design by John Johnston.

RUSSELL SAGE FOUNDATION
112 East 64th Street, New York, New York 10021
10 9 8 7 6 5 4 3 2

Contents

Contributors

Sissela Bok is Distinguished Fellow at the Harvard Center for Population and Development Studies.

Obie Clayton, Jr. is Director of the Morehouse Research Institute and Associate Professor of Sociology, Morehouse College, Georgia.

Wilbur Watson is Research Associate at Morehouse Research Institute.

Stephen Graubard is Professor at Brown University and Editor of *Daedalus*.

Robert A. Dentler is Faculty Fellow at the William Monroe Trotter Institute, University of Massachusetts at Boston.

Reynolds Farley is Research Scientist at the Population Studies Center, University of Michigan.

Ronald F. Ferguson is Senior Research Associate at the Malcolm Wiener Center for Social Policy and Associate Professor of Public Policy at the John F. Kennedy School of Government, Harvard University.

William Darity, Jr. is the Cary C. Boshamer Professor of Economics at the University of North Carolina at Chapel Hill.

John Sibley Butler is Professor of Sociology and Management at the Unviersity of Texas at Austin.

Walter R. Allen is Professor of Sociology at the University of California at Los Angeles.

Joseph O. Jewell is a student in the sociology doctoral program at the University of California at Los Angeles.

Susan Welch is Dean of the College of Arts and Sciences at the University of California at Los Angeles.

Michael W. Combs is Associate Professor of Political Science at the University of Nebraska at Lincoln.

Lee Sigelman is Professor of Political Science at George Washington University.

Timothy Bledsoe is Associate Professor of Political Science at Wayne State University.

Samuel Walker is Professor of Criminal Justice at the University of Nebraska at Omaha.

Cassia C. Spohn is Professor of Criminal Justice at the University of Nebraska at Omaha.

Antonio McDaniel is Associate Professor of Sociology and Member of the Population Studies Center at the University of Pennsylvania.

Doris Wilkinson is Professor of Sociology at the University of Kentucky.

Preface and Acknowledgments

This book is intended to provide an interdisciplinary perspective on race relations and social change in the United States since the 1940s. The essays have been selected for their comprehensive and thoughtful analyses of the effects of racial discrimination in American society. The book is designed for use as either a main or a supplemental text for courses in sociology, race relations, urban studies, political science, and other disciplines touching on social problems related to race. The individual chapters examine a variety of issues, including education, political and economic participation, and gender relations. This breadth, I believe, will help to illustrate how pervasive the issue of race remains in contemporary America.

The research necessary to produce this volume could not have occurred without the financial support of several foundations. I am particularly grateful to the Foundation for Child Development, the Ford Foundation, the Rockefeller Foundation, and the AT&T Foundation. I would also like to express my sincere appreciation to the Russell Sage Foundation, and its President, Eric Wanner, for their financial and editorial assistance. The staff of the Russell Sage Foundation has consistently provided helpful insights and fair criticisms regarding the manuscript and guided it through final production.

Finally, I would like to thank my administrative assistant, Iretha Stoney, for her deft handling of the correspondence associated with the book. Stephen Graubard, of *Daedalus*, proved to be a valued contributor, editor, and friend, and I am deeply indebted to him. Thanks go as well to my colleagues at the Morehouse Research Institute and Morehouse College. And, most importantly, I am grateful to my wife, Amy, and my children, Michael and Kristen, for their support and patience during the many hours I devoted to this project.

Obie Clayton, Jr.

Sissela Bok

Foreword

AN AMERICAN DILEMMA REVISITED was the title my father Gunnar Myrdal had given to his final, unfinished book. His aim was to reexamine all that had gone into writing *An American Dilemma,* to reevaluate its conclusions in the light of how race relations in America had evolved in the ensuing decades, and "to express my worried thoughts about the future development."[1]

But the task proved too great. In 1985, at the age of eighty-seven, increasingly immobile and blind, and unable to carry out or even oversee the research and the revisions that he knew were needed, he decided not to submit his manuscript for publication.[2] He wrote to André Schiffrin, his publisher, that, as an old author, he could not in good conscience sign off on a book once he knew that he could not go over the proofs.

My father used to say that some people were better than their books, whereas others were not as good as their books. As a child, I was perplexed by this distinction. How did he arrive at it? And what yardstick could he possibly be using? What kind of goodness, I later wondered, did he have in mind? But one thing seemed certain: his own preference. No matter what the personal sacrifice, he would rather leave behind him at least one great book than the memory of a life that, however worthy in other respects, had produced only mediocre writings.

This was the passionate scholarly commitment that he brought to the writing of *An American Dilemma.* Nothing less could do justice to the power and complexity of the problems he had been asked to tackle. He would sacrifice many pleasures, and much that most of us regard as indispensable to our lives and relationships, to have a chance to produce work that truly contributed to human knowledge and to the common good. When asked by my sister, Kaj Fölster, what had been the greatest moment of his life, my father answered that it had been when he finally stood at the Princeton train station, "with the manuscript for the *Dilemma* in my hands—ready! All that I had lived for."

In 1938, Dr. Frederick Keppel of the Carnegie Corporation asked my father to come to the United States to study "the American Negro Problem."[3] Keppel's courage, honesty, warm-heartedness, and imagination impressed

my father deeply. Keppel insisted that my father begin his study by traveling through the South rather than settling down to do library research on
race issues. My father soon recognized Keppel's wisdom in forcing him to
confront the realities of discrimination right away: "I was shocked and
scared to the bones by all the evils I saw, and by the serious political implications of the problem which I could not fail to appreciate from the beginning."[4]

It was clear from the outset that the problem my father had been asked
to study, far from affecting blacks alone or simply dividing blacks and
whites, was lodged in the hearts of all Americans: "It is there that the interracial tension has its focus. It is there that the decisive struggle goes on.
This is the central viewpoint of this treatise."[5]

This struggle generates the dilemma in the book's title. How can
Americans square the nation's lofty ideals—the American Creed—with the
base realities of racial discrimination? How can they claim to respect the
dignity of all persons, equality, and the inalienable rights to freedom, justice, and a fair opportunity, while countenancing pervasive violations of the
dignity of blacks and of their rights to that freedom, that justice, and that
fair opportunity?

> The Negro in America has not yet been given the elemental civil
> and political rights of formal democracy, including a fair opportu-
> nity to earn his living, upon which a general accord was already
> won when the American Creed was first taking form. And this
> anachronism constitutes the contemporary "problem" both to
> Negroes and to whites.[6]

My father saw no reason why the contradiction between principles and
practices could not be overcome.[7] The challenge for the nation lay in living
up to its principles by altering its practices. Merely stating the dilemma,
however, would do little to bring about such a change. Only by exposing
the underlying conditions to full view and by exploring the details of possible remedies could the process of change be set in motion.

For this purpose, he assembled a remarkable team of social scientists to
conduct meticulous research on all facets of the problem and to write preliminary drafts for a number of the chapters. Among these collaborators
were Ralph Bunche, Franklin Frazier, Charles S. Johnson, Otto Klineberg,
Arnold Rose, and Dorothy Swaine Thomas. In reminiscing about his collaboration with them, my father would often speak of the rare intellectual
camaraderie that he experienced with these coworkers. To be sure, there
were disagreements over what direction to take and what parts to include
or leave out. He was never an easy person to work with, and some expressed

resentment at his pressing them as hard as he pressed himself. But the magnitude of the challenge and the fact that so much of the writing had to be done in wartime could easily have derailed the project had he not been so determined to bring it to closure.

It is no wonder, given the priority my father always gave to authorship, that an important part of the dialogue I myself had with him concerned writing and scholarship. His insistence that human problems call for interdisciplinary study, combined with his rigorous and probing devotion to the crafts of research and writing, constitute part of what I see as his intellectual legacy. There is a moral side to that legacy as well: the concern to do justice to the complexity of problems such as those surrounding race and the duty to speak the truth as he saw it.

"At least I have never written anything I could be ashamed of," he would say, toward the end of his life, as he thought back over his work. Humble as this statement may sound, it is one that far from all scholars can honestly make. It, too, conveys the honor and personal responsibility that he associated with authorship.[8]

Such a view, however, implies no naive belief that any scholar could ever get at the full "truth" about any matter. Social scientists have to be as wary of all the influences that distort their own research as of the biases and rationalizations that they aim to expose among others. Throughout his life, my father pursued the inquiry into how valuations influence research and into possible means of minimizing, though never eliminating, resulting errors. As I look over my correspondence with him, I am struck by how often he brings up this issue, urging me to take it seriously in my own work. In a letter to me when I was beginning my doctoral studies in philosophy, he wrote:

> I am very excited that you are turning to the ethical problems in philosophy. Please read leisurely my *Political Element in the Development of Economic Theory* and my *Value in Social Theory*. Do not skip my "Postscript." . . . I am asking you this not in order to influence your development. You shall have your own life and not be under the pressure of my thoughts, but I do believe that it is civilized that you know something about how I have been living with this problem of the moral element in scholarly work since my youth. Remember what I point out in the P.S., that I do not feel I have solved the problem—only that I am nearer the truth than my contemporaries.[9]

It was that same "problem of the moral element in scholarly work" that he brought up in talking about the parts of *An American Dilemma* that he considered crucial to addressing *any* complex human problem. It will not do, he suggested, just to sit yourself down in front of whatever you see as the facts, to carry on with your research uncritically, and then to proceed to propose policies, solutions to the problems you address. And you will not have the energy and the courage to persevere without some framework of value premises such as the American Creed to buttress your conviction that change is possible and that your efforts can actually bear fruit. But that very framework is one you can never take for granted, never simply accept from your predecessors or your cultural tradition, and never leave unexplored, lest you risk damaging the integrity of your research.

I can hear him say the same to us now, as we reexamine the issues of race and community in the United States: some that remain dispiritingly similar to those he wrote about and others that are bewilderingly new. Without examining the value premises we bring to our research and policy proposals, we Americans shall be less able to explore these issues with the seriousness that they deserve, and therefore less able to do everything in our power to overcome the dilemma between the ideals of the American Creed and the realities of racial discrimination and all the evils it has brought in its wake.

There were three parts of *An American Dilemma,* my father would often say, that laid the foundations for that work as for *Asian Drama* and his later studies: the pitfalls and challenges that valuations and beliefs posed for social scientists studying issues as complex as those having to do with race in America; the interaction among the factors producing the complexity; and the sober Enlightenment ideals that he cherished to the end of his life in spite of much discouragement about the course of human affairs. Over the years, he would repeatedly suggest that I study these three parts:

> Read my first two Appendices about facts and valuations and beliefs! . . . *then* let's talk about valuation and bias and integrity in the social sciences.

> Read the third Appendix about the "principle of cumulation" and vicious circles, *then* let's talk about the ways in which discrimination, poverty, poor health care, unemployment, and other factors interact.

> Read the last paragraphs of the book and consider its last word, "Enlightenment," *then* let's talk about the possibility of bringing about genuine reforms.

Of the three parts, the one that he saw as most fundamental to all research was the first: the scrutiny, in the first two Appendices to *An American Dilemma,* of the pitfalls and challenges posed by valuations and beliefs.[10] He drew a distinction between beliefs—the ideas people have about reality—and valuations[11]—the ideas that people have of how reality ought to be:

> A person's beliefs, that is his knowledge, can be objectively judged to be true or false and more or less complete. His valuations—that a so-

cial situation or relation is, or was, "just," "right," "fair," "desirable," or the opposite, in some degree of intensity or other—cannot be judged by such objective standards as science provides. In their *"opinions"* people express both their beliefs and their valuations. Usually people don't distinguish what they think they know and what they like or dislike.[12]

Different valuations, moreover, are often in conflict, as in the views of many Americans regarding race. Efforts to deny such conflicts can result in distorted beliefs regarding reality and in the adherence to biases or hidden value premises. When it came to the race issue, my father found these distortions and biases as common among scholars and social theorists as among others, to the great detriment of rigorous social study. "Throughout the history of social studies," he would point out, "the hiding of valuations has served to conceal the inquirer's wish to avoid facing the real issues."[13] This inclination was part of human nature and not to be wondered at:

> When people try to deny, to the outside world and to themselves, that they live in moral compromise and that they ceaselessly and habitually violate their own ideals, they are customarily brought to falsify their perception of reality in order to conceal this from themselves and others. About this, I first became truly aware as a scholar through my work with *An American Dilemma*.[14]

The resulting difficulties for anyone attempting to do research or to make public policy are daunting. My father returned to these difficulties repeatedly in later writings.[15] The problem, he suggested, can never be fully eradicated. All we can do is strive to be as aware as possible of the inevitable limitations, subjectivities, and biases in how we perceive the outside world and our own feelings. Scholars, especially, owe it to themselves and to the public to be as open as possible about the valuations guiding their own research. To this end, he proposed that they should introduce "explicitly stated, specific, and sufficiently concretized value premises" from the outset of a study.[16]

In the case of his American study, my father found that the task was made easier by the fact that the American Creed, with its Enlightenment ideals, was already so clearly known and taught throughout American society. Later, he would conclude that this had been an unusual case, not repeated, for example, in working on his later book, *Asian Drama*, where he found societal valuations to conflict in a much more confusing manner. But no matter what the difficulties, he continued to insist on two requirements without which social scientists could not legitimately study the biases of others: they must make every effort to probe their own unexamined stereotypes and other forms of what he called "opportunistic beliefs"—beliefs that allow them to hold conflicting valuations about, for instance, race and justice, without fully acknowledging the conflict; and they must account openly for the value premises on which they base their research and the steps of reasoning which they employ.

Striving to counter the force of all that goes into skewing perception and deliberation, my father aimed to address the role of values in complex human problems in as rigorously scientific a manner as possible. He hoped thereby to acknowledge the pervasive role of values in human affairs while at the same time stepping back to study them in as objective a manner as he could. To the extent that he succeeded, he would avoid the collapse into simplistic relativism and its byproducts: irrationality, obscurantism, and, too often, the fatalism and intellectual defeatism of so many social scientists about the problems of race, in his day as in ours.[17] Instead, he meant to open his work to the same rigorous criticism to which he subjected that of others, and in this way to help advance the collective body of research and policy-making as far and as fast as possible.

The second part of his book to which my father frequently referred me was the third Appendix, entitled "A Methodological Note on the Principle of Cumulation."[18] This principle, often called that of the "vicious circle," ought, he suggests earlier in the book, to be developed into a main tool in studying social science. The more general term is preferable, a footnote points out, since the changes can work in a desirable direction as well as in an undesirable direction.[19] The principle of cumulation, which he characterizes as a main explanatory theme throughout the book, concerns equilibrium and change in the relationship between interdependent factors:

> White prejudice and discrimination keep the Negro low in standards of living, health, education, manners, and morals. This, in turn, gives support to white prejudice. White prejudice and Negro standards thus mutually "cause" each other. If things remain as they are and have been, this means that the two forces balance each other. Such a static "accommodation" is, however, entirely accidental. If either of the factors changes, this will cause a change in the other factor, too, and cause a process of interaction where the change in one will continually be supported by the reaction of the other factor. The whole system will be moving in the direction of the primary change, but much further. This is what we mean by cumulative causation.[20]

My father had used theories of equilibrium and change in earlier writings in economics.[21] These theories, which have "given us, for the first time, something which approaches a real theory of economic dynamics," he now works out in a more general scheme for the study of social change.[22] In essence, when a number of different debilitating factors, such as discrimination, poor housing, poor health care, and poor schooling affect one another, an equilibrium of sorts can develop that either locks those most severely affected into their predicament or shifts into a downward spiral, a "vicious circle"; but when change for the better is brought to bear on any one of the factors, the effects can be reversed, and a "virtuous circle" can affect the other factors as well.

Intuitively, this view of cumulative causation is powerful, not least as a counter to the counsels of despair that are understandable enough as reactions to prolonged and seemingly intractable social problems. When it comes to the problems of race in America or to other complex linkages of human problems, it is clear that there is not just one factor at play but many interlocking ones. And so long as it is possible to break in at any one point and begin to set in motion more generalized effects for the better throughout the system, there can be no room for defeatism.

Without such a possibility of shifting the equilibrium, and without the examples of so many persons willing to break into the cycles of despair and set in motion changes for the better, none of us might continue to work at social problems. Here again, my father saw a special role for social science in offering a systematic, rational approach to coordinate disparate efforts and to help mobilize large-scale social change. There could be little reason to attempt such change haphazardly. And those who held forth simple remedies for complex problems were not to be trusted. Interrelations are in reality much more complicated than in our abstract illustrations. And

> [i]t is likely that *a rational policy will never work by changing only one factor,* least of all if attempted suddenly and with great force. . . . This, and the impracticality of getting political support for a great and sudden change of just one factor—is the rational refutation of so-called panaceas.[23]

Panaceas and other one-factor solutions, such as those stressing the economic factor as all-important, cannot bring about the desired rational change for the better. "In an interdependent system of dynamic causation there is no 'primary cause' but everything is cause *to* everything else."[24]

In spite of this emphasis, it is often mistakenly thought that my father suggested that any one change could set in motion an entire "virtuous circle," and that there existed some simple, reified, interlocking system for reformers adept at social engineering to manipulate.[25] Clearly, the phrase "social engineering" that he used in earlier writings and in *An American Dilemma* does not help in this regard. But whereas today the phrase has connotations of misguided efforts at technocratic control, my father defined it more neutrally as "the type of practical research which involves rational planning."[26] In the years before coming to America to begin work on his book, my father had, with my mother Alva Myrdal, been instrumental, through such research and planning, in launching a broad set of reforms that came to be known as the Swedish welfare state.[27]

Even in my parents' early writings, the phrase never had the technocratic connotations that it has now assumed. By the time he came to write *An American Dilemma*, my father already had something much more fluid, much subtler in mind than anything resembling a rigid engineering model. He knew, moreover, that what he was learning challenged much of what he had taken for granted. In a letter to Gustav Cassel, his former professor and mentor, he wrote:

> I feel that I am making contact with certain fundamentals in the tragedy of humanity. I cannot yet say that I see clear lines before me. I still feel as if I am swimming in an ocean. . . . I have to dive more deeply than ever into a foreign culture. Even if it is tiring it makes us happy. After all, it is an extraordinary and rare expansion of the personality that we are living through.[28]

Try as I may, I cannot recall ever having heard either of my parents use the expression "social engineering" in conversation during the postwar decades. Yet it has proved irresistible as an epithet for conservative critics to attach to their world view. Others, however, have chosen to bypass the phrase itself and to focus on the underlying theory concerning social change. They have found especially fruitful the view that one can postulate not only vicious but also virtuous circles, in which changes among different but interdependent forces affect one another respectively for the worse or for the better.

This perspective has mattered greatly to me in pursuing my own work, as has my father's critique, both of defeatist acceptance of the status quo with respect to complex human problems and of the faith in one-factor solutions. Rarely have I seen the need for an approach such as his, simultaneously constructive and wary of simplistic answers, as much as in analyzing the debate about the uniquely high levels of violence in America, compared to other industrialized nations. In this debate, scholars as well as policy advocates too often stress some one factor, such as firearm availability, poverty, family breakdown, drugs, or entertainment violence, as being the one and only factor requiring attention; or else they reject all efforts to bring about change with respect to any one of these factors and thus collapse into intellectual defeatism very like the pessimism decried by my father on the part of so many scholars with respect to the evils of segregation.

The third and final part of *An American Dilemma* that my father often stressed is that of its final paragraphs, and especially the last word of the last paragraph: "Enlightenment." The emphasis on the Enlightenment ideals that he espoused from his student days lends support and energy to the first two parts that I have discussed—so long as they are entertained together. The ideals were those of justice, liberty, rationality, the power of people to bring about change in their condition, and the consequent possibility of progress for individuals, groups, nations, and indeed all of humanity.

These ideals were, in one sense, what made it so important for him to tackle the problems having to do with race in America, and later those of European cooperation after World War II, world poverty and exploitation, and the resistance to wars such as those in Vietnam and Afghanistan. His awareness grew of how societies as well as individuals can regress as well as progress—sometimes regress to such bestiality that the very epithet is a slur on the animal kingdom. This is one reason why he agreed so strongly with Dr. Martin Luther King, Jr., that political advocacy and movements for social change must be nonviolent at all times; and why he thought King's stand against the war in Vietnam was fully consonant with his rejection of violence by all sides in the civil rights struggle.[29]

Lars Ingelstam, a younger Swedish colleague and friend of my father, said of him after his death in 1987:

> Gunnar Myrdal wanted to see himself as an analytical intellectual, but there was in him an unbending desire to bring about change, an insistence that the world could be arranged in a more rational manner.[30]

It has become fashionable to decry the Enlightenment values that inspired such engagement on the part of intellectuals. Many speak of the naïveté, if not downright dangerousness, of Enlightenment thinkers who spoke of preferring rational approaches to problems, of the possibility of progress, and of the perfectibility of human beings and societies. But my father's devotion to Enlightenment values was always tempered by the first two factors mentioned earlier—his searching awareness of human limitations and of all the obstacles to rationality and objectivity, along with his understanding of the complexity of interacting forces.

He regarded sheer uncritical faith in rationality and progress and human perfectibility as indeed naive. And he stressed that few of the greatest Enlightenment thinkers cherished any such confidence, untempered by all that can skew rationality and derail progress. To be sure, they saw progress as possible; but few thought it would come about soon, much less automatically. To be sure, they also wrote of the improvability (the word "perfectibility" that is carelessly attributed to them as a group was much less common) of human beings and society; but, again, few thought that such changes could come about except through immense efforts.

My father never saw a reason to change the last word in *An American Dilemma*. He stood to the end by the convictions expressed in the last three paragraphs of that book:

> Social study is concerned with explaining why all these potentially and intentionally good people so often make life a hell for themselves and each other when they live together, whether in a family, a community, a nation, or a world. The fault is certainly not with becoming organized *per se*. In their formal organizations, as we have seen, people invest their highest ideals. These institutions regularly direct the individual toward more cooperation and justice than he would be inclined to observe as an isolated private person. The fault is, rather, that our structures of organizations are too imperfect, each by itself, and badly integrated into a social whole.
>
> The rationalism and moralism which is the driving force behind social study, whether we admit it or not, is the faith that institutions can be improved and strengthened and that people are good enough to live a happier life. With all we know today, there should be the possibility to build a nation and a world where people's great propensities for sympathy and cooperation would not be so thwarted.
>
> To find the practical formulas for this never-ending reconstruction of society is the supreme task of social science. The world catastrophe places tremendous difficulties in our way and may shake our confidence to the depths. Yet we have in social science a greater trust in the improvability of man and society than we have had since the Enlightenment.[31]

NOTES

1. Gunnar Myrdal. *An American Dilemma Revisited.* Unpublished draft, 2.
2. Instead, he asked that the manuscript be available at the Arbetarrörelsens Arkiv in Stockholm, Sweden, where the rest of his papers are kept.
3. For accounts and analyses of this undertaking, see Walter Jackson. *Gunnar Myrdal and America's Conscience* (Chapel Hill: University of North Carolina Press, 1990); Ellen Lagemann. *The Politics of Knowledge: The Carnegie Corporation, Philanthropy, and Public Policy* (Middletown, Conn.: Wesleyan University Press, 1989); and David W. Southern. *Gunnar Myrdal and Black-White Relations: The Use and Abuse of "An American Dilemma," 1944–1969* (Baton Rouge: Louisiana State University Press, 1987).
4. Gunnar Myrdal. *An American Dilemma,* twentieth anniversary ed. (New York: Harper & Row, 1962), p. xxv.

5. Ibid., p. lxxi.

6. Ibid., p. 24.

7. I draw, in this paragraph and the following one, from Chaps. 8 and 9 of Sissela Bok. *Alva Myrdal: A Daughter's Memoir* (Reading, MA.: Addison-Wesley, 1991).

8. For a bibliography of Gunnar Myrdal's works through 1981, see Kerstin Assarsson-Rizzi and Harald Bohrn, eds. *Gunnar Myrdal: A Bibliography, 1919–1981,* 2d ed. (New York: Garland Publishing, 1984). See also Gilles Dostaler, Diane Ethier, and Laurent Lepage, eds. *Gunnar Myrdal and His Works* (Montreal: Harvest House, 1992).

9. Letter from Gunnar Myrdal to Sissela Bok, 23 July 1962, referring to Gunnar Myrdal. *The Political Element in the Development of Economic Theory* (London: Routledge & Kegan Paul, 1930); and Gunnar Myrdal. *Value in Social Theory: A Selection of Essays on Methodology,* ed. Paul Streeten (London: Routledge & Kegan Paul, 1958).

10. Myrdal. "Appendix 1. Note on Valuations and Beliefs." *An American Dilemma,* pp. 1027–1034; reprinted in Myrdal. *Value in Social Theory,* pp. 71–86; Myrdal. "Appendix 2. A Methodological Note on Facts and Valuations in Social Science." *An American Dilemma,* pp. 1035–1064; reprinted in Myrdal. *Value in Social Theory,* pp. 118–153.

11. He preferred the term "valuation" thus specified, to "value," which he found looser and more confusing.

12. Myrdal. *An American Dilemma,* p. 1027.

13. Gunnar Myrdal. *Asian Drama: An Inquiry Into the Poverty of Nations* (New York: Pantheon Books, 1968), p. 32.

14. Gunnar Myrdal. *Hur styrs landet?* (*How is the Land Governed?*) (Stockholm: Rabén och Sjögren, 1982), p. 263. My translation.

15. See, especially, Gunnar Myrdal. *Objectivity in Social Research* (New York: Pantheon Books, 1967).

16. Myrdal. *An American Dilemma,* p. 1043.

17. For a discussion of Myrdal's views on this subject, see Michel Rosier. "On the Hypothetical Character of `Moral Premises.'" In Dostaler, Ethier, and Lepage, eds. *Gunnar Myrdal and His Works,* pp. 174–88; and Jacques Peltier. "Myrdal and Value-Loaded Concepts," in ibid., pp. 188–205.

18. Myrdal. *An American Dilemma,* pp. 1065–1072; reprinted in Myrdal. *Value in Social Theory,* 198–205.

19. Myrdal. *An American Dilemma,* p. 75.

20. Ibid.

21. Writings for which he was awarded the 1974 Nobel Prize in economics.

22. Myrdal. *An American Dilemma,* p. 1065.

23. Ibid. p. 77.

24. Ibid. p. 78.

25. See, for example, Jackson. *Gunnar Myrdal and America's Conscience,* p. 197.

26. Myrdal. *An American Dilemma,* p. 1044.

27. The book by Alva Myrdal and Gunnar Myrdal in which they proposed these reforms is *Kris i Befolkningsfrågan (Crisis in the Population Question)* (Stockholm: Bonniers, 1934).

28. Gunnar Myrdal, letter to Gustav Cassel, January 1939. My translation.
29. The two met only once, when Dr. Martin Luther King, Jr. and Mrs. Coretta King came to my parents' Stockholm apartment for dinner in December 1964, the day after King received the Nobel Peace Prize in Oslo.
30. Lars Ingelstam. "Kampen mot cynismen: minnesord om Gunnar Myrdal." Unpublished comments made 2 June 1987; quoted in Sissela Bok. "Introduction." In Dostaler, Ethier, and Lepage, eds. *Gunnar Myrdal and His Works*, p. 3.
31. Myrdal. *An American Dilemma*, p. 1024.

Obie Clayton, Jr. · *Wilbur Watson*

Introduction

AN AMERICAN DILEMMA REVISITED grew out of a symposium hosted in 1994 by Morehouse College and the Morehouse Research Institute. The symposium was conceived in memory of Gunnar Myrdal, author of the monumental study *An American Dilemma: The Negro Problem and Modern Democracy* (1944), from which the symposium drew its title. In his classic work, Myrdal developed a detailed historical, social, and economic inquiry into the status and life chances of African Americans during the period between the Great Depression of the 1930s and World War II. One of the products of the Morehouse symposium is this volume featuring essays by participants in the symposium. The chapters in this book assess the status of African Americans in various areas of contemporary American society since Myrdal's research and writings of the 1930s and 1940s. The authors address the interactions of race with the political, economic, educational, and justice institutions in the United States. Related issues such as gender and demographic shifts are also discussed.

Most of the problems that Myrdal saw as critical to the plight of African Americans remain prevalent: poverty and unemployment continue to be unacceptably high; crime and delinquency are rampant in our cities and suburbs; and racial discrimination and prejudice continue to divide Americans. When Myrdal's book was first published, racial segregation was widely accepted as a structural feature of everyday life in the United States. The belief among whites that they were innately superior to blacks was reinforced by the separate and unequal public accommodations in schools, employment opportunities, housing, and other accoutrements given legal sanction by the 1896 *Plessy v. Ferguson* decision which upheld segregation with its "separate but equal" ruling. Racial polarization in the United States was exacerbated by the inability, or unwillingness, of the federal, state, and local governments to enforce the laws of the land, especially the Fourteenth and Fifteenth Amendments to the Constitution. Blacks were repeatedly thwarted in their attempts to achieve equal and humane public accommodations. This, combined with de jure segregation in all vital areas of life contributed to the persistence of racial prejudice and discrimination.

Many African Americans gave up hope that any real change would occur in the South, where prejudice and discrimination were worst, and moved North in search of better futures. This sense of hopelessness is frequently cited as the major cause for the mass migration of African Americans from the South throughout the century. In 1900, only 10 percent of African Americans lived in northern cities; by the mid-1960s 50 percent resided in northern cities.

Many economists and historians refer to the decades after 1940 as a watershed for African Americans—a time of building, creativity, and economic progress. These decades, however, also witnessed the rise of a large African American underclass. Migrating African Americans often lacked the resources and education that employers demanded and ended up settling in inner cities under conditions of high unemployment and abject poverty, which were often worse than the conditions they had sought to escape in the South. This migration coincided with an awareness of a host of new urban social problems created by white flight: the migration of jobs out of the central city; the construction of highways, which often destroyed neighborhoods; and increases in crime, delinquency, and school dropout rates.

In *The Truly Disadvantaged*, William Wilson (1987) suggests that the ghetto poor, a group which is disproportionately African American, have become divorced from the lifestyle associated with American culture. Wilson argues that because members of this urban underclass are both spatially and culturally isolated from the middle class, they are denied the opportunity to adopt middle-class values and norms. This residential segregation has allowed generations to grow up without hope for advancement. Racial prejudice compounds the problem. Bobo and Klugel (1991) found that whites still perceive African Americans as more willing to live on welfare and as less intelligent and career-oriented than whites. Other recent studies (Ferguson, 1994; Reich, 1992) suggest that African Americans are losing ground in today's labor market. To make the preceding point more salient, unemployment among African Americans is now significantly higher than it was during the 1940s. According to the authors of *A Common Destiny* (Jaynes and Williams, 1989), the unemployment rate among black and white men was virtually equal in the 1940s, with only 1 man in 10 among both blacks and whites unemployed. By the 1980s, however, fewer than 8 in 10 black men were employed, while the unemployment rate among white men remained virtually unchanged. The same study illustrated that white women are more likely to be employed than black women. Another way of expressing the same finding is to examine the unemployment ratio of black to white workers. This ratio was 1.69 in 1948, but had increased to 2.32 in 1983 (Clayton, 1992).

The writings in this volume do not argue that no economic gains were achieved by African Americans from 1940 to 1980, but rather that improvements were concentrated in a relatively short time span, between the late 1960s and mid-1970s, when federal antidiscrimination laws were being strictly enforced. This federal activism led to a dramatic increase in the number of African Americans employed by federal contractors or in firms subject to affirmative action requirements. However, the advancements appear to have waned or ended entirely in the mid-1970s. Moreover, since the 1980s there has been a public backlash against any set-aside programs based on race, and the courts have generally ruled that these programs are unconstitutional.

At the heart of this book is the question of whether the presence of an African American "underclass" has become a permanent feature on the American landscape. Have we become, as Gunnar Myrdal argued in 1944, a caste-ridden society which passes the same social status from generation to generation? If the answer to these questions is yes, what are the implications for racial equality and economic parity? This book will examine the factors that have lead to declining economic conditions for many African Americans, and it will suggest ways to improve their economic standing. The authors examine the complex interactions among the problems that contribute to the disadvantaged position of African Americans in today's society: prejudicial attitudes limit African Americans' access to jobs and housing; residential segregation isolates African Americans, which can breed negative attitudes and behaviors on both sides of the racial divide; high unemployment and low wages limit access to many of the basic amenities taken for granted by other Americans.

In chapter 1, Stephen R. Graubard frames the historical background within which Myrdal's research took place. Graubard argues that even though animosities between blacks and whites have declined somewhat, race remains a pressing problem in the United States. In contemporary America, factors associated with race have increasingly been confused with structural changes in the economy, economic dislocations of workers, and changes in social class and lifestyles. Graubard shows how this social-historical and economic background shapes so many of America's race-related social problems.

In chapter 2, Robert A. Dentler examines what strides African Americans have made in the political arena. When Myrdal conducted his research, African Americans residing in the South were effectively excluded from the political system by the legalized discrimination of the Jim Crow laws, persistent prejudice, and violence. The violence faced by African Americans during the 1940s was almost as frequent as it was after Reconstruction. Although laws have changed and African Americans are widely enfranchised, Dentler illustrates that African-American political power has not matched their electoral participation.

The causes and problems of residential segregation are the topic of chapter 3. Like Myrdal, Reynolds Farley suggests that racial residential segregation is one of the key factors leading to the educational and economic disadvantage of African Americans. In essence, many African Americans are stuck in poverty due to their cultural and spatial isolation. Farley demonstrates that with improvement in their socioeconomic standing and with limited migration to small cities, segregation declines.

In chapter 4, Ronald Ferguson attempts to explain the differentials in earnings between African Americans and whites. Ferguson examines the "skills mismatch" caused by the limited or inferior education and job training available to African Americans. This mismatch limits their ability to compete for high-skilled entry level jobs, and many end up in the lowest paying service and retail labor markets. Many African Americans also suffer from a "spatial mismatch," as blue collar jobs move from the central cities where most African Americans live. To reduce economic disparity among entrants in the workforce from different racial backgrounds, Ferguson calls for increased support for—and accountability from—the institutions that should inspire, train, and educate our youth.

Chapter 5 addresses the central question of whether a large black underclass has become a permanent phenomenon in the United States. William Darity, Jr., asks whether social mobility in this country has slowed significantly over the course of the century. If so, what are the prospects for achieving racial equality? These questions were central to Myrdal's research. As Myrdal wrote, "White prejudice and discrimination keep the Negro low in standards of living, health, education, manners, and morals" (Myrdal, 1962). But Myrdal thought that Americans would ultimately abandon discriminatory practices and uphold the American creed: "One implication of their belief in the principles of democracy and Christianity is that they are more susceptible to the more specific and practical consequences of these principles." It has been fifty years since Myrdal penned those words, and, as Darity writes, American society remains segregated and unequal.

In chapter 6 John Sibley Butler examines how social forces affect the acquisition of skill and success in labor markets. Butler points out that, when Myrdal wrote, assimilation was the dominant measure of success for black entrepreneurs. Since then, however, research has pointed to the importance of "self-contained communities" for the development of professional and business classes within the context of larger societies. Reexamining American history from this perspective shows more successes among African Americans than previously observed. Butler also calls for more attention to programs designed to produce successful, independent businesspeople in today's changing economy.

Either directly or indirectly authors of each of the preceding chapters stress the importance of education in the battle for racial equality. Unfortunately, as Walter R. Allen and Joseph O. Jewell discuss in chapter 7, education is an area where African Americans have not fared well over the past several decades. According to Allen and Jewell, the best educational opportunities have been most available to the privileged and rich. Unless we rethink our educational policies, many young African Americans will enter the twenty-first century unprepared to participate fully in American life.

In chapter 8, Clayton examines the role of the churches during the civil rights movement. I believe that minimal interaction between the black and white churches prolonged the battle for social integration, and that religion was often used to justify the status quo. Despite their great potential for effectiveness, both black and white churches generally responded to the civil rights movement with silence. Myrdal observed similar problems, but despite the reluctance of many churches and churchmen to actively participate in the Civil Rights Movement, he saw hope:

> It is true that the church has not given much of a lead to reforms but has rather lagged when viewed from the advanced positions of Negro youth and Negro intellectuals. But few Christian churches have ever been, whether in America or elsewhere, the spearheads of reform. That this fundamental truth is understood—underneath all bitter criticism—is seen in the fact that Negro intellectuals are much more willing to cooperate with Negro churches than white intellectuals with white churches (Myrdal, 1961).

Churches have become more activist since the 1970s, and urban ministries are now focal points in most denominations, but much work remains to be done if the churches are to become true spearheads of reform.

Chapters 9, 10, and 11 are concerned with crime and the application of justice among African Americans. Susan Welch and her collaborators (chapter 9), and Samuel Walker and Cassia Spohn (chapters 10 and 11 respectively) suggest that increased crime among African American youth cannot be overlooked when studying the economic disparities between black and white Americans. Likewise, social and economic conditions must be considered when examining crime. African Americans are involved in criminal activities at an alarming rate, primarily because of poor job prospects and higher labor force dropout rates. As Myrdal observed, "Most people discuss crime as if it had nothing to do with social conditions and was simply an inevitable outcome of personal badness" (Myrdal, 1944). Poor employment opportunities, especially in the inner-cities, contribute to the lack of hope for a decent job among many youth. For others, the pay for available jobs is so low that many individuals leave the labor force and turn to illegitimate or illegal markets. The criminal record that many ultimately receive places them at a disadvantage in the labor market, creating what William Wilson (1987) called the "left behinds."

The number and proportion of African Americans in prison constitute a grave problem. There are more African American men under correctional supervision than there are in colleges and universities (Bureau of Justice, 1989; U.S. Department of Education, 1990). Given such a startling statistic, it is unlikely that an inner-city child does not know someone who is or has been in prison. This phenomenon has serious implications for the youth in these communities, who often view "doing time" as an initiation rite. These chapters demonstrate that, despite improvements in the administration of justice, true justice will not have been served until the underlying social and economic inequalities between whites and blacks are addressed.

To understand the nature of racial conflict in the United States it is also necessary to understand the demographic transformations that have accompanied the social construction of racial differences and racial acceptance. In chapter 12, Antonio McDaniel illustrates how the population of the United States has changed over time and how these changes have led to social problems. McDaniel believes that racial conflict and competition have been hallmarks of American society since European settlers encountered established Native American populations in the fifteenth century, and that they are unlikely to vanish in the foreseeable future.

The final chapter deals with the intersection of racial inequality and an equally salient social problem: gender inequality. In the tradition of Myrdal, Doris Wilkinson writes that, along with racism, class oppression and sexism pervade American culture. Myrdal drew many comparisons between the status afforded women and African Americans. Specifically, Myrdal stated that when studying discrimination and prejudice directed at "Negroes" one must examine another disenfranchised group, women: "Their present status, as well as their history and their problems in society, reveal striking similarities to those of the Negro" (Myrdal, 1944). Wilkinson believes that racism, sexism, and class differences are crucial variables in the mapping of life experiences. Furthermore, any discussion of racial and structural differentiation exclusive of gender leaves a void in our knowledge base and hence in our comprehension of racial realities.

Whether explicitly or implicitly, each chapter in this book illustrates the deleterious effects of racism and prejudice, which have eased only slightly since Myrdal wrote *An American Dilemma*. Animosities between blacks and whites persist, although less entrenched than in the years preceding the civil rights movement of the 1960s. *An American Dilemma* made a seminal contribution to the field of social research on racial relations. This volume was conceived as a report card on where the United States stands on the same issue today. While the focus of this book is on African Americans, the significance of the issues is not limited to African Americans. Many of the problems at hand, which have gone unnoticed or unresolved since the 1940s, have a new urgency in light of the massive, racially diverse immigration of the last two decades. Despite the daunting magnitude of the problems associated with race in the United States, America cannot afford to allow significant numbers of its citizens to lose hope, to give up on the myriad opportunities of American life. Somehow we must find workable solutions to an enduring American dilemma.

Stephen Graubard

1

An American Dilemma Revisited

IN CHOOSING TO COMMEMORATE the fiftieth anniversary of the publication of Gunnar Myrdal's *An American Dilemma*, Russell Sage Foundation is doing more than simply celebrating the magisterial scholarly work of another age. It is asserting, simply but emphatically, that no issue is more crucial to the country today than the relations between the races—relevant to every aspect of American life—and that few matters of such moment are being discussed less candidly, less openly. Some, imagining that their sexual freedom is a faithful index of the country's twentieth century liberation from Puritan and Victorian mores, little realize how reticent and confused they have become on all manner of other more sensitive subjects. Race has become America's forbidden theme, with "bell curves" and other such nonsense substituting for serious discussions of real national and international problems. No study of race relations in the United States comparable to Myrdal's has been published since 1944, though the problems that Myrdal and his colleagues addressed more than half a century ago—moral, economic, social, and political—may be more acute today than they were when the Carnegie Corporation commissioned its inquiry in the summer of 1937.

It is extraordinary that there has been no successor study to that of Myrdal, that no foundation or corporate group has to this date recognized the need for a fundamental reinvestigation of what is incontestably the most serious problem that plagues American society today. The Myrdal study, undertaken in the midst of the country's worst economic depression in history, called for collaboration between a foreign scholar, little known in the United States when he started his work, and a remarkable group of American social scientific colleagues, black and white, who gave him a great deal more than information, allowing him to witness and describe a scene that had no precise parallel anywhere in Europe.

As Walter A. Jackson makes abundantly clear in *Gunnar Myrdal and America's Conscience: Social Engineering and Racial Liberalism, 1938–1987*, American social scientists had made full and elaborate investigations into the nature of race relations in the United States many years before Gunnar Myrdal arrived to take charge of the ambitious study commissioned by the

Carnegie Corporation. Myrdal, indeed, profited enormously from the work of these scholars, moving substantially beyond them, however, in the kinds of recommendations he made. A political activist himself, he did not come with the conviction that all social scientific inquiry had to be value-neutral, that the scholar's first obligation was to avoid making public policy recommendations, that there was some positive advantage in not entering into the political arena.[1]

Coming from a European tradition where social science was expected to serve political and social ends—which did not mean that it had to be ideological or biased—Myrdal shared few of the American social scientists' beliefs that objectivity, in the manner of the natural sciences, ought to be the scholar's first responsibility. For Myrdal, the paradigms of the natural sciences did not provide the intellectual models that he felt compelled to adopt or imitate. Many American scholars who had written on the tangled and contentious issue of race relations refused to think of themselves as social reformers. For them, such an attribution would have been no distinction at all. They aspired to do something more difficult and more serious, to carry on as uninvolved scholars—latter-day monks of a sort, ascetics—who simply consulted the evidence and reported their findings to the community of scholars.

One of the great philanthropic institutions of the day, the Carnegie Corporation, founded in 1911 and still carrying on in certain of the traditions set by Andrew Carnegie, knowing the difference between philanthropy and charity, but at the same time seeing no fundamental conflict between its commitment to the pursuit of knowledge and active social engagement, saw the possibility of creating a unique niche for itself by initiating a scholarly study of American race relations. That such a body should have accepted the obligation to concern itself with race, knowing the incendiary character of the issues involved, that in the end it should have expended well over $300,000 in doing so—a figure comparable to several millions in 1995 dollars—suggests something of the importance that President Frederick Keppel of Carnegie and his trustees attached to the race project.

The proposal for such a study had come as early as 1935, originally from Newton D. Baker, a Carnegie trustee who had served as mayor of Cleveland and secretary of war in the Wilson administration, who knew more than many of his colleagues about the complexities of race in a society recently tested in the crucible of war. Keppel, while hospitable to the idea, believed that the race question was so "charged with emotion" that no American scholar could be entrusted to provide the principal intellectual focus for such an inquiry. Almost a century after the greatest foreign observer, Alexis de Tocqueville, came to write about the American democracy, Keppel launched a search to discover a twentieth century analogue to Tocqueville.

While he might have wished for a latter-day James Bryce—thought by many to have been the second of the great nineteenth century commentators on the United States—Keppel knew that scholars coming from Europe's imperial centers, France or Great Britain, would be unacceptable in the America of the 1930s. As he explained in the foreword to the Myrdal volume,

> . . . since the emotional factor affects the Negroes no less than the whites, the search was limited to countries of high intellectual and scholarly standards but with no background or traditions of imperialism which might lessen the confidence of the Negroes in the United States as to the complete impartiality of the study and the validity of its findings.[2]

Keppel and his colleagues, who might have been caricatured by a later generation as well-born, affluent, white Protestant males, with little first-hand knowledge of either the black bourgeoisie or the working class that had already made Harlem a near-black enclave in New York, who knew even less about conditions below the Mason-Dixon line, their birthplaces and political experience notwithstanding, were concerned to produce an accurate and objective study that would find favor among whites and blacks in the South as well as in the North. Because 75 percent of blacks were still living in the South at the time, they looked for a man prepared to school himself in the very special conditions that prevailed in that part of the country. In the late 1930s, to study blacks in America was to study the South. However, it was not a regional expertise that they were searching for; as Keppel explained, they hoped to discover "someone with a fresh mind, uninfluenced by traditional attitudes or by earlier conclusions."[3] Given these conditions, particularly those that excluded scholars from the so-called imperial countries of Europe, their search naturally led them to look for a scholar in Switzerland or Scandinavia.

In the end, they settled on Gunnar Myrdal, a young Swedish economist who had spent a year in the United States as a Rockefeller Fellow in 1929–1930, witnessing both the Wall Street crash and the beginning of the world economic depression. That Myrdal held a chair as professor at the University of Stockholm, was an economic adviser to the Swedish government, and was a member of the Swedish Senate, were all cited by Keppel as obvious qualifications for the arduous task the foundation had assigned him. Given Myrdal's youth—he was not yet 40—and that his experience with the study of race was negligible, it became important to dwell on his public affairs credentials. That the Carnegie invitation came at the time when Myrdal was preparing to come for his second visit to the United States, having been invited to give the prestigious Godkin Lectures at Harvard, suggested that he was beginning to be recognized on both sides of the Atlantic as a public-spirited individual whose reputation as a social economist had already given him a certain renown.

Keppel, careful and diplomatic at all times, knew how limited Myrdal's familiarity with the race issue was, and why it was essential that he, in his capacity as president of Carnegie, pay tribute to the scholarly work of American social scientists who had made race a matter of great concern to themselves. If, as he explained, there "was no lack of competent scholars in the United States who were deeply interested in the problem and had already devoted themselves to its study,"[4] this did not invalidate the foundation's wish to vest the direction of its ambitious study in a foreign scholar whose objectivity and independence could be relied on. Myrdal was expected to recruit a team of experts of both races, whom he would consult, who would assist him in his research: he would seek to avail himself of the best talent in the country, wherever he found it. Myrdal learned very early that many of the most talented were young men like himself, engaged in historical, psychological, anthropological, and economic research on various aspects of race relations. Many, with academic bases in the Negro colleges and universities of the South—at Howard or Fisk, for example—lived in a scholarly world and published in academic journals scarcely known to those who inhabited the Ivy League, but familiar to the small numbers who pursued comparable social scientific research in certain of the private and public universities of the South and Middle West, at Chicago, Northwestern, Wisconsin, and North Carolina, to name only a few.

America had developed a strong social science tradition, centered in a handful of universities; issues of culture, class, race, and prejudice were not neglected subjects in Depression-ridden America. Indeed, when Myrdal came to publish his 1,483-page book, the list of books, pamphlets, periodicals, and other material referred to in *An American Dilemma* covered some 36 pages in very small print. The social sciences, as practiced in the United States, might still, by certain standards, lack the theoretical distinction of the best of Europe's scholarship, but an even casual study of authors, titles, and publication sites suggested that the United States, in respect at least to the study of race relations, was in no way laggard, simply following in the wake of European research. Myrdal came to a country where he had much to learn but also a great deal to give.

An American Dilemma: The Negro Problem and Modern Democracy was not the labor of an accomplished journalist who simply transcribed his many conversations, or of a scholar who read widely but stayed tucked away in a library. Rather, it was the work of a young scholar who took certain risks by traveling in a segregated South in the company of a radical young black political scientist, Ralph Bunche, who was to achieve international eminence and the Nobel Peace Prize some years later, who, with others, engaged in constant dialogue with his Swedish colleague. Myrdal depended heavily on the investigations of others, and indeed gave several, in very difficult economic times, their first opportunity to do research and publish. The group of scholars, of both races, some established, others barely known at the time, cited by Myrdal in his Preface included, among many others, Margaret Brenman, Sterling Brown, Barbara Burks, Allison Davis, J. G. St. Clair Drake, E. Franklin Frazier, Melville J. Herskovits, Charles S. Johnson, Otto Klineberg, Ira D. A. Reid, Edward Shils, and Louis Wirth, not to mention Kenneth Clark, Arnold M. Rose, Samuel Stouffer, and the social statistician who accompanied him from Sweden, Richard Sterner.

For those familiar with the work of the greatest number of these scholars, there can be no surprise that they did not always agree among themselves, even on fundamental issues, or that they did not all look upon the final product with the same degree of enthusiasm. If it was Myrdal's task to learn from all of them, he understood very early that there was no way for him to compromise or bridge the differences between a Bunche and a Herskovits—friends though they might be—the latter recognized to be one of America's leading anthropologists, the former a young unknown professor at Howard. Herskovits, with his firm belief in the importance of African culture in shaping the mind-set and habits of American blacks, wishing to develop in the United States an "interdisciplinary enterprise with a comparative perspective,"[5] was not likely to persuade another of Myrdal's gifted collaborators, E. Franklin Frazier, who chose to see American black culture and life in a very different light. The intellectual disputes in the team recruited by Myrdal could never be charted along simple racial lines. Blacks differed with blacks; both differed with whites, or at least certain among them; and all had a number of reservations about their leader, and they were not contained in the jaundiced characterization of Myrdal as the "Swedish Simon Legree."[6] Those words, uttered by the youthful Bunche, himself a driven man of herculean energy, told as much about the frenetic pace of the project as it did about the perpetual demands of its foreign leader, a good friend of Bunche, who never ceased to admire what he perceived to be his independence and courage.

As Walter Jackson makes clear in what is today the best account of the intellectual and methodological differences between those who served as advisers, but also among those who were frozen out of the Carnegie enterprise, issues relating to integration and assimilation figured prominently for a number of Myrdal's colleagues, were almost secondary for others. While some wished principally to investigate the question of race relations, being relatively unconcerned with formulating recommendations calculated to influence public policy, others cared deeply about the conditions that existed, finding them abominable, wishing only to change them.[7] Within the Myrdal team, even before World War II created yet new fissures, there were substantial differences about what the book should say, how it should be said, and who its intended audience might be. Questions that have plagued a good number of the more limited studies on race relations published since *An American Dilemma* existed in an acute form even then.

Myrdal presided over a contentious crew that did not simply defer to his opinions. Yet, he was incontestably chief of the enterprise, and it is not insignificant that when the book appeared in 1944, he was sole author, though the title page carried the meaningful additional phrase, "with the assistance of Richard Sterner and Arnold Rose." The book was Myrdal's, though parts of it were written by other hands. Samuel Stouffer, for example, had been substantially involved, particularly during the periods when Myrdal was absent from the United States, making his perilous way across the submarine-infested Atlantic to his home and family in Sweden. *An American Dilemma*, a unique description of American race relations during the era of the Depression, carried the story into the first years of World War II. In describing a segregated South, still living in the shadow of the Civil War, a booming North, gradually being released from some of the worst effects of the Depression—with blacks in great number flocking into its cities in search of work, as they had also done during World War I—American society was still characterized by its poverty and want, perhaps most conspicuous among blacks but common also to many whites. Whether describing the lives of black men and women, sharecroppers in the South, or menial factory workers in the North, Myrdal criticized a set of economic and social conditions that he found offensive, which bound millions to intolerable conditions of penury. His more determined concern, however, was to explain how the United States had come to betray its own founding principles, accepting that great numbers of its citizens should live under inhumane conditions, at variance with the country's stated ideals.

Committed by its Enlightenment, Protestant, Christian, and English legal values to what Myrdal called the American Creed, he saw this idealism as the cement that held the disparate nation together. Myrdal knew that the moral obligations imposed by the Creed had been flouted for centuries. Black men and women were denied the fundamental liberties guaranteed by the founding myths of the republic; even in the midst of war, with all the promises implicit in the Atlantic Charter, blacks were denied the freedom and dignity they were entitled to as citizens of a democratic republic. What sense did it make for the United States to insist on its democratic principles when it treated millions in the way that it did? Myrdal, the citizen of a neutral state, Sweden, ashamed at what his country felt compelled to do to keep Hitler's armies out, allowing the Germans to transport men and military equipment across its territory to Nazi-occupied Norway, looked for a higher level of performance from an America at war with Nazi Germany. He wrote *An American Dilemma* in some part, at least, as a call for the United States to take seriously the democratic creed that formed such an integral part of its civil religion, never so denominated. Myrdal, with all the authority that a long italicized paragraph could provide, made his principal purpose explicit when he wrote:

> The American Negro problem is a problem in the heart of the American. It is there that the interracial tension has its focus. It is there that the decisive struggle goes on. This is the central viewpoint of this treatise. Though our study includes economic, social, and political race relations, at bottom our problem is the moral dilemma of the American—the conflict between his moral valuations on various levels of consciousness and generality. The "American Dilemma," referred to in the title of this book, is the ever-raging conflict between, on the one hand, the valuations preserved on the general plane which we shall call the "American Creed," where the American thinks, talks, and acts under the influence of high national and Christian precepts, and, on the other hand, the valuations on specific planes of individual and group living, where personal and local interests; economic, social, and sexual jealousies; considerations of community prestige and conformity; group prejudice against particular persons or types of people; and all sorts of miscellaneous wants, impulses, and habits dominate his outlook. . . . The Negro problem is an integral part of . . . the whole complex of problems in the larger American civilization. It cannot be treated in isolation.[8]

If *An American Dilemma* had been only a jeremiad, a call to white men to abandon their racism, it would have greatly embarrassed those in the Carnegie Corporation who had funded the study. Given Myrdal's own interests, it was inconceivable that he would wish to write or give his name only to an elaborate bill of complaints. The work, in fact, existed on several planes; on one level, it could be read as a warning to Americans of the dangers they ran by continuing to ignore the injustices inflicted on blacks; riots and worse were a very real possibility if conditions continued as they were, and Myrdal intended for his book to sound a tocsin. On another level, it was an analysis of black society and black culture, as Myrdal and his associates interpreted them, basing their views largely on what they had witnessed in the South, informed also by what they had learned from reading the copious literature on race relations extant at the time in the United States.

The uniqueness of the study is admirably captured by Walter Jackson:

> In contrast to many American social scientists of the period, Myrdal bluntly and forcefully condemned racial oppression, particularly seg-

regation and discrimination in the South. Totally absent from "An American Dilemma" was the vague rhetoric of racial adjustment, deference to southern white folkways, and silence or equivocation on the social equality issue that had characterized so many foundation-sponsored studies of black–white relations. Yet Myrdal did not engage in the kind of crude South-baiting that had awakened regional defensiveness in the past. His status as a foreign observer, his emphasis on the American creed as a functioning part of the nation's culture, and his treatment of race relations in an international context during wartime allowed him to avoid the appearance of singling out the South for censure.[9]

If Myrdal expected that his even-handedness—his avoiding some of the more conventional denunciations of southern white practices along with his studied unwillingness to sentimentalize any aspect of black life and experience, refusing in any way to ignore the iniquities created by the nation's failure to practice its Creed—would provide him with protection against certain kinds of criticism, he was proved wrong. While the greatest number of reviewers were effusive in their praise, others were more reserved. Convention dictated that some, cited by the author for their help, should not choose to review it at all. While Lewis Gannett in *The New York Herald Tribune* compared the work with that of Tocqueville and Bryce, and *Time* made the same comparison a fortnight later, the reviews in *The New York Times, The New Republic*, and *The Saturday Review* were no less favorable, with reviewers, white and black, of the intellectual distinction of Reinhold Niebuhr, Robert Lynd, Henry Steele Commager, J. Saunders Redding, E. Franklin Frazier, and the "dean of American Negro studies," W. E. B. Du Bois, vying with each other to praise the work, speaking of its seminal importance. Although such praise was common, it was by no means universal, particularly among southern reviewers, including a number who might, because of their liberal inclinations, have been expected to react more favorably.[10]

The work, because of its theoretical as well as its empirical qualities, could not fail to attract the attention of those partial to such inquiry. Sociologists, psychologists, historians, and economists felt an obligation to comment on Myrdal's methods and findings. Some, like the young Robert Merton, for example, expressed serious reservations about Myrdal's American Creed, in which he had placed such great stock. Writing a major essay on Myrdal's work in 1949, Merton thought the theory might be "seriously misleading for social policy and social science." In his view, if people violated the Creed sufficiently, those violations became themselves what he called an "institutionalized evasion of institutional norms," thereby effectively minimizing the power of the Creed. Myrdal, however unwittingly, in Merton's opinion, had exaggerated its influence.[11]

Gordon Allport, the senior social psychologist at Harvard, whose work, *The Nature of Prejudice*, enjoyed enormous renown at the time of its publication in 1954, seemed more sympathetic to the principal argument in the Myrdal tome. For Allport, the American democratic ethos carried very great weight; it was, in his view, a mistake to underestimate its power. As he argued, from the perspective of a psychologist concerned with stigma and intolerance, "the quickest way to deflate a bigot was to show him that his prejudice violated the Christian-democratic creed." In a letter to Kenneth Clark, written in 1953, Allport said, "People really know that segregation is un-American, even the masses in the South know it." Allport believed that if the Supreme Court took a position against segregation, that decision would eventually carry the day. This, however, did not make him at all sanguine about what interracial contact would do to reduce prejudice; the conditions for that to happen were substantially more complex than those outlined by Myrdal.[12]

If traditional academics were on the whole overwhelmingly favorable in their comments, reluctant to find fault with what they took to be a serious work of scholarship, this was not the position of those who proudly proclaimed their intellectual allegiances to be on the Left. The young Marxist historian, Herbert Aptheker, published a short book—essentially a pamphlet—on Myrdal's many inadequacies in 1946 and reprinted it in 1977. Entitled *The Negro People in America: A Critique of Gunnar Myrdal's An American Dilemma*, Aptheker, like others of Myrdal's critics, found flaws in his historical interpretation. He and others criticized what they believed to be his failure to give sufficient attention to the economic factors that perpetuated the system of discrimination and injustice, and not only in the South. Myrdal, though a prominent Social Democrat in Sweden, had not, in their view, been sufficiently attentive to the ways in which the capitalist system inevitably brought oppression in its wake. Scarcely less serious, in Aptheker's opinion, was Myrdal's failure to represent and portray black culture correctly; the proposition that blacks were essentially passive, incapable of resistance, offended Aptheker. Myrdal, in his view, simply did not know or understand the strengths of the black culture.[13]

Doxey Wilkerson, one of Myrdal's collaborators in *An American Dilemma*, who chose to make no mention of that now-embarrassing fact, wrote the introduction to Aptheker's book, dismissing Myrdal's work as "corporation-financed" and "pseudo-scientific." According to Wilkerson, "The Negro question has now become one of the most crucial and fundamental issues confronting our nation. Not only are the lives and liberties of fourteen million Negro citizens in dire jeopardy but the fascist pattern of terror by which they are oppressed threatens to spread and destroy the freedom of all Americans." Black oppression, in Wilkerson's view, was profitable;

hence it was maintained, particularly at those times when it was threatened. The "long, gradual never-ending process of 'education'"—the education of the white majority—was not what Wilkerson was prepared patiently to wait for. Myrdal's book, in Wilkerson's view, was an "ideological monstrosity," and had found its corrective in the work of Aptheker.[14]

Whether Myrdal was greatly disconcerted by such criticism from the Left it is difficult to know, but one may presume that the exaggeration of its language provided him with a certain immunity to the barbs so liberally issued. The more significant fact, certainly, is that the Carnegie Corporation itself, his sponsor and funder—its officers and trustees—never really seemed to take pleasure in Myrdal's accomplishment. Keppel had died in 1943, before the book was published. Others in Carnegie, who had helped significantly with the project, including Donald Young, who was later to serve as president of the Russell Sage Foundation, were surprisingly circumspect, saying almost nothing in public. Given that Young was advising the War Department on race issues at the time, his reticence might be explained by the nature of his war service, except that in both his correspondence and the oral history he prepared for deposit at Columbia University, he told another, less flattering, story. Young believed that Myrdal had not "made any contribution to the understanding of race relations…in a scholarly sense."[15] This, for him, was the supreme offense.

Others, who also chose not to comment in public—Melville Herskovitz, Samuel Stouffer, and Edward Thorndike, to name only three of the more prominent advisers—had other reservations about the book, which they circulated privately. A number of individuals who are alive today, who knew these or other of Myrdal's collaborators, would be in a position to tell more about their misgivings. Whether such recollections would in fact throw light on why the Carnegie Corporation chose not to celebrate Myrdal's achievement, it is difficult to say. One might be left with nothing more than what Waldemar Nielson, in his not very flattering portrayal of the large American foundations, chose to write. Nielson, noting that Walter Jessup, Keppel's successor as the Carnegie president, "entirely divorced himself from the book," thought it strange that while "there have been many examples of a foundation turning its back on its failures," in this instance "the Carnegie Corporation turned its back on a triumph."[16] Why?

Myrdal, and those who had worked with him, not least the young black scholars whom he had engaged, expected publication of the book to lead to greater research opportunities. This did not happen. Walter Jackson states the matter concisely: "One of the effects of the Myrdal project was to dry up foundation money for major studies of race relations and of Afro-American communities and culture for the next twenty years."[17] The story of why this happened has yet to be written—Jackson's own very brief account, with its description of how Young wrote to the foundations urging them not to engage in further research on the subject, but to focus instead on the "point of contact between groups, such as at the factory, in the store, at school, in the city street, or on the bus," does not begin to tell the tale of why foundation funding for fundamental research on race relations dried up in the years after World War II and has never been seriously renewed since then.[18]

A far more important story, however, is the political one, dealing with how Roosevelt, Truman, and Eisenhower perceived civil rights issues, and why their administrations acted in the way they did in the years from 1933 to 1960. Franklin Roosevelt's own attitudes and policies in respect to racial issues have been frequently explored, but a new generation of historians may be expected to look more closely and more critically at how he managed his affairs in this very sensitive area. Roosevelt, considered by most to be a friend of the blacks—any photograph of the crowds waiting along the railroad tracks to watch the train bearing his body from Georgia to Washington, D.C., or weeping in the streets of the capital as the cortege passed by, tells its own story—was sufficiently sensitive to congressional opinion to know that it would not respond positively to major proposals to enact civil rights legislation. Dependent on southern Democratic senators and representatives, whose number and seniority alone guaranteed their influence, Roosevelt knew what kinds of support he might expect of such men, why he would be foolish even to attempt to challenge them in matters where he could not hope to win their votes.

Just as he carefully calibrated his foreign policy innovations to take account of what a suspicious, recalcitrant Congress would in the end approve, so he took great pains to avoid repeating in domestic policy the kinds of mistakes he made in his Supreme Court–packing intervention, which cost him so dearly and ended so disastrously. In proposing legislation calculated to assist those in difficulty, men and women at risk in many segments of American society—refusing to single out blacks or any other minority— Roosevelt showed characteristic political acumen. Determined to build a new kind of Democratic party, dependent on the support of constituencies, ethnic, racial, and social, not previously tied very securely to the party, Roosevelt pursued a tactic intended to make his New Deal reforms a permanent feature of the American political landscape.

Developing, however inchoately, new concepts of social welfare, suited to the depressed economic conditions common in his time which so adversely affected the overwhelming majority of the country's citizens, Roosevelt catered to a working-class America stricken by unemployment, whose wages were low, who had few advantages over the poor farmers who sought to scratch a meager living from their inadequate holdings. That

Eleanor Roosevelt, by her own highly publicized actions, made the president appear to be the friend of the common man—the phrase obviously included women and blacks, among others—showed something more than White House solicitude for the obviously disadvantaged citizens of a country still reeling from the effects of a world economic catastrophe. It expressed the capacity of both to understand certain political necessities, common to a time when most American citizens lived close to the margin, when their conditions of life made the building of political coalitions difficult. In a society where so many were in fact competing for so little, the potentialities for conflict between hostile groups, ethnic and racial, each striving for its own share of an inadequate economic pie, had to be counteracted by making it appear that all were in the same boat, that none were being treated preferentially.

Now that we know a great deal more about the gravity of Roosevelt's illnesses, how serious indeed was the deterioration in his health by the spring of 1944—facts artfully concealed at the time, scarcely figuring even in the presidential election campaign of that year—one can only guess at what would have happened had Roosevelt died in April 1944 rather than in April 1945.[19] Had his successor been Henry Wallace, purportedly much more partial to pressing for civil rights legislation, there is no reason to believe that major new civil rights laws would have been enacted. The vice president's reputation in the South was never very high; indeed, it was one of several reasons why he was passed over for the vice presidential nomination in 1944. The introduction of major reforms of the kind suggested by Myrdal in *An American Dilemma* required something more than support from the White House. It called for changes within Congress, within the public consciousness, and nothing that happened during World War II suggested that such changes were in fact taking place. While northerners, dispatched to southern army camps might look with surprise (or even contempt) at what they saw, the indignities suffered by black men and women in a segregated society, this did not translate into the change of heart that Myrdal had called for.

This became obvious during Harry Truman's more than seven years in the White House. Although Truman tried to create a permanent Fair Employment Practices Commission, he failed to win congressional approval. Indeed, it was only a series of racial incidents and lynchings in the South that made Truman aware that a number of his inherited New Deal constituencies were restive, demanding something more than what had satisfied them during Roosevelt's time in office. In creating the President's Committee on Civil Rights, Truman did what Roosevelt had refused to do after the race riots of 1943. Led by Charles Wilson, the president of General Electric, it was comprised of the kinds of men and women who at the time regularly served on such bipartisan commissions. With representatives of labor and industry, it included two white liberal southerners and two blacks, women as well as men, with a Catholic bishop, a Jewish rabbi, and the presiding Episcopal bishop joining the president of Dartmouth and one of the country's distinguished civil liberties attorneys, Morris Ernst, as well as several other presumably influential individuals whose reputation for probity could be counted on.[20]

Their report, "To Secure these Rights," submitted in October 1947, might have come straight out of Myrdal's own work. In no fundamental way did it contradict what Myrdal had said just three years earlier. For the President's Committee, "the American heritage of freedom and equality," as expressed in the Declaration of Independence and the Bill of Rights, legitimated the country's democratic traditions, the American Creed that had so preoccupied Myrdal, which he knew was being violated every day. The blacks were not the only minority suffering abuse. If Roosevelt had sought to provide social and economic protection to many, rarely choosing to distinguish among those who would purportedly profit from his New Deal legislation, the men and women who advised Truman sought to do the same in the field of civil rights. Discrimination, unacknowledged by those who did not experience it, was rife in America, affecting many more than just black men and women in the South or elsewhere. Catholics, Jews, Mexican Americans, Japanese Americans, Native Americans, and others were also suffering indignities and injustices that were intolerable. It was neither economically advantageous nor morally safe for the country to allow conditions of this sort to persist.

Like Myrdal, the President's Commission on Civil Rights saw the moral issue as central. Knowing that the country was much preoccupied with what was increasingly perceived to be a growing Soviet menace, they argued that the lynchings in the South gave "excellent propaganda ammunition for Communist agents." More importantly, because they understood how the American "democratic ideal" was being threatened by practices that shamed the nation's claim to being free and just, they insisted that the country recognize how its failure to live up to its ideals might cause it to lose out in its struggle with the Soviet enemy. The stakes were too high for the country to go on with business as usual. The committee's recommendations included almost all the civil rights laws and regulations that were adopted in time, including, in Jackson's admirable summary, "an antilynching law, an FEPC, abolition of the poll tax, legislation against discrimination in voter registration, an end to segregation in the armed forces, legislation against segregation in interstate transportation, and a cutoff of federal funds to any public or private agency practicing discrimination or segregation." The committee saw as their ultimate objective the "elimination of segregation, based on race, color, creed, or national origin, from American life."[21]

Congress, in 1948, had no interest in such a program, and Truman recognized what his Missouri upbringing ought to have told him—race was an issue too sensitive to be dealt with in so enlightened and revolutionary a manner, even when global and domestic advantages could be adduced. It was only the votes at the Democratic party convention—in a platform battle led by Hubert Humphrey—that produced a civil rights plank that wholly incorporated the President's Committee on Civil Rights recommendations. That Truman chose to run on this plank, that he was forced to compete not only with his Republican party adversary Thomas Dewey but also with both Henry Wallace and Strom Thurmond, in the end garnering more votes from blacks than Roosevelt had ever managed to secure in his four electoral battles, suggested a propensity for risk-taking on the president's part that could never be thought common. Winning by slim margins the electoral votes of several crucial states—California, Illinois, and Ohio— Truman understood what the black vote had made possible, his triumph over Dewey. Blacks and whites, working together, had given him his victory. Truman knew this, but it gave him no additional leverage with Congress, still firmly opposed to most of the measures that white liberals and blacks believed to be necessary for the country. In 1953 when Truman left office, his greatest achievement in the area of civil rights was his desegregation of the armed forces, achieved through executive order.[22]

In the Eisenhower years no effort was made to introduce legislation that would in any significant way incorporate the ideas of *An American Dilemma*. Still, the most important event of the period, certainly as relating to civil rights, was the *Brown* v. *Board of Education of Topeka, Kansas*, decision, handed down by the Supreme Court on May 17, 1954. Chief Justice Earl Warren, in citing the writings of Myrdal, Frazier, Clark, and other social scientists to explain why segregated schools damaged black children and why they could no longer be countenanced, gave Myrdal's magnum opus an importance it had never previously enjoyed. Although the Court asked that desegregation "proceed with all deliberate speed," it refused to set deadlines. The president, for his part, simply remained silent, and southern opposition to the Court decision gained momentum. For most of the next decade, certainly during the last six years of Eisenhower's presidency, the issue played itself out principally on the television screens of the country, much more than in the courts or in the Congress. Still, the Myrdal idea was alive, legitimated by the highest court in the land, given its most important political support by the growing reputation of the black leader Martin Luther King, Jr., as evidenced in his 1963 "I Have a Dream" speech.[23]

The story of how Kennedy was led, after very substantial hesitation, to embrace the cause of civil rights, responding in terms familiar to any reader of Myrdal, has been frequently told. So, also, the violent events that occurred in Alabama, Mississippi, and Georgia, which caused national and international consternation, made perhaps even more dramatic by the peaceful civil rights marches initiated by Martin Luther King, Jr., and the violence they provoked, led Kennedy to make proposals he would not have considered when he first entered the White House. Walter Jackson captures the significance of this epic spring:

> In his [Kennedy's] framing of the civil rights issue as a moral question, in his conception of the black struggle as a demand for individual civil rights, in his emphasis upon the doctrine of equality of opportunity, and in his assumption that skin color, rather than culture, was the only thing that separated black from white Americans, Kennedy faithfully reiterated the liberal orthodoxy that Myrdal had helped put in place twenty years earlier. His use of quantitative evidence and reference to the class and caste system revealed the extent to which social science ideas had penetrated the consciousness of educated Americans. The president's warnings of violence if nothing were done, and his emphasis upon the international implications of domestic racial inequality, and reference to the Nazi "master race" theory all recalled the conclusions of *An American Dilemma*.[24]

Never had a book based on research sponsored by an American foundation, written in a quite different historical era, enjoyed such repute, or been given so belated and cordial recognition. Never, indeed, did the leading foundations, so long shying away from the race issue, whether or not out of a concern to follow the advice of those not wholly enchanted with what Myrdal and his associates had written, move so rapidly into reverse gear, starting again to make funds available for the study of race. However, there was little inclination to do in 1963 or 1964 what the Carnegie Corporation had done so courageously in the late 1930s, making a clear commitment to the importance of scholarly investigation of what were incontestably sensitive issues, none more complex perhaps than those that touched black–white relations. No new Myrdal, foreign or American, was commissioned to launch an in-depth study of the country's race problems after 1963; no such study exists even today when so much has changed both in the country and in the world.

It may be useful to reflect on why this is so. In one sense, the reason is fairly obvious. Though 1963–1965 was a tragic time in the history of the country—not only because of the assassination of yet another American president but also because of the riots in Watts and elsewhere—it was also a time of hope for those who imagined that a new day might at last be dawning in respect to race relations in the United States. Lyndon Johnson, with his extraordinary sensitivity to political currents, recognizing how the assassination might be used to press Congress to pass civil rights legislation—representing it as a memorial to the slain president—knew how to use his large Democratic party majorities in both houses to insist on those objectives being realized at once. Resorting to television, Johnson intuited what his "bully pulpit" in the White House provided; and he was not disinclined to use it. This, however, did not satisfy his insatiable appetite for change. At the Howard University 1965 commencement, before the Watts riots, Johnson promised even more substantial changes; in his view, providing equal opportunity was only the beginning; the ultimate objective had to be a society of equals.[25]

In 1965, also, *Dædalus* published the first of two volumes on "The American Negro" (almost the last time when the term Negro could be used without giving offense)[26] containing an optimistic foreword from the President of the United States. No one could have anticipated the events that would follow, events that would lead to the shattering of the alliance between blacks and whites, so critical in producing the civil rights legislative revolution of the 1960s. The *Dædalus* issues carried any number of warnings, but these were scarcely heeded. It was much more convenient to believe, along with many in the mass media and on university campuses, years later, that Johnson's errors in pursuing the war in Vietnam rather than his much-touted "war on poverty" destroyed his credibility and in the end his administration. All such analysis, however, did not explain why so many blacks, outraged by conditions in their urban ghettos, suddenly took to the streets, what the effects of their violence on white opinion proved to be. Nor did they consider why Myrdal's collaborator, Ralph Bunche, chose to represent Watts as an "unspeakable tragedy," the "bitterest fruit of the black ghetto."[27]

When President Johnson wrote his foreword, Watts had already happened. Johnson said:

> It will not be enough to provide better schools for Negro children, to inspire them in their studies, if there are no decent jobs waiting for them after graduation. It will not be enough to open up job opportunities, if the Negro must remain trapped in a jungle of tenements and shanties. If we are to have peace at home, if we are to speak with one honest voice in the world—indeed, if our country is to live with its conscience—we must affect every dimension of the Negro's life for the better.[28]

If such words were intended to calm rebellious spirits, to inject some reason into an increasingly overheated dialogue, if they spoke in the idiom of Myrdal, they failed to have their intended effect. The riots of the summer of 1966 in Chicago, Cleveland, Brooklyn, Omaha, Baltimore, San Francisco, and Jacksonville continued into the next hot summer, with even more disastrous loss of life in Newark and Detroit. Among blacks there was increasing talk not only of Baldwin's *The Fire Next Time*, a work of 1963, but of Black Power and black anger. The "politics of insult" became the characteristic politics of the day, with terrible consequences for a nation understandably hostile to those who preached or practiced violence. Old political alliances were broken; new ones—pledged to fundamental social reform—were never made.

While former Myrdal associates like Bunche might choose to characterize Black Power negatively, as a "sloganized, grossly oversimplified exploitation of the disillusionment of Negro Americans...which would have neither meaning nor impact without the ghettos," others were less certain, and more importantly, less ready to speak out.[29] If Bunche dismissed Black Power separatism as "racist and escapist," believing that only the breakup of the black ghettos could provide security to the nation—some version of what President Johnson's National Advisory Commission on Civil Disorders (the Kerner Commission) also recommended—there was thought to be too great ambiguity in all such proposals; they were considered by many to be hopelessly utopian.[30] Indeed, as voices were raised on every side, and as Martin Luther King, Jr.'s assassination in April 1968 served to create yet new uncertainties about the future relation of the races, it became increasingly difficult to speak candidly on any of the issues that had once concerned Myrdal. He, like so many of his associates, receded into obscurity, made more painful this time by the fact that so many of the issues they had originally raised were still so largely unresolved.

Foundation and other funding for large-scale scholarly studies of race, for the second time in the century, rapidly dried up. As support for urban studies disappeared, race ceased to be a subject of serious social scientific thinking. While arms control studies continued to command foundation and governmental support, the violence of the inner city, and the hazards posed by it to the larger society, became the subject increasingly of journalism. Scholars receded from a field in which they had so recently been heavily committed.

In the new Republican presidential era that opened with the election of Richard Nixon, which continued with two brief Democratic party intervals, when Jimmy Carter sat in the White House and when Bill Clinton took over in 1993, the silences and reticences of politicians and others, black and white, on issues of race became positively ominous. Safety lay in saying little, in doing nothing. If the War on Poverty concluded with neither victory nor celebration, if it receded as just one more rhetorical invention, characteristic of a Cold War political climate, the more significant fact was that the urban ghetto ceased to be a subject that commanded public attention. It receded from general political discourse, which did not mean that individual acts of violence held no fascination for those who continued to receive their daily diet of news from television, radio, or the more agitated tabloid press. The American urban ghetto, with its burned-out buildings and drug raids, became a recognizable icon in the country's culture by the early 1970s. Individuals were no longer prepared to speak candidly on the conditions that existed, not even on the errors committed in what many considered to have been the halfhearted efforts made to create an integrated society. As for proposed remedies to the social and economic conditions that made the cities of America a national disgrace—all this seemed to be beyond repair. While some spoke heatedly of "political correctness," discovering it in the colleges and universities of the country, another more insidious kind of "political correctness" insinuated itself into the country. Its name was "evasiveness." The country scarcely knew what to do to remedy the abuses that the mass media constantly alluded to. A kind of paralysis descended on the country, not least because so few knew what could be done, and even fewer thought there would be an advantage in speaking of their doubts too openly. Although individual articles might command respect, their common theme no longer enjoyed the kind of attention that had been given Myrdal's work when the Chief Justice handed down his historic opinion. So, while the essay by Daniel Patrick Moynihan on "Employment, Income, and the Ordeal of the Negro Family" prefigured much later general discussion on the crucial importance of parenting, his suggestion that the "fundamental problem is the position of the [black] male" did not provoke disagreement.[31] No one seemed offended by the suggestion; no one knew what to do about it.

If St. Clair Drake, one of the original Myrdal associates, called for a "radical shift in American values and simultaneous adjustments of economy and society," citing his former chief's belief that there must be "an unqualified commitment to provide every individual and every family with an adequate income as a matter of right," these sentiments simply reinforced the message that James Tobin, a future Nobel Laureate, was also concerned to make. For Tobin, as for several of the others, what the federal government chose to do would in very substantial part determine whether racial equality was achieved. That, in 1966–1967, still seemed to be a possibility. Or was it all a liberal chimera?[32]

James Q. Wilson came very close to saying so. He wrote:

> While it may be true that Negroes and whites have a common interest in ending unemployment, improving housing and education, and resisting technological displacement, a stable and enduring alliance to attain these objectives will not be easily achieved. The only major po-

litical mechanism by which poor whites and Negroes have in the past been brought into alliance—the big-city machine—is collapsing; except for a few large industrial unions, no substitute has yet appeared.[33]

Harold Fleming put the matter even more bluntly; if, as he believed, "the federal executive tends to innovate forcefully and effectively only in response to an evident sense of national urgency," it became important to accept the fact that

> no administration, however wisely or humanely led, is likely to initiate far-reaching action in the face of public indifference, to say nothing of hostility. The quality of federal civil rights performance, then, depends directly on the ability of Negro Americans to dramatize their cause in such a way that it enlists the support of other influential segments of the society. Obvious though it may be, this conclusion has been explicitly rejected by some of the militant Negro leadership and is often ignored by others of both races.[34]

It was Oscar Handlin who imagined that the civil rights legislation had in fact produced a social revolution. Handlin said: "Desegregation will not solve any of the important economic, social, and political problems of American life; it will only offer a starting point from which to confront them." He did not expect Negroes "to merge into the rest of the population in the next few decades"—many of the more radical blacks were insisting at the time that they had no interest to join what they saw as a putrefying white man's society, but Handlin saw no need to counter such argument. He was satisfied to remind his readers that "Those who desire to eliminate every difference so that Americans will more nearly resemble each other, those who imagine that there is a main stream into which every element in the society will be swept, are deceived about the character of the country in which they live."[35]

Ralph Ellison, in very different terms, seemed to be saying almost the same thing:

> I defend the subculture, because I have to work out of it, because it is precious to me, because I believe it is a vital contributing part of the total culture. I do not think I want to deny that. If I did, then I would have to throw away my typewriter and become a sociologist. I also believe that the subculture and the larger culture are interrelated. I wish that we would dispense with this idea that we are begging to get *in* somewhere. The main stream is in oneself. The main stream of American literature is in me, even though I am a Negro, because I possess more of Mark Twain than many white writers do.[36]

In the last two and a half decades, there have been no volumes comparable either to what Myrdal aspired to do, or what, with infinitely smaller
resources and success, the American Academy managed to do in the mid-
1960s, again with the support of the Carnegie Corporation. Scholarship on
race relations has not been in a very flourishing state. Journalism, with its
contemporary penchant for investigative reporting, has found few compelling stories to tell about the relations between the races. Theory, never
journalism's strongest suit, and in any case suspect, has been overtaken by
discussion of inexpensive quack remedies—instant cures—for the country's many ills, including crime, teenage pregnancy, drug addiction, delinquency, and the like. Larger issues, relating to the city and its pathologies,
the races, and their mutual recriminations and fears, are submerged in a
politics that has become banal, interesting principally when it involves public or private scandal.

Myrdal, to almost the end of his life, hoped to revise his great work, to
bring it up-to-date. It was not to be. Ethnicity and "identity politics" have
a new meaning in an America which introduced affirmative action originally to redress certain historical wrongs against African Americans, which
has seen the concept expanded to include women, Hispanics, Native
Americans, the disabled, and others. In today's world, while party political interests may make tax reduction, capital gains tax reform, federal bud-
getary control, prayer in the schools, and any number of other such issues
paramount—and while any or all such issues may make a very great difference in who is nominated and who wins the presidential elections of
1996—they are all matters of small moment, not to be compared with those
that relate to education, public safety, health, and well-being of the diverse
populations that today constitute the American commonwealth.

These are the issues that ought to concern the nation—they are the ones
that ought to be argued about. They all involve that rarely uttered word,
race, memorialized in a heavy tome no longer in print in any edition, hard-
cover or paperback. Myrdal's great work—testimony to the extraordinary
effects of the Great Depression and World War II on a society, in his mind,
desperately seeking to live up to its principles—calls out for major revision,
to take account of all that has happened to the United States, fundamentally transformed by the Cold War, incapable of taking in or rejoicing in
what has taken place in the world since 1989.

Last year, in Rome, *Dædalus* convened a conference that brought together
men and women from Africa, Asia, Europe, and North America to consider
how the problems of race and ethnicity now play themselves out on the
world stage. It is not insignificant that it should have been a Swedish institution, the Institute for Futures Studies, in collaboration with the American
Academy of Arts and Sciences, that recognized the need for summoning
such a conference, and indeed provided the funds to make it possible. The

impetus for the meeting was Myrdal's own classic work. In the letter of invitation that went out to men and women concerned with conditions in South Africa, India, and Japan, France, Germany, Sweden, Italy, and the United Kingdom, Canada and the United States, Russia, the Czech republic, and Ukraine, I wrote:

> Fifty years ago, Gunnar Myrdal wrote *An American Dilemma*, giving what may still be the most extensive study ever made of race relations in the United States. Today, one half-century later, the American dilemma has become the world's dilemma. This is not to suggest that the race question in the United States resembles that increasingly common in Europe, Africa, and Asia, but only that race, ethnicity, and national sentiment enjoy a salience today that they never previously commanded. Indeed, issues of homogeneity and heterogeneity are recognized to have quite new dimensions, and not only because of their religious and cultural dimensions in individual nation-states.
>
> Our concern is with stereotypes and stigmas, but also with the larger issues that relate to prejudice and bias, that create such injustice and inequity in the contemporary world. Given the unprecedented events now occurring in Central and Eastern Europe—and not only in Russia—it is possible for some to portray the ethnic and nationalist upsurge as relating principally to the demise of all manner of controls exercised by authoritarian Communist leaders. The situation in the West, in Europe and the United States, belies such simple analysis. We need to explore the economic, social, and psychological conditions that perpetuate racial and ethnic division, that create such feelings of insecurity and rage. We need to analyze why the democratic instruments of contemporary politics are so incapable of dealing with the consequences of this yearning for identity, often a masked nostalgia for a very different world than that made up of individual homogeneous nation-states.

If, as is hoped, those who gathered in Rome, men and women of several generations coming from a wide range of academic and professional disciplines, are able in time to publish an issue on "The World's Dilemma: Race and Ethnicity," it will be one more way to commemorate Myrdal's historic text, a collaborative work in the best sense of the term, reflecting a time when men and women of different races could speak to each other candidly.

NOTES

1. Walter A. Jackson. *Gunnar Myrdal and America's Conscience: Social Engineering and Racial Liberalism, 1938–1987* (Chapel Hill and London: University of North Carolina Press, 1990), pp. 10–35. Jackson writes: "During the first three decades

of the century, American philanthropic foundations had come to play a significant role as planning agencies, undertaking studies of subjects that neither
government nor corporations chose to support." Jackson's account of the circumstances that led to the Carnegie Corporation's decision, dealing with every
aspect of the book's composition and reception, is very full. An equally excellent account is provided by David W. Southern. *Gunnar Myrdal and Black-White
Relations: The Use and Abuse of An American Dilemma, 1944–1969* (Baton Rouge
and London: Louisiana State University Press, 1987), pp. 1–27.

2. Frederick P. Keppel. "Foreword," in Gunnar Myrdal. *An American Dilemma:
The Negro Problem and Modern Democracy* (New York and London: Harper &
Brothers, 1944), p. vi.

3. Ibid.

4. Ibid.

5. Jackson. *Gunnar Myrdal and America's Conscience*, pp. 100–108, 120–132. These
pages tell a great deal about Myrdal's relations with his collaborators; they are
equally revealing on the intellectual differences between those who assisted
him.

6. Brian Urquhart. *Ralph Bunche: An American Life* (New York and London: W.W.
Norton, 1993), pp. 81–91. Urquhart's chapter on *An American Dilemma* carries
the subtitle, "A slave for the Swedish Simon Legree."

7. Southern. *Gunnar Myrdal and Black-White Relations*, pp. 29–48. Southern's chapter, "The Ordeal of Collaboration, 1939–1943," is filled with interesting and important data; so, also, is the following chapter where he concerns himself with
the effects of World War II and increasing militancy among blacks who recognized the contradictions between waging a war against fascism abroad and
the toleration of racism at home. Myrdal, Southern argues, was particularly
sensitive to these issues; so, also, were many of his black colleagues.

8. Myrdal. *An American Dilemma*, pp. xlvii–liii. Myrdal's "Introduction," though
awkwardly written in places, is a powerful statement of his major premises
and conclusions.

9. Jackson. *Gunnar Myrdal and America's Conscience*, pp. 187–188.

10. Ibid., pp. 241–271. See also Southern. *Gunnar Myrdal and Black-White Relations*,
pp. 71–99. Each gives interestingly different accounts of the work's reception.
My own differs somewhat from Jackson's. I do not, for example, accept that
the book was essentially a "jeremiad," though it had much that might make it
appear to be that.

11. Southern. *Gunnar Myrdal and Black-White Relations*, pp. 202–203.

12. Ibid., pp. 203–204.

13. Herbert Aptheker. *The Negro People in America: A Critique of Gunnar Myrdal's
An American Dilemma* (New York: Kraus Reprint, 1977). The book was useful
to many who have written on Myrdal, not least for Aptheker's penetrating and
provocative comments on those who praised Myrdal's work, but also on those
who found fault with it.

14. Ibid., pp. 7–16. The whole of Doxey Wilkerson's brief Introduction is worth
reading if only because it so admirably expresses the rhetorical "excitements"
of the Left immediately after the war.

15. Jackson. *Gunnar Myrdal and America's Conscience*, pp. 261–264; Southern. *Gunnar Myrdal and Black-White Relations*, pp. 86, 120. Jackson's account of Young's role is significantly different from Southern's.

16. Quoted in Southern. *Gunnar Myrdal and Black-White Relations*, p. 104.

17. Jackson. *Gunnar Myrdal and America's Conscience*, p. 263.

18. Ibid., p. 264. Young believed, in Jackson's words, that the "key questions for the postwar period were why prejudice and discriminatory behavior exist and what kinds of programs might be devised to reduce or eliminate such behavior. He doubted that the social scientists specializing in race relations, particularly the `warhorses' who had been working in the field had anything new to say."

19. A new generation of Roosevelt biographers, following in the tradition of Geoffrey Ward, who in his two magnificent volumes, *Before the Trumpet: Young Franklin Roosevelt, 1882–1905* and *A First-Class Temperament: The Emergence of Franklin Roosevelt*, treated only the period before Roosevelt entered the White House, can be expected to probe much more deeply into Roosevelt's politics, much as British biographers and historians are doing with Winston Churchill. That "revisionism," which could easily degenerate into a kind of ideological warfare, given the contemporary political climate, cannot be hagiographic in the old tradition, but it must seek to establish the political context for what Roosevelt felt himself able to do. On Roosevelt's personal life, as distinct from his politics, Doris Kearns Goodwin. *No Ordinary Time: Franklin and Eleanor Roosevelt: The Home Front in World War II* (New York: Simon & Schuster, 1994), pp. 491–497, needs to be read. Her material on Roosevelt's illnesses adds significantly to our understanding of the last year of Roosevelt's life.

20. Southern. *Gunnar Myrdal and Black-White Relations*, pp. 113–125; also, more briefly. Jackson. *Gunnar Myrdal and America's Conscience*, pp. 273–279. These accounts need to be supplemented with David McCullough. *Truman* (New York: Simon & Schuster, 1992), pp. 586–590.

21. Jackson. *Gunnar Myrdal and America's Conscience*, pp. 276–277.

22. Ibid., p. 278.

23. Ibid., p. 296.

24. Ibid., p. 297.

25. Ibid.

26. "The Negro American." *Dædalus* 94 (4) (Fall 1965) and "The Negro American— 2." *Dædalus* 95 (1) (Winter 1966). The most complete analysis of the two *Dædalus* issues, as they appeared in Kenneth B. Clark and Talcott Parsons, eds. *The Negro American* (Boston: Houghton Mifflin, 1966), is in Southern. *Gunnar Myrdal and Black-White Relations*, pp. 271–275. He also writes about the *Dædalus* issue, "Color and Race." published in 1967, and republished as a book by John Hope Franklin, ed. *Color and Race* (Boston: Beacon Press, 1969). See Southern. *Gunnar Myrdal and Black-White Relations*, p. 276.

27. Urquhart. *Ralph Bunche: An American Life*, pp. 440–445.

28. Lyndon B. Johnson. "Foreword to the Issue," *Dædalus* 94 (4) (Fall 1965): 744.

29. Urquhart. *Ralph Bunche: An American Life*, pp. 446–449.

30. Ibid.

31. Daniel Patrick Moynihan. "Employment, Income, and the Ordeal of the Negro Family," *Dædalus* 94 (4) (Fall 1965): 760.

32. St. Clair Drake. "The Social and Economic Status of the Negro in the United States." *Dædalus* 94 (4) (Fall 1965): 771–814; and James Tobin. "On Improving the Economic Status of the Negro." *Dædalus* 94 (4) (Fall 1965): 878–898.

33. James Q. Wilson. "The Negro in Politics." *Dædalus* 94 (4) (Fall 1965): 961.

34. Harold C. Fleming. "The Federal Executive and Civil Rights: 1961–1965." *Dædalus* 94 (4) (Fall 1965): 945.

35. Oscar Handlin. "The Goals of Integration." *Dædalus* 95 (1) (Winter 1966): 284.

36. Ralph Ellison. "Transcript of the American Academy Conference on the Negro American—May 14–15, 1965," *Dædalus* 95 (1) (Winter 1966): 436–437.

Robert A. Dentler

The Political Situation and Power
Prospects of African Americans
in Gunnar Myrdal's Era and Today

GUNNAR MYRDAL'S *An American Dilemma* (1944) stands as a monumental achievement in the annals of social scientific reporting on race relations. It has been severely criticized for embodying a white liberal ideology and for denigrating African Americans by portraying them as mere reactors to institutional white racism rather than as creators and carriers of a great subcultural tradition. It has outlasted those criticisms, valid as they are, however, and continues to be read, studied, and used in policy interpretations to this day. *An American Dilemma* also provides us with a good baseline from which to examine change or the absence of change in race relations over the course of 50 years. In this chapter, we shall use it, with some caveats and revisionist considerations, as such a baseline to assess the contemporary and future political sociology of the African American situation.

Gerald David Jaynes and Robin M. Williams, Jr., worked on this question in their report commissioned by the National Research Council (1989). We shall use some of their findings on the political status and participation of African Americans. However, as Aldon Morris noted in his review of their book,

> The lack of theoretical explanations of racial inequality and race relations, even at the middle range, constitutes its greatest weakness. We should learn once again that a theoretical framework is crucial in the study of complex social phenomena because, to a large degree, it determines what kinds of questions we ask and helps differentiate the trivial from the profound. *Common Destiny* does not grapple with the hard questions concerning black-white relations. [1990, p. 655]

This chapter differs in three respects from *Common Destiny*. It focuses as narrowly as possible on the political situation of African Americans 50 years after Myrdal, introducing points about social structure and the economics of power only when essential to this focus. The key issues for Myrdal are the key issues today: strategies of political organization; prospects for extensive electoral participation; and ways to gain shares in the national power structure.

The chapter stays close to the main propositions advanced by Myrdal in his Chapter 23 on "Trends and Possibilities," and it borrows and applies concepts from a middle range sociological theory as part of interpreting and projecting current trends. The term *Negro* is herein used when referring to the Myrdal era and book; the term *black* is used when drawing on reports that use that designation; and the term *African American* is adopted for all other portions of this work.

MYRDAL ON UNIFIED BLOC VOTING

Myrdal believed that Negroes would have to vote as a unified bloc to achieve significant political power. Reasons for this included the fact of disenfranchisement in the Deep South, the wide range of states with virtually no Negro residents, and the fluidity of Negro relations with the Republican and Democratic parties of the time. Myrdal hoped that middle- and upper-income Negroes would find ways to bargain collectively because their caste condition gave them inherently shared interests with all other Negroes.

Myrdal saw that Negroes exerted little or no influence on national power relations and were instead manipulated by white leaders within the major parties. On the local level, he recognized that the needs of Negroes were mediated politically by Negro politicians who were, in effect, the ward managers who delivered votes for personal gain and for small concessions on behalf of ghetto services. Myrdal, in Chapter 23, was not predicting a trend toward increased Negro power; rather he was grasping at straws in a palpably desperate hope that Negroes might find ways to unify their political community so profoundly as to break out of this divided, reactively manipulated arrangement.

MYRDAL'S STRATEGIC DIVISION OF LEADERSHIP LABOR

To make this aim more workable, Myrdal suggested that Negro leaders should plan to divide political labor between them such that one stratum of leaders would identify with one of the major parties while a second stratum remained independent and became the prestigious negotiators of important national policy issues. Even while advancing this proposition, he realistically identified the obstacles to its realization. "One [obstacle] is the internal rivalry among leaders in a frustrated group," Myrdal wrote. "Power becomes so dear when there is so little of it. Cynicism becomes so widespread among ambitious individuals whose way upward is blocked," (p. 507). By the time he added other impediments, the likelihood of implementing his vision was, by his own admission, barely above zero.

NO THIRD PARTY FORMATION

Myrdal explored and then dismissed the possibility that Negroes would ever embrace fascism or other totalitarian parties of the right. He was less certain about any future propensity toward left-wing radicalism, however. He noted that the propaganda and recruitment efforts of the American Communist Party, efforts that flourished during the Depression and flowered as active pro-Soviet friendship drives from 1939 to 1944 made some headway but never "succeeded in getting any appreciable following among Negroes in America" (p. 508).

As a European social scientist, Myrdal was keenly mindful of how the American polity was organized almost exclusively, so far as the exercise of power relations and the accumulation of influence were concerned, around a two-party system. Consistent with his theory of post-slavery Negro history, he argued that Negroes would continue indefinitely to seek to bid for influence from within that system and not by creating alternatives.

Myrdal did believe, as W.E.B. Du Bois had done from the turn of the century on, in bargaining with both parties. David L. Lewis (1993) has shown us that Du Bois was a "maverick socialist" rather than a Socialist Party adherent from the days of Eugene Debs through the turmoil of World Wars I and II. Du Bois campaigned for Democratic Party presidential nominee Woodrow Wilson, against the grain of the mass of Negro Republicans and in defiance of his own socialist credentials.

Myrdal had a firm understanding of the hold that Republican Party leaders had on Negroes from the Civil War until the advent of the Depression. He also foresaw the conditions under which African American participation in the New Deal Democratic Party as the party of liberal reform would continue to evolve rapidly after World War II. He hoped that this would permit many "Negro politicians [to] be released from the dilemma of double loyalty to the party and to the Negro group. This would remove to a certain extent one of the fundamental causes of political cynicism and corruption among Negro politicians" (p. 511).

Precepts about political organization for Negroes in the 1940s have little relevance for questions of organization in the 1990s, however. For example, at the state level in Myrdal's time, political party structures within the two-party system were dominant. There were few independent voters, whereas today that group comprises a large portion of each state's electorate.

National power relations were grounded in state parties as they are not so grounded today. And the exercise of party will over the actions of individual officials was more influential and disciplined than it is today.

THE CENTRALITY OF SUFFRAGE

The denial of the right to vote was, as Myrdal argued in several chapters of his book, the pivotal source of the Negro's status and life condition of extreme deprivational subdominance in the South. He quotes from Du Bois and argues that the broad range of Negro leaders and intellectuals, from the most cautious and conservative to the most daring and liberal, had long maintained that suffrage was the essential key to future racial progress.

Myrdal saw that the forces working to secure full voting rights for Negroes were too vast to be denied fulfillment in the postwar years. He forecast that the conservative strategy in the South of emphasizing state's rights would be defeated. He did not go so far as to trace in the likely consequences of the attainment of full suffrage; indeed, he recognized that "Most Southern Negroes seem to keep their minds turned away from the whole matter. As we have shown, they have, indeed, good reasons for lack of political interest" (p. 513). But Myrdal did foresee that an acceleration in political participation would follow enfranchisement. He foresaw accurately the rising force of federal intervention in issues of voting rights and the eventual collapse of the South's line of state's rights defense. Indeed, he slyly, if timidly, suggested that white politicians in the South could avoid ultimate humiliation in this only by initiating reforms before they could be introduced by the federal establishment. Myrdal wrote that southern white conservatives would continue to oppose full suffrage until their illusions were shattered by legal action and political competition. And Myrdal predicted that full suffrage would be achieved within a decade after the close of World War II.

TRANSITION TOWARD SUFFRAGE

Gunnar Myrdal and his associates did their research at a time we now realize was a turning point in the political history of African Americans. The second period of Reconstruction had been underway for three decades. The device of the grandfather clause, one of the bulwarks of Negro disenfranchisement in the South, was struck down in *Lane* v. *Wilson* in 1939. In 1941 the Supreme Court in *U.S.* v. *Classic* decided that primary elections were subject to federal control, setting the stage for the *Smith* v. *Allwright* decision: "Under our Constitution the great privilege of the ballot may not be denied any man by the State because of his color" (321 US 1944: 661–662). Literacy tests and poll taxes as well as virulent forms of coercive denial, such as retaliation against those who tried to register, were still widely practiced in 1942, but Myrdal could see how surely the barriers to suffrage were being felled by the Supreme Court. The Court ruled in 1953, just a decade after Myrdal made his prediction, in *Terry* v. *Adams*, that racial exclusion from the so-called pre-primary as well as from primary elections was unconstitutional. With *Brown* v. *Topeka* in 1954, many kinds of related legal barriers were destroyed. The force of the Fourteenth and Fifteenth Amendments was revived as surely as it had been put to sleep 60 years earlier.

THE VOTING RIGHTS ACT

Important civil rights gains were achieved in the immediate aftermath of World War II: the beginnings of judicial demolition of the disenfranchisement of African Americans throughout the South; the striking down of racial covenants in residential housing policies; and the integration of the armed forces. Further progress was slowed by the advent of the Cold War. Neither the Truman nor the Eisenhower administrations did much more than previous administrations had done to improve racial justice or to meet African American needs.

Congress passed a Civil Rights Act in 1957 and strengthened it a bit in 1960. Thurgood Marshall commented that these statutes were not worth the paper they were printed on, but in hindsight we can see that they were symbolic forerunners of the great Civil Rights Act of 1964.

The 1954 *Brown* decision triggered substantial early changes in political participation among Negroes in one important respect: It spurred an otherwise gradualistic process of change (Dentler 1991). As Citizens Councils formed to resist the implementation of the *Brown* decision, and as the Ku Klux Klan began to ride again, blacks responded with collective action, breaking from the stereotype in which they had been cast since 1867 as a compliant, self-segregated, and manipulable subpopulation. White reactions to the *Brown* decision, in fact, defiant and evasive as they were, helped ignite the black revolution in the South and the rise of the civil rights movement.

The first nationally broadcast occasion of the movement's rise was the Montgomery bus boycott; the second was the series of marches and protests employed by Martin Luther King, Jr., and other black leaders to draw whites into the movement nationwide. This mobilization succeeded in marshaling a coalition of biracial groups, including some white elites in the labor, church, and academic establishments of the day.

Myrdal appraised accurately the headway that was being made from 1937–1943 by the NAACP Legal Defense Fund in the federal courts. He

traced out the ways in which World War II would change the political economy of American in a direction beneficial for Negroes. However, he did not
predict, nor did other social scientists of his time, the advent of a powerful,
vast, and transformative social movement of African Americans.

The *Brown* decision, the movement, and the 1963 March on Washington,
combined with the accession of Lyndon Johnson to the presidency, created
conditions for the passage of the Civil Rights Act of 1964. Titles I and VIII
built on the progress that had been made earlier in enhancing political rights
of minorities. Title I was aimed at undermining the use of literacy tests in
granting voting rights and tried to provide universal standards for qualifications for voting nationwide. Title VIII created federal monitoring mechanisms for keeping track of voter registration and voting statistics in every
state. But in all of its other particulars the act focused on essentially nonpolitical rights. It did not attack the still formidable barriers to full suffrage.
Albert Blaustein and Robert Zangrando (p. 575) reported that the registration of Negroes in Alabama rose by only a few percentage points, from 14.1
percent to 19.4 percent, between 1958 and 1964; and Mississippi, historically the most closed state, increased only from 4.4 percent to 6.4 percent.
Teams of attorneys from the NAACP Legal Defense Fund, the American
Civil Liberties Union, and groups of attorneys in Mississippi and Alabama,
meanwhile, continued to press for the elimination of the suffrage barriers.

These efforts, the civil rights movement, and the intensifying impact of
the *Brown* decision and the Civil Rights Act culminated in the single most
decisive legislative action for African American political rights since
Reconstruction: the Voting Rights Act of 1965, which struck down all tests
or other devices used to qualify a person as a voter, including literacy. It
also set up federal machinery intended to monitor and enforce voter registration and fair polling procedures in seven "covered states" in the South
under examiners employed by the U.S. Civil Rights Commission.

Between 1965 and 1975 white southern political leaders attempted to
reintroduce in state and local legislation virtually every device that had
been used after the second Reconstruction to evade and delay the impact
of the Fourteenth and Fifteenth Amendments (Davidson 1992, pp. 39–42).
Each strategy had to be countervailed in the courts. Appellate courts and
the U.S. Supreme Court protected the meaning and implementation of the
Act until 1980, when a sharply divided Supreme Court decided in *City of
Mobile* v. *Bolden* to narrow the scope of the Act and to impose a trial standard of intent to discriminate. Congress revised and amended the Act in
1982 after enormous political force had been mobilized by civil rights
groups.

In spite of year-by-year attacks on the Civil Rights Act, it continued to
enlarge and enhance African American electoral rights profoundly. The U.S.

Civil Rights Commission reported in 1975, a decade after its passage, that the percentage of eligible blacks registered in the covered states increased from 29 percent in 1964 to over 56 percent in 1972. A later study revealed that the proportion of all black elected officeholders in the covered states grew from less than 0.5 percent in 1968 to 5.6 percent in 1980.

Further evidence of this progress is even more impressive:

> Between 1964 and 1988 the percentage of voting-age blacks registered in the eleven southern states increased from 43.3 percent to approximately 63.7 percent. Black registrants in the five Deep South states increased in the same period from 22.5 to about 65.2 percent. The gap in black-white registration narrowed dramatically by one reckoning . . . from 47.1 to −4.4 points (indicating a black rate higher than the white one. . . . The number of black elected officials increased from fewer than 100 in 1965 in the seven originally targeted states to 3,265 in 1989. In 1989 blacks in these states comprised 9.8 percent of all elected officials as compared with about 23 percent of the voting-age population. [Davidson 1992, p. 43]

Jaynes and Williams report that black voter participation has increased across all social strata:

> Since 1978 there has been a significant reduction in the impact of socioeconomic status as a determinant of black turnout. . . . In 1984, blacks at the lowest levels of education and income outvoted similar whites by 9 to 12 percentage points; at the upper end of the status scale, black and white turnout was about equal. Blacks aged 35 or younger were 7 to 9 percentage points more likely to vote than whites of the same age. Overall, the 1980s have seen a dramatic mobilization of lower status blacks with a previously marginal attachment to electoral politics. For example, first-time black registrants between 1982 and 1984 were disproportionately composed of young people with high levels of racial consciousness. . . . The trend toward mobilization of lower status blacks is not mirrored in the white population: between 1978 and 1984, the determinants of white turnout remained fairly constant. [1989, pp. 235–236]

OTHER ASPECTS OF VOTER PARTICIPATION

Myrdal's vision of full suffrage was realized within the first decade following passage of the Voting Rights Act of 1965. His dateline had been set too early but not his emphasis on the critical significance and urgent necessity of full suffrage. He was also impressively accurate in the particular trends he summarized and projected forward in Chapter 23. Full suffrage arrived, as he said it would. African Americans have, quite consistently and overwhelmingly, stayed within the two-party system; they have not, to any noteworthy extent, moved toward movements or parties of the radical Left or Right. The question of whether African Americans have come to vote in a unified bloc, as Myrdal recommended, is much more complicated. Attorneys and political scientists alike refer to the contemporary features of bloc voting in three overlapping concepts: vote dilution, racially polarized voting, and bloc voting by race. Each should be distinguished from disenfranchisement, although statistically there is little difference.

The Voting Rights Act, especially as amended in 1982, proscribes actions that have the effect of diluting the outcomes of minority voting in most elections. Indeed, gerrymandering of districts, malapportionment, and various types of at-large elections, were among the devices that, even before passage of the Civil Rights Act, were struck down by the federal courts because they violated the Constitution. Court cases contesting new and ingenious schemes to achieve dilution have continued to this day (Grofman 1992, pp. 197–229). Sheila Ards and Marjorie Lewis categorize the most common racial dilution tactics as: cracking (dispersing large concentrations of minorities among several districts), stacking (combining several concentrations of minority population along with a greater white population to assure a white majority), and packing (combining minority voters into one or more districts to minimize the number of districts controlled in elections for state and local offices (1992, p. 29).

Myrdal thought of unified bloc voting as a tactic for Negroes to achieve electoral leverage. Those who advocated and helped achieve the Voting Rights Act of 1965 believed that the Act would diminish the significance of race in politics. The two ideas, though closely interrelated, are not the same.

Racially polarized voting provides an indicator of the extent which the race of the voter, not necessarily of the candidate, determines the outcome of an election. Polarized voting is, according to Laughlin McDonald (1990, pp. 74–75), "omnipresent" throughout the country. It results when voters cast their votes as a function of their race. Thus, polarization results from bloc voting, but not in the sense Myrdal meant.

In an essay on voting equity, Lani Guinier wrote:

> To overcome white bloc voting that consistently defeats the choices of black voters, voting rights activists have endorsed as a remedial strategy the creation within the larger electorate of some majority-black election districts. The exclusive remedial focus, however, ignores the broad-based participatory and transformative politics implicit in the original vision of the civil rights movement that led to passage of the Voting Rights Act in the first place. Even at its most impressive, the remedial focus has failed to produce real transfers of power. [1992, p. 289]

However, as their voting mass has grown, African Americans have performed as a bloc in the way Myrdal prescribed by becoming the swing vote in countless local, state, and federal elections:

> Of the three elections won by the Democratic party since 1960, John Kennedy, 1960; Lyndon Johnson, 1964; and Jimmy Carter, 1976, the black vote has been pivotal in two, in 1960 and 1976. In 1960, the black vote was critical in fifteen states that totaled 209 electoral votes for Kennedy, more than two-thirds of the total he needed to win. Nationwide, Kennedy won 70 percent of the black vote. In 1976, southerner Carter won only 45 percent of the white vote in the South, but won more than 90 percent of the black vote. [Lusane 1992, p. 9]

Bill Clinton, moreover, was elected with less than 45 percent of the popular vote nationally but with more than 90 percent of the African American vote. And the political logic of full suffrage, stimulated by Jesse Jackson's registration drives, the modest successes of his Rainbow Coalition, and his extraordinary performance as a vote-getting presidential candidate in 1980 and 1984, culminated in 1992 in the election of forty African Americans to the U.S. Congress.

This number is more than half of all black members who have served in Congress in the nation's history. This achievement included the election of Carol Mosley-Braun to the U.S. Senate from Illinois, where her success stemmed in part from substantial and widespread white voter support. State and local successes in 1992 were equally great in numbers and in political surprises. Among the latter, for example: Pamela Carter became attorney general of Indiana, and Jackie Barrett was elected sheriff of Fulton County, Georgia! Douglas Wilder's triumph in being elected governor of Virginia in 1988, as well as David Dinkins's election as mayor of New York City, suggest that we are entering an era where the color line in elections will be breached more and more frequently.

AFRICAN AMERICAN POWER

Chicago's long-term Congressman William Dawson used to declare that "a voteless people is a hopeless people" (*Jet,* November 23, 1992, p. 51). This adage was countered by the equally true observation, expressed in his long career as a loyal member of the Cook County Democratic Party machine, that people can win the vote in a democracy and still be rendered relatively powerless politically. To what extent, therefore, has the power potential of African Americans changed in the 50 years after Myrdal?

Gunnar Myrdal, like most of the scholars on race relations and ethnicity in America, assumed that the racial hierarchy in America was best explained

by the psychological vestiges of the institution of slavery and the corresponding social and ecological history of white domination and exploitation. Although the color line has been breached in elections in recent years,
it is also true that political trends during the 1980s forced a reconsideration
of Myrdal's point of view (Jackson 1990). As Anthony J. Lemelle points out
in his review of a book by Ralph C. Gomes and Linda Faye Williams (1992):

> The title of the work (*From Exclusion to Inclusion: The Long Struggle for
> African-American Political Power*) is a misnomer in two senses: the
> African-American political experience, according to the authors' analy-
> ses, is more accurately described as from exclusion to illusion, and it
> is never demonstrated that the masses of black Americans wished for
> inclusion in U.S. political institutions, though some did. . . . The logi-
> cal support for the bias of inclusion is that more inclusion is synony-
> mous with more progress. . . . In the end, there is only an apology for
> the fact that the election of more blacks has been accompanied by de-
> terioration in the quality of African-American life. [Lemelle 1993, p. 63]

Benjamin B. Ringer and Elinor R. Lawless (1989) challenge the popular notion that there is a universalistic, inclusive, and meritocratic American
Creed and that modernization gradually widens fulfillment of the Creed
in real social life, leaving racial inequality as a marginal product of aber-
rant behavior and the vestigial ravages from the past. The point of view
they dispute is the core source of policy hope in *An American Dilemma*, as
it has been the guiding source of the integrationist, non-nationalistic cor-
pus of civil rightists since the Civil War. This vision tends to minimize the
mechanisms of sociocultural hegemony, in which every facet of American
society, however vast and vital or tiny and trivial, is structured—that is, pre-
designed—to perpetually reproduce racial hierarchy and racial/ethnic
structural dominance by whites. If Gomes, William, Ringer, and Lawless
are correct, the thesis of hegemony is that there is no way for the African
American subpopulation to "catch up" in terms of power shares. There is
a grain of truth in this thesis, but it is countervailed by the dynamism and
relative openness of a multiethnic, postindustrial society like America.

   Robert Dahl demonstrated long ago (1957) that comparisons of the power
of individuals or groups involve much more than membership in a ruling
elite. There are not only differences in the basis or source of power and in
the means used to employ power, Dahl noted; there are also more pertinent
questions of power comparability and in scope of power. Postmodern
America is much too complex and power-fragmented a polity to enable us
to rely on a simple formulation of power sources alone. Contrasting political power relations in Myrdal's era with those of today, Dahl concludes
that those relations are now extremely fragmented, systemically uninte-

grated, incomprehensible, and volatile (Dahl 1993). He finds that power once concentrated in the White House and the Congress as well as in a network of establishments such as the church, the chambers of commerce, and civil rights organizations, has been transferred at many points to the political action committees and to the interest groups that control them. Dahl also notes a great intensification in the scope and importance of direct communications between leaders and the public, particularly through television and radio news and talk shows, while the representational and deliberative processes common to public policy-making have been diffuse, spread out, and very hard to trace or interpret. Elected leaders and the party organizations that elect them are less influential and more subject every year to single-issue lobbies, he argues.

The effect of these changes on power, then, is akin to changes in economic and community structures since 1965. African American leaders became mayors of cities just as cities were plummeting into economic and social disorganization. Other African American leaders have entered the Congress, the Cabinet, and the advisory groups closest to the president at a time when the federal political system, as Dahl puts it, "seems to lack any well defined systemic properties." As they have participated more and more extensively and strategically in electoral politics in the current era, however, the power structure and relations between its units, has become opaque as well as disjointed. Primed to exert power and to obtain an equitable share of influence over policy, African American leaders today are still not based in any numbers in the groups where policy influence is most often exerted.

The civil rights movement, which began to swell in Montgomery in 1955, reached the peak of its impact on racial politics and national policy just a decade later. A year before his death, Martin Luther King, Jr., wrote:

> The practical cost of change for the nation up to this point has been cheap. The limited reforms have been obtained at bargain rates. There are no expenses, and no taxes are required, for Negroes to share lunch counters, libraries, parks, hotels, and other facilities with whites. Even the psychological adjustment is far from formidable. . . . Even the more significant changes involved in voter registration require neither large monetary nor psychological sacrifice. . . . The real cost lies ahead. The discount education given Negroes will in the future have to be purchased at full price if quality education is to be realized. Jobs are harder and costlier to create than voting rolls. The eradication of slums housing millions is complex far beyond integrating buses and lunch counters. [King 1967, pp. 5–6]

In the aftermath of the burning of Watts in 1965, when political as well as physical renewal was so slow as to have been barely begun by the time of the riot in South Central Los Angeles 27 years later (Dentler 1992), social scientists came to recognize that changes take place in some very specific racial power relations, such as enfranchisement or the integrating of lunch counters, so long as they do not cost a great deal in money or in the preservation of white dominance. Reconstructing Watts in 1965 would have cost at least $1 billion, and reconstructing Los Angeles after the 1992 riots would have cost at least $5 billion. Nothing approaching these sums has been invested.

It is in this sense that, as Lerone Bennett, Jr., put it in 1982, in the case of African Americans "everything has changed but nothing has changed." Terribly significant yet low-budget policy changes have brought new dignity, self-respect, and symbolic equality of social treatment, but they have not impacted substantially on the solution of extreme deprivation in jobs, housing, and quality of education. Voting rights, increasing participation, and the election of many African American leaders to political office have thus not transformed the power status of black Americans in general.

SEARCHING FOR EXPLANATIONS

John Rex and David Mason (1986) edited a useful collection of the currently prevailing theories in England and North America. Rational choice theory (Hechter in Rex and Mason 1990; and Chong 1991) is highly favored among political scientists, although most sociologists tend to prefer a different approach.

Key components of sociological theory are expressed in the concept of internal colonialism (Blauner 1969; Davidson 1973, Hechter 1974) which combines the ideas of involuntary entry into a society; transformation of the original culture that is considered inferior into a version of the dominant culture; political and economic domination by other groups; and victimization through prejudice and discrimination.

Theorists of internal colonization all converge around the notion that the political formula governing power relations in a nation-state changes in concert with changes in the social structure. Thus, as the structural mobility of African Americans has accelerated since 1960, so the political strategies of the white-dominated major parties have changed. The Republican southern strategy cultivated white movement out of the Democratic Party in the South by careful manipulation of racial polarization. The strategy was pivotal in electing Richard Nixon, Ronald Reagan, and George Bush, as well as many members of Congress.

The polarization exploited by the Republicans was made possible by the African American outmigration from the South and the white demographic growth of the Sunbelt. The Democrats inherited African American support somewhat by default. No other population subgroup in the nation has unified so solidly around Democratic candidates and platforms: Jimmy Carter lost the white majorities in border and southern states in his 1976 election but more than offset this loss with black votes. Jesse Jackson demonstrated in 1980 and again in 1984 how far minority bloc unity could impel a candidate, but he also further polarized party politics at the state as well as the federal level.

The other aspect of this process, which is consistent with the theory of internal colonialism, is that Republicans, with occasional exceptions, of course, have treated the African American bloc as a kind of colonial set of political outcasts to be avoided in the search for increased advantage among whites, while Democrats have been able to count on the bloc and taken it for granted, making very minimal concessions in promises or exchanges.

Bill Clinton counted on overwhelming black voter support in his 1992 campaign, but his prospects for victory were so fragile that he spent most of his campaign energies courting white suburbanites. He has yet to recognize his political indebtedness to racial/ethnic minority voters. Indeed, his swift repudiation of the nomination of Lani Guinier, an advocate of sophisticated proportionalism in voting, and his even swifter firing of Surgeon General Joycelyn Elders, symbolize his tactics in handling racial power relations during his first administration.

President Clinton's record is more mixed than this suggests, however. His cabinet included two African American secretaries, Ronald Brown and Mike Espy, who resigned in October 1994. Secretary Brown is under Justice Department investigation at this time and may be forced to resign. Housing Secretary Henry Cisneros, a Mexican American, began to implement strategies to make urban housing projects more secure and to disperse poor minority families from such projects into better housing in the suburbs. These and other housing policy initiatives were severely impeded 2 years later, however, as Clinton moved to dissolve or merge more than half of all federal housing programs as part of proposed federal savings. Clinton also responded favorably to intense pressure from African American leaders to strengthen his involvement in the Haitian crisis.

Most of the power struggles involving domestic policies which the Clinton Administration has faced have turned on questions of how to avoid being outflanked by the right-wing groups. Before the 1994 gubernatorial and congressional elections, most political commentators speculated that a slow swing of the pendulum from the right toward the center had begun. After the Republican Party won a majority in the House and the Senate, however, this speculation proved to be misguided, as the strong swing to the right which had begun in 1970 and intensified in 1980 culminated in an electoral transformation. By January 1995 the African American Congressional Caucus had nowhere to turn.

Alex Willingham (1992) shows how voting policy has come to affect major party strategies between 1965 and 1992 and summarizes how the Reagan and Bush administrations succeeded in politicizing voting access. He also illuminates the ways in which both parties now focus on competing for support from the class- and race-restricted electorate, which comprises the real arena in which to win votes by policy appeals. That arena excludes the so-called urban underclass, referred to most recently by President Clinton as the "outerclass."

Enfranchisement has arrived; elected officials who are African American will soon approximate the share of the group in the adult population nationwide; and political involvement of wealthier and professional-class African Americans has accelerated tremendously during the last quarter of the century. However, political equality continues to elude the vast majority of African Americans.

Jaynes and Williams (1989) distinguish between the politics of civil rights and the politics of allocation. We have covered the former's impact on the political situation of African Americans and concur that this arena is perennial and requires more-or-less perpetual vigilance if gains are to be preserved. According to John Hope Franklin (1993), great effort was expended during the Reagan-Bush era to divert and eliminate the gains made so recently. All of politics, however, concerns allocations, whether of goods, values, benefits, or rights, and to this extent the civil rights arena is just one among many in which African American needs and interests are exercised. We focus on this arena because it was pivotal historically, but also because so much has been accomplished within it and so little else has occurred.

Our theoretical perspectives and recent political trends at the national level combine to suggest why it is that the power share of African Americans has grown so little while electoral participation and impact has increased greatly. As African Americans have relocated to the North and West, and as the strata of middle- and higher-income households have left the cities of all regions for suburbia, the demographic concentration that made the black church and rural southern black households a major force in the civil rights movement has ended. In a multiethnic society where the proportions of Hispanic households will exceed that of African Americans by the year 2010, moreover, and in a polity of greatly modified power concentrations across parties and interest groups, there is no longer a distinctive or singular black establishment. Simultaneously, the black church has lost much of its hold on younger urban households and is in the same long-term period of membership decline that characterizes established white denominations.

The social problems and economic challenges crying out for remediation, meanwhile—criminal justice reforms, health and welfare service reforms, educational improvements of a deep and enduring quality, and urban development, including jobs and housing—are, as King warned, very costly and difficult to marshal the political will to make into funded policies.

The Republican southern strategy redesigned regional and national power structures between 1970 and 1990. White liberal and white labor alliances with African American causes were badly fractured by this redesign at the same time that political liberalism in its Democratic Party formulation gave way each year to very different concerns and interests springing up among corporate and white suburbanites everywhere. There was, by 1980, little mileage left in the coalition politics of urban Democrats, labor, and the other groups unified by President Roosevelt during the Depression.

The political outlines of internal colonialism were thus restored and magnified in the 1980s. As African Americans in the declining cities lost the economic gains they had made in earlier decades, the new chaos of gang formation, drug trafficking, armed violence, and hopelessness began to set in. New and revived modes of white racial hatred sprang up around these trends, and as in Myrdal's day, the hatred was grounded in renewed social distance between the races as well as intensified fear of criminal violence. As criminologists Albert Cardarelli and Jack McDevitt commented recently (1994) in their research report, "Crime and Public Safety in Boston," "Boston currently is a city where citizen perceptions do not meet reality. Fear is increasing while crime is decreasing."

An improvement in the share of power exercised by African Americans is unlikely to occur under these conditions. More than a decade of intensifying mistrust, increases in the gap between the white rich and the black poor, and profound changes in patterns of housing and economic location into edge cities, have made a dialogue between racially separate leaders and constituents more difficult by far than was a dialogue in 1965. Indeed, many conservative candidates who ran for office in 1994 found there was mileage to be gained by stressing antagonism toward illegal aliens, welfare mothers, and social programs aimed at helping mitigate urban poverty.

SIFTING ALTERNATIVE STRATEGIES

Prospects for a national improvement in the power shares of African Americans grew dim during the Reagan years and were dimmed further by the economic depression of 1989–1993. They are declining today on some policy questions, such as the future of affirmative action by the advent of a conservative Supreme Court and the Republican Party triumphs in the 1994 elections. While the place of African Americans in the federal cabinet and in corporate board rooms has enlarged substantially, and while the Black Congressional Caucus has grown in numbers if not in power, the wall surrounding the white preserve of power has grown thicker, not thinner, since 1980. Against this backdrop, advocates for a more equitable distribution of power have come to look beyond the power of the vote.

One much discussed and currently implemented strategy is that of the Democratic Leadership Council (DLC) in the late 1980s, whose vice chairman was Congressman William Gray, then chair of the Black Congressional Caucus. The preoccupation of the DLC has been with coopting the policy and ideological center of the electoral spectrum and countervailing the costs of party identification with the policies of the Great Society and with racial/ethnic minority interests.

Thus, Clinton administration proposals have tended to delete or downgrade initiatives for the preservation of affirmative action, urban community development investments, outlays for the reconstruction of South Central Los Angeles, and welfare assistance. These traditional liberal supports are being replaced by those for greatly intensified anti-crime resources, workfare, health insurance, and family values.

The logic is laid out by Paul Starr, who concentrates on a call for an end to major supports for affirmative action policies, but who could be speaking for a much broader range of policies:

> With the positive effects of racial preferences have come many unhappy ones sustaining racism, stigmatizing much minority achievement as "merely" the result of affirmative action, creating a sense of grievance among whites who then feel entitled to discriminate, and blocking the formation of bi-racial political alliances necessary to make progress against poverty. [Starr 1992, p. 14]

In other words, one essentially white liberal strategy alternative after more than a decade of racial conservatism is to perfect and enlarge upon economist Kenneth Arrow's proposition that universal benefits or "everybody wins" social policies are much more likely to succeed than are policies centered upon compensation or investments aimed at subdominant minorities or socioeconomic groups. William Julius Wilson (1990) endorses this strategy in several respects by giving it biracial respectability. This strategy entails a search for ways to increase marginal returns for parts of the ruling white elites by reducing observable alliances with those who have been internally colonized long ago and who cannot mobilize the larger mass of impoverished voters anyway.

The DLC strategy does not ignore African American policy concerns or leave this pivotal constituency outside of its proposals; but the universalism of it will mean that over time African Americans will be unable to catch up to whites within the polity, let alone to exert power as a singularly strategic constituency. The strategy avoids the question put by King in 1967: Would the price of true equalization of the life chances of the races be paid?

More importantly, perhaps, the conservative triumphs in 1994 have thrown the DLC strategy into question and generated serious self-doubt among Democrats themselves.

A second, alternative strategy stems in part from Myrdal's arguments for a unified bloc. The civil rights movement accomplished the revolution in the politics of civil rights. Parts of that movement were turning increasingly toward economic and foreign policy issues at the time it began its decline. Jaynes and Williams remark that there have been vigorous debates over the years about whether the movement will live on as a significant source of influence in policy-making or whether it will give way increasingly to the exercise of policy leadership by elected African Americans in concert with those who, like Vernon Jordan and Ronald Brown, have made their way into the White House and corporate boardrooms.

It seems unlikely that the movement will play a significant role in power relations in the 1990s. It is simply too fragmented and weak. In addition, the power bases of those who might advance the movement are not strong enough to be decisive. Jaynes and Williams give solid evidence to show that black attorneys in Washington's eighteen most prestigious law firms made up 2 percent of the senior partners and 3.7 percent of the associates in 1986, and that black corporate directors comprise fewer than fifty individuals among the boards of the nation's thousand largest corporations. These are merely examples. We might add the still tiny percentage of African Americans who are on historically white college and university faculties across the nation and the even smaller proportions who are gaining entry into doctoral degree programs in the sciences and in engineering. And we might also add the very small share of radio and television stations and channels owned or managed by African Americans. The numbers of power sources and power bases have grown, but not enough to be very influential.

The most urgent and perplexing domestic policy issues for African Americans at both the federal and state levels continue to be employment, health care, welfare, and education investments designed to advance them toward equal status and greatly improved life chances in these domains. Each is technically very complex and must be approached with great care and on a long time horizon. None of these most urgent issues puts the flint to a tinderbox of mass protest by subdominant ethnic or racial minorities, however. Each tends by now, 30 years after the greatest successes of the old movement, to have organizations and followers specialized around one issue, meaning that general-style ingathering is mostly a thing of the past.

The old tools of the movement no longer have much efficacy, either. Marches, boycotts, freedom rides, pickets, and rallies have given way to film and television as the vehicles of power communications in the 1990s. Protests of the older sort tend to be confined to single cities and counties

today. The Black Panther Party, virtually liquidated by the police and the
F.B.I. by the early 1970s, has been revived in a handful of cities, including
Cleveland, Milwaukee, Oakland, and Los Angeles, and it continues the tradition of threats and armed vigilante activity in order to attract and mobilize ghetto support. Louis Farrakhan has intensified the involvement of Black
Muslims in local protests, local organizing, and the use of the media to attract followers and reactions through the rhetoric of ethnic hatred. The comparative vigor of these activities within big cities suggests the extent to which
millions of African Americans continue to feel politically dispossessed.

The second alternative, despite severe limitations, thus consists of re-
newing and redesigning the civil rights movement and of tying the new
movement's leadership and carefully selected domestic policy issues
closely with the growing cadre of African American congressmen and
women and with corporate, legal, medical, and academic elites, however
small, who command resources for organization that far exceed what was
available to the old movement. The strategy includes placing great tactical
emphasis upon mass media communications and media-centered organizing practices now common to the most efficacious interest groups everywhere in America.

Today, interest groups can be manufactured somewhat at will. The organizational means are available as never before if subgroups of individuals coalesce enough to commit to work on single issues. Within civil society,
the black churches provided the institutional means for initiating the civil
rights movement, and black college students formed a second wave of effective investors in organized power. These are not the most likely sources
of civil agency initiatives for the end of the century or for the century ahead.
Other sources will emerge under initiatives from an expanded stratum of
highly educated, wealthy professional and commercial leaders.

The Executive Secretary of the National Association for the Advancement of Colored People (NAACP), Benjamin Chavis, worked diligently
during 1994 to expand very substantially the range of interest groups and
other minority organizations with which the "new" NAACP seeks to co-
align or at least collaborate on particular issues. His efforts have included
well-publicized outreaches to urban gang leaders and to the Nation of
Islam. His board members divided over this approach, while old allies, including key leaders of the American Jewish establishment, dissociated
themselves from it. The controversies sparked media attention and reporting. Reverend Chavis was fired from his position by the board of the
NAACP in August 1994, ostensibly because he spent organization funds
to settle a civil suit brought by a former employee without board notifica-
tion or approval. Subsequently, in October 1994, the NAACP was unable
to meet its personnel payroll nationwide. Myrlie Evers-Williams was
elected chairman of the board early in 1995, and the NAACP began its ef-

fort at reconstruction. It is conceivable that something approximating a social and political movement designed to fit the coming century may evolve from this effort.

Meanwhile, African American leaders, together with political leaders from other ethnic groups, have occasionally explored the possibility of establishing a third national party. Jesse Jackson, in the winter of 1995, began to emphasize that he is an "Independent Democrat" and that he was looking into whether to run for the presidency in 1996 as a third-party candidate. Third-party discussions have become especially intense among left-of-center activists ever since the Republican electoral triumph of November 1994.

Third-party formation is an important possibility, not because it could elect a president or senators in 1996 or even in 2000, but because it could develop and consolidate a constituency large enough and vocal enough to affect social policies in some states and in Washington. What George Wallace did in the 1960s and Ross Perot did in 1992 showed just how influential a party carrying from 10–15 percent of the electorate can become.

It takes from $10 million to $25 million to organize and wage campaigns nationally, however. The question is not whether a constituency of African Americans, other racial and ethnic minorities, and left-of-center activists could be found and mobilized, but whether there are others who would fund its emergence and campaigns. The correlative question is whether the current fragmentation of leadership in African American and in white progressive sectors could be surmounted. Before the Republican take-over of Congress in November 1994, the other grave question facing third-party enthusiasts was whether isolation of liberals and progressives, including African Americans, would deliver the federal government into conservative hands. Now, it is obvious that this can take place with or without withdrawal from Democratic Party ranks; thus, new incentives have been added to the impulse toward third-party formation.

CONCLUSION

This chapter has traced the course of the African American political situation across the last 50 years. Using *An American Dilemma* as its baseline, it has shown how suffrage was won between 1938 and 1982 and how the rate of participation in the national, state, and local polities has accelerated greatly since passage of the Voting Rights Act of 1965.

Because of that participation and the social movement that shaped cultural norms of involvement so profoundly, American political life itself has been transformed. Political party strategies have shifted fundamentally, alliances and coalitions have changed, thousands of new leaders have emerged at all levels of government, and even foreign policy relations, especially in regard to South Africa, have changed profoundly over the second half of the five decades we have explored.

Political power to define and establish domestic social policies has not kept step with levels and quality of participation among African Americans, however. They remain isolated, with important and growing exceptions, to be sure, from the interlocking elites in industry, government, and academia. And the progress in power shares that has been made was set back deliberately and successfully by Republican leaders from Richard Nixon to Newt Gingrich. Even if the progress speeds up during the 1990s, African Americans will continue to lag behind in power equity terms as surely as they lag behind in employment and wealth today.

Three alternative strategies for enlarging that power share were examined. One consists of letting the old rights movement fold its tent and join in the universalistic, centrist, and moderate gradualism outlined in recent years by the Democratic Leadership Council. Here, some of the most pressing needs of the African American population can be met, in theory, by taking quiet and cheerful seats in the middle of the generally white-dominated bus as it drives toward inclusive progress.

A second strategy would consist of redesigning and revitalizing the civil rights movement, organizing it tightly around one social policy issue at a time, and linking it to the growing elite of elected and appointed African American officials, using television as the main instrument of mobilization and influence exchange.

A third strategy would involve formation of a third party on a scale sufficient to control a swing vote of from 10–15 percent of the electorate. This has come under intense examination as an option since the conservative Republican electoral victories of November 1994. Hefty funding and a new, unprecedented level of unity among African American political leaders and left-of-center whites would be the requisites for some measure of success in this strategy.

Some of the many limitations facing those who work to implement this strategy were examined. Nothing less than a recasting of the "political formula" will be required in the future, as the role of the nation-state gives way in the coming century to the role of the world political economy. The emergence of that world system is, finally, a major source of the within-nation conflicts that are raging in so many societies today. Extreme dislocations and volatile transformations of production and exchange functions, transnational corporatism, high technology, and other emerging forces are also generating new levels of resistance to change and new degrees of intergroup tensions. The political sociology of the African American situation should therefore be studied in the decade ahead within the context of world rather than national or local events.

Reynolds Farley

3

Black–White Residential Segregation: The Views of Myrdal in the 1940s and Trends of the 1980s

WRITING FIVE DECADES AGO, Gunnar Myrdal asserted that housing segregation involved discrimination, representing a deviation from free market competition for housing, thereby curtailing opportunities for blacks. He explained why this segregation had detrimental effects:

> It permits any prejudice on the part of public officials to be freely vented on Negroes without hurting whites. . . . It is in Southern cities that Negroes receive few neighborhood facilities such as paved streets, adequate sewage disposal, street lights and so on. [p. 618]

Based on more recent studies, Douglas Massey and Nancy Denton (1993) argue that black–white residential segregation is the key missing link explaining the persistence of black unemployment and poverty. The civil rights revolution of the 1960s had offered hope that longstanding black–white differences would decline and eventually disappear and many changes did occur. Two of the most important were the election of forty African Americans to the 103rd Congress and the appointment of four blacks to President Clinton's cabinet. But on important economic indicators, the improvements have been minuscule. For a score of years, the poverty rates of blacks have been three times those of whites and, despite Title VII or the 1964 Civil Rights Act, the unemployment rate of blacks has consistently been at least twice that of whites. The census of 1990 revealed that young whites were having a more difficult time than their older brothers or sisters or parents in moving into the middle economic class. But, on crucial indicators of employment and earnings, the gap separating young blacks from young whites grew larger the 1980s.[1] If the arguments of Myrdal and Massey and Denton are correct, residential segregation continues to limit the opportunities of blacks.

Cities in the United States have not always been thoroughly segregated. After the Civil War, southern cities attracted a black population, but his-

torical accounts report that many pockets of blacks were scattered across
the urban landscape (Gatewood 1990, pp. 65–66; Green 1967, p. 127; Kellogg
1977; Rabinowitz 1976). And in the North, segregation did not exist as we
now know it. Quite a few poor blacks lived side-by-side with immigrants
in low-cost housing, but urban historians who describe Chicago (Spear 1967,
Chap. 1), Cleveland (Kusmer 1976, Chap. 2), and Detroit (Zunz 1982,
Chap. 6) point out that a tiny cadre of prosperous blacks lived in integrated
neighborhoods. A system of residential segregation had to be designed, imposed, and enforced. It affected blacks much more thoroughly than Asians,
Jews, or other immigrants our society once demeaned.

This chapter describes:

> The development of black–white residential segregation in the
> early decades of this century.

> Efforts to tear down segregation beginning before World War I,
> reaching a high point in the 1960s, and continuing to the present.

> Changes in black–white residential segregation during the 1980s.

> Forces influencing segregation now and into the future.

DEVELOPING AND IMPOSING A SYSTEM
OF BLACK–WHITE SEGREGATION

The Era from the Turn of the Century to World War II

By the 1890s blacks were disenfranchised in the South, the promises of
Reconstruction were vitiated, and Jim Crow became the norm, especially
after *Plessy* (1896) ratified state-mandated segregation. Blacks first moved
to cities in large numbers in an age of Social Darwinism, so whites wished
to maintain a physical distance from them. Between 1910 and the 1930s,
four major strategies were developed, strategies that laid the foundation
for the American Apartheid system (Massey and Denton 1993).

First, laws sought to impose segregation. Middle-class blacks often seek
housing commensurate with their financial capabilities. In 1910 some of
them sought housing in the Druid Hills neighborhood of Baltimore, thereby
crossing an imaginary line separating the races. Baltimore's city council
passed the first residential segregation ordinance specifying that blacks
might move only into some city blocks and whites into others, an ordinance
that served as precedent for similar legislation in at least thirteen other large
southern cities (Johnson 1943, pp. 175–178).

Louisville had such a law at the time of World War I. In an elaborate test
case devised by the NAACP, a white plaintiff sought to overturn the ordi-

nance, while a black litigant sought to uphold it. The Supreme Court in 1917 (*Buchanan* v. *Warley*) gave the NAACP one of their early victories by overturning the law on the grounds that it infringed property owners' rights (Vose 1959).

During World War I the South replaced Southern Italy and Eastern Europe as the source of labor for northern industries. Langston Hughes, living in Cleveland, described what happened there.

> White people on the east side of the city were moving out of their frame houses and renting them to Negroes at double and triple the rents they could receive from others. An eight-room house with one bath would be cut up into apartments and five or six families crowded into it, each two-room kitchenette apartment renting for what the whole house had rented for before.
>
> But Negroes were coming in a great dark tide from the South, and they had to have some place to live. Sheds and garages and store fronts were turned into living quarters. As always, the white neighborhoods resented Negroes moving closer and closer—but when the white did give way, they gave way at very profitable rentals [1993, p. 27].

Whites did not always "give way" peacefully, so violence became the second method used to enforce residential segregation. We had a Red Summer in 1919. That was because Attorney General Palmer thought that Bolsheviks were about to start a revolution here. But "red" refers also to racial bloodshed on the streets, primarily the Washington and Chicago riots. Some blacks sought better housing in white neighborhoods, but they often met violent opposition. The Chicago Commission on Race Relations, led by Robert Park and his student Charles Johnson, analyzed the cause of that riot and reported 58 firebombings of blacks who moved into white neighborhoods on the South Side between 1917 and 1921. One unfortunate black banker, Jesse Binga, was the victim of seven bombings. Chicago police arrested only one white terrorist, and misdemeanor charges against him were dropped (Chicago Commission on Race Relations 1922, pp. 122–135).

In Detroit there were frequent stonings of the homes when blacks moved to white neighborhoods. The most famous racial trial of the 1920s involved Dr. Ossian Sweet, a black gynecologist trained in Europe, who purchased a home on the city's far east side in 1925. He moved in, but an ugly crowd surrounded his home and, after nightfall, began stoning it. The police were there in numbers but did nothing until a shot rang out from the house killing one person in the crowd. At that point, the police arrested Dr. Sweet and his family, charging them with first-degree murder. After two long and much publicized trials, Clarence Darrow won acquittal for Dr. Sweet, thereby establishing the principle that blacks could defend their property. Undoubtedly, the larger

message to the middle-class black community was that they should keep out
of white neighborhoods (Canot 1974, pp. 300–330; Capeci 1984, pp. 6–7; Levine
1976, pp. 163–165; and Thomas 1992, pp. 137–139).

Violence was a generally unacceptable and costly way to maintain segregation—albeit a commonly used one. Thus, a third effective strategy developed. By the mid-1920s, it had become common practice for real estate
brokers to include a clause in deeds specifying that the property could not
be rented or owned by undesirable groups—blacks, Jews or Asians—for a
period as long as 99 years. Homeowners in neighborhoods subject to black
invasion sometimes got together and inserted such restrictive covenants
into their deeds. The Supreme Court, in denying *certiorari* in 1926 upheld
these as permissible private agreements (*Corrigan* v. *Buckley*). While there
is debate about the enforceability of these covenants and many examples
of their violation, there is agreement about their popularity. President
Truman's Committee on Civil Rights found that by the mid-1940s, 80 percent of the residential land in Chicago was covered by restrictive covenants
(Committee on Civil Rights 1947, pp. 68–69).

Finally, federal housing policies encouraged segregation. The economic
chaos of the Depression threatened the tenure rights of that small proportion of households owning their homes. In 1933 President Roosevelt created
the Home Owners Loan Corporation, the first of numerous federal agencies
encouraging home ownership. Modern mortgages with their low down pay-
ments and modest monthly bills became the norm and, for the first time, a
large share of the middle and working classes bought their own homes.

Federal housing agencies created and standardized a national appraisal
system replacing the idiosyncratic ones formerly used in local areas. A central component was the drawing of color-coded maps classifying neighborhoods by their investment prospects: green for the most worthy, blue
for the next best investments, yellow for properties likely to decline in value,
and red for areas where prices had already dropped. Using the theories of
housing economists of that era, it was decided that racially mixed areas and
those neighborhoods that blacks or Jews might enter should be coded in
red, regardless of their actual housing values. This color-coded system and
its descendents continued to guide federal housing policy and investment
decisions until the 1960s (Jackson 1985, pp. 185–186).

Gunnar Myrdal clearly understood the impact of these decisions of the
federal government:

> This matter is a serious one for the Negro. It is one thing when pri-
> vate tenants, property owners, and financial institutions maintain and
> extend patterns of racial segregation in housing. It is quite another
> matter when a federal agency chooses to side with the segregation-

ists. This fact is particularly harmful since the Federal Housing Agency (FHA) has become the outstanding lender in the planning of new housing. It seems probable that the FHA has brought about a greatly increased use of all sorts of restrictive covenants and deed restrictions, which are the most reliable legal means of keeping Negroes confined to their ghettos [p. 349].

Building the Second Ghetto: Residential Segregation after World War II

Following World War II, we had an opportunity to develop more integrated cities. The number of housing units built in the 35 years after V-J day—37 million—was far greater than the number existing in 1940 (U. S. Bureau of the Census 1943, Table 2; 1975, Table N-156). Federal policies strongly promoted new construction and home ownership. Residential integration was feasible but did not occur. Rather, we built a second ghetto or, as a Motown group sang, "Chocolate City, Vanilla Suburbs" (Malbix/ Ricks 1976). Four policies created this segregation.

First, federal financial programs in housing, closely linked to the ethical standards of the real estate industry, censured brokers who introduced minorities to white neighborhoods and encouraged the isolation of blacks and whites (McEntire 1960, p. 245). Although the FHA and the Veterans Administration made loans to blacks, and Fannie Mae's infusion of investments into the housing market helped to improve the quality of housing occupied by blacks, redlining was the rule; and a black who sought to purchase a home in a white or integrated area was disqualified from the desirable federally backed mortgages.

Second, there was some continuation of the intimidation practices—the stoning of homes purchased by blacks in white areas or the forceful removal of blacks as they tried to move in (Hirsch 1983). Many cities had one or more incidents of blacks innocently moving into white areas only to face a hostile crowd of whites. Most whites, however, did not engage in such violence, since they found it easy to leave central cities and buy homes in exclusively white suburbs, using federally backed loans.

Third, in the Northeast and Midwest—much more so than the South— suburban rings include many individual suburbs which, after World War II, generally indicated that blacks were unwelcome. Whites who moved to the suburbs knew that they would live with other whites, send their children to school with whites, and shop with whites. Specific strategies for accomplishing suburban segregation are most fully documented for Dearborn, Michigan (Good 1989); Parma, Ohio (*U. S. v. City of Parma* 1981); and for New Jersey (Lake 1981). They involved some use of the police to intimidate blacks—a strategy recommended by Mayor Hubbard in

Dearborn—but depended much more upon sending a clear signal to central city blacks that they should live elsewhere. The nation invaded and conquered a crabgrass frontier (Jackson 1985) after World War II, but did so with a Jim Crow strategy.

Fourth, federal public housing policy exacerbated residential segregation after World War II. In the 1930s public housing was conceived of on the British model. Poor families were expected to live in public housing temporarily as they mustered the resources to enter the regular housing market. In the 1950s urban renewal became Negro removal as large institutions in older cities—hospitals and universities—sought to rid themselves of black neighbors. A great deal of housing was razed, both during urban renewal and to create the National Defense Highway System, which allowed suburbanites to get quickly to central city jobs. Rather than dispersing blacks to the suburbs, large public housing units were erected, thereby concentrating them and increasing segregation (Adams et al. 1991; Bickford and Massey 1991; Hirsch 1983, pp. 223–227; Lemann 1991, p. 74; and Squires et al. 1987 p. 103). As Lee Rainwater (1970, Chap. 1 and Friedman 1967) observed, public housing by 1960 became the last resort dumping ground for problem families, especially black families headed by impoverished women.

CHALLENGING RACIAL RESIDENTIAL SEGREGATION: THE DECADES SINCE 1960

Writing about the isolation of blacks, Myrdal observed,

> The chances are that, in the South, at least, segregation will have to be accepted in the surveyable future. In the North, on the other hand, there is some chance that the evils of segregation can be removed by means of the gradual abolition of housing segregation itself [pp. 351–352].

There is no evidence that segregation declined in either the North or the South in the two decades after Myrdal wrote, but the 1960s marked a turning point. Old policies were challenged and replaced by new ones that eventually produced modest declines in segregation. While the changes were national in scope, their impact depended upon the characteristics of specific metropolitan areas.

Changes in Federal Housing Policy

Throughout this century, civil rights organizations fought local ordinances as well as federal policies that mandated segregation. In 1948 the NAACP and its allies, especially Jewish civil rights organizations, convinced the

Supreme Court to rule that restrictive covenants could not be enforced by either state or federal courts (*Shelley* v. *Kraemer* 1948). Just over a decade later, while seeking votes in the black community, presidential candidate John F. Kennedy boasted that he could end racial discrimination in housing with the "stroke of a pen." But civil rights groups pressured him for almost two years before he issued a timid Executive Order banning discrimination, exempting all existing housing and all new housing except that built or financed by the federal government (Branch 1988, p. 679). The major achievement was the Fair Housing Law of 1968, although this legislation languished in Congress until Dr. King was murdered in Memphis. This encompassing law was upheld and strengthened by federal court decisions outlawing segregation in all aspects of the sale or rental of housing (*Jones* v. *Alfred H. Mayer* 1968; *U. S.* v. *Mitchell* 1971; and *Zuch* v. *Hussey* 1975). Indeed, the Supreme Court approved using testers and auditors to identify discriminatory practices (*Havens Realty Corp.* v. *Coleman* (1982).

Although enforcement by federal agencies was often lax (Lamb 1984, p. 172), the open housing movement was bolstered by subsequent developments in residential finance. By the 1970s, institutionalized patterns of lending discrimination were first documented and then called into question. Congress passed the Home Mortgage Disclosure Act (HMDA), which proved to be a potent "freedom of information" requirement since it mandated that federally chartered fiscal institutions report exactly where they made or denied loans. Later, its value to the open housing movement was greatly enhanced by requiring information about the income and race of those obtaining or denied mortgages (Fishbein 1992). Studies in Atlanta (Dedman 1988), Detroit (Blossom, Everett, and Gallagher 1988; Everett 1992), and other cities demonstrated that banks loaned much more frequently to white neighborhoods than to economically similar black ones. (For other studies of possible racial discrimination in lending, see Avery and Buyank 1981; Bradbury, Case, and Dunham 1989; Feins and Britt 1983; Leahy 1986; Pol, Guy, and Bush 1982; Shlay 1988; Taggert and Smith 1981; and Wienk 1992.)

In 1977 urban development groups encouraged Congress to pass the Community Reinvestment Act (CRA), which required federally chartered fiscal institutions to meet the credit needs of the *entire* metropolis they served, specifically mentioning low-income areas. A "quiet revolution" occurred as the anti-redlining movement grew into a more powerful community development movement (Bradford and Cincotta 1992, p. 228). As an example of developments of the 1980s, in Atlanta, for 2-1/2 years the Atlanta Community Reinvestment Alliance pressured banks to make more loans to low-income and black neighborhoods. They resisted. In the spring of 1988, the *Atlanta Journal/Constitution* published Bill Dedman's "The Color of Money," demonstrating that Atlanta's banks seldom loaned to such neighborhoods. Within two weeks, a coalition of lenders announced they had $65 million to lend to low- and moderate-income inner-city neighborhoods (Robinson 1992, p. 104; Keating, Brazen, and Fitterman 1994, p. 170). In Pittsburgh, CRA negotiations with Equibank led to a $50 million mortgage program for low- and moderate-income neighborhoods (Metzger 1992).

Later, toward the end of the 1980s, the existing system of state-chartered banks emerged into a system of nationwide banks, as stronger ones bought out smaller ones throughout the country. These mergers required approval from the Federal Reserve Board. Community activists were able to demonstrate that many local banks got their deposits from low-income neighborhoods, but did not lend there and therefore failed to meet their CRA responsibilities. This put great pressure on banks to demonstrate that they complied with all federal laws.

The open housing movement kept the issue of discrimination by brokers and lenders before the public (Saltman 1978, 1980). In 1977 HUD carried out the first national audit study of housing market discrimination (Wienk et al. 1979). Twelve years later, a similar HUD audit study concluded: "...blacks and Hispanics experience systematic discrimination in terms and conditions, financing assistance, and general sales effort in about half of their encounters with real estate agents" (Turner 1992; Turner, Struyk, and Yinger 1991, p. 43). The Federal Reserve Board, prompted by civil rights and community development activists, began investigating lending discrimination using the informative HMDA data. A Boston study discovered that 10 percent of the applications for conventional mortgages by whites were denied. Blacks and Latinos who had financial and demographic characteristics similar to those of whites had a rejection rate almost double: 18 percent (Munnell et al. 1992, Table 8). That particular study was criticized by many who did not believe that federally chartered banks would violate civil rights laws. The findings were so controversial that Fannie Mae commissioned a complete review. Their report begins:

> This study confirms the findings of a 1992 Boston Federal Reserve Bank report that discovered lending discrimination in the Boston area. This study also refutes recent reports that attempt to discredit the original Boston Fed work. . . . In fact, a closer examination of the data reveals an even stronger case of discrimination in the Boston market than was revealed by the original report. [Carr and Megbolugbe 1993, p. v]

The Supreme Court's decision regarding the Chicago Housing Authority (*Hills* v. *Gatreaux* 1976) established the principle that public housing could not be constructed so as to encourage or perpetuate segregation, but this was a hollow victory for the open housing movement. Federal judges ordered scattered site public housing, but few units were built because of both the intransigent opposition of local residents and the lack of federal funds (Chandler 1992). In some metropolises, vouchers, rent supplements, and Section VIII grants were developed to assist low-income households. Although the evidence is mixed, these programs apparently encourage residential integration, as does the Gautreaux demonstration program in Chicago, which provides households eligible for public housing with a voucher they can use wherever they wish (Davis 1993; Gray and Tursky 1986; Lief and Goering 1987, p. 246; Rosenbaum and Popkin 1991; Rosenbaum 1992; Rosenbaum et al. 1991; and Stucker 1986, p. 259).

Changes in the Racial Attitudes of Whites

Because segregation resulted from the unwillingness of whites to remain when blacks entered their neighborhoods, as well as from the reluctance of whites to move into areas that already had blacks, integration awaited a liberalization of white attitudes. This happened gradually. When national samples were first asked about the *principle* of residential segregation, whites endorsed it strongly. As a component of the government's domestic intelligence effort at the start of World War II, the National Opinion Research Center (NORC) asked a national sample of 3,600 whites: "Do you think there should be separate sections in towns and cities for Negroes to live in?" Eighty-four percent agreed (NORC 1942, Question 22). Since the early 1960s, NORC has asked whites whether they agree or disagree with the statement, "White people have a right to keep blacks out of their neighborhoods if they want to, and blacks should respect that right." Just before the Civil Rights Act became law in 1964, 60 percent of whites agreed, but by 1990, only one white in five agreed with such a segregationist principle (NORC 1990, Item 127B; Schuman, Steeh, and Bobo 1985, Table 3).

Endorsing a principle is easier than actually accepting black neighbors. Changes in white attitudes are more than merely about principles. In 1958 Gallup found that 44 percent of a national sample of whites claimed that they would move away if a black moved in next door. When the questions was last asked—in 1978—only 14 percent said having a black neighbor would trigger their flight (Bobo, Schuman, and Steeh 1986; Schuman, Steeh, and Bobo 1985, Table 3.3).

New Housing Construction

In their analysis of changes in the 1940s, the Taeubers (1965, Table 16) found that new construction in a metropolis was associated with increased segregation since it provided opportunities for whites to distance themselves from the blacks who moved into central cities in great numbers. New construction after 1968 had the opposite consequence. The Fair Housing Act had a greater effect in newly constructed suburban developments and apartment complexes than in neighborhoods built during the Jim Crow era. Many older communities have widely known identities, either as places where only blacks live or for their hostility to blacks. Newly constructed areas generally lack such reputations.

Open housing advocates often target such developments for testing and, since 1972, HUD regulations require that developers affirmatively market their properties if they use federally backed loans, meaning that they are sometimes advertised in the black-oriented media (Lief and Goering 1987, p. 238). The 1970s and 1980s were decades of substantial new construction, with 1.8 million units started annually in the earlier decade and 1.5 million per year in the later (U.S. Bureau of the Census 1991b, Table 1269). In Atlanta, for every 100 homes existing in 1980, 48 new ones were built in the decade; in Orlando, 66 new homes in the 1980s for every 100 found there at the start of the decade. In the Rust Belt the situation was drastically different: in metropolitan Chicago and Detroit, 9 new homes for every 100 found there at the start of the decade; in Cleveland and Pittsburgh, just 6 (U.S. Bureau of the Census 1993).

Growth of the Black Middle Class

Theories of residential assimilation stress that the economic success of a group hastens their residential integration with whites. The Duncans (1957, pp. 240–245) found that the blacks likely to pioneer in white neighborhoods were the more prosperous ones, and the Taeubers (1965, p. 76) showed that the greater the increase in the occupational status of blacks in a city in the 1950s, the smaller the rise in segregation.

Between 1940 and the early 1970s, the black middle class grew more rapidly than the white. A minimum criterion for membership might be having a cash income of at least twice the poverty line. The percentage of blacks in such households rose from a minuscule 1 percent in 1940 to 39 percent in 1970. Among whites, the change was from 12 to 70 percent. The decades after 1970 involved slower growth of the middle class. By 1990, 47 percent of blacks and 74 percent of whites were in households with incomes at least double the poverty line (U. S. Bureau of the Census 1972, 1982, 1993).

There is an important recent change. Similar to whites, the income distribution of blacks has became more polarized. In 1968, 5 percent of black households had incomes exceeding $50,000 constant 1990 dollars; by 1990, one black household in eight had that income. Among whites, the shift was from 15 percent with incomes above $50,000 in 1968 to 28 percent in 1990 (U. S. Bureau of the Census 1991a, Table B-10). The proportion of blacks with economic status qualifying them for expensive housing and, presumably, with characteristics mitigating white flight rose in the 1980s.

These four developments—the successes of the open housing and community development movements, liberalization of white attitudes, much construction of new housing since the Fair Housing Law went into effect, and the growth of a black middle class—set the stage for reduced black–white residential segregation.

CHANGES IN BLACK–WHITE RESIDENTIAL SEGREGATION IN THE 1980s

Conflicting conclusions were drawn about segregation trends during the 1970s. Focusing on the largest metropolises, Massey and Denton (1993, p. 83) claimed that "…the nation's largest black communities remained as segregated as ever in 1980." To the contrary, Jakubs (1986) examined all 318 metropolises and found black–white segregation decreased in the majority of them, especially in the younger areas.

To avoid ambiguity, we describe segregation at the beginning and end of the 1980s, using all metropolises having substantial black populations.[2] There is no confusion about what happened. There was a pervasive pattern of modest declines, the average index of dissimilarity falling from 69 to 65. We are using group block data from the censuses of 1980 and 1990 and comparing the residential distributions of blacks and whites with the index of dissimilarity. Should there be total apartheid such that all blacks lived in different block groups from all whites, the index would take on its maximum value of 100. Were individuals randomly assigned to their places of residence, the index would approach its minimum of 0. The index may be interpreted as the percentage of either blacks or whites who would have to shift their block group of residence to eliminate residential segregation. Its value is not affected by the relative size of the groups (Zoloth 1976).

Figure 3.1 shows the distribution of 232 metropolises by black–white segregation scores in 1980 and 1990 (top panel). Segregation decreased in 194 metropolises, and the drop was at least 5 points in 85. In 1980, 14 locations had extremely high scores exceeding 85, but 10 years later only 4 metropolises had scores at that level. In 1980, 29 metropolises could have been classified as moderately segregated if that means a score of less than 55. The number of moderately segregated places more than doubled to 68 in 1990. (For other investigations of racial residential segregation in 1990, see Denton

Figure 3.1

Distribution of metropolitan areas, by residential segregation scores: 1980 and 1990.[a]

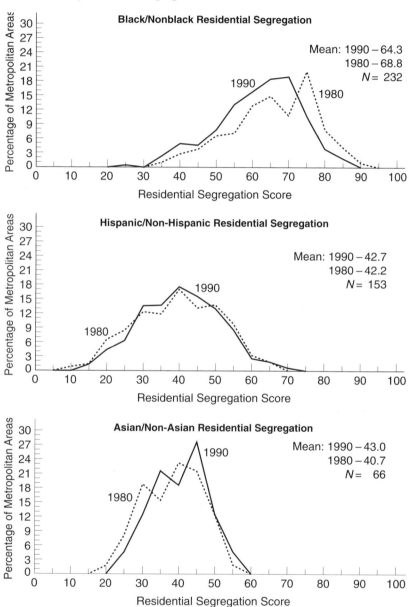

[a]Metropolitan areas for each minority group comparison include those where the minority has a 1990 population of greater than 20,000, or represents at least 3% of the metropolitan area total population.

1992; Harrison and Weinberg 1992; Massey and Denton 1993, Table 8.1; and Weinberg and Harrison, 1992.)

An important distinction is revealed by Figure 3.1. Despite decreases, blacks remain more segregated than the two other large minority groups. In 1990 the average score for Asians and Hispanics was 43, about 20 points lower than for African Americans. Because of the very rapid growth of the Asian and Latino populations, their segregation scores did not decline in this decade, indeed, the average index increased for Asians. Thus, the trend toward somewhat less residential segregation is restricted to blacks. (For an analysis of the segregation of Asians and Latinos, see Frey and Farley 1993.)

To indicate variation in 1980 and 1990, the most- and least-segregated places are listed in Table 3.1. Of the 15 metropolises where black–white segregation was greatest in 1990, 11 are older midwestern industrial centers and 2 are retirement communities in Florida. A decade earlier, the list of most segregated locations was dominated by midwestern places, but it also included 7 Florida retirement locations. Five of them disappeared from the list as their populations grew and the new housing built there was less segregated.

The list of least-segregated metropolises is dominated by places whose economy depends on the Armed Forces: Anchorage, Clarksville, Fayetteville, NC; Jacksonville, NC, and Lawton appeared on the list both years, while Cheyenne, Fort Walton Beach, Honolulu, and Killeen were on the 1990 list. The university towns of Lawrence and Charlottesville had little segregation in 1990, and Columbia, MO, was among the least segregated a decade earlier. Two metropolises exceeding one-half million—Honolulu and Tucson—as well as San Jose with 1.5 million population and Anaheim with 2.5 million population were on the 1990 list of integrated places, suggesting that some large places are not highly segregated.

The segregation level in a metropolis—and its change between 1980 and 1990—depends upon ecological, economic, and social factors, including the history of race relations in the area, the rate of both geographic and social mobility of blacks and whites, the housing stock, possible discrimination by real estate brokers, and the attitudes and financial capabilities of both races. The following four factors are particularly important.

Age of the Metropolis

The age of a place has consistently been related to racial and socioeconomic segregation (Frey and Speare 1988 and Schnore 1965). As Massey and Denton (1987, p. 818) observed, "Cities built up before the Second World

Table 3.1

Metropolitan areas with greatest and least black–white residential segregation: 1980 and 1990.

	1980	D		1990	D
METROPOLISES WITH GREATEST SEGREGATION					
1.	Bradenton	91	1.	Gary	91
2.	Chicago	91	2.	Detroit	89
3.	Gary	90	3.	Chicago	87
4.	Sarasota	90	4.	Cleveland	86
5.	Cleveland	89	5.	Buffalo	84
6.	Detroit	89	6.	Flint	84
7.	Ft. Myers	89	7.	Milwaukee	84
8.	Flint	87	8.	Saginaw	84
9.	Ft. Pierce	87	9.	Newark	83
10.	West Palm Beach	87	10.	Philadelphia	82
11.	Ft. Lauderdale	86	11.	St. Louis	81
12.	Naples	86	12.	Ft. Myers	81
13.	Saginaw	86	13.	Sarasota	80
14.	Milwaukee	85	14.	Indianapolis	80
15.	St. Louis	85	15.	Cincinnati	80
	Average	88		Average	84
METROPOLISES WITH LEAST SEGREGATION					
1.	Jacksonville, NC	36	1.	Jacksonville, NC	31
2.	Lawrence, KN	38	2.	Lawton	37
3.	Danville	41	3.	Anchorage	38
4.	Anchorage	42	4.	Lawrence, KN	41
5.	Fayetteville, NC	43	5.	Fayetteville, NC	41
6.	Lawton	43	6.	Clarksville	42
7.	Honolulu	46	7.	Anaheim	43
8.	Anaheim	47	8.	Ft. Walton Beach	43
9.	Charlottesville	48	9.	Cheyenne	43
10.	Clarksville	48	10.	Honolulu	44
11.	Colorado Springs	48	11.	Tucson	45
12.	San Jose	48	12.	Danville	45
13.	El Paso	49	13.	San Jose	45
14.	Columbia, MO	49	14.	Charlottesville	45
15.	Victoria	49	15.	Killeen	45
	Average	45		Average	42

War have ecological structures that are more conducive to segregation, with densely settled cores and thickly packed working class neighborhoods."

We determined when the largest city in a metropolis first attained a size of 50,000 and used that to classify places by age. For Baltimore and New Orleans, this occurred decades before the Civil War, while other presently large metropolises, including Atlanta and Los Angeles, satisfied this criterion toward the end of the last century. Some large places are post–World War II in their age: Anaheim, Ft. Lauderdale, and Riverside; while the youngest reached the metropolitan rank after the Fair Housing Law: Daytona Beach and Anchorage, for example.[3]

Figure 3.2 shows that older metropolises were most segregated, and differences by age were substantial. In 1990 the average segregation score was

Figure 3.2

Black–white residential segregation scores, for metropolises classified by age: 1980 and 1990.

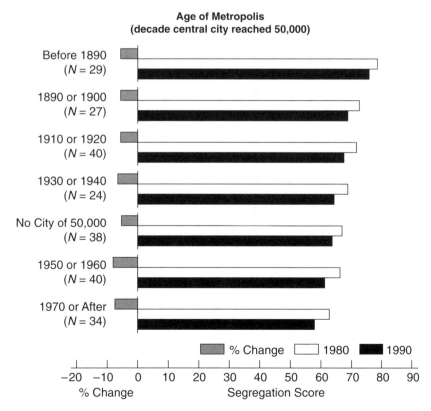

76 in places whose central cities were large a century ago, but only 61 in the newest locations. Declines in segregation—indicated by the bars to the right of the vertical line in each figure—were largest in the youngest metropolises, but were certainly not restricted to such places. Even in the older metropolises, black–white segregation fell in the 1980s.

Functional Specialization

Metropolises differ in their economic bases, which influences segregation in three ways. First, the stock of housing may be directly linked to functional specialization; that is, university towns or those around a military post will differ from manufacturing centers. Second, the educational attainment and social characteristics of the population depend upon a community's economic base. Finally, the effectiveness of open housing legislation may differ from one location to another because of differences in their population composition and their housing stock.

The 232 metropolises were classified according to the following specializations (Farley and Frey 1994):

(a) Retirement communities on the basis of the percentage of their population aged 65 and over.

(b) Durable goods manufacturing communities on the basis of the industries of their employed workers.

(c) Non-durable goods manufacturing communities on the basis of the industries of their employed workers.

(d) Governmental communities on the basis of employment characteristics.

(e) University communities on the basis of enrollment rates of their populations aged 18 to 24.

(f) Military communities on the basis of the share of their labor force employed by the Armed Forces.

(g) Mixed communities were those not classified into any of the specialized categories listed above because of their highly diversified economic base.

Figure 3.3 shows the average black–white segregation scores for the metropolises classified by functional specializations. Retirement communities—all but three of them in Florida—had high levels of segregation. Few older blacks possess the requisite savings to move into such areas, so their older populations are overwhelmingly white. Additionally, Fitzgerald's 1981 study of such a place in Florida found that the residents moved there

Figure 3.3

Black–white residential segregation scores, for metropolises classified by functional specialization: 1980 and 1990.

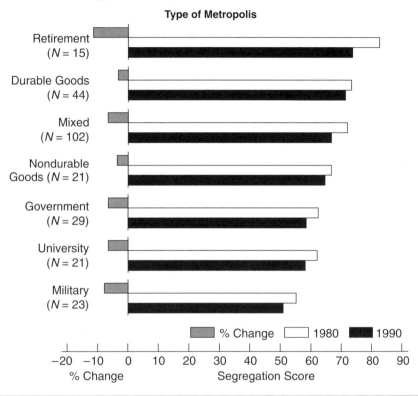

from cities in the Northeast and Midwest that had histories of racial strife, so they looked forward to racially homogeneous white areas. Despite their high levels of segregation in 1980, there were decreases in the decade.

Of the 44 metropolises specializing in durable goods manufacturing, 41 are located in the Midwest or Northeast. Cleveland, Detroit, Flint, Gary, and Saginaw have been among the most segregated since World War II (Taeuber and Taeuber 1965, Table 4). Nevertheless, there was a modest drop in segregation in such places between 1980 and 1990. Many non-durable goods manufacturing centers specialize in textiles, chemicals, or food products, and three-quarters of them are in the South. Residential segregation was not too extreme in them in 1980 and declined modestly in that decade.

Government, university, and military locations attract populations which differ—especially in educational attainment—from metropolises that have

manufacturing as their base. Many residents in university and military locations spend only a few years there, so their attachments to neighborhoods
may be ephemeral, and those living in dormitories, barracks, or homes on
base may be assigned to their places of residence.

Segregation was moderate in governmental metropolises. Neighborhoods in metropolitan Washington, on average, were more mixed than
those of most large manufacturing centers. Fifteen of the 29 government
centers are state capitals and, by the mid-1980s, 35 states had fair housing
laws similar to the federal legislation (Lamb 1992). Quite likely, those enforcing these laws live in state capitals.

Most university metropolises are moderate in size, but their black and
white populations were residentially mixed. Southern university cities, including Athens, Charlottesville, Gainesville, and Lubbock, had unusually
low scores; and in the Midwest, Ann Arbor, Champaign, Columbia, and
Lawrence were among the least segregated. Because racial attitudes are
linked to education, we expect whites in such locations to be quite accepting of black neighbors. But structural factors also play a role. Wineberg's
1983 analysis of Gainesville shows how racial changes at a university overturned entrenched segregation. The University of Florida attracted black
students, many of them choosing to live off-campus in apartments that had
previously been closed to blacks. The school also recruited black professionals who opted to reside, not in the impoverished black section, but in
previously white neighborhoods consistent with their status.

Metropolises dominated by the military are the most unusual: they had
low levels of segregation in 1980s, but these declined to even lower levels
in 1990. This was encouraged in some places because blacks are assigned
to integrated quarters on base or live in apartment complexes that have
demonstrated, to the satisfaction of the local commander, that they do not
discriminate. Even large metropolises whose economies depended on the
military—Norfolk with 1.4 million and San Diego with 3.5 million—had
relatively low levels of black–white residential segregation.

Region

Region is used because of its link to the structure of local governments.
Northeastern and Midwestern states in the nineteenth century granted
town officials much independent authority. Suburban communities sprung
up early this century and, after World War II, more suburbs were incorporated and developed their own land use regulations, zoning ordinances,
police forces, and schools. When whites began leaving central cities in the
1950s—a migration hastened by the presence of blacks in cities (Frey 1979,

1984)—they found suburban communities that had either histories of animosity toward blacks or which responded to the wishes of their residents by developing segregation strategies (Newton 1993, pp. 123–124). This did not happen elsewhere. At the end of the nineteenth century, state legislatures in the South reorganized local governments because of their fears that black voters might unite with poor whites in a populist movement. Local authority was often vested in countywide governments subject to state control. As a result, few southern cities are surrounded by dozens of independent suburbs, and zoning and policing decisions are made at the county level. School districts in most southern states are drawn along county boundaries, encouraging residential integration in those many school systems subject to federal court desegregation orders. Southern whites seldom have the option of moving into a white suburban community with an exclusively white school system. Additionally, southern states had permissive annexation laws. Recognizing the suburban trends and wishing to raise tax revenues, administrators in southern cities annexed their fringes after World War II, which was almost impossible in the Midwest or Northeast. Older cities along the West Coast—Los Angeles, Portland, and San Francisco—have systems of local government similar to those of the Midwest, but newer cities in that region—Phoenix, San Bernadino—annexed outlying areas, a factor linked to their lower segregation.

Figure 3.4 shows average segregation scores by region and percent change during the 1980s. At the start of the decade, places in the Midwest averaged 13 points higher than those in the least segregated region—the West. Segregation fell in all regions but much more in the rapidly growing South and West than in the Northeast or Midwest. The gap between the highly segregated Midwest and the more integrated West increased to an average of 16 points: 71 in the Midwest, 55 in the West in 1990. Only 4 of the 28 western metropolises—Denver, Los Angeles, Oakland, and Portland—had scores exceeding 65 in 1990 but, in the Midwest, 48 of 61 had such extensive segregation.

New Construction

This variable is linked to segregation since homes and apartments built after 1969 came onto the housing market when discrimination was illegal. Places with much of their housing stock constructed recently, we expect, will be less segregated than those where most of the homes and apartments were built either before the Depression or just after World War II, when the nation built its segregated "Second Ghetto" (Hirsch 1983). To index this, we used new dwelling units built 1980 to 1989 as a percentage of the housing stock counted in 1980.

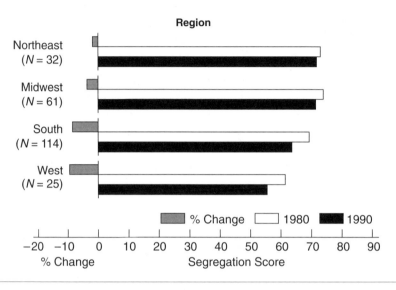

Figure 3.4

Black–white residential segregation scores, for metropolises classified by region: 1980 and 1990.

Figure 3.5 illustrates the relationship of new construction to segregation. Metropolises with many new homes and apartments were less segregated in 1990 than those where new construction was rare. In 58 metropolises, housing built during the 1980s was 24 percent or more of the existing stock. Only 6 of these had segregation scores exceeding 75, and all of them were Florida retirement centers. But 21 of the 59 metropolises in which new construction counted for less than 9 percent of the existing stock had scores about 75. All of them were in the Northeast or Midwest, except for two old industrial centers in the South—Beaumont and Gadsden. Note in Figure 3.5 that the percentage decline in black–white segregation was greatest where there was much new construction.

Explaining Changes in Segregation in the 1980s

Black segregation from whites was essentially unchanged in Detroit and Gary in the 1980s, but fell by 11 percent in Los Angeles, by 20 percent in Fort Worth, and by 8 percent in Atlanta. What accounts for these variations? We sought to explain the changes in the 1980s using the four ecological variables discussed previously.

Figure 3.5

*Black–white residential segregation scores, for metropolises classified
by new housing construction in the 1980s: 1980 and 1990.*

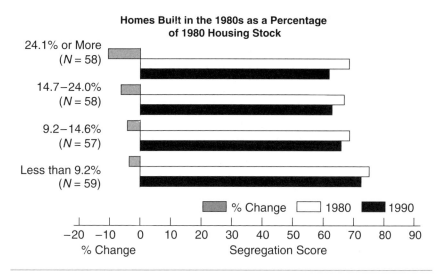

Factors other than ecological variables help account for whether
black–white segregation persisted or declined. Where the black–white gap
in economic status decreased, we expected declines in segregation. To assess this, we calculated the mean household income of blacks as a percentage of whites' for 1980 and 1990. We then subtracted the 1980 percentage
from that of 1990 and found that, despite the growth of the black economic
elite, the average income of black households fell further behind that of
whites. In 1980, black households in these metropolises averaged 65 percent as much income as whites; in 1990, only 62 percent as much. The ratio
of black-to-white household income increased in only 55 of the 232 metropolises (Farley and Frey 1994, Tables 2 and 3).

Because whites are reluctant to live in neighborhoods with many blacks,
some metropolises are easier to integrate than others. Suppose that there is
a history of segregation in one place such that whites live in neighborhoods
which, on average, are only 2 percent black. In another, integration may
have occurred so that whites live in neighborhoods where 12 percent of the
residents are black. If the racial attitudes of whites have liberalized in recent decades, whites in the highly segregated metropolis might not be upset
if a few more blacks came to their neighborhoods since they would still be
overwhelmingly white. In the other metropolis, white resistance to inte-

gration may be greater since it may appear to whites that their neighborhoods are being overrun by African Americans.

Data from the census of 1980 were used to calculate an index measuring the exposure of whites to black neighbors (James and Taeuber 1985; Lieberson 1981; and Massey and Denton 1987, 1988). To summarize the situation in a metropolis, we determined the percentage of blacks in the typical block group of whites in 1980. This index assesses the probability of whites contacting blacks on their block and thereby measures white "exposure" to black neighbors at the outset of the decade. On average, whites in the 232 metropolises lived in block groups in which 6 percent of the population was black. In southern locations with numerous blacks and moderate levels of segregation, whites resided with many blacks; in Tallahassee, whites lived in neighborhoods where 18 percent of the residents were black; in Richmond and Norfolk, 13 percent. In northern locations, whites were much less "exposed" to black neighbors. In Kansas City and Detroit, they lived in areas where only 4 percent of their neighbors were black; in Chicago and Milwaukee, just 3 percent.

In a statistical analysis (Farley and Frey 1994, Tables 2 and 3) we assessed the independent effects of the variables we described. The dependent variable was the rate of change in segregation in the 1980s; that is, percent change in black–white residential segregation. Net of other factors, only two types of functional specialization were significantly related to changes in segregation. The shift to lower levels was particularly slow in retirement communities, resulting from their housing stock and the attitudes of their older white residents. And military locations, which had exceptionally low levels of segregation in 1980, had unusually large declines during the decade.

New construction was a powerful force promoting integration. Suppose that in one metropolis the amount of new construction equaled 5 percent of the 1980 housing stock while, in another, it equaled 30 percent—roughly the difference between Buffalo and Charlotte. This difference produced an additional net 4 percentage point decline in segregation. Turning to the economic indicator, we found that if the income of black households rose vis-à-vis that of whites, segregation decreased, but the consequences of such changes were small and not significant.

Region had a strong net effect on segregation: it declined significantly more in the South than in the other regions. This comes about, we believe, because of the absence of many independent suburbs surrounding cities in the South. In addition, the court-ordered integration of schools occurred primarily in the South, and where these school districts involved both cities and suburban rings, whites had fewer options to flee.

The measure related to the attitudes of whites, that is, white exposure to African Americans on their block at the start of the decade had a substantial impact upon segregation changes. The higher the proportion of blacks in the neighborhoods of whites in 1980, the less the decline in segregation. Imagine two metropolises that were similar in other regards, but in one whites lived in block groups that were, on average, 2 percent black—Boston, for example—while in the other, whites lived in block groups where 12 percent of the residents were black—New Orleans. This difference translated into a net 6 percentage point difference in the rate of decline. The higher the proportion of blacks in the neighborhoods of whites in 1980, the less the decrease in segregation, strongly suggesting that whites tolerate a few black neighbors but become uncomfortable with many.

To account for changes in segregation in the 1980s, it is necessary to consider local conditions. First, the past maintains segregation in older metropolises. It is the political geography, economic specialization, and housing stock that perpetuate segregation, especially in the Northeast and Midwest (Hershberg et al. 1981). Second, housing construction was strongly associated with declines in segregation, suggesting that the Fair Housing Law of 1968 and subsequent legislation may have had an effect. Finally, the attitudes of whites undoubtedly limit how much integration can be achieved. Massey and Gross (1991) claimed that reductions in segregation in the 1970s were confined to those metropolises where blacks were so few in number that they could be accommodated in white neighborhoods without threatening whites. In the 1980s declines were not limited to places with few blacks but the largest decreases occurred where blacks made up a small percentage of the neighborhood of the typical white.

FORCES INFLUENCING RESIDENTIAL SEGREGATION NOW AND IN THE FUTURE

Were the changes of the 1980s the start of a trend toward much lower levels of segregation, or will blacks and whites continue to be isolated from each other? On the positive side, several trends suggest more integration.

(a) For the first time, leading players in the nation's financial system—the Federal Reserve Board and Fannie Mae—are taking a stronger stand against discrimination in mortgage lending, and the Department of Housing and Urban Development is promoting integration more now than it had years ago.

(b) The late baby boom birth cohorts of blacks and whites now entering the housing market are more extensively educated than were earlier birth cohorts. Because education is strongly correlated with liberal racial attitudes, particularly the endorsement of principles of equity, we assume there will be a greater potential for integration.

(c) The new African American migration pattern revealed by the 1990 census—an outmigration of blacks from older metropolises with histories of racial strife, such as Chicago, Detroit, and New York—and into newer, rapidly growing metropolises, such as San Bernadino, Orlando, and Phoenix—means that blacks are moving away from highly segregated places and into more integrated ones (Frey 1993).

(d) In light of finding that new construction is associated with declines in segregation as the stock of older housing is gradually replaced, we expect greater integration.

Why does segregation persist and what might be done to provide African Americans with equal opportunities in the housing market? Two opposing views—and their policy implications—are strongly defended. George Galster (1986, 1988, 1990, and 1992), John Yinger (1986) and previous investigators (Pearce 1979) argue that discrimination in the marketing of housing first created and now maintains segregation. They cite many investigations reporting that white and African American home seekers are steered to different neighborhoods, and that mortgage funds are more available to whites than to comparable blacks (Bradbury, Case, and Dunham 1989; Carr and Megbolugbe 1993; Munnell et al. 1992; Turner, Struyk, and Yinger 1991; and Yinger 1991). If laws severely punished such discrimination, they hypothesize, it would stop and the result would be neighborhoods in which blacks lived alongside whites.   ·

The opposing view contends that the preferences of blacks and whites—not discriminatory practices—maintain segregation. In *The Declining Significance of Race,* William Julius Wilson (1978, pp. 140–141) asserted that income was overtaking skin color as a determinant of where blacks lived, and claimed that those who had the financial resources and wished to do so could move into suburbs, implying that segregation was becoming voluntary. Subsequently, William Clark (1986, 1988, 1989, and 1991) analyzed residential preferences and concluded that both blacks and whites wished to live in neighborhoods in which their race was numerically dominant. Supposedly, segregation levels would remain elevated even if real estate dealers and lenders complied with fair housing laws because both races would seek neighborhoods where they feel comfortable; that is, where there are many members of their own race and not many of the other. Reducing segregation apparently awaits a change in racial preferences, rather than larger fines for brokers and bankers who violate the Fair Housing Act.

Living with Blacks on the Block: The Preferences of Whites

The Multi-City Study of Urban Inequality is analyzing the causes of residential segregation in Atlanta, Boston, Detroit, and Los Angeles (Farley et al. 1994). One important aim is to adjudicate between the two explanations for persisting segregation. In this chapter, I report findings from Detroit. In both 1976 and 1992, the University of Michigan's Detroit Area Study selected random samples of adults and asked numerous questions about residential segregation, racial issues, attitudes, and demographic characteristics. In both years, the African American population was oversampled. The 1992 investigation included 750 black respondents and 789 others—almost all of them white (Steeh 1993).

To determine the preferences of whites, we presented every respondent with five cards, each showing 15 homes (see Figure 3.6). We asked them to imagine that they lived in an all-white neighborhood, a realistic assumption for most, using the center home as theirs. They were then shown a second card indicating one home occupied by a black household and 14 by whites. We asked them how comfortable they would feel if their neighborhood came to resemble that minimally integrated neighborhood. If they said "very comfortable" or "somewhat comfortable," they were presented with cards showing larger proportions of blacks until a card elicited a response of "somewhat uncomfortable" or "very uncomfortable" or they came to the majority black neighborhood. (For a summary of 1976 findings, see Farley et al. 1978.)

There are reasons for cautious optimism about whites' changing attitudes. In 1976 three-quarters said they would be comfortable living with one black family, but in 1992 this rose to 84 percent. By 1992, 7 out of 10 whites claimed that they would feel comfortable if their neighborhood had the racial composition of the entire metropolis; that is, 12 white and 3 black households. This information is shown in Figure 3.6. As the ratio of blacks to whites rose, the comfort of whites declined and, quite clearly, most whites—in both years—felt uncomfortable when they were the racial minority. Just 35 percent of whites in 1992 said they would be comfortable in an 8 black/7 white neighborhood, but this was a significant increase from 28 percent in 1976.

Residential integration will never occur if there is extensive "white flight." We sought to measure whether whites would leave if blacks moved into their neighborhoods. We took the first card showing mixed neighborhoods which elicited a response of "uncomfortable" from a white and asked if he or she would try to move away should their neighborhood come to have the racial composition pictured. If they said no, we presented them with the card showing the next higher representation of blacks and repeat-

70

Figure 3.6

Attractiveness of neighborhoods of varying racial compositions for white respondents, Detroit area studies: 1976 and 1992.

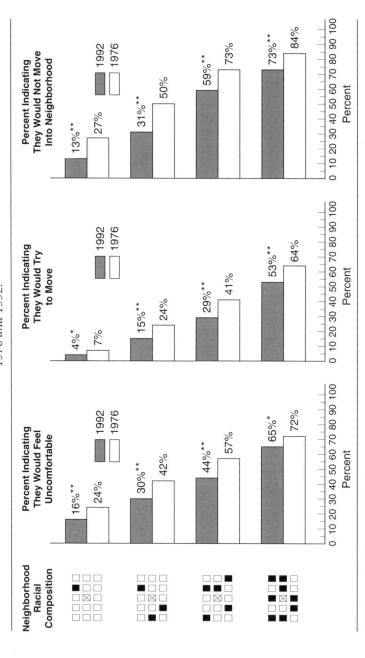

*Difference significant at .05 level.
**Difference significant at .01 level.

ed the question about moving away. Responses are shown in the middle of Figure 3.6. This question was posed to the 65 percent of white respondents who said they would feel uncomfortable if their neighborhood came to look like one of the mixed areas portrayed on the cards but the base for these percentages is the total white sample.

Few whites would try to leave if one black entered their area. In 1992 only 4 percent would do so, a significant drop from the 7 percent 14 years earlier. If Detroit area residents selected their neighborhoods randomly, the typical area would be approximately 12 white/8 black. Fifteen percent in 1992 said they would try to leave such a neighborhood, suggesting that the overwhelming majority of whites would remain, which implies that whites are willing to accept a representation of blacks equal to that of metropolitan Detroit. Higher proportions of blacks, however, led more whites to say they would try to leave, and in 1992, as in 1976, the majority of whites would try to move away from a majority black neighborhood, although even here there was a significant liberalization of white attitudes.

Because integrated neighborhoods will remain racially mixed only if some whites replace those blacks and whites who move away every year, we assessed the willingness of whites to move into mixed areas. Each respondent was presented with the five cards and asked if there were any neighborhoods they were willing to move into should they find an attractive home they could afford.

Are Detroit area whites willing to move into neighborhoods which already have black residents? The answer is "yes" if there are just a few, but "no" if they are many. In 1992 almost 90 percent of whites said they would consider moving into a neighborhood with 14 white and one African American resident (see Figure 3.6). Considering the neighborhood resembling the racial composition of the metropolis—3 blacks and 12 whites—about 7 out of 10 would move in. The racial tolerance of whites has a limit, and areas with 5 or 8 black households were not attractive to whites in either year. White demand for housing in a neighborhood is clearly affected by its racial composition.

Living with Whites on the Block: The Residential Preferences of Blacks

Few, if any, Detroit neighborhoods went from black to white, so it was pointless to ask African Americans if they would be upset by the arrival of whites. Thus, the residential preference questions for blacks differed from those for whites. We showed blacks five diagrams of neighborhoods varying in composition from all-black to all-white as illustrated in Figure 3.7.

Figure 3.7

Attractiveness of neighborhoods of varying racial compositions for black respondents, Detroit area studies: 1976 and 1992.

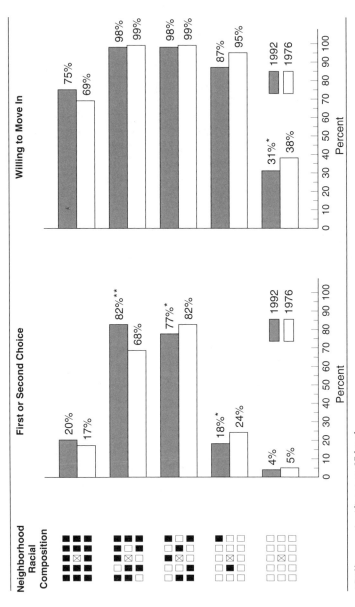

*Difference significant at .05 level.
**Difference significant at .01 level.

Blacks were asked to imagine that they were searching for a home and had found a nice one they could afford. This was designated at the center of each neighborhood. They were then given the cards and asked to rank the neighborhoods from the one most attractive to them to the one least appealing. Figure 3.7 reports the percentage of blacks who rated each neighborhood as their first or second choice.

When the residential preferences of Detroit blacks in 1976 and 1992 are compared, we find little change. Most African Americans preferred areas that were racially mixed, but which already had a substantial representation of blacks. The ideal neighborhood was one in which blacks composed at least one-half of the residents. Figure 3.7 reports that there have been statistically significant declines in the proportion of blacks who ranked the "3 black/12 white" or "7 black/8 white" neighborhood as their first or second choice, and a significant increase in the percentage who highly rated the "11 black/4 white" area as their first or second choice.

Because whites will not move into majority black neighborhoods, if residential integration is to occur, blacks will move into largely white areas. Are African Americans willing to be the pioneers who change the racial composition of an area, or do they strongly prefer already integrated areas? We gave the cards to blacks and asked them to imagine they had been searching for a home and found one they could afford. It could be located in any of the areas shown, ranging from all-white to all-black. We then asked them which neighborhoods they would be willing to enter.

Almost all blacks said they would move into neighborhoods that already had blacks. There were no significant changes between 1976 and 1992 in the willingness of blacks to move where there already were African Americans. Figure 3.7, however, shows that racially mixed neighborhoods were more popular with blacks than the all-black area. There was some black opposition to the all-black neighborhood since 31 percent of blacks in 1976 and 25 percent in 1992 said they would not move into an all-black neighborhood.

Most Detroit area blacks are reluctant to be the first of their race in a white neighborhood. Less than one-third of the 1992 respondents were willing to take this risk, a significant decrease from the 38 percent who were willing to move into an all-white neighborhood in 1976.

Lest a reader think that whites and African Americans have very similar preferences and that these perpetuate segregation, I stress that blacks are much more willing to move into neighborhoods where they are the minority than are whites. Note that one-third of blacks report their willingness to be the pioneer who integrated an all-white area. Only 29 percent of whites were willing to consider moving to the 7 white/8 black neighborhood. Presumably few, if any whites, would be willing to pioneer in Detroit's many all-black areas. Furthermore, the racial mix that mirrors the Detroit metropolis—3 blacks/12 whites—commands much more approval among blacks (87 percent) than it does among whites (69 percent), a difference that is highly significant.

CONCLUSION

Gunnar Myrdal (1944) described how the residential segregation of blacks limited their opportunities by denying them services provided to whites. Massey and Denton (1993), writing almost one-half century later, stressed the consequences anew and argued that the current residential isolation of most blacks is a key reason for their lack of economic success. The civil rights revolution of the 1960s effectively challenged those discriminatory policies that excluded most African Americans from the mainstream of society including those in the housing market that kept blacks and whites in their own neighborhoods. Whites, for the most part, now endorse the principle that blacks should have equal opportunities including the right to live wherever they afford.

Agreement with the principle of equal housing opportunities did not, in itself, reduce residential segregation. But there were important changes during the 1970s and 1980s that led to lower levels of black–white segregation, including new laws, much housing construction, some expansion of the black middle class, a continued change in the racial attitudes of whites, and the migration of blacks to new and rapidly growing metropolitan centers less riven by race. Social and economic trends may encourage even more residential integration in the future but it is highly unlikely that the next census will report that segregation of blacks declined to the much lower levels now observed for Latinos and Asians. Evidence from the Detroit study, as well as the analysis of segregation change in 232 metropolises, suggests that most whites are uncomfortable when more than a few blacks enter their neighborhoods. Additionally, very few whites are willing to move into neighborhoods with more than small numbers of blacks. Blacks, in the Detroit study, were much more willing to live in integrated neighborhoods than whites, but many were reluctant to be the pioneers who entered a previously all-white neighborhood. These findings imply that the reductions in black–white segregation will be modest.

NOTES

1. Between 1980 and 1990, the proportion of white men aged 19–29 who had finished school who were employed went up from 86 to 87 percent; among similar black men it dropped from 67 to 64 percent. Black men in this age group who worked in 1979 earned, on average, 73 percent as much as white men; in

1989, 71 percent as much. Among young white women who had completed school, the percentage employed went up from 64 to 72 percent, while among black women the rise was from 56 to 57 percent. In 1979 black women, on average, earned 95 percent as much as white women; in 1989, 85 percent as much.

2. Figure 3.1 shows indexes of dissimilarity computed from data for block groups comparing one group, i.e., Blacks, Asians, or Latinos, to all other persons. Block groups averaged 903 residents in 1980 and 564 in 1990. They give a more sensitive picture of segregation—and higher segregation scores—than do indexes based upon census tracts which average about 5,000 residents.

Indexes of segregation were calculated for all metropolises in which the minority group made up at least 3 percent of the residents or in which there was a minimum of 20,000 members of the minority group in 1990.

Geographically constant metropolises were used, consisting of the counties or parishes defined for the 1990 enumeration. Note that data other than those shown in Figure 3.1 compare the distributions of those who said they were black by race to those who said they were white by race. In 1990, 6 percent of those who said their race was white went on to identify themselves as Hispanic on the separate Spanish-origin question, while 3 percent of those who identified themselves as black by race went on to identify themselves as Spanish in origin (U. S. Bureau of the Census 1993).

3. Thirty-five metropolitan areas defined for 1990 had no central city that ever reached 50,000. Three metropolises—Nassau-Suffolk and Orange Counties, New York, and Monmouth-Ocean, New Jersey—had no central city.

Ronald F. Ferguson

4

Shifting Challenges: Fifty Years of Economic Change Toward Black–White Earnings Equality

WHEN GUNNAR MYRDAL published *An American Dilemma* in 1944, three of every four Negroes in the United States lived in the South. The reigning ideology in the South, mirrored to a substantial degree in the nation at large, was white supremacy. Decade after decade, the leading proponents of white supremacy decreed that Negroes had neither the right nor the human potential to participate on a par with whites in the economic and political life of the nation. White citizens broadly subscribed to this dictum, as did many blacks. Consequently, a full eight decades after the formal abolition of slavery, social, political and economic opportunity for black Americans remained severely circumscribed.

In some ways, the South's racial caste system was even more restrictive than the institution of slavery. As Myrdal wrote:

> Before Emancipation it was in the interest of the slave owners to use Negro slaves wherever it was profitable in handicraft and manufacture. After Emancipation no such proprietary interest protected Negro laborers from the desire of white workers to squeeze them out of skilled employment. They were gradually driven out and pushed down into the "Negro jobs," a category which has been more and more narrowly defined.[1]

Thus limited, blacks in the early 1940s trailed far behind whites on virtually every important social and economic indicator. Blacks attended poorly equipped schools and for only half as many years as did whites. The average black male earned less than half as much as his white contemporary. He labored, more often than not, in the most menial and low-wage jobs and received less pay than comparable whites, even when doing the same work. Such was the custom in 1944.

Fifty years later, in 1994, remnants of white supremacist ideology continue to color the thoughts and behaviors of whites and blacks alike, but the most pernicious customs are largely outdated and most are violations of federal law. Further, beyond formal legal structures, the civil rights and Black Power movements have achieved for African Americans a presence in public affairs and elective offices that few could have conceived of at the time that Myrdal wrote.

Still, legacies from three centuries of enforced social and economic subordination abound: economic advantage and disadvantage still correlate with race much more than might happen by chance; social relations between the races remain clumsy, suspicious, and fragile. Moreover, tenets of conventional wisdom regarding the causes of racial economic inequality, some of which are increasingly obsolete as contemporary explanations, are legacies of the past as well.

This chapter reviews explanations for changes in earnings inequality between black and white males since *The American Dilemma.* In addition, it aims to inform conventional wisdom concerning sources and remedies for inequality between black and white labor force participants in the 1990s and beyond. While reviewing patterns for all age groups, it concentrates on young adult males. The chapter contends that the most strategically relevant fact for understanding and reducing remaining wage and employment differences between young black and white male adults is that the basic skills (basic reading and math) of young black male workers are not today, on average, as well matched to shifting patterns in the market demand for labor as are the basic skills of young whites who have the same years of schooling and live in the same regions. For young males in their twenties and early thirties, research of the late 1980s and early 1990s suggests that economic disparities between blacks and whites due to differences in skill and behavior outweigh those associated with other proximate causes.

Measurable racial disparities in skills and apparent commitment to work are complex manifestations of deep-rooted historical and contemporary social forces that produce self-fulfilling prophecies of poor performance for many African American youth and adults alike. These forces include the demeaning and discouraging messages that society delivers to black males as a group and the long tradition of excluding black workers from many positions for which they have had the qualifications. Discouraging messages that communicate lack of welcome and low expectations to black male youth, buttressed by inadequate schools and talk "on the street" that the economic game is "rigged," foster skeptical and often half-hearted engagement by many black youth, and some adults as well, in "mainstream" activities that purport to prepare them for expanded opportunity.[2]

Substantially reducing racial disparity among young adults in the labor market requires supporting *and* holding accountable the institutions that should inspire, educate, and nurture African American children.[3] In addition, it requires continued vigilance against racial bias in the world of work which, when it happens, serves to validate young people's expectations that the game is rigged against them even when they do their part to prepare and perform. Given the complexity of the social forces that affect the acquisition of skill and success in labor markets, and given that social forces are malleable, I reject any assertion that the remaining differences in skill among blacks and whites that this chapter explores are genetically predetermined (as some pundits are again suggesting) or that society should acquiesce and be content to tolerate them.

The chapter covers two periods: 1940–1975 and after 1975. It reviews the pattern of black economic progress since *An American Dilemma* and the most important explanations for the pattern that economic research has offered. The discussion for the period after 1975 focuses mostly on the experiences of younger workers. After 35 years of relative progress from 1940 through 1975, the economic status of older black workers stabilized relative to whites. That of younger workers, however, deteriorated.

PROGRESS FROM 1940–1975[4]

Let us begin by establishing the general pattern of economic change for which this section provides a causal story. Five decades of the decennial census provide the data for Figure 4.1.[5] Figure 4.1 permits the reader to distinguish progress within individual 10-year cohorts from the progress that accrued because each successive cohort of blacks entered adulthood on a more equal social and educational footing with whites than the one preceding. The vertical axis of Figure 4.1 measures average weekly earnings for blacks as a percentage of those for whites. The horizontal axis shows the census years 1940–1980. The dark diagonal line up the center represents the composite earnings ratio for 16–64-year-olds. The narrower and flatter lines portray the patterns for 10-year cohorts that entered the labor market during consecutive decades. The label on each line shows the decade that the cohort entered the adult labor force.

Figure 4.1 shows that improvement for blacks relative to whites came from progress both within and between cohorts. However, the pattern was uneven over time. The 1940s saw rapid relative progress because heavy demand for labor during World War II broke down barriers that had previously excluded blacks from the types of jobs that they entered during the war. The 1950s were flat within cohorts, but the composite pattern was slightly positive because the young men who entered the market had higher relative earnings (i.e., relative to their white peers) than the older men who retired. The 1960s produced progress for all cohorts. The 1970s saw progress through mid-decade, but a

Figure 4.1

Black weekly wage as percentage of white adult males: 1940–1980.

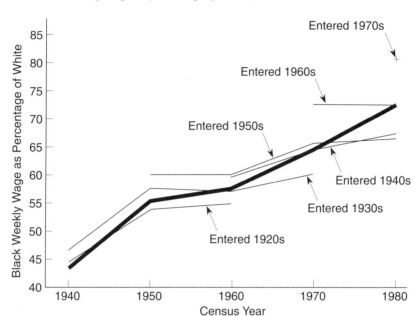

Source: Constructed from data in Table 8 of J. Smith and F. Welch. "Black Economic Progress Since Myrdal," *Journal of Economic Literature,* June 1989.

decline afterward. Hence, the decade ended with relative wage levels for individual cohorts roughly where they began in 1970. Nevertheless, successive cohorts continued to move ahead of those before. The cohort that entered during the 1970s had wages that were higher relative to whites in 1980 than for any previous cohort—over 80 percent of those for same-aged whites.[6]

Three clusters of explanations seem to account for black economic progress relative to whites between 1940 and 1975: black migration away from southern states and rural areas; improvements in the quality and quantity of schooling that blacks received; and the dismantling of discriminatory barriers in labor markets.

Migration

The fact that blacks lived disproportionately in the rural South—the poorest region in the nation—helps to explain why the black–white wage gap for the nation was greater than 50 percent in 1940 and why it rose as blacks left in search of greater opportunity. In 1940, 90.6 percent of blacks in the United States had been born in the South and 74.8 percent still lived there.[7] Only 28 percent of the nation's whites were southerners. Fifty-six percent of blacks in the South lived in rural places, as did 49 percent of the region's whites.

From 1940 through the mid-1960s, blacks abandoned the rural South in massive numbers. They found greater economic opportunity in the urban South and in the cities of other regions. The large difference between what blacks could earn in the South versus other regions was not, however, a permanent condition. Regional differences in the quality of opportunity narrowed substantially after the mid-1960s.

For example, analyses of annual data from the Current Population Survey (CPS) demonstrate that wage rates for black men in the South in 1965 were still 35 percent below those for whites of the same age and the same years of schooling. Outside of the South, the analogous gap was 17 percent.[8] By 1973, the gap for the South had shrunk to between 19 and 20 percent. The percentage difference for blacks in other regions had moved by less than two percentage points. Curiously, and suddenly, the data show a large positive spike in relative improvement for blacks outside the South between 1973 and 1975.[9] During these two years, the black–white wage gap outside the South was cut in half from almost 16 percent down to 8 percent. By 1980, however, the gap outside the South had returned to its 1973 level. Hence, nearly all of the sustained wage gains for black men relative to white men in the 15 years from 1965 through 1980 came in the South.[10] In addition, wage levels in the South for all racial groups, including whites, were slowly catching up with those in the rest of the nation.[11]

Hence, the economic incentive for blacks to leave the South decreased rather dramatically after 1965. The direction of migration reversed during the 1970s with a small net migration back to the South. Today, roughly half of all black Americans live in the South, and over 80 percent live in urban areas.

Younger cohorts of blacks in the South migrated away in larger numbers than did their elders. This helped to increase their wages relative to whites more rapidly. Overall, migrants out of the South comprised 14.6 percent of southern blacks during the 1940s, 13.7 percent during the 1950s, and 11.9 percent during the 1960s.[12] These are lower than the numbers for 20–24-year-olds. Net migration figures show that 26.3 percent of the South's 20–24-year-old black males left the South in the 1940s, 24.5 percent left in the 1950s, and 19.3 percent left during the 1960s.[13]

To summarize, migration was important among the reasons that wages for black males rose relative to those for white males during the period from 1940 to 1965. Smith and Welch estimate that migration boosted the black–white wage ratio by 20 percent between 1940 and 1970 for young men with 5 or fewer years of experience.[14] The gains were smaller for older cohorts who migrated in smaller numbers.

Schooling

Little agreement exists concerning how best to measure school quality. It is clear, however, that gross differences in resources available to black and white children as existed in the South in the earlier part of the twentieth century could not possibly have provided them with equal opportunities to learn.

When Gunnar Myrdal wrote *An American Dilemma*, disparities in educational resources for black and white children in the South were diminishing, but still large. Card and Krueger have assembled data that show average pupil/teacher ratios, term length, and teacher pay for 18 segregated states between 1915 and 1966. These disparities were not inadvertent. For example, Myrdal quotes from a report on teacher salaries:

> An additional argument in favor of the salary differential [between black and white teachers] is the general tradition of the South that negroes and whites are not to be paid equivalent salaries for equivalent work. . . . the custom is one . . . that the practical school administrator must not ignore.[15]

Figure 4.2 shows the patterns that Card and Krueger document.[16] In 1915, blacks shared classrooms with three fellow students for every two in the classes that whites attended. They attended school only two-thirds as many days as whites did. Further, black teachers earned less than half of what white teachers earned. The 50 years between 1915 and 1965 were years of hard-fought battles for educational equity. Those battles produced convergence in at least some measures of school quality.

Figure 4.2 shows that by 1965, black schools in the South had achieved near parity on pupil/teacher ratios, term length, and teacher pay. This convergence along several dimensions of school quality probably helps to explain why younger cohorts in the labor market did better both absolutely and relative to whites than did their fathers and older brothers.[17]

Card and Krueger present evidence of a link between the school resource variables in Figure 4.2—pupil/teacher ratios, term length, and teacher pay—and later adult earnings for men who attended the southern schools that Figure 4.2 represents. Specifically, Card and Krueger estimate rates of return to additional years of schooling for men in nine northern states in 1960, 1970, and 1980, who were born and educated in the South. They show

Figure 4.2

Relative school quality in eighteen segregated states: 1915–1966.

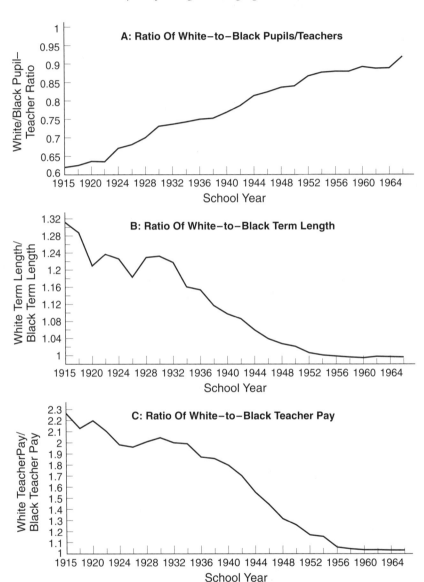

Source: Card and Krueger 1992.

that state-by-state differences between blacks and whites in the economic return to an additional year of schooling are correlated with black–white differences in schooling resources in the southern states at the times that the men received their educations.

Figure 4.3 shows one of the patterns that their work reveals. The vertical axis shows the black–white difference in the percentage increase in income associated with an additional year of schooling. The horizontal axis shows the black–white difference in average pupil–teacher ratios. Although the pattern in the diagram does not prove causation, the correlation is clearly negative: smaller class sizes appear to increase the value of an additional year of schooling.

During the period from 1960 to 1980 that Card and Krueger studied, the relative rate of return to an extra year of schooling for black men educated in the South and working in the North was higher for younger cohorts than for older ones. The rate of return to schooling for the younger cohorts of southern-born blacks was higher not only relative to whites but relative to

Figure 4.3

Difference in rate of return to schooling versus difference in pupil–teacher ratio: 1910–1939 (men born in the South).

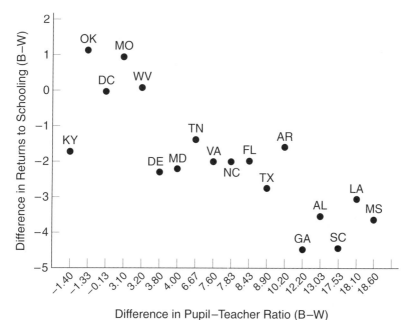

Source: D. Card and A. Krueger. "Schooling Quality and Black-White Relative Earnings: A Direct Assessment." *Quarterly Journal of Economics,* Feb. 1982.

northern-born blacks as well. This increase in the return to schooling as compared with northern-born blacks who worked in the same northern labor markets, suggests that the gain for southern blacks between 1960 and 1980 was not due simply to civil rights pressures on employers. These pressures would presumably have affected all blacks living in the North in a similar way, regardless of the region of their birth. Instead, Card and Krueger argue, the higher rates of return to schooling for the younger cohorts reflect improvements in the relative quality of the schools that younger cohorts of southern-born blacks attended. In addition, the increasing quality of the schools that black youth in the South attended probably helps to explain why younger cohorts chose to attend school longer.

Indeed, the gain in years of schooling for blacks in the United States after 1940 is truly impressive. Since the majority of blacks lived in the South, the national pattern reflects southern progress disproportionately. In 1940, the average 16–64-year-old black male in the United States had only 4.70 years of schooling. The average for whites was 9.38. This difference of almost four years diminished to 1.5 years by 1980. By then, average years of schooling had risen to 12.50 for whites against 11.00 for blacks. For the youngest adults, the difference by 1980 was less than one year.[18] Not only was the gap in average years of schooling closing, the gap in what an extra year of schooling contributed to earning power was closing as well. Some estimates show that blacks and whites with less than 15 years of experience had virtually the same rate of return to an additional year of schooling in 1980.[19]

Civil Rights

While some effects of the civil rights movement on relative earnings may have begun before 1960, most probably came afterward. The topics addressed above—migration, improvements in school quality, and more years in school—leave roughly one-third to one-half of the gain in relative earnings for blacks between 1960 and 1980 unexplained.[20] Research on the link between black economic progress and the civil rights movement has not produced a definitive estimate of how important affirmative action and civil rights enforcement were to black economic gains after 1960. We know, for example, that black employment increased in firms that were federal contractors and subject to federal affirmative action requirements. This improvement was concentrated in the South where black wage gains were greatest.[21] In addition, we know that relative improvements in black earnings between 1960 and 1980 were concentrated between the late 1960s and the early 1970s during a period when formal and informal pressures to provide equal employment opportunity were especially strong. What we do not know with any precision is what percentage of observed improvements in employment outcomes for blacks were due to these and other civil rights pressures. Given that one-third to one-half of the gains after 1960 are not easily explained otherwise, the impact may have been substantial.

Whatever the importance of federal pressure may have been, the period of advancement in labor market outcomes for black males ended, at least temporarily, in the mid-1970s.

THE LACK OF PROGRESS AFTER 1975

By 1975, black males had earnings that were within 8 percent of those for whites who shared the same patterns of working and had equal years of schooling.[22] Since the mid-1970s, however, the level of wage disparity between black and white males older than age 45 has been roughly constant. Disparity among younger males has increased, with younger blacks falling further behind.[23] The possible reasons are complex and not fully understood.[24]

The CPS provides the data that researchers use most commonly to track annual changes in earnings and employment. Based upon analyses of CPS data, several authors have reported the decline in relative earnings for young black males.[25] Figures 4.4 and 4.5 show the percentage gap since 1973 between blacks and whites (black minus white) in usual weekly earnings, holding constant years of schooling and potential experience.[26] Figure 4.6 shows employment–population ratios for men with less than 12, exactly 12, and exactly 16 years of schooling. All of the numbers in Figures 4.4, 4.5, and 4.6 are for young men 18 years old and over, with 9 or fewer years of labor market experience.[27]

Figures 4.4 and 4.5 show that the pattern of change differed across regions and for men with different amounts of schooling. The greatest deterioration in relative earnings was for groups that experienced the most equality in the mid-1970s: college graduates, men in the Midwest, and, to a lesser extent, men in the Northeast.

Figure 4.6 shows that the employment–population ratio deteriorated at least slightly for all but white college graduates after the mid-1970s.[28] However, the only group with large and perhaps permanent deterioration in its position—diverging sharply from employment levels of the mid-1970s— are black high school dropouts. Figure 4.6 shows no time after 1981 when more than 50 percent of black male dropouts in this age range were employed.

Increased Demand for Skill

A partial explanation for the increasing wage disparity between young blacks and whites after the mid-1970s is an increase in the demand for, and the price of, skill.[29] Even though it appears that blacks gradually have been

Figure 4.4

Black–white percentage earnings gap by level of schooling, young men with less than 10 years experience.

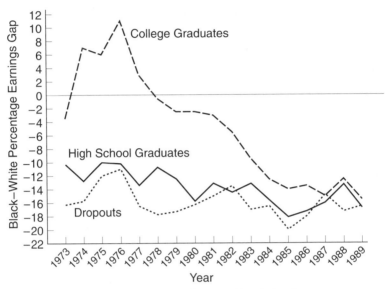

Source: Bound and Freeman 1992. Analysis of Current Population Survey.

closing the gap in skill between themselves and whites,[30] the market "price of skill" (defined below) during this period may have been growing more rapidly than the racial gap in skill has been closing.[31]

Consider a hypothetical example. Imagine that points on a particular test are a good measure of proficiency in basic reading and math skills. Employers buy (or, more accurately, rent) these skills by hiring employees to use their skills in the workplace. In effect, employers are bidding against one another for employees with good basic skills. The "price" of "10 points worth of skill" is the difference in wage rates that the employer pays for the skills associated with the ten points. If the "price of skill" were $0.10 per point in 1980 and rose to $0.25 per point by 1990, then two otherwise identical people whose test scores were 10 points apart could expect the difference in their wages to rise from $1.00 per hour in 1980 to $2.50 per hour by 1990. If the test score gap closed from 10 points in 1980 to become, say, 7 points in 1990, then the gap in wages would not grow to $2.50, but it nevertheless would rise to $1.75. For the wage gap to remain constant at $1.00 in this example, the gap in test scores would have to fall from 10 in 1980 to 4 in 1990.

Figure 4.5

Black–white percentage earnings gap by region (high school or less), young men with less than 10 years experience.

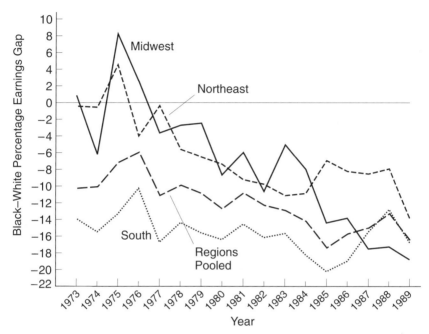

Source: Bound and Freeman 1992. Analysis of Current Population Survey.

Why do we believe that the market value of skill has risen? One piece of evidence is that the gap in earnings between high school and college graduates grew on the order of 1 percent per year during the decade of the 1980s.[32] Card and Krueger report that the percentage gap in earnings between blacks and whites with equal years of schooling tends to move up and down as the percentage gap in earnings between high school and college graduates rises and falls.[33] Another reason to believe that the market value of skill has risen is that differences in wages predicted by differences in test scores that measure basic reading and math scores have, by some estimates, grown. This evidence of the increasing importance of test scores as predictors of earnings, however, is based on data that are not completely appropriate.[34] Hence, while the story is quite plausible, the question remains an open one among researchers.

Figure 4.6

Employment–population ratios, by levels of schooling, black and white males with less than 10 years experience.

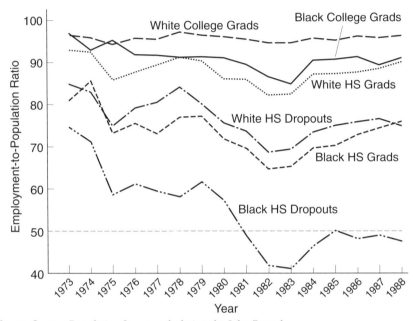

Source: Current Population Survey, tabulations by John Bound.

Skill-Biased Economic Change

Changes in the economy that have impacts on workers that vary according to their proficiencies in relevant skills are examples of "skill-biased economic changes." For example, employment in the United States has been falling in the public sector and in jobs protected by unions. Public sector and union jobs tend to insulate workers from head-to-head competition based on proficiency. Another example is that competition from immigrants and foreign workers in the least-skilled jobs that pay the lowest wages has been increasing. This increase in the supply of low-skilled labor suppresses the wage rate for such workers and thereby increases the cost to any given low-wage worker of not having better skills. Better skills might earn him or her a job in a segment of the labor market not affected so much by immigration. For a third example, modernization in both manufacturing and service sector technology is requiring new modes of workplace organization that entail more learning on the job, more responsibility among rank-and-file workers for managing technology, more reading of manuals, more writing of reports, and more working in groups.[35] These trends appear to be increasing the demand for both cognitive and social skills. Each may be helping to increase wage differences between people at different skill levels.

Bound and Freeman attempt to measure the degree to which some of the factors listed above help to predict the trends in Figures 4.4 and 4.5.[36] The factors that they study include changes over time in location patterns, industrial and occupational employment shares, unionism, and the real value of the minimum wage. All may be causes or consequences of changes in the price of skill, as defined above, and associated increases in economic disparity.

Table 4.1 summarizes what Bound and Freeman find. The "Average Annual Change" at the top of each column represents the average annual change from 1973 through 1989 of average weekly earnings for blacks as a percentage of those for whites, holding constant years of schooling and potential experience. The lines numbered 1 through 5 show how much of the average annual change Bound and Freeman estimate to be associated with each respective category of explanatory variables.

The "Average Annual Change" is most negative for college grads (–1.547 percent per year, in column 2) and for men with 12 or fewer years of schooling in the Midwest (-1.42 percent per year, in column 5). The most important factor for the Midwest is industry. This reflects the disproportionate shift of young black men in the Midwest out of manufacturing as older manufacturing plants closed in older central cities where blacks are most concentrated. The biggest drop for college-educated men is associated with occupation. Numbers not shown here demonstrate that 80 percent of the effect of occupation reflects greater shifts into lower-wage occupations for college-educated blacks than for college-educated whites, and 20 percent reflects reductions in the wages of occupations that blacks already tended to occupy more than whites in the early 1970s. However, even after all of the categories of variables are included, 59 percent of the trend for college graduates remains unexplained in the Bound and Freeman analysis.

The trend in earnings inequality for black dropouts in Table 4.1 is not as negative as that for high school and college graduates. Indeed, the fall in the real value of the minimum wage is sufficient alone to account for the trend. This, however, is not the most important story for black dropouts. First, white dropouts experienced a large amount of erosion in the inflation-adjusted value of their own weekly earnings, so the fact that blacks did almost as well as whites is not grounds for solace. Second, recall the divergent employment trend for black high school dropouts in Figure 4.6. It appears that changes in the relative demand for black labor appeared more

Table 4.1

Annual change in black–white earnings gap as percentage of white earnings for young men attributable to various listed sources (men with less than 10 years of experience: 1973–1989).

| | United States | | | | Region (hs or less) | | |
| | Total | College Grad | High School Graduate | Dropout | Midwest | Northeast | South |
	1	2	3	4	5	6	7
Average Annual Change	-0.565	-1.547	-0.449	-0.208	-1.424	-0.797	-0.241
1. Due to Location	-0.062	-0.167	-0.041	-0.109	-0.188	-0.300	-0.014
2. Due to Industry	-0.058	-0.108	-0.046	-0.106	-0.455	-0.140	-0.062
3. Due to Occupation	-0.109	-0.296	-0.157	-0.018	-0.162	-0.042	-0.106
4. Due to Unionism	-0.027	-0.024	-0.046	-0.047	-0.126	-0.108	-0.058
5. Due to Minimum Wage	-0.097	-0.042	-0.120	-0.203	-0.101	-0.034	-0.181
Total of Lines 1-5	-0.353	-0.637	-0.410	-0.229	-1.132	-0.624	-0.185

Source: Adapted from estimates presented in Table III, Bound and Freeman 1992, p. 213. See text for further explanation.

through changes in weekly earnings (Figure 4.4) for men with high school and college educations and more through falling employment rates for high school dropouts (Figure 4.6)

An important source of job competition for black dropouts is immigration. Immigration is a skill-biased economic phenomenon because it has different effects on workers at different skill levels. Immigrants have increased the supply of labor in low-wage, low-skill segments of the labor market. One study estimates that legal and illegal immigrants together comprised a group equal to 17 percent of high school dropouts in 1975.[37] This number nearly doubled to 31 percent by 1985. The same study calculates that the number of high school dropouts apparently displaced by net imports to manufacturing grew from 1.5 percent to 12 percent over the same period. These numbers are large enough to be partly responsible for the deterioration in employment outcomes that less skilled young workers, especially black dropouts, experienced during the 1975–1985 decade.

The queuing theory of labor demand helps to explain what may be happening to young black males. The theory posits that employers hire from the front of an implicit labor queue. The applicants whom the employer expects will be most desirable as employees are at the front of the queue. The workers whom the employer expects will be less productive or otherwise less desirable are at the back of the queue. Employers will hire them last, if at all.

If employers hire from the front of the queue, and if blacks are disproportionately at the back—behind immigrants and native-born members of other racial groups—then blacks will suffer the greatest deterioration in employment when the number of immigrants grows. Precise estimates of the effect that immigration has on employment for black dropouts are not available. Nevertheless, growth in the size of the immigrant labor force probably helps to explain the trend in employment-to-population ratios for black high school dropouts in Figure 4.6. The chapter returns below to consider some reasons that young black dropouts may be more often at the back of the hiring queue.[38]

A more disaggregated set of industrial and occupational categories in the study by Bound and Freeman would probably have explained an even larger percentage of the trends in earnings inequality. Nevertheless, even at the levels of aggregation that they used, they identified an increasing propensity after 1973 for blacks to occupy less lucrative occupations and to work in industries that offered lower pay. For high school dropouts, some of this appears to be the consequence of increasing competition from immigrants. For high school and college graduates, our analysis suggests that some of the shifting across occupations and industries may be the consequence of changing skill requirements and racial differences in how well blacks versus whites meet those requirements. First, however, a non-trivial share of this shifting is almost certainly the consequence of declining pressure for affirmative action.

Equal Opportunity and Affirmative Action

Declining pressures by the federal government and by other parts of society for equal employment opportunity and for affirmative action probably account for some of the industry and occupation effects in Table 4.1, as well as for some of the trends that remain unexplained. During the early 1970s, affirmative outreach for young minority workers, especially college graduates, was in style. The civil rights movement and the resulting federal laws and regulations significantly reduced the possibility that past customs of racial exclusion could go unquestioned during the 1960s and early 1970s. Many employers in the late 1960s and early 1970s probably responded to the mood of the times and "voluntarily"—without court orders or contract compliance obligations—hired blacks into positions that they had reserved for whites in the past.

Title VII of the Civil Rights Act of 1964 and President Johnson's Executive Order 11246 provided official enforcement powers to the federal government. With these powers, the government put pressure on firms that discriminated against racial minorities and also on federal contractors who may in the past have had no concern for racial balance. Acting under the provisions of Title VII, federal courts awarded damages against firms convicted of racial bias. Hence, for example, *Griggs* v. *Duke Power Company* put the business community on notice that even the appearance of a discriminatory motive—use of an exam that had a racially disproportionate impact and without sufficient job relatedness—could put them at risk for heavy fines and penalties.

Pressures for affirmative action by federal contractors waned during the 1980s. According to Jonathan Leonard, who has studied these issues extensively, " . . . affirmative action under the contract compliance program virtually ceased to exist in all but name after 1980."[39] As partial evidence, Leonard points out that the black share of employment in the early 1980s grew more rapidly in firms that were not federal contractors than in firms that were. He remarks, "It was as though contractors were returning to a growth path they had been forced off by previous affirmative action efforts."

Economic opportunity for racial minorities was not a priority during Ronald Reagan's presidency. Neither, for that matter, were these issues as focal in the Carter administration of the late 1970s as they had been in the

Johnson administration of the late 1960s. Hence, even in the absence of changes in the actual performance of federal enforcement agencies, it seems reasonable to expect that employers after the late 1970s may have, as Leonard suggests, returned for the most part to the patterns that they would have followed in the absence of federal pressure.

Changes from the 1970s to the 1980s in the relative occupational distributions of young blacks and whites are consistent with this interpretation. In the 1970s young black college graduates were as likely as their white counterparts to be in managerial and professional occupations. By the late 1980s they were 13 percent less likely than young whites to be in these occupations.[40] Black high school graduates lost ground as well. In the 1970s young blacks had more than their share of jobs as operatives but less than their share of craftworker positions. By the late 1980s the percentage of young black workers in operatives was the same as that for whites, and blacks had lost even further ground as craftworkers.[41]

THE IMPORTANCE OF SKILLS AND BEHAVIORS

Audit studies of hiring practices that send equally qualified blacks and whites to apply for the same job openings find that whites receive more job offers by small but nevertheless important margins of difference.[42] The need to comply with caste-based custom, however, is no longer a standard explanation as it may have been 50 years ago. Instead, both employers who discriminate and many researchers who seek to explain employers' behaviors usually point to what researchers call "statistical discrimination."[43]

By definition, statistical discrimination based on race is when employers use race as a signal of potential productivity and hire whites over blacks even when the two appear otherwise equal. In any particular example, an employer's assumption that race is a valid signal of skill and behavior may be correct, or not. Still, if he expects on average to be correct, he will continue the practice. Although rational for employers, statistical discrimination is illegal and unfair to its victims. It gives each black male an additional burden of proof to carry: the burden of proving that he is an exception to whatever stereotype against young black males that the employer might carry in his head.

It is true that young black males *on average* rank lower than whites on dimensions that are unobservable to employers at the time of hiring but which help to predict later productivity on the job. These initially "invisible" characteristics may sometimes include basic reading and math skills as well as some employment behaviors, such as absenteeism and the propensity to quit.[44] Hence, employers who discriminate in an effort to select the most productive workforce may, on average, be following a profit-maximizing strategy. Attempting to change employers' screening strategies without also changing the skills and behaviors that produce and confirm those strategies is an expensive and potentially unworkable policy both for employers and for society at large. Conversely, permitting employers to practice a strategy of statistical discrimination is unfair to the black males unjustly excluded from jobs. From a societal perspective, neither alternative is desirable. This remains an American dilemma.

Basic Skills and Wages

Data from the National Longitudinal Survey of Youth (NLSY) are the only nationally representative data that include measures of basic reading and math skills as well as the variables that researchers need to estimate standard wage and employment equations. The NLSY began with a sample of 12,000, 14–22-year-old respondents in 1979. Half were males. Interviewers have revisited the original sample each year since 1979. Ninety-five percent of the sample completed the Armed Services Vocational Aptitude Battery (ASVAB) in 1980. Here, I report results using a composite score called the Armed Forces Qualifications Test (AFQT). The AFQT is a composite score formed by summing the scaled scores from tests of arithmetic reasoning, word knowledge, paragraph comprehension, and half the score from a speed test of numerical operations. Hence, it is essentially a test of basic reading and math proficiencies.

Several authors have reported how well the AFQT score helps in predicting otherwise unexplained differences between blacks and whites in hourly wage rates.[45] For this chapter we conducted an analysis of wage rates for 1988–1992[46]. This analysis computes estimates of hourly earnings based on data for 1,745 young men (1,136 white and 609 black) aged 23–35 years. Each man reported earnings for the "current or most recent job" for each of the 5 years.[47] We used the wage on the most recent job at the time of the interview, averaged across the five years of 1988–1992.[48] The footnotes provide technical details.

The estimates that form the basis of this discussion include controls for years of schooling, census region, central city versus suburban versus rural residence, and years of potential experience.[49] This is the same type of estimation procedure that Bound and Freeman used in estimating the numbers that Figures 4.4 and 4.5 report.[50]

Results.[51]   When our estimates do not include the AFQT score among the explanatory variables, the estimated wage differences between blacks and whites resemble those that Bound and Freeman found (see Figures 4.4

and 4.5) for the late 1980s in their analysis of data from the CPS. When test scores are not controlled, the unexplained racial difference in earnings for the late 1980s is between 13 and 20 percent in their analysis using the CPS as well as in our analysis using the NLSY. One-half to three-quarters of this difference disappears, however, once the analysis takes account of differences in basic skills as measured by the AFQT score.

Figure 4.7 shows three different methods of demonstrating the importance of reading and math skills (AFQT scores) in accounting for

Figure 4.7

Percentage difference between predictions: wage if treated as black versus wage if treated as white with and without controls for AFQT test scores for men aged 23–35: 1988–1992.

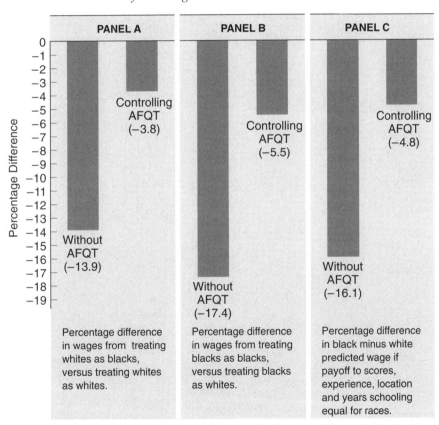

Source: Author's calculations using National Longitudinal Survey of Youth. See text for further explanation.
Note: Length of each bar is shown in parenthesis.

black–white differences in hourly earnings. Each panel of Figure 4.7 shows two bars. The longer bar in each panel is from estimates that exclude the AFQT score, and the shorter bar is from estimates that include it.[52]

Regression coefficients estimated from the data for a given racial group reflect the "rules" in the market that determine wage rates for members of that group. We can use the rules estimated for one group to simulate what the average wage rate would be for people of the other group, if that other group were subject to the same treatment in the market as the first group. Panels A and B of Figure 4.7 rely on this technique.

For example, "treating blacks as whites," for purposes of prediction, means taking the rules estimated on the data for whites and applying those rules to the raw data for blacks. This simulates what the average wage would be for blacks if the market treated them as whites. An analogous statement applies for treating whites as blacks.

Panels A and B of Figure 4.7 show that the apparent differential in the consequences of being treated as black versus as white diminishes when the AFQT is included in the analysis. Without the AFQT, whites have predicted wages that are 13.9 percent lower and blacks have wages that are almost 17.4 percent lower, if they are treated as blacks instead of as whites.[53] Including the AFQT brings these differences down to -3.8 for whites and to -5.5 for blacks.

Panel C of Figure 4.7 uses the estimation procedure that Bound and Freeman used for the numbers in Figures 4.4 and 4.5. It uses equations that pool blacks and whites together and include a variable that captures the black–white difference in earnings that is otherwise not accounted for. The close similarity between Panel C and the other two panels of Figure 4.7 shows that regressions that pool the races together and use a variable to capture the unexplained racial difference, as in Panel C, produce essentially the same results as the more cumbersome procedure of estimating separate equations for the racial groups, as in Panels A and B.[54] Without including the AFQT, Panel C estimates that the unexplained gap between blacks and whites is 16.1 percent. With the AFQT, it become 4.8 percent.[55]

Figure 4.8 applies the method that Panel C of Figure 4.7 uses, but for separate regions and education levels. Panels A, B, and C of Figure 4.8 use a separate equation for each region.[56] The AFQT score predicts roughly two-thirds of the remaining black–white wage gap in the Northeast, three-fourths of the remaining gap in the Midwest, and half of the remaining gap in the South. The South has the largest remaining gap at 10 percent after the AFQT is in the analysis and 20 percent before.[57]

Panels D and E of Figure 4.8 show results separately for men with 12 or fewer years of schooling and for men with 13 or more years. The estimated gap in earnings before the AFQT is in the analysis is -17.4 percent for men

Figure 4.8

Black–white percent difference in wage rate with and without controls for AFQT test scores for men aged 23–35: 1988–1992.

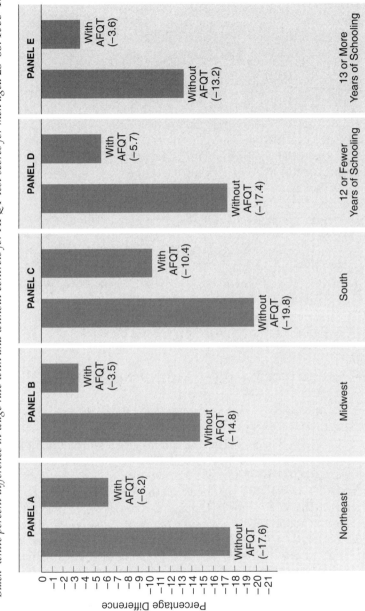

Source: Author's calculations using National Longitudinal Survey of Youth. See text for further explanation.
Note: The length of each bar is shown in parenthesis.

with 12 or fewer years. Introducing the AFQT reduces the gap to -5.7 percent—a reduction of two-thirds. For men with 13 or more years of schooling, the gap of -13.2 before including the AFQT drops to -3.6 afterwards—a plunge of almost three-quarters.[58]

To summarize, Figures 4.7 and 4.8 show that reading and math skills measured by the AFQT are important predictors of black–white wage differences. The gap in relative earnings is between 3 and 6 percent after taking the AFQT into account, except in the South where the gap is 10.4 percent.

Figures 4.4 and 4.5 show that the greatest erosion in relative earnings after 1973 was outside the South, in the Midwest and Northeast, and for college graduates. The gaps that Figure 4.8 display, after taking the AFQT into account, are too small to support the proposition that the erosion after the mid-1970s was mostly the result of increasing racial bias. Instead, the erosion probably results from some combination of the following: an increase in the market value of skill (e.g., the types of skills that the AFQT measures); or the deflation of an affirmative-action "bubble" that temporarily inflated wages for young blacks to be above those of whites with similar skills in the 1970s. These interpretations are not inconsistent with those in the Bound and Freeman analysis discussed above. With an average wage gap of roughly 5 percent in 1988–1992 (Figure 4.7 after taking the AFQT into account), an explanation of the trends in Figures 4.4 and 4.5 that rests on increased discrimination simply is not plausible.

SKILLS, BEHAVIORS, INCARCERATION, AND WORK[59]

The typical African American male works fewer weeks per year than his white male counterpart (recall Figure 4.6). The analysis below uses the NLSY to test several hypotheses concerning differences in employment between blacks and whites aged 23–31 who had 13 or fewer years of schooling in 1986–1988. Together, these hypotheses account for virtually all of the disparity in weeks worked per year between the least skilled young black and white males in the NLSY sample. Using no explanatory variables other than location and schooling leaves an unexplained black–white difference of about 3 months per year, with blacks working less.[60] With a number of additional explanatory variables included, the remaining unexplained difference is on the order of 1–3 weeks per year for men in the least complex jobs. This difference is not statistically distinguishable from zero. The difference is larger for more complex blue-collar jobs. Before explaining this statement, however, we introduce the other explanatory variables in the analysis.

Measures of both skill and behavior in this analysis help in predicting black–white differences in employment for young men with less than 13 years of schooling. Clearly, these differences in skill and behavior are associated with differences in schools, family backgrounds, youth peer cultures, and other pre-labor-market institutions. Hence, the lack of equal opportunity for employment success may begin even before youth enter the labor market, causing them to enter the market less well prepared than their white counterparts. Discrimination in the allocation of resources for youth development gives way to other forms of discrimination against adults. Our results suggest that discrimination during the adult years includes greater discrimination against blacks with criminal histories than against similar whites. It also may include patterns of human relations in the workplace which, other things equal, lead blacks to quit more frequently than whites in occupations that require more skill.

Skills. Skill-related measures in this analysis of weeks worked per year include the AFQT score, the NLSY interviewer's rating of the respondent's comprehension during the interview, and a complexity rating for the respondent's occupation in the year before the analysis.[61] All three variables come from an earlier year. Each is a statistically significant predictor of weeks worked and helps to explain racial disparity in employment for young males. Black–white differences in the AFQT score predict roughly 3 weeks less employment per year for blacks, and the interviewers' rating predicts an additional 1 week less, for a total of 1 month from these two sources.

Behaviors. Research in sociology and anthropology demonstrates that socialization processes differ within and across communities. Even in the poorest neighborhoods of the most burned-out central cities, many children receive the nurturance and protection that they need to mature and prosper. However, many schools, families, and community institutions lack the social and material resources to cope successfully with the all of the youth development challenges that they face. Negative influences that tend to distract youth from wholesome development and from investing in their own futures can overwhelm the defenses that parents and their allies can muster. Mischief and crime are often the consequences.

Results from my research with the NLSY show that two indices related to crime are important in predicting weeks worked. The first measures whether the respondent was ever incarcerated in the years prior to the analysis. The second is an "incarceration-likelihood index" that uses prior behaviors and other background factors to estimate the likelihood that the respondent has ever been incarcerated. The two measures—actual past incarceration and the incarceration-likelihood index—are simultaneously strong predictors of how many weeks per year young men work. This pair of variables is important in explaining black–white differences in employment. Young black males are more likely than young white males to experience incarceration. Moreover, actual prior incarceration has twice the negative effect on weeks worked for blacks as for whites.

Prior incarceration for a young white male predicts that, other things equal, he will work an average of 2 months less per year than a young white male who has no history of incarceration. For young black males, the average difference between those with and without prior incarceration is 4 months per year. This measured effect of actual prior incarceration on weeks worked probably reflects both labor supply behavior (including reincarceration) and, on the demand side, employment discrimination that penalizes blacks who have criminal records more than it penalizes similar whites. Even for men with a history of incarceration who were *not* reincarcerated during the 1986–1988 study period, the effect of prior incarceration is more than twice as negative for blacks as for whites: roughly 1 month per year less work for whites and more than 2 months per year for blacks.

The strongest predictors of incarceration are all either locational or behavioral. Behaviors that help in predicting incarceration are expulsion from school, unwed fatherhood, age of first intercourse (earlier is worse), income from crime during adolescence, drug use, and dropping out before completing high school. Race, test scores, attitudes, family background, and local unemployment rates help in predicting these behaviors, but they do not help in predicting incarceration once the listed behaviors are controlled. Aside from indices associated with individuals, the incarceration rate in the geographic area where a young man lives is an important predictor of incarceration, explaining 30 percent of the black–white differences in incarceration rates. This signals the importance of local difference in law enforcement practices, youth cultures, or other features of local environments.

Among the indices of adolescent behavior that predict incarceration, only income from crime shows a statistically significant relationship to local unemployment (for the year during adolescence when the income from crime was earned). However, self-reported income from crime during adolescence does not differ much by race. In contrast, for example, the average age of first intercourse is more than 1 year earlier for blacks, bears no relationship to the state of the local economy, and is an important predictor of later incarceration.[62] The same is true for unwed fatherhood. These empirical results suggest that both economic and noneconomic forces predict differences in behavior that lead to mediocre labor market outcomes. Black–white differences in actual and predicted incarceration in this analysis account for an average difference between *all* blacks and whites in the sample (not simply those who have been incarcerated) of roughly 1 month per year in time employed.

Together with the 1 month estimated to be due to skill differences, this adds to a total difference in time employed of 2 months per year between black versus white 23–31-year-old males with 13 or fewer years of schooling.

Quit Rates.   Among the unanticipated findings from this work is that the black–white difference in job-resignation rates for non-college-educated males in their twenties increases with occupational complexity—the quit rate for young blacks rises with occupational complexity and that for young whites falls.[63] In a multivariate statistical analysis that includes a number of controls, the difference between blacks and whites in the effect on employment of raising occupational complexity (as measured in the job held in 1985) predicts an average difference in employment of between 4 and 5 weeks per year for young blacks and whites during the period 1986–1988. Again, this pattern is measured with years of schooling, test scores, and other background variables held constant.

Table 4.2 shows the pattern in the raw data. It divides the jobs that men with 13 or fewer years of schooling occupy into two categories—"low skill" and "high skill." This splits the sample rather evenly. The table covers three years, 1986–1988. The NLSY interviewed respondents three times during

Table 4.2

Reason for leaving most recent job:
percentages for black and white males with less than 13 years of schooling (taken at first survey date during 1986–88 when respondent had left most recent job, men aged 23–31 during 1986–1988 (columns 1, 2, 4, and 5 each add to 100 percent).

	"Low Skill" Occupations			"High Skill" Occupations		
	Black	White	Black–White Difference	Black	White	Black–White Difference
	1	2	3	4	5	6
Percent Laid Off	10.95	10.91	0.04	6.32	5.12	1.20
Percent Job Ended	3.38	3.20	0.18	6.54	1.46	5.08
Percent Quit	14.01	7.13	6.88	19.05	5.15	13.90
Percent Fired	6.81	2.37	4.44	3.04	1.69	1.35
Percent Other	2.19	1.31	0.88	1.18	0.98	0.20
Percent Employed at All 3 Survey Dates	62.66	75.08	12.42	63.87	85.60	21.73

Source: Compiled by author from National Longitudinal Survey of Youth.

this period. The table tabulates the reason each respondent gave for leaving the last job. The answer comes from the first of the three interviews during this period at which the respondent reported that he was not currently employed. The bottom line of the table shows the percentages of blacks and whites who had jobs at all three interview dates, and who therefore never gave a reason for leaving a job. The percentage of blacks employed at all three dates is virtually the same for the "high skill" occupations (62.66 percent) as for the "low skill" occupations (63.87 percent). For whites, the percentage employed at all three dates rises from 75.08 in the "low skill" to 85.60 in the "high skill" jobs. Remarkably, roughly half of the blacks unemployed from the higher skill occupations report that they quit their last jobs. The comparable number for blacks in the lower skill occupations is roughly one-third. One-third is also the proportion of quits for unemployed whites in both high- and low-skill jobs.

The fact that increasing job complexity has different effects on employment longevity for blacks and whites reinforces the general proposition that skill differences are central in explaining racial differences in employment for young males, but, especially here, the mechanisms are not transparent.

We have previously stated that after taking account of explanatory variables, the remaining unexplained difference in weeks worked for the least skilled blacks and whites is roughly 1–3 weeks. This difference of 1–3 weeks applies to men in the least skilled jobs. For a job of average complexity, we need to add the 4–5 weeks per year of higher unemployment for blacks than whites associated with the occupational complexity of the average job that blacks without college educations occupy. Whether one counts the 4–5 weeks associated with occupational complexity to be "explained," because it is associated with a particular meaningful variable (occupational complexity), or "unexplained" because we do not understand why the black–white difference in this relationship exists, depends upon one's purpose.

Certainly, this effect is "unexplained" if one's purpose is to shape an intervention. A speculative explanation is that blacks and whites in the workplace are sometimes caught in a cycle of negative and self-fulfilling expectations: blacks expect that whites will expect less and will be less supportive to them than to whites; whites expect that blacks will have chips on their shoulders and will be less cooperative; each lives down to the other's expectations, and each thereby finds his expectations confirmed. If blacks respond by quitting, as Table 4.2 suggests that they often may, then they accumulate less experience and, over time, the deficit in their experience may further harm their employment prospects and performance. Human relations across racial lines in the workplace, especially blue-collar workplaces, present issues that deserve much more attention than they currently receive. Current ethnographic work by other researchers may help to explain the workplace dynamics associated with these interesting and important patterns.[64]

SUMMARY

World War II opened new employment opportunities for African Americans. It brought growth in earnings that did not disappear when the war was over. While the causes shifted, the positive momentum of progress continued from the 1940s through the 1960s as younger blacks led a mass migration away from the rural South. Some settled in southern cities; others migrated farther to the cities of the North where, until the mid-1970s, economic opportunities were far superior.

Thanks to the civil rights movement, economic progress for blacks accelerated in the South after the mid-1960s. For the first time, more blacks returned to the South than left it during the 1970s. In addition to its many other achievements, the civil rights movement was a major force behind decisions by Congress and the president to enact Title VII of the Civil Rights Act of 1964 and Executive Order 11246. Both of these measures apparently helped to sustain income growth for blacks relative to whites well into the mid-1970s. These civil rights measures helped to ensure, for example, that blacks would receive the growth in earnings that they deserved, commensurate with the gains that they were achieving in academic attainment. Blacks gained on whites in educational attainment and in various measures of school quality through the entire period after 1940. Researchers agree that this probably accounts for between one-quarter and one-half of the progress that blacks achieved in closing the gap in earnings, even without explicitly accounting for civil rights pressures. After the mid-1970s, progress toward closing the gap in earnings stopped. In fact, for younger blacks, the trend reversed. Disparity grew.

A number of economic shifts have been identified as contributing factors by other authors. They include racially disparate shifts in industry and occupational employment patterns, among others, that contributed to growth in racial disparity among young workers after 1975. Several may have common roots in the growing value of skill and in reduced federal pressure for affirmative action. Several, such as changing technology, the falling minimum wage, declining unionism, and increased immigration, help to account for why the value of skill has grown both within and across racial groups.

This chapter presents an analysis that helps in judging the likely importance of skill differences in accounting for deterioration in earnings for young black males relative to whites after 1975. First, it estimates the black–white gap in earnings for 23–35-year-old males that remains unexplained for 1988–1992 after accounting for years of schooling, potential experience, and several measures of location. For example, a composite estimate (Panel C of Figure 4.7) shows a gap of 16.1 percent. Comparable numbers from the mid-1970s are much smaller: an estimate from 1975 for men with 0–9 years of experience, displayed in Figure 4.5, indicates a difference of 6 percent, for 1989 the estimated difference is 16 percent. (The latter number is not statistically distinguishable from the 16.1 percent estimated here using a different data set.) Thus, the apparent erosion in relative earnings after 1975 is on the order of 10 percent.

After accounting for reading and math skills by inserting a test score into the analysis, the otherwise unexplained 16.1 percent difference in average hourly earnings that this chapter estimates for 1988–1992 diminishes to a residual 4.8 percent. Hence, a black–white earnings gap of 11.3 percent over and beyond that explained by differences in years of schooling,—the difference between 16.1 and 4.8—appears to be accounted for by black–white differences in the reading and math skills that the test score measures. Because of data limitations, we do not know what an estimate that controlled for test scores would have shown for the early 1970s.

The National Assessment of Educational Progress shows that basic skills for black high school students have been rising relative to those for whites since at least the early 1970s. Hence, the increase from -6 percent (for 1975) to -16 percent (for 1989) in the disparity in wage rates between young blacks and whites (as measured without controlling for test scores) is probably not because blacks' skills have deteriorated. Instead, either the value of skill rose after 1975 faster than the black–white gap in skill closed—thus inflating the financial significance of remaining skill differences—or blacks in 1975 were earning more than whites who had similar qualifications and the apparent erosion of earnings after 1975 was simply bringing them back in line. Either or both explanations may have some merit.

Based on the evidence, these explanations for what happened after 1975 seem more plausible than one that relies on an increase in discrimination. If an increase in discrimination were the major explanation for the increase of 10 percent described above in black–white earnings disparity, then one should expect an unexplained gap in earnings that is larger than 4.8 percent for 1988–1992. Recall that 4.8 percent is the black–white gap in earnings that this paper estimates for 1988–1992 after accounting for differences in basic skills (again, before accounting for back skills, the gap is 16.1 percent).

Therefore, while this chapter notes the continuing importance of discrimination and endorses the vigorous enforcement of civil rights laws, the findings point to other explanations for the increase in disparity after 1975. Similarly, black–white differences in employment levels for men with 13 or fewer years of schooling reflect various skill and behavioral differences, including a greater propensity to resign from occupations that require more skill. The latter pattern may be a response to racial bias in the social relations of work for more complex occupations. It warrants further investigation.

CONCLUSION

Most important disparities in opportunity may occur before young people even enter the labor market—in the provision of schooling and other resources that influence skill-building and the socialization of youth. These include not only current disparity in the quality of schooling and recreation and discouraging messages from society at large but also racial inequities in past generations of institutions that prepared parents and grandparents for their roles as teachers and care givers. Certainly, efforts to fight unfair racial bias in hiring and promotion must continue. However, interventions to strengthen schools, families, and other institutions that prepare children for adulthood must take center stage in responding to the economic disparities that remain among young adults in the 1990s.

These are different times from the 1940s, 1950s and 1960s. The job now is to to utilize more effectively the legal and institutional resources that the civil rights and Black Power movements helped to put in place. The dream that inspired these movements was that African Americans might lead more healthy, happy, and productive lives, free from the hardships and degradations of social and economic subordination. The dream has not fully come true. Indeed, America may never cast off completely the ideology of white supremacy. Similarly, social class interests that align with wealth and privilege will remain challenges to many visions of social fairness and equity. Nevertheless, the evidence that this chapter reviews demonstrates that progress for black Americans over the past 50 years has been remarkable. In the face of resistance, discipline, courage, and perseverance have paid dividends. The same will be true in the future. As African Americans whose parents and grandparents taught this lesson to us, we much teach it to our children and insist that they put it to practice.

On the last page of *An American Dilemma,* Myrdal writes:

> The rationalism and moralism which is the driving force behind social study, whether we admit it or not, is the faith that institutions can be improved and strengthened and that people are good enough to live a happier life....To find the practical formulas for this never-ending reconstruction of society is the supreme task of social science. The

world catastrophe places tremendous difficulties in our way and may shake our confidence to the depths. Yet we have today in social science a greater trust in the improvability of man and society than we have ever had since the Enlightenment.

NOTES

1. Myrdal. *An American Dilemma,* p. 222.
2. On oppositional behaviors by stigmatized minorities, see, for example, Ogbu 1978. On discouraging and demeaning messages, see Ferguson and Jackson 1994.
3. Developing this point is beyond the scope of the present paper. However, I have written more on this theme in Ferguson 1991b; Ferguson and Jackson 1994; and Ferguson 1994. Also see Mincy 1994.
4. This section goes through 1975 because that is roughly the time that improvement ceased to occur. However, much of the actual discussion in this section goes through 1980 because 1980 was a census year. The section relies on work by a number of previous authors who have considered the questions with which this section deals. Most important among these are Smith and Welch 1989; Donohue and Heckman 1991; and Card and Krueger 1992.
5. The data for this graph come from Smith and Welch 1989. See their footnote 5, page 522, for details on the way that they drew this sample from the census public use data files.
6. Decreases in labor force participation have been larger for blacks than for whites and this may lead to an overestimate of progress in relative earnings. Donohue and Heckman 1991, citing studies reviewed in Heckman 1989, report estimates that "selective attrition of low wage blacks from the labor force likely accounts for 10–20 percent of black measured wage gains from the mid-1960s through the mid-1970s." Also, Smith and Welch 1989 attempt to correct the estimated ratio of black-to-white male wages for selective attrition and conclude that it "explain[s] at most a minor part (roughly 5 percent) of the observed increase in black-white male wages between 1970 and 1980." William Darity, Jr. and Samuel Myers (see Darity 1980 and Darity and Myers 1980) were among the first to raise the concern that changes in labor force participation might distort simple black–white economic comparisons.
7. Smith and Welch 1989, Table 15.
8. Based on Donohue and Heckman, Figure 6. Note that these percentages are for gaps in hourly wages holding constant years of schooling, while those in Figure 4.1 are for weekly wages and do not hold years of schooling constant.
9. This spike appears in Donohue and Heckman 1991, Table 6, which represents 20–64-year-old males. A similar but smaller spike appears in the numbers from Bound and Freeman 1992, for men with 0–9 years of experience. These numbers from Bound and Freeman appear here in Figure 4.5. Figure 4.4, also based on numbers presented by Bound and Freeman 1992, shows a huge spike for black college graduates between 1973 and 1976. Relative earnings for young black males in Figure 4.4 jumped from an average of 4 percent below

that for whites in 1973 to an average of 11 percent above that for whites in 1976.

10. Donohue and Heckman.

11. See Table 2 in Donohue and Heckman, constructed from Tables A.1 and A.2. in Smith and Welch 1986.

12. Farley and Allen 1987, Table 5.1.

13. Donohue and Heckman, footnote 13, using data from U.S. Commission on Civil Rights 1986, Table 5.2.

14. Smith and Welch 1989, Table 20.

15. Ibid., p. 215. This passage is quoted by Myrdal from a report on teacher salaries for which he does not provide further reference.

16. Card and Krueger 1992, Figure 1, p. 168.

17. Convergence along other dimensions, including the quality of teachers' preparation to teach, may still be some distance from being achieved. See Ferguson 1991a and 1991b.

18. In 1980, the percentage of 25–34-year-old males who were high school graduates or better was 87.2 for white males and 75.3 for black males. By 1992, the percentage of 25–34-year-old males who were high school graduates or better was up to 82.2 percent for black males against 86.3 percent for white males. Source: Bureau of Labor Statistics, 1992.

19. Smith and Welch 1989, Tables A.1 and A.2.

20. According to Heckman and Donohue, this is also true after accounting for a possible upward bias in estimates of black progress, due to the disproportionate decrease in labor force participation during this period by blacks who would have had lower earnings if they had worked.

21. See, for example, Ashenfelter and Heckman 1976 and Leonard 1984a and 1984b.

22. See Heckman and Donohue 1991, Figure 6. Also see Bound and Freeman 1992, shown here in Figure 4.5 for young men with less than 10 years of experience.

23. This different pattern by age level is shown and discussed by Boozer, Krueger, and Wolkon 1992, Table 13.

24. One extensive review of explanations for why young black men are doing worse in the labor market is Moss and Tilly 1991. Moss and Tilly express skepticism that skill differences could be among the causes. This is because, by most measures, skill differences between young blacks and whites have been diminishing. This author and others argue that skill differences could easily constitute most of the story if the market value of skill has been growing more rapidly than skill differences have been closing. The evidence is not definitive. See the discussion here in the text.

25. See, for example, Juhn, Murphy, and Pierce 1991; Rogers 1993; Bound and Freeman 1992; Smith and Welch 1989; Card and Krueger 1992.

26. "Potential experience" is the number of years during which a person could "potentially" have been working and accumulating experience. Most researchers measure it as the smaller of (a) age minus years of schooling minus six, or (b) age minus 18. Hence, experience for years when the respondent was under age 18 or enrolled in school do not count.

27. The data for Figures 4.4 and 4.5 are from Table 1 of Bound and Freeman 1992. The data for Figure 4.6 was provided to this author directly by John Bound.

28. White college graduates were also the only group that did not experience decline in the real purchasing power of its earnings.

29. Juhn, Murphy, and Pierce 1991 were among the first to construct an indirect test of this hypothesis. They compared the pattern from 1963–1987 in average earnings for blacks relative to those for a particular category of whites—whites at the years-of-schooling level that put them at the same percentile in the overall earnings distribution as the average black worker in 1963. (Note that these whites had less education than the average black.) This was a period of growing inequality even among whites. The authors found that blacks' earnings tracked closely on those of the white comparison group. The results of their empirical test suggest that the forces responsible for blacks' average earnings falling behind whites' average earnings may be the same as the forces responsible for the increasing earnings disparity among whites. This force, they suggest, is the increasing demand for skill and the growing differential in pay that employers are willing to offer to more skilled workers.

    Some see an inconsistency in this explanation versus those offered by Bound and Freeman 1992, discussed in this paper below and illustrated here in Table 4.1. We argue, however, that Bound and Freeman illuminate the channels through which growth in the price of skill has occurred and that there is no necessary inconsistency.

30. See Mullis and Jenkins 1990 and Dossey, Mullis, Lindquist, and Chambers 1988.

31. Bound and Freeman 1992 report in their footnote 6 that the gap in earnings during the 1980s was roughly the same with or without controls for years of education. This was not because blacks did not continue to close the gap in schooling. Instead, it was because the rate of return to additional years of schooling (especially post–high school) was increasing. This offset the positive relative earnings effect of increased years of schooling, because it made the remaining gap in schooling more important as a source of earnings disparity between black and white males.

32. For more on the growing inequality in the economy during the late 1970s and 1980s see Katz and Murphy 1992; Murphy and Welch 1992; Levy and Murnane 1992; Mishel and Teixeira, 1991; Moffit and Gottschalk 1993; Blackburn, Bloom, and Freeman 1990; Bound and Johnson 1992, and Krueger 1993.

33. Boozer, Krueger, and Wolkon express skepticism that an increase in the value of skill is responsible for the increase in disparity between young black and white males. The gap in skill between older blacks and whites is greater than that between younger blacks and whites. Hence, Boozer, Krueger, and Wolkon argue that one should expect an increase in the value of skill to cause the disparity among older workers to increase by more, and in fact it changes hardly at all. They acknowledge the argument that older workers may be more well-established in their positions and not as vulnerable to changes in the economy as younger workers.

34. See, for example, Murnane, Willett, and Levy, March 1994. The present author has written a working paper (Ferguson 1993) showing for 23-year-old males that the measured impact of test scores on wages grew during the 1980s and that this helps to explain the increase in racial earnings disparity. However, I have refined these estimates and now find higher coefficients on test scores in the early 1980s than I had previously estimated. It is clearly true that test scores in the NLSY predict racial earnings differences that are difficult to predict without test scores. We show this in the present paper. However, if the effect was already strong in the early 1980s, it may not explain the trend in earnings disparity during the 1980s decade. Resolution on this question concerning the trend is difficult, given the character of available data.

35. Employers are reporting these changes in a project that this author is conducting with an associate, John Ballantine.

36. Bound and Freeman 1992.

37. Borjas, Freeman, and Katz 1989. Also see Borjas, Freeman, and Lang 1991.

38. See Kirshenman and Neckerman 1991 for an extensive report on interviews with employers regarding their perceptions of and attitudes toward young black workers in Chicago. White and black employers alike in their study regarded young black workers, on average, to be the least dependable workers.

39. Leonard 1990.

40. Reported in Bound and Freeman 1992, p. 215, and footnote 13, based on their analysis of CPS data. Also see Cotton 1990 for a related discussion.

41. Ibid.

42. Studies by Michael Fix et al. at the Urban Institute.

43. See extensive interview findings in Kirshenman and Neckerman 1991.

44. Ferguson and Filer 1986 report higher absenteeism rates for blacks than for whites in the Current Population Survey. Blacks have higher quit rates than whites in the National Longitudinal Survey of Youth.

45. See: O'Neill 1990; Neal and Johnson 1994; Maxwell 1994; Ferguson 1993; Ferguson 1991b. The findings reported in Ferguson 1993 have since been modified to reflect larger estimated returns to test scores even in the early 1980s than the paper originally found. Hence, the trends in the "price of skill" that the paper reports are too steep, but the finding that test scores account for much of the racial difference in earnings by the late 1980s still stands.

46. The AFQT score here is standardized to have a mean of zero and a standard deviation of one for each individual age group. Hence, the score used is a measure of each respondent's proficiency at the test date relative to his same-aged peers. Since the youngest person at the time of the test was aged 14, and little reason exists to expect that the *rank order* of basic skills changes much among a population after age 14, the age-standardized AFQT score that we use is probably a good measure of young adults' proficiencies relative to their peers. For a discussion of why academic test scores are related to earnings and of the stability of the relationship between test scores and earnings even if scores are measured at young ages, see Chapter 5 of Jencks 1979. If these

test score data collected in 1980 are not accurate measures for the late 1980s and early 1990s, then the measurement error will cause the findings to underestimate the effect of the measured skills in explaining wages.

47. In order to do the most representative analysis, we exclude the supplemental samples of poor whites, identified by sample identification numbers 2 and 9 in the NLSY. Including these would cause blacks to appear more well-off relative to whites than they actually are. We also exclude members of the special military sample identified by sample identification numbers of 15 and over. To avoid distortions due to student or military status, we exclude men who were enrolled in school as of May 1 of any survey year from 1988–1992 or who had military income during this period. Men with reported hourly earnings of less than 1 or more than 75 dollars per hour were dropped (these constituted less than 1 percent of the sample).

48. Wages are in 1988 dollars. The natural logarithm of the average real wage for the 5 years is the dependent variable and each man in the analysis contributes one observation to each estimated regression equation.

49. Years-of-schooling controls are dummy (0,1) variables for individual years of schooling. This allows the effect of years of schooling to be nonlinear. Potential experience is essentially a measure of age. We measure it in the standard way: it equals age minus years of schooling minus 6, if years of schooling exceeds 12; and it equals age minus 18 if years of schooling is less than 12. The location controls are individual 0,1 variables for each of the four major census regions, and 0,1 variables to measure rural versus central city versus suburban location.

50. In other analyses we have tested the importance of other family background variables. Generally, once test scores are in the analysis, contributions of family background variables to equations for employment outcomes are small and statistically insignificant. Including other variables does not change the bottom-line conclusions of the simpler analysis reported here. Where family background measures are most important in a more extensive analysis, is in predicting the test scores. Mothers' and fathers' years of schooling, characteristics of the fathers' occupation, and the number of educational resources in the home are all important predictors of the AFQT test score that we use here.

51. This discussion of results is intended to be accessible to a general audience. Some of the technical details are in the footnotes, but the full pattern of results is not shown here. Readers may write to the author for a copy of the full regression results.

52. We estimated four equations to construct Panels A and B of Figure 4.7: one that used the data for whites only and excluded the AFQT from the explanatory variables; a second that used the data for whites only but included the AFQT; a third that used the data for blacks only without the AFQT; and, a fourth that used the data for blacks only and included the AFQT among the explanatory variables. Again, all estimates include controls for years of schooling, Census region, central city versus suburban versus rural residence, and years of potential experience.

53. Differences between panels A and B are due to differences in blacks' and whites' average characteristics, not differences in their treatment. Differences

in *treatment* are reflected in the length of each bar, since each bar represents the difference between being treated as black or white.

54. Statistical tests do not reject the null hypothesis that these two approaches are equivalent.

55. The t-statistic on the 16.1 percent is 8.21; the t-statistic on the 4.8 percent is 2.08. The adjusted R-square statistic is .2845 for the regression that excludes the AFQT and .3302 for regression that includes it.

56. Pooling the regions together in regressions and using 0, 1 variables to capture the black-white differential for each region produces essentially the same pattern in estimates of racial differences. We report results from separate regressions primarily to assure readers that the estimated patterns really do apply separately to each region. Results for the West are not shown because the sample size for blacks in the West is too small to make the estimates reliable. We find that the AFQT score in the West matters as much for predicting wages as for the other regions, but the estimated black–white difference has a very large standard error because of the small number of blacks in the NLSY's Western sample. Men from the West are, however, included in estimates that pool all regions, such as those in Figure 4.7 and in Panels D and E of Figure 4.8.

57. We cannot know for sure whether this difference represents unequal treatment. It may be that blacks are different in a way that our estimates do not measure, that they live in lower-wage cities, or that their referral networks do not contain information about the same quality of jobs as for whites. Analogous statements apply for estimates that suggest nearly equal treatment.

58. The -3.6 has a t-statistic of 0.87, such that this estimate of -3.6 is not statistically distinguishable from zero.

59. The research paper that presents these findings more formally is currently in progress. What follows is simply a summary of findings.

60. All of the regression results for total weeks worked are from Tobit regressions that take account of truncation at both 0 and 52 weeks per year.

61. Racial bias does not appear to be important in the interviewer's rating: race is not a predictor of the interviewer's rating once test scores, years of schooling and social background factors are controlled. The occupational complexity measure comes from the occupation that the respondent had in 1985, not the occupation that he has during any of the three years 1986–1988 for which the analysis aims to explain the number of weeks worked.

62. It seems reasonable to speculate that youth who engage in early sexual activity, especially boys, may be distracted away from other more developmentally appropriate activities by the increased preoccupation with finding more opportunities to repeat the experience.

63. The occupational complexity ratings come from a factor analysis of job characteristics, conducted as part of a study for the Dictionary of Occupational Titles. The rating is a composite measure of a number of different distinguishable characteristics of jobs, constructed in the early 1980s using 1970 standard occupational classification codes.

64. The Russell Sage Foundation is currently supporting a cluster of research projects among which are both quantitative and qualitative studies that may shed light on these issues.

William Darity, Jr.

The Undesirables, America's Underclass in the Managerial Age: Beyond the Myrdal Theory of Racial Inequality

IN 1944, GUNNAR MYRDAL opened Chapter 17 of *An American Dilemma*, "The Mechanics of Economic Discrimination As a Practical Problem," with the following decidedly pessimistic commentary:

> The picture of the economic situation of the Negro people is dark. The prospects for the future . . . are discouraging. The main practical problem must be how to open up new possibilities for Negroes to earn a living by their labor.[1]

Today, we must ask whether blacks will be significant participants in twenty-first century America. Opening up jobs from which African Americans have been excluded by historic and ongoing discriminatory practices remains an important issue, but subordinate to the more comprehensive nature of discrimination that portends exclusion of an entire racial/ethnic group from this nation's future.

Since World War II, federal antidiscrimination measures have been adopted of a scope that Myrdal and his collaborators hardly anticipated in the early 1940s. In fact, in Myrdal's Chapter 17 great concern was expressed that the piecemeal adoption of efficacious nondiscriminatory policies by individual employers, cities, and/or states would lead them to be overrun by "Negroes":

> Suppose that an individual employer would entirely ignore the race of those applying for work at his shop and would consider just the individual capacities of the job-seekers, white or black. The fact that most other employers exclude Negroes means that the individual employer would have a disproportionate number of Negroes applying for his jobs. The rumor about his unusual behavior would draw Negro workers from other localities, and he might soon find a majority of

Negroes on his labor force. The consequence might be that his establishment would be shunned by white labor, and it is not impossible that the result would be an almost all-Negro shop. The best he can do if he wants to favor the Negro, without having to face such consequences, is to fix the percentage of Negro workers; but that means giving up the principle of selecting Negro and white workers on an individual basis.

White workers, of course, are up against the same problem, and they have even more reason to be concerned about it than have the employers. Every individual municipality, and even every state, is in a similar situation. Let us imagine that a certain state, by means of strongly enforced legislation, would succeed in abolishing most racial discrimination in the economic sphere. If similar strong measures were not taken simultaneously by other states as well, the result would be a tremendous increase in in-migration of Negroes to that state.[2]

Myrdal's concerns about all-black workshops, cities, or states—under circumstances where blacks locate to benefit from marked economic advantages—seem dated. He constructed a hypothetical circumstance under which quotas are an alternative to the "all-Negro shop," but ironically, these quotas were to be adopted in a nondiscriminatory environment to keep the numbers of (presumably *qualified*) blacks down! And, in principle, the national antidiscrimination measures should have obviated Myrdal's "Negro in-migration" problem altogether. Preventing excessive "Negro in-migration" into particular states has not, however, proven to be the major legacy of the civil rights era.

As I have observed,

> . . . discrimination in its most encompassing sense continues to be operative. Although laws have been passed to make certain of such practices illegal, these laws have been largely circumvented, ignored, or gradually rolled back. In many instances the laws have not touched critical sites of discriminatory activity. To the extent that American society is intensely hierarchical, there is an incentive for members of ascriptively differentiated groups to coalesce and carve out occupational and status niches. Antidiscrimination laws certainly were not designed to level the hierarchical structure of U.S. society; hence the driving motive for discrimination as exclusion remains strong.[3]

It was Myrdal's failure to undertake a serious class-analytical study of American society in conjunction with the phenomenon of racial disparity that contributed to his inability to identify the material basis for racial/ethnic discrimination in the society's hierarchical structure. Indeed, Myrdal's

vision of "the mechanics of economic discrimination" is so strongly driven
by perception, attitude, and ideology that one must presume that if the political will had evolved to adopt antidiscrimination measures in the United
States, racial prejudice on the part of the white political majority must have
been sharply in decline.

For Myrdal the explanatory core of *An American Dilemma* lay in what he
termed "the 'principle of cumulation,' also commonly called the 'vicious
circle,'" an analytical scheme drawn from physics which Myrdal felt had
potential for wide application in the social sciences.[4] The vicious circle refers
to the downward or negative spiral precipitated by the adverse effects of
initial white prejudice and associated limitations on black workplace opportunities:

> The vicious circle of job restrictions, poverty, and all that follows with
> it tends to fix the tradition that Negroes should be kept out of good
> jobs and held down in unskilled, dirty, hot or otherwise undesirable
> work. Residential segregation and segregation at places of work hin-
> der whites from having personal acquaintance with Negroes and rec-
> ognizing that Negroes are much like themselves. In the eyes of white
> workers the Negroes easily come to appear "different," as a "low grade
> people," and it becomes a matter of social prestige not to work under
> conditions of equality with them. The fact that Negroes actually work
> almost only in menial tasks makes it more natural to look upon them
> in this way. The occupations they work in tend to become déclassé.[5]

Beliefs about "the Negro" become a self-fulfilling prophecy, leading Myrdal
to characterize the pattern of job restriction as a "self-perpetuating color
bar."

But the nature of this theoretical approach leaves the door open for the
emergence of a cumulative process leading to a virtuous circle of improvement for blacks. Myrdal wrote:

> If . . . we assume that for some reason white prejudice could be de-
> creased and discrimination mitigated, this is likely to cause a rise in
> Negro standards, which may decrease white prejudice still a little
> more, which would again allow Negro standards to rise, and so on
> through mutual interaction. . . . The original change can as easily be
> a change of *Negro standards* upward or downward.
>
>   . . . A rise in Negro employment, for instance, will raise family in-
> comes, standards of nutrition, housing, and health, the possibilities
> of giving the Negro youth more education, and so forth, and all these
> effects of the initial change will, in their turn, improve the Negroes'
> possibilities of getting employment and earning a living. The original
> push could have been on some other factor than employment, say, for

example, an improvement of health or educational facilities for Negroes. Through action and interaction the whole system of the Negro's "status" would have been set in motion in the direction indicated by the first push. Much the same thing holds true of the development of white prejudice. Even assuming no changes in Negro standards, white prejudice can change, for example, as a result of an increased general knowledge about biology, eradicating some of the false beliefs among whites concerning Negro racial inferiority. If this is accomplished, it will in some degree censor the hostile and derogatory valuations which fortify the false beliefs, and education will then be able to fight racial beliefs with more success.[6]

Presumably the political successes of the civil rights movement should have gone hand-in-hand with dramatic changes in white attitudes, which should then have triggered a major upturn in the social and economic "standards" of African Americans. In the early 1970s there were economists who claimed that the previous two decades had, indeed, been a period of dramatic economic progress for blacks. That being the case, the Myrdal framework would predict that the subsequent decade should have been one of continued comparative advance. But not only has the "dramatic progress" interpretation of economic data by race been challenged substantively, no one can make a serious claim that the 1980s displayed a further decrease in racial economic disparity.[7]

Moreover, the black–white gap in the United States does not ratchet up and down with every detectable change in white racial beliefs, as Myrdal's hypothesis would have it. A diminution in white prejudice does not mean that blacks can instantly enter fields from which they were excluded previously. Furthermore, the existence of antidiscrimination measures does not mean that such measures will be implemented forcefully.

Even Myrdal recognized that discrimination was functional, not merely capricious, in preserving occupational turf for the discriminators. The goal of white labor is to render black labor a noncompeting group:

> When once the white workers' desires for social prestige become mobilized against the Negroes in this way, when they have come to look upon Negroes as different from themselves and consequently do not feel a common labor solidarity with them, "economic interests" also will back up discrimination. By excluding Negroes from the competition for jobs, the white workers can decrease the supply of labor in the market, hold up wages and secure employment for themselves.[8]

But such "economic interests" are secondary props in Myrdal's theoretical framework where racial attitudes take center stage. In this respect the

Myrdal theory, despite its institutionalist flavor and the novelty of the cumulative causation story, is not far removed from the conventional, neoclassical economists' approach to racial restriction in labor markets, which finds its anchor in a "taste for discrimination" on the part of one group toward the other. The neoclassical theory of discrimination remains subject to the charge that, if members of both groups on average have the same capabilities to perform the work, employer competition eventually will lead to segregated workforces but no difference in pay across the groups. Therefore, the neoclassical approach *theoretically* does not yield as a stable outcome persistent economic disparity. Precisely the same charge can be made about Myrdal's analysis.

Oliver Cox, in a profound critique of *An American Dilemma*, characterized Myrdal's emphasis on attitudes—the "American Creed," racial beliefs, etc.—as a "mystical" approach to race relations. Cox proposed instead that race and discrimination must be understood in the context of class relations in the United States and the policies pursued by ruling classes, North and South, to preserve their political control over America. In the process, Cox introduced the argument that discrimination was at base a product of the capitalist class's pursuit of a divide-and-rule strategy vis-à-vis the working class.[9]

Cox's critique is brilliant but suffers from two limitations. First, the divide-and-rule argument tends to minimize the agency of white laborers in pursuing their own interests in engaging in discrimination, "economic interests" that even Myrdal acknowledged might lie behind their efforts to exclude blacks from preferred lines of employment. Second, and more fundamental, Cox's analysis of the American class structure tends to be bipolar—capitalists and workers, in all their ethnic and geographic varieties. But the dynamics of twentieth-century America, particularly from the Great Depression onward, is best understood from the standpoint of a tripartite class structure. In a related vein this more complex class structure must account for the place of the so-called underclass, a term now routinely used in the popular print media.

In what follows, my analysis situates racial disparity and discrimination in a context that goes beyond Myrdal in the direction charted by Cox but with the intent of overcoming the two shortcomings of Cox's approach noted immediately above.

The central questions are: Is the presence of an underclass, disproportionately black, a permanent phenomenon? Has American society, on the verge of entry into the twenty-first century, become a caste-ridden civilization, reproducing the same social status from generation to generation for those both at the bottom and at the top of America's hierarchy? Has there been a hardening of the arteries of social mobility in America over the course of the current century? And, if so, what are the implications for racial inequality?

To address these critical questions requires a systematic inquiry into the class transformation that American society has undergone since the close of the nineteenth century. This has been a class transformation that has meant the supplanting of the authority of financial power and monied property by the authority of mental power and knowledge property. It is a transformation that has been noted by a wide variety of observers who, nevertheless, have failed to explore in comprehensive fashion the nature of its implications for intergenerational transmission of social status and the efficacy of public policies ostensibly intended to uplift the poor. The transformation in question is the transition from the capitalist mode of production to managerial society.

At a Senate hearing held in 1968 on "The Nature of Revolution," commenting on a paper by Louis Hartz, Senator Claiborne Pell asked Hartz:

> Another point that struck me was the progress of society as it moves along. Through your paper I think I detected that you moved from a feudal stage where power is based basically on land, to another stage which is the bourgeois or capitalistic stage, where power is based on the possession of machinery, or the capital with which to buy machinery. But you left it a little up in the air, because nothing is final, and nothing is permanent as to what the evolution of this trend is. Would you agree with Ken Galbraith's [John Kenneth Galbraith] theory that the next stage would be where the possession of mere money per se or ownership is not as important as the mental capacity to provide the direction for the intellectual and managerial estate which is now coming to the fore in our country? Therefore, it is more and more the managerial and intellectual groups that are the ones that are becoming dominant. Do you see this trend going on, or do you disagree with this interpretation of your paper?[10]

Hartz's response was unambiguous:

> I would not say that that trend is in my paper. However, that does not mean that I do not believe there is something in that. I believe that this is and has been a development in American economic life.[11]

In a recent book, Harvard political economist Robert Reich, currently serving as U.S. Secretary of Labor, has partitioned the United States (and the global) occupational structure into three broad categories: "routine production" jobs, "in-person server" jobs, and "symbolic analyst" jobs. According to Reich the first category, which includes the traditional well-paid, blue-collar jobs, is in demise; the second category, which includes retail sales workers and hospital care providers, is in a holding pattern; while the third category, which includes academics and artists, is in ascension on a global scale.[12]

In more substantively class-analytical examination of the changing patterns of social stratification in the modern world, Ehrenreich and Ehrenreich have examined the rise of the professional-managerial class, while the late Nicos Poulantzas referred to "the new petty bourgeoisie," Alvin Gouldner characterized the rise to social dominance of intellectuals and the intelligentsia as the rise of a "new class," and David Lebedoff refers to "the new elite."[13] All of these studies, developed from a Marxist perspective on class, long predate former Vice President Quayle's concerns about "the cultural elite." As we will discover below, somewhat surprisingly, the former Vice President's concerns have a substance even he is unlikely to fathom.

At least one further example of a general social analyst who has detected the sea change in social relations in the modern world is worth nothing. When asked in an interview conducted by Edward Reingold, "What kind of a new century are we in, then?" Peter Drucker replied:

> In this twenty-first-century world of dynamic, political change, the significant thing is that we are in a post-business society. Business is still important and greed is as universal as ever; but the values of people are not business values. Most people are no longer part of the business society; *they are part of the knowledge society.* If you go back to when your father and mine was born knowledge was an ornament, a luxury—and now it is at the very center. We worry if the kids don't do as well in math tests as others. No earlier civilization would have dreamed of paying attention to anything like this.[14]

Indeed, we live in the era of selection by performance on IQ and other standardized tests. Measured or "general" intelligence was largely irrelevant to the world that preceded the current century.[15] As we move to the close of the half-millennium ushered in by Columbus's voyages of discovery, we also are coming to the close of the era of dominance of the business enterprise.

The continuing successful transition from capitalism to what Senator Pell called "the managerial estate" is obscured by developments in Eastern Europe, which have been taken as a signal of the collapse of socialism on an international scale and the rejuvenation of the regime of private enterprise. In fact, what is masked by surface events is the ongoing preeminence of the intellectuals, intelligentsia, and the technocrats. The surge toward political reform, the embrace of democraticization, the attempt to overturn totalitarian governance, the call for the unleashing of "market forces," in fact mean a turn from the control of one group of social managers predisposed toward political and economic bureaucratic authoritarianism to a different group predisposed toward electoral politics and greater reliance on the private sector. And many of the free marketeers still find political authoritarianism quite appealing.

In particular, the artistic/artisanal wing of the Eastern European intellectual community has a pronounced presence among the post-COMECON leadership. Vytautus Landsbergis of Lithuania is a pianist, musicologist, and biographer of Lithuanian composer Mikalous Ciurlonis. Václev Havel of Czechoslovakia is a playwright and short story writer. Poland's Takusz Mazowieski was a journalist who worked for Solidarity's newspaper. Eastern Germany's Lothar de Maziere worked as a lawyer but also played in a philharmonic orchestra in East Berlin.[16]

Marx's fundamental law of motion for bourgeois society—the law of the tendency of the rate of profit to fall—led to his famous conclusion that capitalism would come to an end under the weight of its own contradictions.[17] This conclusion has been deemed false even by Marx's leftist sympathizers who see the power of corporate capital in every facet of their lives, often failing to investigate carefully their own position within the social matrix. Unquestionably, the working class has not attained power in the United States, nor, arguably, anywhere else for that matter. But the end of capitalism need not usher in a "dictatorship of the proletariat."

Instead, the winding down of capitalism and the winding up of managerial society ushers in a "dictatorship of the intellectuals and intelligentsia." Marx's prediction of closure to capitalism can unfold without empowerment of the masses. Indeed, the nature of "actually existing socialism" in Eastern Europe prior to the 1990s is suggestive of the bureaucratic anonymity of a particularized version of managerial society rather than Marx's vision of socialism.[18]

The newly ascendant managerial class finds its basis for power in its control over knowledge and information. It exercises its authority via access to decision-making positions within the cluster of institutions that coalesce under the labels of government, the universities, think tanks, and nonprofit foundations. Its functional role—the role that gives it its class character—is its ability to give voice to the identity of, explanation for, and potential solutions of social problems, as well as its capacity to direct cultural and ideological developments. The essence of its class activity is the production of ideas. What delineates the members of this class from others is the combination of specialized, expert knowledge with advanced educational credentials. Indeed, passage through the upper reaches of the university system is the incubator for membership in the managerial class.

This produces a sharp contrast with the once dominant bourgeois class. For the older class found its basis for power in its control over finance and production. It exercised its power via access to the decision-making positions within the business enterprise, i.e., the corporation. Its functional role lay in its ability to introduce new productivity-enhancing techniques. The essence of its class activity has been the appropriation of profit. What has delineated the members of this class from all others has been their great wealth. To the extent that the management task for the corporation has passed to well-paid graduates of MBA programs, there is further evidence of the shift in power toward a distinctive managerial class, whose overriding objective is to engage in thoroughgoing social management.

The direction in which things have turned is reflected in the association between social status in modern America with the acquisition of degrees and/or having studied or worked at the "top" institutions with the "best" persons. Admiration, respect, and envy center more strongly upon the accumulation of credentials than the accumulation of wealth. The attention that post–World War II economists have devoted to Adam Smith's concept of "human capital" is indicative of this social shift in emphasis from acquisition of financial wealth to acquisition of educational credentials, although economists tend to conflate the two since one of the perquisites of advanced education is typically an above-average income.[19]

The overworked term *networking* also comes into play here. Networking, or an individual's personal contacts, determine whether or not he or she becomes attached to the "best" persons who can then bestow authority and credibility. Members of groups who are outside the prestige networks never can get in the game, and the discriminatory nature of the exclusion is masked by their lack of the "best" references and "best" degrees. Reputation-building is tied closely to the pattern of connections with those who already are acknowledged as the established experts.

Myrdal's Chapter 17 focuses in an undifferentiated manner on the nature of discrimination across industrial pursuits. He makes no attempt to consider separately the character of discrimination involving professional-technical activities. And it is perhaps telling that while Richard Sterner and Arnold Rose are listed as collaborators (not co-authors) on the cover page of *An American Dilemma,* none of his black collaborators is listed. The most notable omission is Ralph Bunche, who was involved intimately in the project. Nevertheless, the formal imprimatur of collaborator was not to be added to Bunche's list of credentials.

Although it is well understood that ethical considerations are marginalized in the pursuit of profit from the street level drug traffic to the Wall Street offices of stock traders playing on inside information, it is less widely recognized that advanced educational credentials are valued so highly that cheating to get them is becoming commonplace. A recent issue of *The Wall Street Journal* exposed the extent of cheating at prestigious Taylor Allderdice High School, as students found ways to open dictionaries during S.A.T.s and even got their principal to change report card grades to enhance their chances in competing for National Merit Scholarships.[20] The *Journal* leaves the impression that the phenomenon is not unique to Taylor Allderdice; the Educational Testing Service, the organization that supervises the design and administration of the S.A.T., investigates 3,200 cases of possible cheating annually.[21]

Perhaps the much-maligned values of the urban underclass are not so very different from members of more affluent American social classes. Within their class context, there are many persons who will do whatever it takes to achieve the highest rung on the *available* pecking order. And it is the managerial class's ladder that increasingly provides the highest attainable rungs for overall social preeminence.

Autonomy of the managerial class, whose members can move back and forth between the public and private sectors, is contingent on an expansive arena for government action. The crisis of the Great Depression, creating the opening for the inauguration of the New Deal, provided a springboard for managerial independence from the leash of corporate capital. Additional post–New Deal policy interventions—in particular the Great Society programs of the 1960s—further extended the prerogatives of the managerial class. Unlike the business interests' preference for limited government within a "structure of natural rights," the managerial class's impulse always has been toward unlimited government and, hence, unlimited terrain for managerial planning.[22]

Aside from a 16 percent growth rate in the 1960s, the size of the federal government's workforce has remained fairly stable over the course of the post–World War II era. On the other hand, the composition of federal government employment has changed dramatically since 1960, toward an increased preference for persons with Reich's "symbolic-analytic" skills. Between 1960 and 1980 the number of engineers in the federal government rose more than 50 percent to 98,931, the number of computer specialists rose 600 percent to 46,361, the number of attorneys rose 100 percent to 15,532, and the number of social scientists, psychologists, and welfare workers rose 230 percent to 58,166.[23]

Taking all levels of government employment (federal, state, local) as a proportion of total employment, the rupture in social structure borne by the 1930s and 1940s is quite evident. The ratio of government employment to total employment was no more than 6–7 percent prior to 1930. By the 1950s the proportion had risen to the 10–12 percent range. In the 1960s the proportion rose into the 13–15 percent range; in the 1970s the proportion rose into the 16–17 percent interval. By the start of 1980 the ratio was approaching 20 percent! In the 1980s the ratio dipped back toward the 15 percent level, a point to be explored in greater detail below. Between 1929 and

1989 overall employment rose by 146 percent, but employment in government jobs rose 474 percent![24]

It is ironic that the ascendant class now is in a position to assess how much space should remain for corporate activity. The historical origins of the managerial class can be traced to the decision of the corporate elite in the late nineteenth century to develop a cadre of professionals to perform a supervisory function with respect to the working class both inside and outside the factory. Corporate finance and corporate interests went hand-in-hand with the professionalization of medicine, social work, engineering, the law, and higher education; the new professionals at the turn of the century were, indeed, corporate capital's progeny.[25]

But these were unruly progeny who seized the chance to gain independence from capital when the Great Depression facilitated the opportunity to expand the state. The expansion and character of the managerial state later was to pose important difficulties for corporate capital. These difficulties were articulated in the form of complaints over a rising wage floor attributed to social transfer programs, an over-reaching regulatory apparatus, and excessive wage demands by trade unions, particularly in the 1970s when corporate capital undertook a pronounced withdrawal from productive investment (a capital strike).

The growth slowdown posed a crisis, for the managerial class had to address how to get growth started again—which brought to the surface a critical ideological division among its members. The crisis also provided a political opportunity for corporate capital to stage a counterrevolution in an attempt to restore the old order and to return their unruly progeny to their rightful place as capitalist functionaries.

From this perspective the Reagan administration's activities, and in a more clumsy fashion the Bush administration's activities as well, can be interpreted as a major arm of a capitalist counterrevolution. Reaganomics in its hypothetical ideal form sought to recreate the labor market conditions of the 1920s and the climate that would promote an old-fashioned capitalist boom. The fall in the proportion of total employment attributable to government jobs in the 1980s is indicative of a counterrevolutionary thrust seeking to contain the growth of the public sector.[26]

But restoration of the market atmosphere of the 1920s subjects the economy once more to the boom and bust cycle so characteristic of unrestrained industrial economies. Concurrent deregulation of the financial markets points toward renewal of the structural conditions that existed in the 1920s. The danger that the capitalist counterrevolution—ostensibly intended to promote economic recovery—actually might lead the economy down the road toward depression is only one of the contradictions of the current phase of class struggle.

A second contradiction concerns the fact that to gain electoral support, the Reagan and Bush administrations had to forge an alliance with the working class, the latter generally disgruntled with the liberal agenda of the past 40 years. The alliance was created over the style, if not the substance, of Republican positions on issues like (1) the status of the family, (2) the quality of education, (3) social stability and the nation's moral climate, and (4) the adverse impact of a deficit finance inflationary spiral on "the American dream." Such alliances are fragile since they purport to bring together classes that at bottom are fundamentally antagonistic. It also should be noted that the managerial class built the New Deal and the Great Society by forging a similar alliance with the working class.

The final major contradiction is that corporate capital has had to rely on members of the managerial class—the class it seeks to discipline—to mount the ethical and ideological case for its own full restoration to power. With regard to economic policy alone Reaganomics was able to draw upon a fairly disparate band of conservative economists, ranging from Arthur Laffer to Murray Weidenbaum to Martin Feldstein to William Poole. Whereas, in the early twentieth century such economists could be regarded as "hired guns" for the business interests, today it is less clear who is in control of whom. The centrality of their professional status gives even the least independent-minded economists a tendency to try to demonstrate that they are in fact independent-minded.

There are members of the managerial class who speak for corporate capital not solely because of the pecuniary advantage (which can be substantial) but out of intellectual conviction. This reveals both the strength and the weakness of the class. The element of strength is the exceptional pragmatism and ideological flexibility of the members of the managerial class. The element of weakness enters because the class finds itself deeply torn over numerous issues, especially the issue of how much of a role to assign to corporate capital in the managerial age.

The division within the managerial class can be embodied broadly in the conflict of the broad outlines of Republican economic policy versus the Democratic Party's gravitation toward some variant of New Industrial Policy. The former professes to produce economic growth by resurrecting the "free and natural" operation of the marketplace with reliance on decentralized private investment decisions. The latter professes to introduce industrial planning on a formal basis in the United States. The specifics of NIP vary from plans to have labor, business and government engage in collaborative national planning to plans to introduce selective investment by the public sector to plans to introduce full scale public sector investment and workers' control of industry. The split remains a division over the residual role for corporate capital in the new age.

The members of the managerial class are professionals with portfolios. It is the criteria for entry into the professions that dictate the terms of inclusion and exclusion from this social class. It is not being argued here that the standards are illegitimate vis-à-vis the tasks the professional is to perform—although sometimes they are—but the meeting of these standards is what separates the members of this class from the rest of the population.

Professional positions for the members of the managerial class are to be obtained on a "merit" basis. After all, it is customary for the social managers to espouse a vision of the ideal society that throbs with the images of a pure meritocracy. A companion theme is the social managers' tendency to advocate the creation of full conditions of equal opportunity—the notion that all with the desire and ability should have access to the appropriate set of tests that, should they pass them, will permit them entry to the professions. Thus, the managerial class conceives of itself as an open class; all those who display sufficient "merit" can be admitted as members.

But who is most likely to demonstrate "merit"? The managerial class is disproportionately comprised of those who are academic high achievers. Growing evidence is at hand that academically high-achieving youths typically are children of academically high-achieving parents.[27]

Robert Reich characterizes 80 to 85 percent of young people in the United States as receiving either virtually "no education" or "a poor one." But, says Reich, the remaining "15 to 20 percent…are being perfectly prepared for a lifetime of symbolic-analytic work."[28] Reich goes on to describe the nature of the education and the social background of these "fortunate young people":

> The formal education of the budding symbolic-analyst follows a common pattern. Some of these young people attend elite private schools, followed by the most selective universities and prestigious graduate schools; a majority spend childhood within high-quality suburban public schools where they are tracked through advanced courses in the company of other similarly fortunate symbolic-analytic offspring, and thence to good four-year colleges. But their experiences are similar: Their parents are interested and involved in their education. Their teachers and professors are attentive to their academic needs. They have access to state-of-the-art science laboratories, language laboratories, interactive computers and video systems in the classroom, language laboratories, and high-tech school libraries. Their classes are relatively small; their peers are intellectually stimulating. Their parents take them to museums and cultural events, expose them to foreign travel, and give them music lessons. At home are educational books, educational toys, educational videotapes, microscopes, telescopes, and personal computers replete with the latest educational

software. Should the children fall behind in their studies, they are delivered to private tutors. Should they develop a physical ailment that
impedes their learning, they immediately receive good medical care.[29]

While other countries, Japan and those in Europe for example, offer a higher
quality of education for broader segments of its population, Reich says "no
other society prepares its most fortunate young people as well for lifetimes
of creative problem-solving, -identifying, and brokering."[30] The phenomenon of caste—not in Myrdal's sense but in Cox's sense of the term—in the
selection of America's "symbolic-analytic" elite is plainly apparent.

Such a phenomenon was evident as early as the mid-1950s to Horace
Mann Bond. Bond was curious about the social distributive effects of reliance upon standardized tests for identification of young people with talent. The National Merit Scholarship Corporation's 1956 report provided
a summary table listing the winners' reports of their fathers' occupations.
By comparing these reports with the total numbers of males in each of
the occupational categories, Bond could assess how "productive" each
occupational group was in generating winners of National Merit awards.

The results demonstrate clearly that the standardized tests used for selecting winners of National Merit Scholarships tended to identify young
people whose fathers tended to be members of America's highly educated,
professional strata. As Bond observed:

> . . . an American child whose father was a librarian had, in 1956, 1,120
> times the chance to win a National Merit Scholarship than a child
> whose parent was a laborer had. The odds against a child whose fa-
> ther is in one of the farming occupations were 30–1 to win a National
> Merit Scholarship in competition with a child of one of the profes-
> sional occupations. While 168,000 physicians produced twenty-six
> scholars, 972,300 carpenters produced seven; 516,300 machinists
> produced three; 289,140 plumbers produced two; and 1,376,910
> truckers produced three.[31]

Bond also reported that only *one* child reported having a father who was a
laborer, despite the fact that there were 3.6 million men who held such an
occupational status in 1956. On the other hand, there were 234 scholars
among the children of 3 million men who were professional, technical, and
kindred workers.[32]

Because the National Merit Scholarship Corporation's report also indicates from which high school each of the winners came, Bond was also able
to conclude that *no* black child from segregated southern high schools received an award.[33] Nor was there any evidence that there were black students from the South among the 4,000 finalists either![34] Bond doubted that

the class and racial background of the scholars could be attributable to innate heredity:

> ... I cannot bring myself to believe that the odds against "high scholastic aptitude" for various occupations even remotely resemble the genetic distribution of capacity in the persons concerned . . . Nor can I believe that there is no child—among the 10 million Negroes of the American South—with a "talent potential" worthy of search and subsequent development.[35]

Bond believed something else was going on—that the National Merit Scholar data pointed toward class immobility. An optimist about prospects for mobilizing the educational system to enhance social mobility, Bond was hopeful that reforms of schooling would further broaden the base of persons who could be identifiable as "talented." But that is precisely why the widespread diffusion of quality education is a political question. If quality education were to be provided to the now less fortunate 80–85 percent of America's youths, it would erode the present tendency to select into the managerial class the sons and daughters of the current members of the managerial class. Indeed, the task of screening for the available slots in the managerial elite would become quite problematic if there was a genuine diffusion of "symbolic-analytical" skills across the entire population.

A policy optimism similar to Bond's actually underlies the pessimistic findings in a study undertaken by Charles Manski on behalf of the Democratic Study Center. Manski found that growth in college enrollment over the past decade has been concentrated among more affluent young people. Partitioning the population into five groups on the basis of family income, Manski found that the lowest quintile was the only group with a smaller proportion of its children in college than at the start of the 1980s. Nevertheless, the proportion of low-income high school graduates attending four-year colleges remained stable at 26–27 percent, while the proportion of children from upper-income families attending four-year colleges rose from 56 to 60 percent. The study suggests that the decline in enrollment among the poorest young people was due to reduced federal financial aid.[36] The inference is that if federal financial aid rose, college enrollment among the poor would expand significantly, and the cause of interclass mobility would be enhanced.

This perspective fails to recognize the fundamental rigidity underlying the changed nature of social stratification in American society, a rigidity that was beyond the view of the Myrdal team, perhaps because of the ideological frame of their study and the time period of their study. Today it is clearer that highly educated and comparatively affluent parents are better able to endow their children with the resources, from infancy and early childhood, to position them for renewed access to the overclass. Even prior to cutbacks in federal financial aid, half the proportion of low-income students was attending four-year colleges than were affluent students.

If it were possible to have a completely nondiscriminatory regime on the basis of race or class—a pure equal opportunity environment—this would simply lock in the inequalities that are determined by differential background advantages which better educated parents can bestow upon their children.[37] The Nobel laureate in economics Arthur Lewis observed in this context:

> Despite all the talk of social mobility, the open door, and equality of opportunity, the main effect of schooling on class structure has been to retain middle-class jobs for middle-class children, since middle-class parents are better than working-class parents at getting their children through schooling and past the usual tests.[38]

Here is a Myrdalian cumulative process with substance, operating across generations to preserve and widen class-cum-race differences.

Horace Mann Bond based his optimism concerning interclass mobility on another body of data that he felt ran counter to the implications of the National Merit Scholarship data. Bond undertook his own investigation of the occupational standings of the fathers and paternal grandfathers of 300 black Americans holding doctoral degrees by the mid-1950s. He obtained responses that gave him data on 266 fathers and 89 paternal grandfathers. He found that out of the 266 observations on fathers, over 41 percent held positions as professional, technical, and kindred workers, disproportionately consisting of ministers and teachers, while about 19 percent of the 89 observations on grandfathers consisted of professional, technical, and kindred workers. Identification of grandfathers' occupations was more difficult because most of the subjects' grandparents were slaves; therefore the occupations listed were based upon post-emancipation employment.[39] Bond said, "the rapid emergence of an intellectual elite among former slaves shows how quickly the American magic can work."[40]

But Bond already limited his view to a highly select group of blacks, whose experiences were exceptional, by taking a retrospective look at the family heritage of that small group of blacks who had earned doctorates. The intergenerational link that is suggestive of dramatic upward mobility really is between grandfathers and fathers, although the confidence in the findings is reduced by the sharp attrition in information on paternal grandfathers. Moreover, for the first generation out of slavery to find that out of 89 men, about 17 held professional, technical, or kindred employment suggests that this was an unusual group of persons as well. However, the lost information probably is more likely to apply to cases of paternal grandparents who had low status occupations, which would reinforce Bond's optimism.

But once we get to the fathers' generation the transmission of social status takes on the more familiar lock-step fashion. As Bond acknowledged:

> A social and intellectual elite takes form, evolving in two generations from an apparently unstratified population—principally composed of slaves, with a small minority of scarcely more privileged free persons of color. In the relatively short span of two generations, the parental occupations of our holders of doctorates, listed in the decade 1910–1919, closely approximate the parental occupations of our National Merit Scholars, as reported in 1956 (41 percent of the fathers of black doctorate holders were professional, technical, and kindred workers while 45 percent of the fathers of NMS winners had the parallel occupational classification).[41]

On the basis of a small and select sample, Horace Mann Bond, nonetheless, has uncovered an important pattern. With the expanded development and importance of the managerial class, interclass mobility has *declined* in the United States. There was, arguably, a greater degree of interclass mobility under mid- to late nineteenth century capitalism than there was during the mid-twentieth century with the consolidation of managerialism.

Again this rigidity, leading to the inability to move those at the lower tiers of the American social ladder readily to higher tiers, was outside the vision of the Myrdal team. Consequently, Myrdal could speak of a symmetrical ease with which society can switch from a vicious to a virtuous circle of race relations with a marginal change in white beliefs. The perspective advanced here asserts no such symmetry exists; it is much easier to maintain a downward spiral than to get into an upward spiral.

Still, an illusion of substantial interclass mobility in the United States remains commonplace. It has been fostered, in part, by the mythology of white ethnic immigrant ascension. But, in general, white ethnic immigrant groups arriving at the turn of the century whose descendants have proven to be high achievers typically were better educated and more skilled than groups whose descendants have not done as well, even if all arrived in poverty. Careful attention to the prior class position of the successful groups in their countries of origin suggests that they "broadly have displayed *lateral* rather than *upward* mobility in their movement from abroad to the United States."[42]

For example, Jewish Americans have the highest income among all white ethnic groups in the United States. Although Jewish immigrants entered the United States in poverty at the turn of the century, Goldscheider and

Zuckerman have pointed out that "[t]he proportion of Jews who declared upon entry to the United States that they were laborers, farmers, or servants averaged less than 25 percent in 1900–1902 compared to 80–90 percent of the other immigrant groups," adding that "In 1910 and 1914, for example, about 90 percent of Croatians, Slovenians, Finns, Greeks, Hungarians, Poles, Russians, and Italians compared to 20 percent of the Jews were laborers, farmers, or servant."[43]

The more recent successes of youths from Asian immigrant families display a similar connection. A 1987 study in *Time* of Asian American students is revealing. Psychologist Julian Stanley found that out of 292 preteens who scored high on the math portion of the Scholastic Aptitude Test, one-quarter of the students were Asian Americans. Seventy-one percent of their fathers and 21 percent of their mothers held doctorates or medical degrees, in contrast with 39 percent of the fathers and 10 percent of the mothers of non-Asians. The same article reports that a 1965 immigration law eliminated U.S. exclusionary quotas and "brought a surge of largely middle-class Asian professionals—doctors, engineers, and academics from Hong Kong, Taiwan, South Korea, India, and Philippines—seeking economic opportunity." On average, these families have done well economically and academically in the United States. But *Time* also found that the predominantly lower-class immigrants from Indochina largely remain in poverty, and *their* children are often dropouts from U.S. schools.[44]

Previous estimates of intergenerational income correlations suggested a phenomenon of "regression toward mediocrity," i.e., that there was negligible correlation, .2 or less, between fathers' and sons' income. But the most recent research indicates that the earlier estimates were biased downward by measurement error, unrepresentative samples, or both. The revised estimates now establish that the intergenerational correlation between incomes is *at least* .4, reversing the prior assumption that there is a high degree of income mobility in the United States.[45]

Of course, there are exceptional individuals, but in modern America, increasingly, ethnicity is destiny. The boundaries of the income and occupational distribution intertwine with more rigid patterns of intergenerational replication of class status. It is within this context that prospects for the underclass need to be understood.

The underclass is the most deprived and least utilized fraction of the working class. Disproportionately black and spatially concentrated in communities beset by intense degrees of poverty, the American underclass is conceptually equivalent to Marx's "lumpen" element of the proletariat. Given the hypothesis that American society is characterized by declining interclass mobility, the presumption here is that notions of uplifting the underclass—indeed uplifting the working class generally—are exercises in mystification on a par with Cox's characterization of *An American Dilemma* as a mystification of American race relations.

In the mid-1980s Arthur Lewis undertook a simple arithmetical exercise with respect to racial inequality. He asked how many above-median earnings jobs would be required for blacks to achieve equality in median earnings between blacks and whites. Using 1980 data Lewis found that there was a deficit of 2 million above-median earnings jobs for blacks, which Lewis said was not a large number of jobs, only about 2 percent of the total number of jobs available in the US economy during that year.[46]

But Lewis never identified the source of the jobs. Would they be entirely new jobs, or would nonblack workers have to be displaced? How would the resistance of white labor to competition be handled in the latter case? Would the jobs continue to be available beyond the year of inauguration? Would they be public sector jobs, or would they be generated by the private sector? Would they be a mere $1 above the median or substantially above the median? And which blacks with below-median earnings would be the ones to receive the jobs that would place them above the median?

The same questions can be raised with respect to the notion of transforming the *class* status of the underclass via the provision of nonunderclass employment. Indeed, why not seek to uplift all persons below the poverty line or within 150 percent of the poverty line, either by providing higher quality employment or improved schooling and training, or both?

These rhetorical questions are intended to tease out the extent of the generally unstated commitment to hierarchy and social inequality. For the capacity to "uplift the poor" is dependent upon the degree of rigidity of the system of social stratification. With a comparatively rigid system of stratification someone must fill all the slots, including the slots at the very bottom. The distribution of relative class status inherently takes on the qualities of a zero sum game, particularly if we view class structure as largely predetermined and only slowly changing—rather than being continuously generated anew on the basis of individual self-investment decisions, as the conceit of the human capital theorists would have it. Or, as Myrdal's conceit would have had it in 1944: Just have strongly enforced antidiscrimination measures and blacks can readily enter new arenas.

The central question must be who is willing to take the place of the existing members of the urban underclass? Who will trade places with the black poor? Or, more generally, which members of the managerial class are willing, at least temporarily, to switch places with members of the working class? Or, still in this vein, how many members of the managerial class are willing to uncompromisingly support the diffusion of quality education, with more resources per capita going to the education of the children of the underclass—rather than their own?

Even the genesis of the black urban underclass bears further testimony to the powerful effects of caste in American society. Nicholas Lemann's study of the great black migration from the deep South portrays the movement of ambitious blacks of essentially peasant backgrounds seeking to make new lives in northern cities, with a specific emphasis on Chicago. Although policies made in Washington, D.C., did little to improve their prospects, Lemann argues that their class origins in the deep South cast the long run die for the migrants.

For in a sense, their class status in the context of southern plantation agriculture was replicated in the context of a northern industrial center. Consistently deprived of quality education on the plantations, to serve the ends of the planters under the sharecropping system, the migrants came to the North without the advantages of, say, Jewish immigrants to the United States in the 1890s or Asian immigrants to the United States in the 1960s.[47] The lack of those advantages would harden their status and their children's and grandchildren's status at the bottom of the nation's hierarchy.

To break with the effects of caste cannot be accomplished without addressing the question of hierarchy in managerial society and the question of who is to be included and who is to be excluded. Race and ethnicity become critical markers, dictating relative group preparedness for active and critical participation in the age of science and technology.

While black Americans constitute about 12 percent of the U.S. population, blacks hold only 1.5 percent of the approximately 75,000 doctorates in science and engineering. Similarly Native Americans constitute close to 1 percent of the U.S. population but hold only 0.1 percent of all science and engineering doctorates. Hispanics are now about 9 percent of the U.S. population while holding only 1.7 percent of science and engineering doctorates. In contrast, whites are 75 percent of the U.S. population but hold 88 percent of the doctorates, and Asians are only 3 percent of the population but hold close to 9 percent of the doctorates.[48] Among whites holding doctorates those numbers are filled disproportionately by Jewish Americans and Irish Catholic Americans.

And the flow of new Ph.D.s holds little promise for a change in these conditions. Between 1982 and 1992 the number of doctorates awarded to African Americans in all fields fell from 1,047 to 951, a 9 percent decline to 2.4 percent of the total awarded. For black males alone the decline was 20 percent to 386.[49]

A similar pattern is evident with respect to professional/managerial employment. While 54 percent of men and 52 percent of women aged 25–54 of Russian (Jewish) ancestry held professional/managerial positions in 1990, the proportion for black American men and women was only 14 percent and 20 percent, respectively.[50] Thus, on the basis of race and ethnicity, "outcast" groups can be identified—groups whose members cannot be expected to play a major role, or even a minor role, in the unwinding of the managerial age.

The most thoroughly excluded members of the "outcast" group, say, for example, the black underclass, may find other policies besides spatial isolation and deprivation of adequate welfare support (as a precursor to workfare) directed toward them. While capitalism in its laissez faire mode necessarily possesses an ambivalence on the population question, the social managers possess a growing inclination to view population as something to be controlled and reduced.

Under capitalism a growing population replenished the reserve of labor and potentially helped contribute to market expansion. Capitalism's relative surplus population or industrial reserve army was necessary, serving simultaneously to restrain the strength and demands of the employed fraction of the working class and to guarantee that capital could hurl workers quickly into newly expanding sectors without having to remove them from other sectors. But the reserve of labor, especially the least frequently employed "stagnant" element, often was undisciplined, prone to street crime, and lived in neighborhoods that were a tinder box for social tensions. From that vantage point some ideologues for the bourgeois system could argue for population control to "fine-tune" the reserve of labor.

Nevertheless, given the necessity of a reserve, capital as a whole maintained an ambivalent posture toward population control. Capitalism's spokesmen would be likely to advocate population control unhesitatingly only if it could be targeted at those elements of the reserve beyond "hope"— those persons never likely to be subjected to the capitalist labor process and always likely to be socially disruptive.

However, for the managerial class the necessity of a working class is merely attributable to the pragmatic consideration that even the current advanced state of machine technology does not yet allow production to be conducted without human labor. But the momentum of technical change renders more and more labor superfluous. Redundancy of labor sets in, having the starkest implications for those least likely to find employment, the "lumpen" fraction of the working class or the underclass.

From the perspective of the managerial class, the "excess population" that carries over with the decline of capitalism is truly extraneous. And the most extraneous will be the element at the very base of the working class, the black underclass. These are managerial society's most obvious "undesirables." Rather than support them indefinitely (or fear them indefinitely) the following policies become possibilities: (1) further efforts to transform and enlighten underclass through better education (but not *much* better education, because that could undermine the security of the status of overclass children), (2) continued efforts to contain and spatially isolate the underclass, (3) continued efforts to provide welfare support for them but in a more restrictive fashion, (4) reduce the numbers of the underclass via population control (i.e., silent genocide), and (5) encourage the underclass to emigrate to Third World countries (e.g., empty the black ghettos of the United States with an officially sanctioned Back to Africa movement). Thus far, more attention has been drawn to the first three rather than the fourth, although the fourth option is attracting more and more interest, ostensibly on the grounds of cost-effectiveness.[51] I suspect that we will hear more and more about the fifth option in the near future.

In an earlier paper where I explored the implications for surplus population of the rise of managerial society, I suggested that the law of population in the new age would be "The Law of the Progressive Elimination of Undesirable Population." Under capitalism, the surplus population, and any segments of it that are undesirable, must be identified relative to capital's valorization requirements. But under managerialism, the existence of a surplus population is a holdover from the *ancien regime,* and the undesirables are identified according to the tastes and preferences of the managerial class.[52]

It could be a matter of whim, or it could be a matter of crude calculation. If it is the latter, the managerial class will ask: Are they too expensive and too dangerous to take care of indefinitely? And if the answer is in the affirmative, steps to prune the numbers of the underclass—beyond the attrition attributable to diseases like the AIDS virus—will be pursued.

In this sense, then, the underclass need not be a permanent fixture in the social order, but its disappearance will not be due to actions to uplift the underclass. Rather it will be due to what amounts to a genocidal strategy, wherein the underclass literally is gradually eliminated, creating a new bottom tier of the American hierarchy. And after all, that is the nub of matters, whether the American system of social stratification will be allowed to continue without challenge, the challenge that Myrdal's famous report never deigned to broach.

NOTES

1. Myrdal, p. 380.
2. Ibid., p. 381.
3. William Darity, Jr. (with Jeremiah P. Cotton and Herbert Hill). "Race and Inequality in the Managerial Age." In Wornie Reed, ed. *African-Americans: Essential Perspectives* (Westport: Auburn House, 1993), p. 34.
4. Myrdal, p. 75. Also see Appendix 3, especially pp. 1066–1069.
5. Ibid., p. 391.

6. Ibid., p. 76.

7. Darity, op. cit., pp. 35–57. To the extent that there was an increase in the numbers of the "black middle class" in the 1960s, it was largely due to the expansion of social welfare programs under the aegis of the Great Society. The growth in the "black middle class" is linked directly to their capacity to take professional, administrative, and technical positions in running public social welfare programs. See Michael K. Brown and Steven P. Erie. "Blacks and the Legacy of the Great Society: The Economic and Political Impact of Social Policy." *Public Policy* (Summer 1981): 308–309.

8. Myrdal, p. 391.

9. Oliver Cox. *Caste, Class and Race: A Study in Social Dynamics* (New York: Monthly Review Press, 1959) (originally published by Doubleday in 1948), pp. 509–538.

10. U.S. Senate, Committee on Foreign Relations, hearings: *The Nature of Revolution,* February and March, 1969, p. 36.

11. Ibid., p. 36.

12. Robert Reich. *The Work of Nations: Preparing Ourselves for 21st Century Capitalism* (New York: Vintage Books, 1992) pp. 208–224.

13. See Barbara Ehrenreich and John Ehrenreich. "The Professional-Managerial Class." In Pat Walker, ed. *Between Labor and Capital* (Boston: South End Press, 1979); Nicos Poulantzas. "The New Petty Bourgeoisie." *The Insurgent Sociologist* (Summer 1979); Alvin Gouldner. *The Future of the Intellectuals and the Rise of the New Class* (New York: Seabury Press, 1979); and David Lebedoff. "The Dangerous Arrogance of the New Elite." *Esquire* (August 29, 1978). Also see in a related vein, Jean-Christophe Agnew. "A Touch of Class." *Democracy* (Spring 1983): 59–72.

14. "Facing the 'Totally New and Dynamic': An Interview with Peter Drucker by Edward Reingold." In Otto Johnson, exec ed. *The 1991 Information Please Almanac* (Boston: Houghton Mifflin Company, 1991), p. 42, emphasis added.

15. Lebedoff, op. cit., pp. 20–21.

16. See Don Kirk. "Maestro Directs Lithuania." *USA Today* (March 27, 1990): A2; and Juan J. Walte. "Intellectuals Rise to Top in Eastern Europe." *USA Today* (March 27, 1990): A2.

17. Karl Marx. *Capital, Volume 3* (New York: Vintage Books, 1981), pp. 317–375. In this connection, Reich's, op. cit., p. 6, observation on the profitability and performance of American corporations over the course of the past quarter century is consistent with the relative decline of industrial capitalism in this country, at least: "It is now a commonplace . . . that large corporations are no longer as profitable as they were twenty-five years ago. From a peak of nearly 10 percent in 1965, the average net after-tax profit rate of America's largest nonfinancial corporations declined in the 1970s, bounced back somewhat between 1982 and 1985, and then resumed its downward slide. When adjusted for inflation, the highest Dow Jones Industrial Average of the bullish 1980s, reached in August 1987, was actually below its peak of January 1966. Further, America's 500 largest industrial companies failed to add any American jobs

between 1975 and 1990, and their share of the civilian labor force dropped from 17 percent to less than 10 percent during the same interval."

18. See, e.g., Rudolf Bahro's study of "actually existing socialism," *The Alternative in Eastern Europe* (London: New Left Books, 1978). An explicit treatment of the bureaucratic elite under "actually existing socialism" as a "new class" with characteristics akin to what is described as the managerial elite came as early as the late 1950s; see Milovan Djilas. *The New Class: An Analysis of The Communist System* (New York: Frederick Praeger, 1957). The classic statement of the emergence of the managerial class on an international scale is contained in James Burnham's widely misinterpreted book, *The Managerial Revolution: What Is Happening in The World Today* (New York: John Day Co., 1941). For a more complete development of the view that the end of capitalism need not mean the rise of the proletariat, also see the discussions in William Darity, Jr., Ronald Johnson, and Edward Thompson. "The Political Economy of U.S. Energy and Equity Policy." In Hans Landsberg, ed. *High Energy Costs: Assessing the Burden* (Washington D.C.: Resources for the Future, 1982), pp. 170–219; and in Erik Olin Wright. "Capitalism's Futures." *Socialist Review* (March/April, 1983).

19. Highly representative of the contemporary economist's impulse is Nobel Laureate Theodore W. Schultze's book, *Investing in People: The Economics of Population Quality* (Berkeley: University of California Press, 1981).

20. Gary Putka. "Blackboard Jungle: A Cheating Epidemic at a Top High School Teaches Sad Lessons." *The Wall Street Journal* (June 29, 1992): A1, A4–A5.

21. Gary Putka. "ETS Tries to Discourage Cheating With Help of Statistics and Tipsters." *The Wall Street Journal* (June 28, 1992): A5.

22. On corporate capital's attitude toward government, see Thorstein Veblen. *The Theory of Business Enterprise* (New York: Scribners, 1904), p. 376.

23. Kathy Sawyer. "Uncle Sam's New Look: A Workforce in Transition From Clerks to Technocrats." *The Washington Post* (August 4, 1980): A7.

24. Calculations performed by the author based upon data in U.S. Bureau of the Census. *Statistical Abstract of the US 1991* (Washington D.C.: U.S. Government Printing Office, 1991), pp. 305, 329.

25. See Ehrenreich and Ehrenreich. op. cit., passim. Also see E. Richard Brown. *Rockefeller Medicine Men: Medicine and Capitalism in America* (Berkeley: University of California Press, 1979); and Thorstein Veblen. *The Higher Learning in America: A Memorandum on the Conduct of Universities by Business Men* (New York: Hill and Wang 1957) (originally published in 1918).

26. In the 1980s government employment continued to grow but by less than 1 percent per annum, while total employment grew at an average 2 percent annual rate. The impact of the capitalist counterrevolution on the social work profession came early. In 1972 only 3.3 percent of all social workers were employed in the private sector, whereas by 1983 the proportion had risen to 12 percent due to "reductions in public funding, as well as expanding [private sector] opportunities." See Jacqueline Trescott. "The New Breed of People Who Help." *The Washington Post* (November 27, 1983): K1. A similar push was

evident in the medical and health services field with the development and implementation of various proposals to "privatize" the delivery of such services. See Judith Feder et. al. "Health." In Isabel Sawhill and John Palmer, eds. *The Reagan Experiment* (Washington D.C.: The Urban Institute Press, 1982).

27. Dan Morgan. "A Mixed Message on Education From the Home of `The Bomb.'" *The Washington Post* (October 19, 1980): A1-A2.

28. Reich. op. cit., p. 227.

29. Ibid., pp. 227–228.

30. Ibid., p. 228.

31. Horace Mann Bond. *The Search for Talent* (Cambridge: The Graduate School of Education, Harvard University, 1959), p. 23.

32. Ibid., pp. 26–27.

33. Ibid., p. 22.

34. Ibid., p. 22.

35. Ibid., pp. 26–27.

36. Pat Ordovensky. "Poor Are Still Shut Out of College." *The USA Today* (August 27, 1992): D1.

37. Christopher J. Ruhm. "When 'Equal Opportunity' Is Not Enough: Training Costs and Intergenerational Inequality." *Journal of Human Resources* 23(2) (Spring 1988): 155–172.

38. W. Arthur Lewis. *Racial Conflict and Economic Development*, (Cambridge: Harvard University Press, 1985), p. 58.

39. Bond. op. cit., p. 28.

40. Ibid., p. 52.

41. Ibid., p. 31.

42. William Darity, Jr. "What's Left of the Economic Theory of Discrimination." In Steven Shulman and William Darity, Jr., eds. *The Question of Discrimination: Racial Inequality in the U.S. Labor Market*, (Middletown: Wesleyan University Press), pp. 343–344, emphasis in original. Also see Andrea Tyree. "Reshuffling the Social Deck: From Mass Migration to the Transformation of the American Ethnic Hierarchy." In J.R. Blau and Norman Goodman, eds. *Social Roles and Social Institutions: Essays in Honor of Rose Laub Coser* (Denver: Westview Press, 1991). Tyree (p. 213) finds using data from the General Social Survey that "the current [economic] ranking of white ethnic groups is a positive function of hierarchical position at the turn of the century."

43. Calvin Goldscheider and Alan S. Zuckerman. *The Transformation of the Jews* (Chicago: University of Chicago Press, 1984), p. 166. Stephen Steinberg also has reported on the skilled character of Eastern European Jewish immigrants that "gave them a decisive advantage over other immigrants." See Stephen Steinberg. *The Ethnic Myth: Race, Ethnicity and Class in America* (Boston: Beacon Press, 1981), p. 101.

44. Jennifer Hull, Jeannie Park, and James Willwerth. "The New Whiz Kids." *Time* (August 31, 1987): 42–51.

45. See Gary A. Solon. "Intergenerational Income Mobility." *American Economic Review* 82(3) (June 1992): 393–408, and David J. Zimmerman. "Regression

Toward Mediocrity in Economic Stature." *American Economic Review* 82(3) (June 1992): 409–429.

46. Lewis, op. cit.

47. Nicholas Lemann. *The Promised Land: The Great Black Migration and How It Changed America* (New York: Vintage Books, 1992), pp. 1–58.

48. Robert C. Johnson. "Black Underrepresentation in Science and Technology." *Trotter Institute Review* (Winter/Spring 1991): 13–18.

49. Frank James (Knight-Ridder news service). "The Educating of America: Black Ph.D. Recipients—Prospective Faculty Members—Are On Decline." *The Durham Herald-Sun* (February 13, 1994): G6, G10.

50. William Darity, Jr., and William Winfrey. "Interethnic Disparity Across Census Divisions, 1980–1990." Paper prepared for the Housing and Urban Development conference on "Regional Growth and Community Development," held at the Omni Shoreham Hotel, Washington, D.C., November 18, 1993.

51. Paul Sommers and Laura Thomas ("Restricting Federal Funds For Abortion: Another Look." *Social Science Quarterly* 64(1) (March 1983): 340–346) explicitly have made a case for preserving the availability of federal funds for abortions for low-income women to reduce the long-term costs of social transfer programs. Also see the discussion in Salim Muwakkil's essay in *In These Times,* June 12–25, 1985, p. 6. Two years ago *The Philadelphia Inquirer* editorialized that Norplant implants as "foolproof contraception could be invaluable in breaking the cycle of inner city poverty." "Poverty and Norplant: Can Contraception Reduce the Underclass?" *The Philadelphia Inquirer* (December 12, 1992): A18.

52. William Darity, Jr. "The Managerial Class and Surplus Population." *Society* (November/December 1983): 54–62.

John Sibley Butler

6

Myrdal Revisited:
The Negro in Business,
the Professions, Public Service,
and Other White Collar Occupations

IN THE YEARS since Gunnar Myrdal published his work, there have been many changes in the area of race relations. A massive civil rights movement provided people of African descent with the basic constitutional rights that other Americans had enjoyed for centuries. Racial integration of housing, though varying across the country, has been accomplished. Despite all of the changes, *An American Dilemma* stands as a baseline for the analysis of race relations in America. The purpose of this chapter is to reexamine Myrdal's analysis of business and professional African Americans.

When Myrdal examined the collected data on the Negro in business, the professions, public service, and other white collar occupations, his interpretation of the data was influenced by the theoretical frameworks of his day. His interpretation was also influenced by the structure of segregation and the overall reality of race relations in America. As we reflect on Myrdal's work, we must also consider how relevant theoretical ideas allow us to look at Myrdal's original data. We must also use recent theoretical insights to project the future of blacks in business, professions, public service, and other white-collar occupations.

This chapter follows the original outline that was presented by Myrdal in his Chapter 14. The first section is thus concerned with his overview of blacks in business, the professions, public service, and other white collar occupations—his operational definition of who these people are. The second section concentrates on specific kinds of occupations—business enterprises, financial institutions, black teachers, blacks in the medical profession, and blacks on stage, screen, and in music.

MYRDAL'S THEORETICAL FRAMEWORK

Myrdal started his Chapter 14 by partitioning the black wage earner from those who were called professionals and other white collar occupations. This distinction was based on the total exclusion of black professionals from professional opportunities in the larger society, or what Myrdal called the white middle or upper classes. Myrdal's analysis brought together racial customs and laws. He noted that

> The position of the Negro in business, professions, public service, and white collar jobs is far different from that of the Negro wage earner. As a wage earner the Negro is excluded from many trades; where he works, he is commonly held down to the status of laborer and is excluded from skilled work. But there are always possibilities for him to enter these jobs, and he is always struggling to do so. In the occupations traditionally associated with upper- or middle-class status, the exclusion policy is usually much more complete and "settled"; this is because it is fortified by "social" considerations, as well as by economic ones.[1]

This distinction between wage workers and black professionals is important because he noted that even under segregation, black workers had aspirations of moving up the ladder to better jobs. But black professionals, whether business people or medical doctors, had no opportunity to use their professional expertise.

Following in the tradition of earlier analysis of the black community during this time period, Myrdal correctly placed business people and other black professionals outside the overall American economy. The economic ramifications, as noted by Myrdal, were great:

> The exclusion from the larger white economy means a severe restriction of the opportunities for Negroes to reach an upper- or middle-class status. It represents one of the main social mechanisms by which the Negro upper- and middle-classes are kept small. It also makes the occupational distribution in those classes skewed: while the Negro community gives places for a fair number of Negro preachers, teachers, and neighborhood storekeepers, it does not offer much chance for civil engineers and architects. The latter have to work in the white economy which does not want Negroes in such positions. The Negroes' representation among managers of industry, if anything, is still smaller.[2]

This competitive disadvantage faced by the black business people and other professions created a dual experience within their ranks. On the one hand, segregated markets of professionals, such as ministers, morticians, and beauticians, were generally respected. But the black storekeeper could not compete with the white storekeeper. This was also true of the black doctor and the black lawyer. But without segregation, noted Myrdal, the entire black middle class could not exist; he wrote:

> This means that the entire Negro middle- and upper-class becomes caught in an ideological dilemma. On the one hand, they find that the caste wall blocks their economic and social opportunities. On the other hand, they have, at the same time, a vested interest in racial segregation since it gives them what opportunity they have.[3]

In 1930 Myrdal reported 254,000 black workers in white collar and higher occupations. This meant that one out of fifteen black workers in nonagricultural pursuits had a status higher than that of wage earner. In the white nonfarm population, Myrdal noted, two out of every five workers were in business, managerial, professional, and white collar jobs. Between 1910 and 1930 the number of black workers in such occupations increased. But Myrdal showed that the corresponding increase of white workers had been greater, so the relative position of blacks did not improve. In 1910, of all professional, managerial, and clerical workers, 1.8 percent were black. In 1930 this percentage was 1.7 percent. Between 1910 and 1930, there was only a 1 percent increase in the professional, businessman, and white collar worker categories for blacks.

Table 6.1 reports the data since Myrdal for blacks in white collar and higher occupations. Although the census categories have changed since 1930, Table 6.1 provides an excellent measurement of the changes. Even a cursory glance at the table illustrates the fact that things have not changed significantly.

For example, in 1930 the number of blacks (males and females) in professional occupations was 115,765.[4] In 1970 that number was 633,615. Although the absolute numbers increased, one can see that the percentages have increased only slightly. The percentage of blacks in the professional category in 1930 was 3.9 percent, and by 1970 that percentage was up slightly to 5.4 percent.

The major increases in the number of black workers have come in the category of clerical, sales, and kindred workers. In 1930 males represented 1.3 percent and females .07 among clerks and kindred workers. For 1980 these percentages increased to 6.7 for males and 8.6 for females. Looking at the table shows a steady increase for years presented.

For 1980 the census combined the categories of professional and proprietors, managers and officials. During Myrdal's time, the category was just professional persons; this category shows an increase to 5.9 percent.

Table 6.1

Black workers in business, professional, and white collar occupations: 1940, 1950, 1960, 1970, 1980.

	Professional and Semiprofessional Workers			Proprietors, Managers, and Officials			Clerical, Sales, and Kindred Workers		
	Males	Females	Both	Males	Females	Both	Males	Females	Both
Number of Black Workers									
1940	53,312	65,888	119,200	37,240	10,914	48,154	58,557	20,765	79,322
1950	75,090	104,280	179,370	71,130	25,950	97,080	116,760	80,850	197,610
1960	115,683	178,690	294,373	65,346	25,867	91,213	194,664	197,263	391,927
1970	244,655	388,960	633,615	121,949	48,007	169,956	430,120	825,514	1,255,634
1980[b]	546,271	770,809	1,317,080				712,342	1,639,737	2,352,079
Blacks as a Percentage of All Workers									
1940	2.80%	4.50%	3.60%	1.10%	2.60%	1.30%	1.30%	0.70%	1.10%
1950	2.50	5.30	3.60	1.70	3.80	2.00	4.40	1.80	2.80
1960	0.30	0.80	0.40	1.40	3.30	1.70	6.20	3.00	4.10
1970	3.50	8.30	5.40	2.30	4.40	2.60	6.10	6.50	6.30
1980	4.10	8.60	5.90				6.70	8.60	7.90

Source: U.S. Bureau of the Census, *The Labor Force, Sixteenth Census of the United States: 1940, Population*, Vol. 3, Pt. 1; U.S. Bureau of the Census, *U.S. Census of the Population: 1950*, Vol. 4, *Special Reports*, Pt. 1, Chap. A, "Employment and Personal Characteristics"; U.S. Bureau of the Census, *U.S. Census of the Population: 1960. Subject Reports. Occupational Characteristics*; U.S. Bureau of the Census, *U.S. Census of the Population: 1970. Subject Reports. Occupational Characteristics*; U.S. Bureau of the Census, *U.S. Census of the Population: 1980. Subject Reports. Occupation by Industry*.

[a]Figures for 1940 are of employed persons. Figures for 1950–1980 are of the experienced civilian labor force.

[b]In the 1980 census, the professional and semiprofessional workers were combined with proprietors, managers, and officials to form the category of Managerial and Professional Specialty Occupations. Clerical, sales, and kindred workers are considered to be in technical, sales, and administrative support occupations.

When Myrdal examined categories within different occupations, he found that blacks had slightly better chances in the professions than in other occupations in this group. Thus, in 1930 the number of black professional workers was higher (116,000) than that of clerical workers (83,000). Among whites, there were almost three clerks and kindred workers for every professional. Myrdal noted that blacks had as much as a 4 percent representation among the professional workers because of the segregated southern school system and the segregated church.

Myrdal's data show that teachers and ministers account for about two-thirds of all black professional workers. Black small-business owners occupied an intermediate position between these two groups, numbering 56,000, making up about 1.5 percent of all American businessmen.

MYRDAL'S OVERVIEW AND THEORETICAL CHANGES IN THE STUDY OF ETHNIC AND RACIAL GROUPS SINCE 1944

Before we move to Myrdal's analysis of different categories of what he calls middle class blacks, it is important to consider the concept of "success" and how that success is acquired in American society. Two major frameworks stand center stage in racial mobility today. The first, which has guided much of the research in racial mobility in America, is that of assimilation. This model is still dominant today. The second framework is called middleman theory; it has developed a systematic research literature during the last 10 years. Both frameworks are important and contribute to our understanding of race and ethnic relations.

During the intense segregation of the time period in which Myrdal performed his analysis, the explanation of poverty and inequality in America dominated social science literature. The major question posed has always focused on why certain individuals and groups are more successful than others in attaining economic stability in this country. The "economic ladder" analogy, or the assimilation model, has been offered as the definitive reason that certain ethnic groups, such as Koreans and Jews, have reached great economic heights. Put simply, this argument holds that over the years America initially welcomed ethnic groups who started as laborers on the economic ladder but who, over time, worked themselves out of poverty and into the "middle class." Countless studies have shown how the Irish, the Italians, and the Poles came to America and, through hard work, realized their dream of economic stability. This dominant paradigm, or way of modeling research, represents the classic illustration of how groups and individuals successfully adjust to American society.

During the days of segregation, or the time when the Myrdal Report was completed, the perspective was also theoretically applied to black Americans and projected as a model for black success. Put differently, segregation locked this group in a tight opportunity space and took away the opportunity for blacks to move up the economic ladder. In more recent years, the "climbing the ladder" perspective has been applied to blacks, even to the extent of treating them like an immigrant group. As with European ethnic groups, an emphasis is placed on blacks moving to major industrial centers, where they work hard to generate economic success and gain, thereby, access to "middle class" status. Certainly, some blacks have followed this model and achieved economic success.

Although the "climbing the ladder" perspective of adjustment to America is still dominant in the minds of most Americans, new research on the relationship between self-help and successful economic adjustment to America is adding a wealth of knowledge to our understanding of this process.[5] Indeed, the findings of this research should enhance our understanding of how groups and individuals trade up from poverty and achieve economic and occupational stability. More importantly, the prevalent theory coming out of this self-help research is proving to be a universal one that applies to all groups regardless of ethnicity and race. This research is redefining self-help as the prime factor in adjustment to the American dynamic.

One of the most interesting research findings on ethnic America is that certain groups have achieved more economic stability then others. For example, research has consistently shown that Japanese Americans, as a group, have the highest income in America today. Researchers refer to this as the "miracle success story." But the positioning of the Japanese in America's income distribution pattern is no miracle at all. In reality, it is due to their adjusting their self-help capacities to American society. And other groups who adjusted in the manner of the Japanese have exhibited the same kind of entrepreneurial success. An emphasis on business enterprise and institutional building is universal. These self-help traits are in stark contrast to those of the Irish and Italians, who made their adjustments by joining America's massive labor force. But when unions were broken up or neutralized, many Italian and Irish neighborhoods were thrown into economic turmoil. The independent and self-reliant Japanese, by and large, escaped this fate.

In a major research effort entitled *The Economic Basis of Ethnic Solidarity*, Edna Bonacich and John Modell show how, in the face of discrimination and racist ideology, the Japanese adjusted to America.[6] Arriving between 1899 and 1907, they worked first as farm laborers and domestic servants. But by 1909 there were at least 3,500 Japanese-operated enterprises in the western states. The great majority were service-oriented enterprises—boardinghouses, barbershops, poolrooms, tailor and dye shops, shoe repair shops, and laundries. They also owned many farms. Another study entitled *Latin Journey*, by Alejandro Portes and Robert L. Bach, shows how many Cuban Americans adjusted to America in the same manner by developing small-scale enterprises. The same historical pattern can be seen with Eastern European Jews (although all Jews did not adjust to America in this manner). The Jewish pattern of adjustment can be found in the work of Walter P. Zenner, who, in 1980, wrote "American Jewry in the Light of Middleman Minority Theory" for *Contemporary Jewry*.[7] Studies showing similar adjustment patterns are beginning to appear concerning Haitians and Koreans.[8] These groups developed ethnic enclaves that contained both residential homes and business enterprises. This is unlike most other ethnic groups who, for the most part, developed only residential communities.

The significance of this growing body of research lies in the sociological implications that may be applied to future generations of the groups who adjusted to America through self-help. For example, it has been shown that these groups emphasized the importance of education. When their children entered the labor market, they tended to enter as professionals who were entrepreneurial by nature. While the parents were small shopkeepers in the service sector, their offspring were more likely to be lawyers, doctors, dentists, educators, or business people with advanced degrees.

The children of groups that adjusted to America by self-help are less likely to depend directly on the larger society for their economic stability. They are less likely to be affected by the ups and downs of the American economy. Whereas ethnic groups who adjusted to America by depending on jobs provided by large-scale industry rode the seesaw of the marketplace, so, too, did their offspring who followed them into the factories and mills.

Groups in the self-help tradition are also known for ethnic solidarity. Community organizations are created that teach children to appreciate both their culture and the concept of self-help. This preoccupation with self-help and economic stability often alienates groups and individuals of the larger society. Thus, anti-Semitism is a product of both the refusal of the Jewish group to give up its identity and assimilate in the larger society *and* its attainment of economic stability. This is also true of anti-Japanese sentiments that developed on the West Coast prior to World War II, and it is becoming true of the Vietnamese in America today. The Vietnamese, like other groups that adjusted through self-help, are laying the foundation for future generations with an emphasis on education of their offspring. Thus, in the future, we shall see that second- and third-generation Vietnamese will more likely be professionals in the tradition of the earlier self-help groups.

In my *Entrepreneurship and Self-Help Among African Americans: A Reconsideration of Economics,*[9] I asked the question: Did African Americans (who also at the turn-of-the-century adjusted to America by self-help and business enterprise) produce the same kind of offspring as other ethnic groups who adjusted in the same manner? The mere asking of the question, before I began this research, sent chills up my spine, and as the data burst forth, the answer became a resounding "yes!" Put another way, there is really no difference between the offspring of African Americans today whose parents, grandparents, and great-grandparents adjusted to America by self-help and the offspring of other self-help ethnic groups. This statement holds despite the historical presence of racism and discrimination. The research contained in my book should revamp our entire perspective on race and economic stability in American society. In understanding how this conclusion was reached, one must take a fresh and comparative approach to the subject of race and inequality in America.

Let us begin with the fact that before the Civil War many free blacks made their living as owners of small shops. In the late 1700s, for example, Philadelphia was a community abounding in both small and large African American enterprises. Philadelphia's James Forten, for example, became a millionaire making sails. Also during this time, Baltimore was one of the main centers of commerce for African American enterprises. What is significant about this city is that over 40 percent of these entrepreneurs were ex-slaves who had been purchased out of slavery by loved ones who had saved enough money to free them. In Cincinnati, African Americans owned engineering firms, brick factories, and other small enterprises. African Americans in New York were also very active in business enterprises between the Revolutionary and Civil wars. They owned some of the best restaurants on Wall Street and were known for their expertise in tailoring. Free blacks in southern cities developed service enterprises (such as catering) that were so superior that they monopolized the field. The primary adjustment pattern at this time was through the formation of business enterprises. African Americans were functioning in much the same way as Jews did in Europe. They, too, were a small business–oriented people operating in an atmosphere of racial hostility.

Like other groups that adjusted to America in this way, this entrepreneur-oriented group of African Americans developed a strong sense of the importance of education. They began developing schools and encouraging education for their children as early as the 1830s. When W. E. B. Du Bois was doing turn-of-the-century research for his book, *The Philadelphia Negro,* he noted that there was an "upper-class" group among blacks. No doubt these were descendants of the entrepreneurs who established themselves early in Philadelphia's business enclave.

After the Civil War, when millions of African Americans were "freed" from slavery, the major question of the period was how this new group of citizens would adjust to American society. The celebrated debate between Booker T. Washington and W. E. B. Du Bois over which course to follow is indicative of the conflict during that period. Washington stressed the development of business enterprise as the primary pattern of adjustment to America. Although Washington is identified as the major proponent of this form of adjustment, he was, in fact, adhering to the business traditions already established by free African Americans prior to the Civil War. His Negro Business League, started at the turn of the century, was really a natural extension of pre–Civil War African American organizations that were prevalent in communities geared toward enterprise. Because Washington was "soft" on protesting for civil rights, he has gone down in history as the Uncle Tom of the race. His speech at the Atlanta Exposition came at a time when white southerners, through Jim Crow laws, were reclaiming the South by reintroducing slavery—in all but name. It was in this speech that he struck a deal whereby whites would support the development of African American enterprise if blacks would not protest for civil rights. Because of this deal, Washington's speech has been referred to as the Atlanta Compromise. He compromised civil rights for white support of business enterprise. Among other things, he argued that blacks should concentrate on industrial education (practical) rather than higher education (arts and sciences). While Du Bois also recognized the importance of business enterprise (indeed Washington adopted many of Du Bois's ideas on economic development), he has been portrayed by historians as a guardian of civil rights and Washington's major nemesis.

For our discussion it is not important to debate the ideology of Washington and Du Bois. What is important, however, is that following the Civil War, African Americans did adopt different patterns of adjustment to American society. The first type of adjustment, under the realities of racism and discrimination, concentrated on the development of business enterprises. These enterprises differed from those before the Civil War because Jim Crow now restricted them to black communities. The second type of adjustment consisted of joining the American workforce in the tradition of European ethnic groups. Working in the larger workforce meant competing for a job in the industrial North or working as servants and domestics in both the North and South. Both types of adjustment, in the face of hostility, were successful. Those who succeeded in rising above the poverty level, those who concentrated on self-help, institution-building, and entrepreneurship developed values that were in the tradition of self-help groups, such as the Japanese and the Jews, while those who adjusted to the larger economy drifted up when it was up and down when it was down.

The self-help group of African Americans developed a strong emphasis on education for their children: the offspring of the black entrepreneurial, self-help tradition are more likely to be professionals. This pattern began to develop strongly during the period of the 1920s and continues today. Thus, it is not uncommon for African Americans today who are in the self-help tradition to rise from poverty and become second-, third-, and, indeed, fourth-generation college graduates. The importance of education has been passed from generation to generation among blacks who adjusted to America through self-help. Also, like the Japanese and the Jews, descendants of this groups are less likely to be found in unemployment lines in America.

Another interesting value developed by these self-help groups is an absolute respect for black institutions. After all, it was their foreparents who built, maintained, and cherished these institutions. Evidence shows that they have never considered these institutions inferior in any way. This phenomenon, which is mostly southern, accounts for the fact that many offspring of this self-help black group still proudly attend African American universities and colleges. In my present ongoing work, *Standing On Shoulders*, I examine the families who have been attending these colleges for four generations. It is clear that until the 1960s most professionals, such as doctors and lawyers, were produced from this self-help group of African Americans, and that, for continuing generations, the role models have been family members and other important members of the community.

These people trace their historical rise from poverty to small enterprises developed in the African American community, professional experiences in one-race settings (hospitals, schools, etc.), and to the strong value placed on education. Put simply, the roots of their success in America, through the generations, have been "home-grown." Atlanta, Chicago, and Durham are still vital black business enclaves because of the continued momentum from turn-of-the-century successes in such areas as insurance, banking, and newspaper, magazine, and book publishing.

The vast majority of African Americans who adjusted to America in the larger economy worked hard to develop economic stability. But like European ethnic groups, as a collective group, they did not develop the same kind of attitude toward self-help and education. Like the Irish and Italians in larger American cities, their lot was affected by the twists and turns of the American economy. Because their offspring were repeatedly told that excellent jobs were available after a high school education, they were not as well prepared academically as those African Americans who adjusted by self-help. This is not to say that college education has not become important to this group of blacks. But unlike their self-help counterparts who have a strong tradition of education, those who adjusted to America by entering the larger society began attending colleges in large numbers in the 1960s. What is interesting is that this group owes its educational success more to the dynamics of change in society than to the dynamics of its own community.

One of the major propositions coming out of this exploration of adjustment to American society is that the effects of economic stability can be passed down to future generations when people faced with poverty add a significant dimension of self-help (community building, importance of education, and the like) to their development.

The major point in the discussion that Myrdal was describing in the chapter on middle-class blacks was a variation of a middleman group within black America, which responded to segregation by creating business enterprises and institutions within communities. That this was done under segregation does not belittle the fact that this group of blacks developed the same kind of self-help attitudes as other middleman groups. But because of segregation, they represent a sort of truncated middleman group.[10] When seen in this light, black accomplishments under hostile conditions blend with traditions of middleman groups around the globe. Throughout the sociological literature, scholars have not known where to put black success in a hostile world. As I noted:

> They . . . have been called the black bourgeoisie, black Brahmans, black elite, and the black upper-class. Whatever they are called, their adjustments to America bear a striking resemblance to middleman minorities throughout history. We formally define the Afro-American middleman group as consisting of those individuals who were entrepreneurs and professionals of the old segregated economy. Both of these groups, significantly, were service-oriented. Entrepreneurs, of course, refer to those who started business enterprises, including the owners of small independent farms. Professionals consisted of doctors, teachers, professors, ministers, and lawyers.[11]

Theoretical changes since Myrdal have shed new light on the importance of excluded groups developing self-contained communities for the development of a business community and a professional class. Indeed, immigrant groups such as the Vietnamese and the Koreans create voluntarily segregated enclaves in order to foster a degree of success. As we proceed with our analysis of the revisiting of Myrdal, we will give a strong consideration to these important theoretical changes which stress the importance of middleman groups.

BLACKS IN BUSINESS

Myrdal's analysis of blacks in business gives a strong consideration to those enterprises that the group controlled prior to the turn of the eighteenth century and how they lost control of them. This was a theme that entered the literature some 30 years before Myrdal's work. For example, in a paper read before the American Historical Society in 1913, Henry M. Minton analyzes the early history of black enterprise in Philadelphia with a concentration on those that had been lost. This paper details the business people of this city and notes that their enterprises were located throughout the city and served black as well as white clients.[12] This fact, which is detailed in all accounts of black business prior to the Civil War,[13] puts black business people squarely in the tradition of middleman groups around the world. Because Myrdal missed this point, and because he did not consider the relationship between oppressed groups and business activity, he could not fully explore the patterns of the data that he analyzed.

Myrdal was writing under the theoretical frameworks of his day. During that time the theory of the concentration of capital was in force; these ideals gave a strong consideration to the declining importance of entrepreneurship in the larger society. So, to understand Myrdal's position and theoretical changes since his publication, we need to understand the theory of the concentration of capital. An understanding of this theory, along with the importance of middleman theory over the years, will really allow us to understand black enterprise over the years.

The theory of the concentration of capital states that the greater the development of the capitalist economic system becomes, the less important entrepreneurs become. This basic idea has its roots in Karl Marx's *Capital*.[14] Marx predicted that small enterprises would not be able to compete with large firms because of the latter's ability to accumulate capital. Although he argued that an "entrepreneurial type" would evolve, it would be insignificant in the overall structure of society.

This reasoning can also be seen in the work of Shumpeter,[15] who concentrated on the process of innovation as the moving force in entrepreneurship. Although Schumpeter understood the importance of innovation, he argued that entrepreneurship had to decline because the process of innovation would be taken over by large-scale firms. Put differently, the concentration of capital in large-scale firms means that they are better equipped to engage in the process of innovation. Because of this, overall entrepreneurship was seen as being insignificant for the future.[16]

Likewise, C. Wright Mills argued the decreasing significance of entrepreneurship in his *White Collar*.[17] Mills's work indicates the continuing influence of this theme, since his work was published 20 years after Myrdal's work.

In the section on the "The Negro In Business," Myrdal saw the same kind of trend data regarding black entrepreneurship. He noted: "The proportion of Negroes among all retail dealers was, if anything, smaller in 1930 than in 1910."[18] He also noted the corresponding trend among entrepreneurship in the overall country. Using sales as an indicator of the decline of entepreneurship, he found that between 1929 and 1939 retail trade in the entire United States declined by 13 percent. For black enterprise the decline was 28 percent.

When the context in which he wrote is considered, and because he did not have middleman theory to guide his work, one can see how the conclusions that he reached 50 years ago would be changed today. Certainly, there was a decline in the process of entrepreneurship in America; these trends provided the data for the concentration of capital theory. But what we have learned since Myrdal is that small-scale entrepreneurship is the avenue for upward mobility for many ethnic groups that come to this country. More importantly, when the theory of middleman minorities is applied to Myrdal's analysis, one can see how his interpretations of the data would change. Let us look at some examples, which cross-fertilize Myrdal's work on ethnic and racial enterprise today, so that we can see the power of changing theoretical frameworks.

During his analysis, Myrdal observed,

> The Negro businessman encounters greater difficulties in securing credit. This is partly due to the marginal position of Negro business. It is also partly due to prejudiced opinions among the whites concerning the business ability and personal reliability of Negroes. In either case a vicious circle is in operation keeping Negro business down.[19]

Myrdal was absolutely correct in his analysis. But in recent years the theory of middleman minorities places an emphasis on a group doing well in the face of hostility by developing small-scale enterprises. A great deal of this research concentrates on how groups develop capital by alternative means when the American banking system failed to meet their needs. Thus, Bonacich and Modell outline the rotating credit system that the Japanese utilize to build enterprises in California.[20] This system was also used by blacks in the late 1900s.

Myrdal did mention what we call middleman ethnic groups today. Using a comparative analysis, he notes that these groups have outperformed blacks in the general economy:

> Particularly interesting is the great number of stores and restaurants operated by Chinese and Japanese. In 1929 they owned one-and-a-

half times as many stores, restaurants, and eating places per 1,000 population as other residents of the United States. Negroes, on the other hand, operated but one-sixth of the number of such establishments as would correspond to their proportion in the population.[21]

This analysis does not consider the fact that blacks were operating under an economic detour. While Japanese and Chinese enterprises were able to develop clients throughout the city, blacks were forced to do business within their own community because of segregation laws. One has to go back to the period before the Civil War to find blacks operating as classic middleman groups with their enterprises throughout the city. The point is that Myrdal was examining a black truncated middleman group, with all of the indications of such a group, and not a middle-class group in the traditional sense of the word.

It also should be noted that the success of black enterprises was related to region. Myrdal noted that black neighborhoods were dominated by the ethnic groups. He wrote:

> Negro areas . . . have a great number of stores and restaurants catering exclusively, or almost exclusively, to Negroes but operated by Jews, Greeks, Italians, and other whites. Sometimes this may be a matter of tradition, since it was only a few decades ago that many of the principal Negro neighborhoods in the North had entirely or predominantly white residents.[22]

Research has shown that even when northern cities did have black business districts, the business people rented from ethnic groups that had vacated the district.[23] In the South, blacks owned the land on which their enterprises were built, and created business communities that were celebrated in the literature. For example, in 1911 Booker T. Washington wrote an article celebrating the business activity of black Durham, North Carolina.[24]

In his book, Myrdal presents his data on the number of black entrepreneurs and white-collar workers in selected trade and service industries for the years 1910 and 1930. The two largest categories are within the wholesale and retail industries. The first is retail dealers (except automobiles). The second largest category includes clerks, salespersons, and other white-collar workers, 27,743. The third largest category includes hotel, boarding-houses, lodging, housekeepers, and managers.

Myrdal's categories reflect the reality of segregation. They are also related to the enterprises of middleman groups throughout the world: the two largest categories are traditional middleman trades. This supports the

Table 6.2

Number of black and white entrepreneurs and white collar workers in selected trade and service industries: 1980.

Industry and Occupation	White	Black
Banking		
Managerial and professional	619,538	187,938
Self-employed	977	8
Technical, sales, and administrative support	1,253,429	140,524
Self-employed	21	0
Insurance		
Managerial and professional	303,139	15,796
Self-employed	4,436	112
Technical, sales, and administrative support	1,365,483	123,696
Self-employed	451	5
Other Finance and Real Estate		
Managerial and professional	339,588	19,403
Self-employed	11,143	205
Technical, sales, and administrative support	1,043,046	40,930
Self-employed	4,924	48
Wholesale Trade		
Managerial and professional	704,820	15,137
Self-employed	23,864	396
Technical, sales, and administrative support	1,856,299	76,716
Self-employed	38,406	830
Retail Trade		
Managerial and professional	1,801,070	76,922
Self-employed	187,399	6,996
Technical, sales, and administrative support	6,670,705	425,206
Self-employed	356,871	11,572
Hospitality (hotels)		
Managerial and professional	147,303	6,256
Self-employed	27,937	364
Technical, sales, and administrative support	144,695	12,131
Self-employed	335	7

Source: U.S. Bureau of the Census, *U.S. Census of the Population: 1980. Subject Reports. Occupation by Industry.*

idea that within the black population, there were blacks who acted like middleman groups. But because of segregation, as noted above, they were a truncated sort of middleman.

This idea is really supported in Table 6.2. Looking at self-employment for 1980, the largest category is retail trade and the second largest category is wholesale trade. This implies a continuity between the findings of Myrdal and more recent data. But the continuity holds only for the middleman-like categories.

Another important point is that in 1980 the number of blacks in hotels, boardinghouses, and lodging was significantly lower than the 1930 figures. This reflects not only the decline of segregation, but also the decline of mom-and-pop-owned boarding establishments in America. While the numbers of black workers in these occupations are similar for 1930 and 1980, the fact that the numbers have remained the same must take into consideration the population growth of the black community.

Table 6.3 presents data for self-employment for agricultural and non-agricultural industries for blacks and whites. These tables were not present in Myrdal's analysis but provide an excellent measurement of self-employment. Starting with 1974, the numbers of black self-employment in nonagricultural industries showed a steady increase to 1992. This was also true for the white self-employed in this category. For the agricultural industry, both black and white self-employment have decreased from 1974 to 1992. Within this decrease, however, black self-employment in the agricultural industry increased between 1984 and 1992. For whites, there were no increases in self-employment during that period. These data illustrate the fact that agriculture is not as important for the determinants of self-employment today as it was 20 years ago. This is true for both the black and white population.

Table 6.3

Number of black and white self-employed, agricultural, and nonagricultural industries: 1974, 1980, 1984, 1992.

Year	Agricultural Industries		Nonagricultural Industries	
	White	Black	White	Black
1974	1,674,000	61,000	5,340,000	259,000
1980	1,578,000	36,000	6,538,000	306,000
1984	1,491,000	29,000	7,245,000	336,000
1992	1,337,000	39,000	7,878,000	415,000

Source: Bureau of Labor Statistics, *Current Population Survey* as published in the *Handbook of Labor Statistics and Annual Updates.*

Black enterprises today are no longer confined to one section of town. The civil rights movement has made it possible for enterprises to be located all over the city. Historically, black enterprises, in the tradition of middleman groups, were more likely to be in the category of service enterprises. But recent trends show a growing diversity among black enterprises.

The locations of the corporate headquarters of the nation's largest black-owned corporations, are in urban areas. These have become areas in which administrative and service duties are the dominant form of economic activity. The growth in corporate administration in central-city business districts has created a need for complementary advertising, computer, accounting, legal, temporary secretarial, and maintenance business services. Employment in these kinds of black firms grew by 224 percent between 1972 and 1987; the number of firms increased nearly five times, and gross receipts grew by 700 percent.[25]

Perhaps the most significant change since the Myrdal report was the legislation spurred by the civil rights movement which was designed to ensure the development of black enterprise. In 1967 the government created the Small Business Administration Section 8(a) program. Under this act, the Small Business Administration is authorized to contract with federal agencies on behalf of small and disadvantaged enterprises. Contracts processed through Section 8(a) increased from $8.9 million in 1969 to $2.7 billion in 1985. As a result of this program, many small and minority-owned enterprises have developed.[26]

The civil rights movement also was instrumental in producing the 1977 Public Works Employment Act, which supplements the SBA 8(a) program, and requires that all general contractors bidding for public works projects allocate at least 10 percent of their contracts to minority subcontractors. These kinds of programs, which had not been in place during the Myrdal years, had a strong positive effect on the ability of blacks to operate enterprises successfully.

But like all things political, the set-aside programs have run into difficulties over the years. Unlike early black enterprises that were independent of governmental programs, black enterprises dependent on the political system for survival are at the mercy of political climates. Thus, during the 1980s the fundamental consent of set-aside assistant programs was called into question. In 1989 the Supreme Court ruled, in *City of Richmond* v. *Croson* that the city of Richmond, Virginia, did not have to set aside 30 percent of each public construction contract for minority enterprises.

This decision had a strong negative effect on minority enterprises in that city. For example, in Richmond during the month of July 1987 when a lower court first ruled against set-aside programs, 40 percent of the city's total construction dollars went for products and services provided by minority-owned construction firms. After the Supreme Court decision, the minority businesses' share of contracts fell to 15 percent, dropping to less than 3 percent by the end of 1988. In Tampa, Florida, the number of contracts given to black-owned enterprises decreased 99 percent for the same time period.[27]

Such dramatic changes in opportunities mean that black business people still face many obstacles. Although many black enterprises are "back on main street," the geographic concentration of firms is highly correlated with large concentrations of the population. California had the highest number of black enterprises (1987) with gross receipts of $2.4 billion. New York was second, with 36,289 firms and gross receipts of $1.9 billion. About 44 percent of gross receipts (185,563 firms and $8.8 billion in gross receipts) were located in California, New York, Texas, Florida, Georgia, and Illinois.[28]

The next significant states in which black enterprises operate include Michigan (13,708 firms with gross receipts of $701.3 million), Maryland (21,678 enterprises and nearly $720 million in receipts), and Pennsylvania (11,728 enterprises with gross receipts of $747.5 million).[29]

Washington, D.C., had the largest share of enterprises owned by blacks—28.3 percent of the firms and 6.3 percent of the gross receipts. Black enterprises had the smallest share of business in the state of Montana, with 0.1 percent of the firms and gross receipts.[30]

When Myrdal published *An American Dilemma*, he used 1939 data and noted that there were 30,000 black enterprises, with total sales of a little more than $71,000,000, which was less than .2 percent of the national total. Although the absolute number of black enterprises has increased significantly, with total gross receipts over $71,000,000, when compared to the business enterprises in general, the total number of gross receipts is very small. Indeed, minority enterprise taken all together represents about 5.7 percent of the total enterprises in America, with gross receipts of about 3 percent of the total gross receipts in the country.

At one time the comparison of ethnic and racial enterprises receipts to those of the larger society was a way to measure the viability of these types of enterprises. But recent research on ethnic enterprises acknowledges the importance of small enterprises in terms of the impact that they have on the education of children and the values that are created. Put another way, the enterprises are seen as important in their own economic light; they are the organizations that keep a group from falling to the bottom of the economic ladder.

This, of course, is one of the central themes of work on middleman minorities and the theory of ethnic enclaves.[31] Put in another way, ethnic enterprises are seen as an unimportant blimp on the economic scene, but as a way that excluded racial and ethnic groups have created opportunities for themselves in hostile situations. Indeed, it is the most recently arrived ethnic groups that remind us of the importance of small enterprises. As the world erupts around them, the United States becomes their economic playing field. Consider the following quotation, which relates to the Cuban experience in South Florida:

> But this is nothing new. The Cubans are just another in the long line of immigrant swarms on the ever-changing American frontier, and their upsurge differs only in speed and number from any other in the continuing saga of American revival. Vietnamese, Central Americans, Lebanese, and even the much abused Haitians are making similar breakthroughs. . . . It has always been immigrants who have revitalized America's faith.[32]

As a result of the importance of business activity within the overall study of racial and ethnic groups, there is more of an appreciation for small enterprises within the black community, regardless of the comparative analysis which concentrates on receipts. As I have noted above, sons and daughters of the early black entrepreneurs made a great contribution to the establishment of a professional class in early America.

Although most of the literature on black Americans downplays the importance of the role of business enterprise in communities,[33] there are indications of change. Scholars are starting to concentrate on the rebuilding of many black communities with a concentration on enterprise.[34] The idea that the black experience is a variation of a middleman group is also becoming established.

Over the last 15 years *Black Enterprise* has published a list of the top one hundred African American businesses. It also discusses business failures and examples of how business successes are achieved. From a historical perspective, the magazine is a recreation of the positive aspects of enterprise that were so prevalent in the writings of the "Tuskegee Machine,"[35] which Booker T. Washington headed. Indeed, it was the Booker T. Washington "Machine" that encouraged many of the enterprises that existed when Myrdal was writing.

Although one can find a list of the top 100 black enterprises over the last 15 years in the magazine, let us look at 1987 for one business category—the top one hundred industrial/service companies. The first thing to note is that the enterprises are very young: 47 percent were founded in the 1970s; 21 percent in the 1980s; 16 percent in the 1960s; 5 percent in the 1950s; and 2 percent in the 1940s. The oldest three companies in the top ten—Johnson Publishing (1942), Motown Industries (1958), and Soft Sheen Products

(1964) traditionally developed products unique to the African American community. Thus, these companies survived legal segregation and the economic detour prior to the 1970s. Another company appearing on this list (#41), founded in the 1940s, also caters specifically to the African American community (hair-care products). The only company on the list that was developed in the early years and not connected to the African American community is Grimes Oil Company, founded in 1940 and a petroleum products distributor. Put more to the point, the economic survivors that were on the *Black Enterprise* list, which were founded prior to the regeneration of African American enterprise, were originally connected to the racial market—a unique economic niche. This was also the niche that Myrdal described since he was discussing black enterprises selling only to blacks.

Perhaps the greatest change since Myrdal vis-à-vis black enterprise is the fact that there are enterprises that serve the entire business community. In addition, there is a greater emphasis on the importance of business education: "The next generation of . . . CEOs are bright, ambitious, well-educated and well-trained. Their challenge: to transform the family business into a diversified professionally managed enterprise."[36]

In a major effort, Thomas Boston has examined the base of what he calls the new bourgeoisie, or the new business class. His research confirms the changing landscape of black enterprises. Concentrating on the city of Atlanta, he looked at the changing nature of enterprises for that city. He found that

> traditional black-owned enterprises, especially those in retail and personal service industries, are rapidly declining. They are being replaced by a new generation of . . . businesses that emerged during the early 1980's. These new enterprises differ by the ethnic diversity of their clientele, the skill and experience of their owners, their location, industry concentration, and financial performance.[37]

The significance of Boston's work is that he shows that the major data source used to analyze black enterprises, the *Survey of Minority-Owned Business Enterprises*, has major flaws which lead to misinterpretations of the performance of black firms, including the number of people employed. The reason for this is that it surveys only small enterprises. Consider the following from Boston's analysis:

> . . . the really surprising revelation is that 325 firms generated 3,250 jobs. Yet the [*Survey of Minority-Owned Business Enterprises*] indicates that total employment in all 11,804 firms in the Atlanta Metropolitan

area is only 6,828. This means that either the 325 firms in our data set account for one-half of all jobs generated by black-owned firms, or that the *Survey of Minority-Owned Business Enterprises* is seriously undercounting the employment capacity of black businesses.[38]

Boston also found significant differences between the *Survey of Minority-Owned Business Enterprises* and the data that he collected. For example, the *Survey of Minority-Owned Business Enterprises* collected by the government found that 46.1 percent of black self-employed people attended college, 26.4 percent graduated, and 13.1 percent went to graduate school. Boston found, in his data, that 74 percent attended college, 55 percent graduated, and 21 percent received a graduate degree.[39] Boston's work shows the need for the development of excellent data sets that will allow the analysis of black business development and performance.

As one enters the twenty-first century, the data are indicating that blacks with college education are making a significant contribution to the establishment of enterprises. But if the black inner-city population is to change, the development of business enterprises is the best way to change some American cities; to make them safe and a place for business enterprise. It is also apparent that years of government programs, which have produced spending in the billions of dollars, have made certain segments of the black population dependent and have taken away some of the incentives for enterprise. Thus today, unlike during Myrdal's time, blacks in poverty are less likely to depend upon the development of business enterprise in order to elevate themselves economically. One must remember that the black population that produced the entrepreneurial spirit between the 1900s and the late 1960s had less education and experience than the present segment of the black population that constitutes the so-called underclass today.

In addition to the methodological problem discussed by Boston, the study of black business today also has theoretical problems. Today's literature on minority business is concerned with the process by which ethnic groups develop, maintain, and expand business enterprises within the economic structure. There is a tendency to compare the development of enterprises without considering the time of entry of the ethnic group. As a result, the results are presented without a strong theoretical background to explain the differences.

This can be seen, for example, in the work of Bates. In an article entitled "The Changing Nature of Minority Business: A Comparative Analysis of Asian, Nonminority, and Black-Owned Businesses," he found that self-employed Asian males outperformed nonminorities and blacks. He explained the results by concentrating on classic economic variables such as weak internal markets which strip communities of entrepreneurial talent.[40]

The idea of looking at the relationship between the demand of markets and the creation of entrepreneurship has not explained the development of entrepreneurial activity in America. Research has shown that demand side theories of entrepreneurship has not been able to explain the proliferation of ethnic or racial enterprises in America. Instead, supply-side theories of entrepreneurship have done a much better job in explaining the development of self-employment in America.[41]

Unlike demand-side theories of entrepreneurship, which concentrate on the classic relationship between demand and supply, supply-side theories concentrate on immigration and the business people that it brings. In a major research effort by Light and Sanchez, a sophisticated analysis revealed the importance of supply-side theories of entrepreneurship.[42]

Light and Sanchez begin with the fact that in every decennial census between 1880 and 1980, the foreign-born systematically exhibit higher rates of self-employment. They further note that foreign members of all racial groups, including people of African descent, are more likely to be self-employed than those born in America. As a result, the longer one lives in America and develops other kinds of opportunities, the less likely one is to be self-employed. As ethnic groups enter the country, they are more likely to be engaged in self-employment if they are entrepreneurial groups; they choose this because they are denied opportunities in the larger employment sector. Instead of choosing bad jobs in that sector, they turn to small-scale self-employment. Alex Portes and Edna Bonacich have demonstrated this fact.

It has also been demonstrated that certain groups within white America, groups that have a history of exclusion, are more likely to be self-employed today. For example, when Jewish Americans are partitioned from the "white" category during data analysis, the incidents of self-employment for white Americans drops considerably. This is why it is important to understand the relationship between the history of hostility toward a group and the nature of entrepreneurship. This methodological problem must be considered when comparing the relationship between ethnicity and the ownership of business enterprise.[42]

At the time of Myrdal's work, the black population developed small enterprises that made significant contributions to their communities. They were instrumental in providing the money to provide for the bricks that built community institutions. In addition to providing money for religious institutions, business enterprises supported more than 200 private educational institutions in the South, ranging from elementary schools to colleges and universities. Today, the black population is showing more of an interest in the importance of business enterprise. It should be remembered that the values that built major institutions under segregation are the same kind of values that have to be developed if one is to solve many problems of blacks in the central city.

PRINCIPAL GROUPS OF BLACK PROFESSIONAL WORKERS

Myrdal's analysis of black professionals was done within the context of segregation, and it shows the following patterns: the largest category was clergyman (16.8 percent of all workers), the next largest was musicians and teachers of music (6.4 percent). The smallest was lawyers (0.8 percent); the second smallest was trained nurses (1.9 percent).

Table 6.4 shows today's figures. Note that the percentage of clergymen has decreased significantly since Myrdal's analysis, from 16.8 percent to 6.2 percent in 1970. On the other hand, trained nurses have increased from 1.9 percent in 1930 to 7.5 percent in 1980.

The percentage of physicians remained constant from 1930 to 1970.

Perhaps the greatest change since Myrdal's work is the participation of blacks in the military. Indeed, opportunities were so restricted within the civilian sector that those blacks who did experience the military saw it as providing more opportunities for advancement than the civilian sector. In 1966, in *Black and White: A Study of U.S. Racial Attitudes Today*, William Brink and Louis Harris were so struck by race relations in the military, as compared to civilian life, that they dedicated a chapter on blacks entitled "A Home in the Service."[44]

A home in the service must be seen in light of the military as an overall opportunity structure. Although the primary function of the military is defense of the country, scholars of this organization recognize that a byproduct of preparing soldiers for participation in war is skills that can be taken back to civilian life. This is all part of the bridging environment although in its broadest form it affects all people who participate in the organization.[45] Indeed, in a seminal essay, Morris Janowitz notes that since its revolutionary origins, military forces have offered second chances to youth from lower-class backgrounds, opportunities for education and personal development for youth who did not have access to schools and for those who had access to those schools but failed. Janowitz notes that these second chances have been especially evident since the development of the large military establishment after World War II.[46]

The effects of the bridging environment have been seen in other data since the publication of the bridging environment thesis by Poston and his

Table 6.4

Number of black workers (black workers as a percentage of all workers).

Occupation	1940[a]	1950	1960	1970	1980
Teachers	66,104 (6.3%)	85,920 (7.6%)	133,852 (8.0%)	227,788 (8.2%)	354,176 (9.7%)
Clergymen	17,487 (12.9%)	18,870 (11.4%)	13,915 (6.9%)	13,739 (6.2%)	
Musicians and Teachers of Music	9,157 (6.2%)	9,540 (5.9%)	9,408 (4.8%)	6,605[b] (6.8%)	
Nurses	7,192 (1.9%)	15,390 (3.2%)	35,240 (5.4%)	66,400 (7.8%)	94,845 (7.5%)
Actors, Entertainers, Dancers, and Athletes	2,467 (4.6%)	3,090 (5.1%)	2,098 (4.2%)	3,732[c] (5.0%)	55,642[f] (4.3%)
Physicians, Surgeons, Dentists, and Veterinarians	5,228 (2.1%)	5,460 (2.1%)	7,643 (2.3%)	8,547[d] (2.2%)	
College Presidents and Professors	2,365 (3.1%)	3,900 (3.1%)	5,910 (3.3%)	16,582[e] (3.3%)	
Lawyers and Judges	1,063 (0.6%)	1,500 (0.9%)	2,440 (1.2%)	3,703 (1.3%)	14,839 (2.8%)

Sources: U.S. Bureau of the Census, *The Labor Force, Sixteenth Census of the United States: 1940, Population*, Vol. 3, Pt. 1; U.S. Bureau of the Census, *U.S. Census of the Population: 1950*, Vol. 4, *Special Reports*, Pt. 1, Chap. A, "Employment and Personal Characteristics"; U.S. Bureau of the Census, *U.S. Census of the Population: 1960. Subject Reports. Occupational Characteristics*; U.S. Bureau of the Census, *U.S. Census of the Population: 1970. Subject Reports. Occupational Characteristics*; U.S. Bureau of the Census, *U.S. Census of the Population: 1980. Subject Reports. Occupation by Industry.*

[a]For 1940, workers include employed persons and experienced workers seeking work. Figures for 1950–1980 are of the experienced civilian labor force.

[b]Musicians and composers.

[c]Actors, dancers, and athletes only.

[d]Dentists, veterinarians, and physicians (medical and osteopathic).

[e]College presidents not included.

[f]Writers, artists, entertainers, and athletes.

collegues and the work of Janowitz. More recent research has shown that veterans earn significantly more, albeit with some exceptions, than their nonveteran counterparts in civilian life.[47] Black veterans continue to earn more than black nonveterans.[48] Given these findings, it is not surprising that the military has been called a home in the service for blacks. It has also increased the earning power of those who have served.

When students of the military looked to explain the conclusions about the military that were established by survey data about blacks perceiving more opportunities in the service, they turned to the unique organizational structure of the military and the opportunities present. The long history of racial segregation was completely turned around when the movement toward racial egalitarianism began. Although issues of racial inequality have always been a part of the military, the issue of segregation rapidly became a nonissue. The rapid transformation in race relations and the opportunities provided to blacks can be explained by the military's rigid hierarchical structure and its historic separation from the larger society.

Being a hierarchical structure, the military is a highly crystallized organization: the distribution of authority comes from a central place and is carried out through a chain of command.[49] The higher one increases in rank, the more power and privileges the individual receives. Especially unique to military organizations is the office of the president, who is not only the chief executive of the country but is also commander-in-chief of the military. Any executive presidential order flows directly to the military without voting or debate. Therefore, once the president gave the order for desegregation, things moved rapidly.

During the period when the military was viewed as providing a "home" for blacks, the service was under conscription. This meant that the concept of civic duty was ingrained in military institutions at the same time that desegregation took place. During the Korean conflict, a cross-section of American youth were brought into the military. Thus, the rapid changes in race relations were the result of different kinds of people coming together, many because they were drafted.

The opportunities that were provided by the military took place when there was almost a complete separation of workplace and residence; the military in essence represented a separate entity. Once the pattern of racial desegregation started, the discontinuous nature of military life enhanced the rapid transformation of race relations. The combination of workplace and residence meant that blacks and whites were forced to live with one another. This racial contact also resulted in more positive racial attitudes between the two groups.[50] When blacks and whites were compared by age, rank, and time in service, the positive attitudes due to racial contact remained intact, even during the difficult racial period of the 1970s.[51]

Since days of the colonies, many blacks have participated in the military. It has provided a sense of economic stability for many black families over the years, just as business enterprise has provided a degree of economic success for middleman groups and the black truncated middleman. More importantly, research leads us to believe that families that make the military a career have a history of producing college graduates within black America.[52]

TEACHERS

Myrdal's analysis of black teachers revealed that the segregated market protected their jobs. But the integration of public schools in the South, as a result of *Brown* v. *Board of Education*, changed the entire teaching profession in the South. Black educators throughout the South paid the highest price for the decision to "integrate." They were systematically replaced in the public school systems throughout the South despite their qualifications.

In 1965 a series of meetings was held by the National Educational Association, which was astounded over reports of the fate of black educators in the South.[53] These meetings were held to establish immediate and long-range plans to halt the massive educational displacement of black teachers. During the meetings it was learned that

Between 1967–68 and 1970–71 school years, more than 6,000 black educators had been displaced. . . . During the current school year ('71–'72), of the more than 1,800 educators who were displaced, 909 were dismissed and the remainder were either demoted, assigned out of their field, or unsatisfactorily placed. The report also noted that many desegregating school districts had initiated the practice of hiring only token numbers of black educators, while the numbers of white educators being employed increased.[54]

Throughout the South, blacks were trying to regroup from the loss of black educators. The Alabama League for the Advancement of Education, concentrating on principals, noted:

When large scale desegregation began, the number of black principals dropped from 620 to 362. The number of white principals dropped also, but overall, the percentage of black principals fell from 35 in 1966 to 25 in 1970. Also, while the hiring of new white principals has remained fairly constant, the hiring of new black principals has dropped to almost none. If the trend continues, within two years there will be no black principals.[55]

The most extensive survey of the eleven southern states about the status of black educators at that time was by the Race Relations Research Center. In 1967 North Carolina had 620 black principals; in 1971, it had 40. Mississippi had lost 250 black principals by 1971. The survey showed that black principals had been given minor administrative jobs which could be called token promotions. By the middle of the 1970s, black teachers across the South became a vanishing breed.

But overall, the number of black teachers has steadily increased from 5.2 percent of all teachers in 1930 to 9.7 percent of all teachers in 1980. Musicians have remained relatively constant since Myrdal's time. Actors, dancers, entertainers, and athletes have also remained constant. These categories of college presidents and professors have remained constant.

CONCLUSION

Myrdal's discussion of blacks in business and the professions was done at a time when segregation was in full force. Although he provided excellent data for business and professional categories, he was limited in his interpretation because he did not seek to understand the data from a perspective that stresses the relationship between oppression and business enterprise.

This theoretical perspective, which was established in a systematic way by Max Weber at the turn of the century and is now called middleman theory, holds that a segment of an oppressed community turns to entrepreneurship and institutional building because of discrimination. It is this population that produces the college-educated population and a professional class. This was especially true of a segment of black America, which because of segregation, can be called a sort of truncated middleman.

When viewed from this perspective, it is not surprising that the numbers of black professionals have not changed significantly over the years. Black professionals, overall, have always been produced by families with strong emphases on education. During the days of segregation, the production of these kinds of people was done by the old truncated middleman (not middle-class). They were entrepreneurs and professionals in the old segregated economy. Consider the following quotation:

> Fathers who were entrepreneurs produced 56 percent of the next generation's professionals and businessmen who were listed in *Who's Who in Colored America*. More importantly, this entrepreneurial sector produced slightly more than half of the college graduates from this community. Those parents who worked in skilled occupations produced the next highest number of college graduates, with 20 percent.

This is followed by the common labor category, which produced 13 percent of the college graduates in the community.[56]

Although changes in the civil rights laws and other federal programs have been designed to increase the number of black professionals, continuing research reveals that the descendants of the old truncated black middleman are still maintaining the tradition of producing black professionals. Even as early as 1937, it was found that blacks who were attending college were in the second generation of college matriculation.[57]

The point is that the values that made blacks successful as professionals in the early days are the same ones that will make them successful today; it does not matter if there is integration or segregation, strong values on the importance of education are more likely to produce a professional class. The only difference is that the opportunity structure today is much broader.

Research in the future should consider the importance of examining the black professional and business class in the tradition of middleman minorities. When this is done, data patterns can be understood from a historical point of view. More importantly, such an approach will show how black families have made sacrifices for their children and have ensured their children's success in an atmosphere that at times can be hostile.

NOTES

I would like to thank Michele Chesser of the University of Texas at Austin for comments and work performed during the preparation of this chapter.

1. Gunnar Myrdal. *An American Dilemma: The Negro Problem and Modern Democracy* (New York: Harper & Brothers, 1944), Chap. 14, p. 304.
2. Ibid.
3. Ibid., p. 305
4. In Myrdal's analysis, wholesale and retail dealers were a separate category. For the census between 1940 and the present, this category was combined with the professional and semiprofessional workers.
5. For a discussion, see John Sibley Butler. "Self-Help and Adjustment to American Society." *Agenda: The Alternative Magazine of Critical Issues.* Neighborhood Policy Institute/The National Center for Neighborhood Enterprise. Washington, D.C. Fall, 1990.
6. Edna Bonacich and John Modell. *The Economic Basis of Ethnic Solidarity: Small Business in the Japanese Community* (Berkeley: University of California Press, 1980).
7. Walter P. Zenner. "American Jewry in the Light of Middleman Minority Theory." *Contemporary Jewry.* 1980.

8. See especially Illsoo Kim. "The Koreans: Small Business in an Urban Frontier." In Nancy Foner, ed. *New Immigrants in New York* (New York: Columbia University Press, 1987).

9. John Sibley Butler. *Entrepreneurship and Self-Help Among Black Americans: A Reconsideration of Economics* (New York: State University of New York Press, 1991).

10. The concept of the truncated middleman captures the fact that before the Civil War, black enterprises were in major business districts of American cities. Thus, their clientele represented people of all races. After the Civil War, they were cut off, or truncated, from the main business districts of America and forced to do business exclusively within their own group.

11. Butler, p. 236.

12. Henry M. Minton, M.D. *Early History of Negroes in Business in Philadelphia*. Read before the American Historical Society, March 1913.

13. See for example, Juliet E. K. Walker. "Racism, Slavery, and Free Enterprise: Black Entrepreneurship in the United States Before the Civil War." *Business History Review* 60 (Autumn 1986): 33.

14. Karl Marx. *Capital*. Vols. 1–3. (New York: International Publishers, 1967).

15. J.A. Shumpeter. *Capitalism, Socialism, and Democracy* (New York: Harper & Brothers, 1942).

16. For an excellent discussion of these issues, see Patricia Gene Green. *A Theoretical and Empirical Study of Self-Employed Women*. Diss. The University of Texas, Department of Sociology, Austin, 1993.

17. C. Wright Mills. *White Collar* (New York: Oxford University Press, 1951).

18. Myrdal. *An American Dilemma*, p. 307.

19. Ibid., p. 308.

20. Bonacich and Modell. *The Economic Basis of Ethnic Solidarity*.

21. Myrdal. *An American Dilemma*, p. 310.

22. Ibid., p. 308.

23. Butler.

24. Booker T. Washington. "Durham, North Carolina: A City of Negro Enterprises." *Independent* 70 (30 March 1911): 642–651.

25. Kenneth Estell, ed. *The African-American Almanac* (Detroit: Gale Research, 1994), p. 674.

26. Ibid., pp. 672–673.

27. Ibid.

28. Ibid., p. 675.

29. Ibid., p. 676.

30. Ibid.

31. See Alejandro Portes and Robert Bach. *Latin Journey*. (Berkeley: University of California Press, 1985).

32. George Gilder. *The Spirit of Enterprise*. (New York: Simon & Schuster, 1984).

33. See especially Bart Landry. *The New Black Middle Class* (Berkeley: University of California Press, 1987).

34. See Robert Woodson, ed. *On the Road to Economic Freedom* (Washington, D.C.: Regnery Gateway, 1987).
35. See, for example, Booker T. Washington. *The Negro in Business* (Chicago: Hertel, Jenkins & Co., 1907).
36. *Black Enterprise,* June 1992, p. 305.
37. Thomas D. Boston. "Black Entrepreneurship and Economic Development: A Case Study of Atlanta." Paper presented at the meetings of the Association for the Study of Afro-American Life and History. November 1994.
38. Ibid., p. 22.
39. Ibid., p. 24.
40. Timothy Bates. "The Changing Nature of Minority Business: A Comparative Analysis of Asian, Nonminority and Black-Owned Businesses." *The Review of Black Political Economy* (Fall 1989): 24–41.
41. Ivan Light and Angel A. Sanchez. "Immigrant Entrepreneurs in 272 SMSAs." *Sociological Perspectives* 30(4) (October 1987): 373–399.
42. Ibid.
43. For a discussion of these methodological problems see Butler. *Entrepreneurship and Self-Help Among Black Americans.*
44. William Brink and Louis Harris. *Black and White: A Study of U.S. Racial Attitudes Today* (New York: Simon & Schuster, 1966).
45. For an analysis of the military as an opportunity structure, see John Sibley Butler and Margaret A. Johnson. "An Overview of the Relationship Between Demographic Characteristics of Americans and Their Attitudes Towards Military Issues." *Journal of Political and Military Sociology* 19 (Winter 1991): 273–291.
46. Morris Janowitz. "Basic Education and Youth Socialization in the Armed Forces." In Roger W. Little, ed. *Handbook of Military Institutions* (Beverly Hills, Cal.: Sage Publications, 1971), pp. 167–210.
47. Dudley L. Poston, Mady Wechsler Segal, and John Sibley Butler. "The Influence of Military Service on the Civilian Earning Patterns of Female Veterans: Evidence from the 1980 Census." In Nancy H. Loring, ed. *Women in the United States Armed Forces* (Chicago: Inter-university Seminar on Armed Forces and Society, 1984), pp. 52–71.
48. Ibid.
49. This analysis followed the discussion by John Sibley Butler. "Race Relations in the Military." In Charles C. Moskos and Frank R. Wood. *The Military: More Than Just a Job?* (Washington, D.C.: Pergamon-Brassey's, 1988), pp. 115–127.
50. Ibid.
51. John Sibley Butler and Kenneth L. Wilson. "The American Soldier Revisited: Race Relations and the Military." *Social Science Quarterly* 59 (3) (December 1978).
52. This thesis is systematically developed in a forthcoming book by Charles C. Moskos and John Sibley Butler entitled *Overcoming Race: Army Lessons for American Society.*

53. This analysis follows John Sibley Butler. "Black Educators in Louisiana—A Question of Survival." *Journal of Negro Education* (Winter 1994): 9–24.
54. Southern Educational Reporting Service. *Southern School News* (April 1965), p. 2.
55. Ibid.
56. Butler. *Entrepreneurship and Self-Help Among Black Americans,* p. 239.
57. Charles S. Johnson. *The Negro College Graduate* (Chapel Hill: The University of North Carolina Press, 1938).

Walter R. Allen · Joseph O. Jewell

7

The Miseducation of Black America: Black Education Since *An American Dilemma*

PUBLISHED IN 1944, amid the massive destruction and racial genocide of World War II, Gunnar Myrdal's *An American Dilemma* stood not only as a challenge to America's democratic principles but also as a firm testament to their promise, conceiving of the American race problem as a moral dilemma in the very heart of the nation's democratic ethos. For him an important part of this dilemma, perhaps the key to its solution, lay in the American system of education: education represented a vehicle for combating racist beliefs as well as for improving black people's material conditions. Myrdal viewed increased educational opportunity for blacks as an important step toward the solution of the American race problem. In the 50 years since the publication of this work, many of the issues it raised remain unresolved, leaving Myrdal's study to persist as a challenge to American democracy, particularly in regards to education. This chapter revisits Myrdal's chapter on black education to examine these issues through a study of trends, themes, and indicators of the progress, problems, and prospects of black education since the publication of *An American Dilemma*. Our hope is to point toward solutions as we elucidate the dynamics of African American opportunity and achievements in education.

From its inception, the black quest for educational opportunity in America has been beset with obstacles—outright opposition through racism, well-meaning white paternalism, as well as internal ideological debates over the goals and purposes of education. Fifty years ago, *An American Dilemma* provided the impetus for change in black education, and since that time numerous events have changed the face of black education. However, despite these events fundamental ideological issues have yet to be resolved. In order to understand the impact of *An American Dilemma* on black education, it is necessary to place this discussion in its proper historical context.

169

SEPARATE AND UNEQUAL: BLACK EDUCATION
AS AN AMERICAN DILEMMA

In 1944 black schools were faced with paternalistic cooperation on one hand and savage inequality on the other. In both the North and the South, the education of blacks was largely controlled by outsiders (i.e., whites), but executed by blacks themselves. From the beginning, the accountability of black schools to the community or population they served was a hotly contested issue.

A considerable portion of Myrdal's chapter on education, "The Negro School," is spent documenting the existing conditions of black education in the South. This was reasonable since in 1944, not only did the larger proportion of blacks reside in the South, but the South's dual school system presented perhaps the greatest challenge to the democratic ethos of American society. Myrdal accurately depicts the state of black education in the South, controlled by southern whites who wished to preserve the racial caste status and northern whites who continued to bear much of the financial responsibility for black education, particularly at the postsecondary level:

> [T]he South now has complete control of Negro education on the elementary and secondary levels. Negroes hold some of the control over their own schools, partly because they help to pay for them by voluntary contributions, but mainly because they are the only teachers now in Southern Negro schools. . . . But ultimate control is held by the White superintendents and school boards, subject only to the few restrictions entailed in accepting federal grants in aid and to the advice of the General Education Board. [Myrdal 1944, p. 893]

At the time of Myrdal's writing, the black population was overwhelmingly concentrated in the South, a region that had traditionally been set apart from the rest of the country by its poor economy, low rate of school attendance, and correspondingly high rate of illiteracy. In the South, racially separate schools were mandated by law under the doctrine of "separate but equal," gleaned from the Supreme Court ruling in *Plessy* v. *Ferguson* (1896). As is well documented by Myrdal and others, the "equal" aspect of this ruling was not enforced or even addressed by state and local governments in the South. The schools for blacks that did exist were consistently short-changed in terms of materials, building construction and maintenance, funding, and the like. Schools in urban areas were often overcrowded, with one school serving a city's entire black population. In rural districts—if there were schools at all—they were often dilapidated, unhealthful one-room versions with even less space than their urban counterparts. However,

Anderson (1988) notes that the development of public secondary education in the South deliberately did not include African Americans. No new high school facilities were made available to black youth despite the fact that in many areas they comprised a large proportion of the state population and, in some counties, were actually the majority population.

Community involvement in the educational system was practically nonexistent at the time of Myrdal's study. Schools for blacks were, for the most part, unresponsive to the communities they served. Rather, these schools were ostensibly used as instruments of social control by the southern white power structure (Anderson 1988). Curriculum was closely monitored by whites, if not controlled by them outright. Segregated schools were entirely staffed by black teachers and administrators who had little or no say in the way these schools were run. So long as their views and educational practices were in line with the beliefs and dictates of the local white power structure, black schools were, for the most part, left to themselves. But the hiring and firing of teachers and staff was entirely under the control and/or supervision of white officials. This control extended to the postsecondary level as well. White southerners monitored the curriculum offered in state-funded colleges, keeping them colleges in name only. In most state colleges for blacks, pre-collegiate courses were offered along with limited vocational and industrial education. White northerners were also involved in the paternalistic control of black education. In the area of higher education, northern white philanthropy had compensated for the lack of state funding for many years by establishing and maintaining quality schools, providing teachers, and funding building construction. Black instructors and administrators were often beholden to those who supported their institutions, dependent upon the charity of others not only for the education of their people but also for their livelihood.

Myrdal's study examined these elements in a critical fashion, pointing to the fact that educational parity in the South as well as in the North had yet to be achieved as late as 1944. Furthermore, Myrdal and his researchers placed much of the responsibility for solving the problems of blacks on the system of education, arguing that it was the key to breaking the vicious cycle of racial discrimination and inequality in American life. However, in the years since Myrdal's study, much has happened to black education. The struggle of blacks to achieve educational parity with whites has long been an issue on the American scene and continues to dominate the dialogue on American education. Since *An American Dilemma* was written, the ideological issues at stake in the quest for black educational parity are no different from those that have faced black institutions of any type since the early days of the struggle for equality: admission into white institutions versus the development and maintenance of separate institutions run by and for blacks; integration versus group pluralism; assimilation versus separatism. These same issues have plagued black leadership for years, most notably in the famed Washington/Du Bois controversy. Since 1944, many formal changes have taken place in black education. But certain fundamental ideological issues have yet to be resolved. In *An American Dilemma*, Myrdal did much to assess the role of race prejudice in hampering the educational goals and attainment of blacks and explained the necessity of removing formal racial barriers in this area. However, neither he nor the civil rights leadership addressed what should be the role of blacks in controlling their own educational destiny. As such, this remains a contested issue.

In the next section of this chapter our attention focuses specifically on the question of racial parity in American education. Fifty years after Myrdal's study, have African Americans achieved true educational parity? To answer this question we will engage in a systematic comparison of blacks and whites on selected indicators of educational attainment. This analysis seeks not only to compare current educational status by race but also gives some attention to important historical trends.

BLACK EDUCATIONAL PROGRESS, 1944–1994: AN EMPIRICAL ASSESSMENT

By World War II African Americans had accomplished one of history's most remarkable transformations by a group of people. In the three generations since emancipation from slavery, blacks had made significant progress in all arenas of life. African Americans had pressed beyond their earlier status as chattel slaves, the property of whites, to contend for full citizenship. This progress was especially pronounced in the area of education. W.E.B. Du Bois described the African American's organized and successful efforts in pursuit of education and group advancement as "one of the marvelous occurrences of the modern world; almost without parallel in the history of civilization" (Myrdal 1944, p. 887).

Myrdal was witness to the significant advances made by blacks in educational attainment. His chapter on "The Negro School" acknowledges the great thirst for education that characterized African Americans after their formal bondage was ended. He asserted that "American Negroes have taken over the American faith in education." School represented for the freedman a Holy Grail by which his freedom would be confirmed. In quoting Booker T. Washington, Myrdal made this point forcefully:

> Few people who were not right in the midst of the scenes can form any exact idea of the intense desire which the people of my race showed for education. It was a whole race trying to go to school. Few

were too young and none were too old, to make the attempt to learn. As fast as any kind of teachers could be secured, not only were day-schools filled, but night schools as well. [Myrdal 1944, p. 883]

In later studies, James Anderson (1988), V.P. Franklin (1992), and Thomas Webber (1978) confirmed that the emphasis among African Americans in the post–Civil War South on education was strategic. Their determined efforts to institutionalize black education specifically, and to establish universal education generally, represented the demonstrated desires of African Americans to educate themselves and their children as a means of "defending and extending" their emancipation (Anderson 1988).

Interestingly, Myrdal provides only scanty empirical information about the educational status of African Americans in his epic study. However, his estimate of illiteracy rates among blacks is revealing, since this statistic was the original measure of education used in the U.S. Census (1979, p. 87). He estimated that by 1860 only 5 percent of slaves could read and write; the literacy rate would have been much higher among free Negroes. Still, Myrdal's empirical figures on this point were unclear and imprecise. We will attempt here to provide more precise empirical information about the level of educational attainment that characterized African Americans at the Second World War. In the process, we will comment on their educational characteristics before and after Myrdal's study was published.

It is reasonable to begin with a consideration of illiteracy rates, referring to the ability of people to read and write, as a fundamental indicator of educational attainment. Table 7.1 shows that in 1890, one generation after emancipation, 61 percent of the African American population was illiterate. By comparison, only 8 percent of whites were illiterate in 1890. The successful efforts among blacks to educate themselves and their progeny is

Table 7.1

Illiteracy rates, by race.

Year	Black %	White %
1890	61	8
1910	33	5
1930	18	3
1947	11	2
1959	7	2
1969	4	1

Source: The Social and Economic Status of the Black Population in the United States: An Historical View, 1790–1978. Washington, D.C.: U.S. Bureau of the Census, 1979, Table 68.

clearly evident by the end of the Second World War, when the illiteracy rate for blacks had dropped to only 11 percent. What had been a difference of over 50 percentage points between black and white illiteracy rates in 1890 was reduced to fewer than 10 percentage points by 1947. Twenty-five years ago, the percentage of African Americans who were illiterate essentially matched the percentage for whites (4 percent versus 1 percent). Today, race differences in illiteracy rates are negligible. African Americans had, in a clear indication of educational progress, "caught up to" whites on this measure of educational attainment.

In order to accurately assess the educational progress of African Americans since the Myrdal study, it will be helpful to employ a wider array of educational attainment measures. Table 7.2 provides statistics on school enrollment by race for persons aged 5–20 years. From 1890 to 1940 the percentage of African Americans enrolled in school virtually doubled, going from 33 percent to 65 percent. Over the same period, the percentage difference between blacks and whites in school enrollment dropped from 25 percentage points to 7 percentage points. These changes provide evidence of substantial gains in educational access and achievement for African Americans. For the past 30 years, race differences in school enrollment have been basically nonexistent. So our second measure of educational attainment also shows substantial black progress over the periods prior to, and following, Myrdal's 1944 study.

An examination of race differences in level of schooling completed adds to our emerging view of dramatic black gains in educational attainment since 1944 (Table 7.3). In 1940 only 7 percent of blacks had completed 4 or more years of high school. For whites the comparable figure was 26 percent. By further contrast, in 1940, 1 percent of African Americans and 5 percent of European Americans had completed 4 or more years of college. As was true with other measures of educational progress, the size of percent-

Table 7.2

Persons aged 5–20 years enrolled in school, by race.

Year	Black %	White %
1940	65	72
1950	79	82
1960	82	86
1970	82	85
1980	86	86
1990	88	89

Source: The Social and Economic Status of the Black Population in the United States: An Historical View, 1790–1978. Washington, D.C.: U.S. Bureau of the Census, 1979, Table 63.

age differences by race had greatly diminished 50 years later. In 1992, 82 percent of black Americans were high school graduates versus 87 percent of white Americans. However, the racial difference in the percentage of college graduates had actually increased since *An American Dilemma*. The percentage of blacks who were college graduates in 1992 had grown to 12 percent as opposed to 24 percent of Whites who were college graduates. It should also be noted that by 1992 there had ceased to be any substantial difference in median years of schooling completed by blacks and whites. As was true for our other measures of educational attainment above, the absolute gains in level of schooling completed since Myrdal's original study have been much greater for blacks than for whites. Thus, African Americans have been in the position of lessening the educational difference or advantage held by whites over blacks.

Table 7.3

Level of schooling completed, by race.

| Year | Percentage of Total Population | | Median Years of School Completed |
	4 Years + of High School %	4 Years + of College %	
	Black		
1940	7	1	5.7
1960	20	3	8.2
1970	31	4	9.8
1975	43	6	10.9
1980	54	9	12.0
1992	81.8	12	12.4*
	White		
1940	26	5	8.8
1960	43	8	10.9
1970	55	11	12.1
1975	65	14	12.4
1980	71.3	19.3	12.5
1992	87.1	24.2	12.7*

Sources: The Social and Economic Status of the Black Population in the United States: An Historical View, 1790–1978. Washington, D.C.: U.S. Bureau of the Census, 1979, Table 70; *1980 Census of Population: General Social and Economic Characteristics.* Washington, D.C.: U.S. Bureau of the Census, 1983, Tables 83 and 123; *Statistical Abstract of the United States: 1992.* Washington, D.C.: U.S. Bureau of the Census, 1993, Table 230; Claudette Bennett, *The Black Population in the United States: March 1992.* Washington, D.C.: U.S. Bureau of the Census, 1993, Table 1.

*Figure taken for the year 1990.

High school completion rates and college enrollment rates provide yet another perspective on the relative educational attainments of blacks and whites in this society. Table 7.4 summarizes these statistics for the period from 1972 to 1992. In a departure from the patterns revealed by other indicators of educational progress, race differences on these measures were more resistant to change over the period in question. In 1972, 30 years after Myrdal, the high school completion rate for whites was 82 percent. This represented an advantage for whites over blacks of 15 percentage points. By 1992, 20 years later, the racial difference in high school completion rates had reduced only by half, to 8 percentage points (whites 83 percent, blacks 75 percent). It is worth noting that among the different race/gender groupings, 1992 high school completion rates were lowest for black males (72 percent) and highest for white females (85 percent).

College enrollment rates reveal different patterns by race than are shown for high school completion rates (Table 7.4). In 1972, 27 percent of African Americans who graduated high school enrolled in college. This rate was only 5 percentage points below the college enrollment rate for white high

Table 7.4

High school completion rates and college enrollment rates, by gender and race/ethnicity: 1972–1992, 18–24-year-olds.

Year	High School Completion Rate			High School Graduates Enrolled in College		
	Total %	Male %	Female %	Total %	Male %	Female %
			White			
1972	81.7	81.1	82.2	32.3	38.6	26.6
1975	83.2	82.7	83.6	32.4	36.4	28.6
1980	82.6	80.6	84.4	31.8	33.8	29.9
1985	83.6	81.7	85.4	34.4	35.8	33.0
1990	82.5	81.1	83.8	39.4	40.3	38.6
1992	83.3	81.2	85.3	42.2	41.6	42.8
			Black			
1972	66.7	63.4	69.6	27.1	33.0	22.5
1975	64.8	61.8	67.1	32.0	32.8	31.5
1980	69.7	66.0	72.6	27.6	26.3	28.6
1985	75.6	72.3	78.4	26.1	27.7	24.9
1990	77.0	75.9	77.8	33.0	34.4	31.8
1992	74.6	72.3	76.8	33.8	29.7	37.5

Source: Carter, Deborah, and Reginald Wilson. *Minorities in Higher Education.* Washington, D.C.: American Council on Education, 1993.

school graduates in the same year (32 percent). By 1992, in contrast with other statistics reviewed here, the white advantage over blacks in college enrollment rates had actually gotten larger. In 1992, 42 percent of Americans of European descent who graduated high school enrolled in college, as compared to 34 percent of African Americans. The race difference had actually grown to 8 percentage points over the ensuing years. Moreover, from 1972 to 1992 the pattern reversed—black women were replaced by black men as the race/gender grouping least likely to attend college after graduating high school.

Any discussion of African American higher educational attainment fails if the role of Historically Black Colleges and Universities (HBCUs) is not considered. Many of these institutions were founded in the shadow of slavery as blacks struggled to define a new place for themselves in this society as freed people. Founded and funded through the joint efforts of northern philanthropists and African Americans themselves, these schools assumed central roles in national efforts to educate blacks. Earlier, these schools provided instruction at the elementary, high school, and college levels. Over time the content of their curricula varied from aspects of agricultural and vocational science to classical instruction. HBCUs were a presence on the American scene when Myrdal conducted his massive study. In 1944 the overwhelming majority of African Americans educated through college had attended and graduated from an HBCU—such was the impact of racially segregated education.

Myrdal spent some time discussing the ideological divide that separated HBCUs into camps associated with Booker T. Washington's emphasis on industrial studies as contrasted with W. E. B. Du Bois's emphasis on classical studies. Ideological debates aside, these institutions shared a heritage defined by external control by whites and a history of economic underfunding and deprivation. Despite these constraints, HBCUs were able to contribute mightily to the higher education of African Americans. Until the 1970s, 20 years after *Brown*, black colleges and universities represented essentially the sole opportunity for the higher education of black people in this country. Although the public and private schools properly labeled historically black presently represent a mere 3 percent of the total 3,200 institutions of higher learning in this country, those schools continue to contribute disproportionately to the production of black college degree holders. In 1980–1981, HBCUs conferred 19,556 bachelor's, 3,185 master's, and 69 doctoral degrees, representing, respectively, 32 percent, 19 percent, and 6 percent of all degrees awarded to African Americans that year (Carter and Wilson 1994, Table 12). Ten years later the figures were equally impressive and disproportionate. In 1990–1991, 27 percent of bachelor's degrees (17,069), 16 percent of master's degrees (2,482), and 12 percent of doctoral degrees (127) earned by African Americans that year were conferred by black schools (Carter and Wilson 1994, Table 12).

In America, economics are tied to educational attainment, or that is what our cultural ethos would lead one to believe. To the extent that a person achieves educationally, it is assumed that she is adding to her human, social, and cultural capital in such a way as to ultimately increase her economic value. Myrdal states this assumption implicitly and explicitly at several places in *An American Dilemma*. In short, the theory presumes America to be a meritocratic society where educational gains will be translated into economic gains, irrespective of a person's race. But race—and class—complicate these matters: "Even among the youths from other poor and disadvantaged groups in the North the ideals implanted by the schools do not fit life as they actually experience it. The conflicts are, of course, accentuated in the case of Negroes" (Myrdal p. 880).

Our focus shifts at this point to a consideration of the economic returns for education that African Americans receive at present. Fifty years ago, Myrdal concluded that blacks did not receive economic returns on their educational attainment commensurate with those paid whites of equal educational status. Figure 7.1 provides a capsule reminder of the pattern of

Figure 7.1

Percentage of persons 25 years old and over, by educational attainment, sex, and race: March 1992.

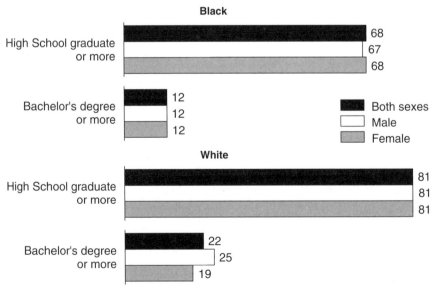

Source: U.S. Bureau of the Census

educational attainment for Americans of European and African descent. In March 1992, 68 percent of blacks 25 years old or over were high school or college graduates, compared to 81 percent of similarly defined whites. For the same cohort, 22 percent of whites and 12 percent of blacks had graduated college or more. Our second figure shows the economic returns that were paid each race/gender/education category in 1991, the previous year. Perusal of Figure 7.2 reveals that the racial disadvantage, in terms of a lesser return to blacks for equal education, pointed out by Myrdal in 1944, continues to be a reality. When the median earnings of year-round, full-time workers by educational attainment, sex, and race are compared, we see that blacks are disadvantaged relative to whites and that women are disadvantaged relative to men. Overall, black high school graduates earned $18,620 annually as compared to the $22,370 earned by whites, a shortfall of nearly $4,000. Taking the comparison one step further, we see that black male high school graduates earned nearly $4,000 more than their female counterparts, while white males who had graduated high school earned over $8,000 more than their white female peers. In descending order, of all high school graduates white males earned most, black males were next, followed by white

Figure 7.2

Median earnings of year-round, full-time workers 25 years and over, by educational attainment, sex, and race: 1991.

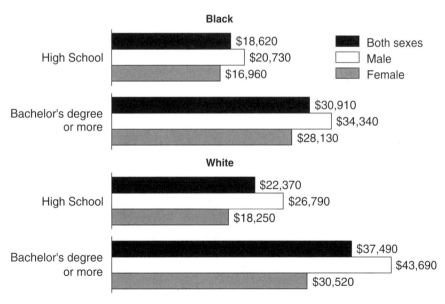

Source: U.S. Bureau of the Census

females. The earnings for black women who had graduated high school were lowest of all the four race/gender groups in this category.

A similar pattern presents itself when we compare the earnings of full-time, year-round workers who had earned a bachelor's degree or more by race and gender. Whites received a premium of nearly $7,000 over blacks with comparable educational attainment ($37,490 vs. $30,910). White males were by far and away the most lucratively compensated race/sex group in this category with annual earnings of $43,690. This figure is much higher than the earnings of college educated black males ($34,340), white females ($30,520), and black females ($28,130). As was the case previously, of the four sex/race groupings with college education, black women were the most poorly compensated.

AN ANALYSIS OF MYRDAL'S TRENDS AND POSSIBILITIES IN BLACK EDUCATION

Myrdal's examination of trends and problems seems, for the most part, to contain accurate predictions for black education in the years following the publication of his study. However, the assimilationist political thrust of the study also limits its predictive power in many areas.

Despite his vivid depictions of the problems facing black education at the time of the study—namely, white southern opposition to black education manifested in segregationist practices and resulting in a dependency upon northern philanthropy—Myrdal accurately foresaw the formal dissolution of the dual school system in the South. The dual system would be an increasingly difficult financial burden for the already strained southern economy. In this connection, Myrdal pointed to an "upward tendency" in the quality of black schools. Real costs were associated with the trend of improvements in the quality and facilities of black education, spurred largely by government involvement and the NAACP's strategic campaign to upgrade black education, particularly on the college and university levels. Myrdal also predicted the virulent racist reactions of lower-class whites to increased black educational access, given that their caste position would be threatened by the dissolution of segregation. On these points, Myrdal's analysis was particularly insightful and accurate. Although Myrdal did not explicitly address the adoption of strictly integrationist schemes to achieve educational parity, the political assumptions of his study definitely supported such a move.

In the chapter entitled, "The Negro Community as a Pathological Form of the American Community," Myrdal argued that the African American community and its culture are essentially "distorted developments" or "pathological conditions" of the general American community and culture. Assimilation, therefore, was held to be the ultimate desirable goal for blacks:

> We assume that it is to the advantage of American Negroes as indi-
> viduals and as a group to become assimilated into American culture,
> to acquire the traits held in esteem by the dominant White Americans.
> [Myrdal, p. 929]

Like most of the social scientists of his era, Myrdal believed in assimilation as the "final solution" to the race problem; he also viewed education
as a means of achieving that assimilationist goal. Education would serve to
change African American culture (i.e., remove its pathological elements)
and eventually bring blacks into the larger American community:

> The trend toward a rising educational level of the Negro population
> in of tremendous importance for the power relations discussed in this
> part of our inquiry. Education means an assimilation of White
> American culture. It decreases the dissimilarity of the Negroes from
> other Americans. [Myrdal, p. 879]

To interpret black culture and the black community as pathological is to
see both as impediments to the solution of the American dilemma. It follows that blacks and whites must go to school together in order for blacks
to become part of the larger American culture through assimilation. In perhaps what was a token gesture to Du Bois, Myrdal quotes his criticisms of
this strategy:

> . . . theoretically, the Negro needs neither segregated schools nor
> mixed schools. What he needs is Education. What he must remember
> is that there is no magic, either in mixed schools or in segregated
> schools. A mixed school with poor and unsympathetic teachers, with
> hostile opinion, and no teaching concerning black folk, is bad. A seg-
> regated school with ignorant placeholders, inadequate equipment,
> poor salaries, and wretched housing, is equally bad. [Myrdal, p. 902]

Despite the fact that Myrdal recognized Du Bois's views on this matter,
his own analysis advanced the premise that black schools are innately undesirable. He defined attempts to incorporate cultural content in black education as problematic and futile. He referred to the "Negro History
Movement" of Dr. Carter G. Woodson as an "essentially propagandistic"
tool against white superiority, a "counterpoison" to white racism with no
real value (p. 752). In short, by arguing that the black community was a
pathological form of the larger American community, and by viewing complete and total assimilation as the "best possible alternative for blacks,"

Myrdal put the stamp of scientific legitimacy on integration as the only means to achieve racial parity in education.

In the wake of *An American Dilemma*'s publication, a number of events took place within the integrationist paradigm that changed the face of black education. The most notable of these events were the school segregation cases, culminating with *Brown* v. *Topeka Board of Education*. Since the late 1930s, civil rights leadership had initiated court cases designed to chip away at the doctrine of "separate but equal," which was the basis of the South's dual school system. This strategy was developed by Charles Hamilton Houston and executed by Thurgood Marshall, both working in concert with colleagues and the National Association for the Advancement of Colored People (NAACP) Legal Defense Fund (McNeil 1983). Fully aware that the professional or graduate education provided for blacks in the South was inferior to that provided for whites, the NAACP sought to force state governments throughout the South to use state funds to live up to the equality implied in "separate but equal." If these states were unable to provide equal or comparable facilities, then integration into existing white institutions would be an unavoidable consequence. This strategy was initiated in 1938 with *Missouri ex. rel. Gaines* v. *Canada* and continued with *Briggs* v. *Elliott* (1948), *Sipuel* v. *Oklahoma State Regents* (1948), *McLaurin* v. *Oklahoma State Regents* (1950), and *Sweatt* v. *Painter* (1950), culminating with *Brown* v. *Board of Education of Topeka* (1954), in which Supreme Court Chief Justice Earl Warren cited *An American Dilemma* as a general source for the basis of his decision. *Brown* had the effect of directly attacking segregation in American education by declaring the doctrine of "separate but equal" unconstitutional. As a result of this decision, the ensuing decades saw the formal dissolution of dual school systems from elementary schools to college levels in the South and in much of the United States.

The eventual control by blacks over their own educational destiny is not addressed in *An American Dilemma* because Myrdal did not view this as a viable alternative or priority. Consequently, Myrdal did not anticipate the black political cultural movement of the 1960s and 1970s, which not only advocated community control of educational institutions but also questioned the validity of the broader American culture and its relevance for black students. Perhaps one of the most striking partings with the integrationist stances of the civil rights leadership was New York City's Ocean Hill-Brownsville Teacher's Strike of 1968–1969. The struggle involved decentralization and local community-based control over the administration of schools within a black and Puerto Rican neighborhood. The Black Power movement and black militancy influenced schools as parents sought more control over the education of their children in an institution that appeared for the most part hostile, if not indifferent, to their present and future well-being.

Protests by parents in the community of Ocean Hill in Brooklyn over school conditions prompted the United Federation of Teachers (UFT) to suggest to the Ford Foundation that the Ocean Hill group be included in a pilot program on decentralization with two other predominately minority schools. As part of an experiment in school decentralization, 30–60 autonomous local school boards were to be created, each with power of budget, curriculum, and personnel and composed of six elected parent representatives and five representatives appointed by the mayor from a list submitted by community groups. Although the city of New York was committed to the policy of decentralization of its operations in an attempt to "deepen and broaden the relationship of the communities to the schools," the UFT opposed the plan on the grounds that it was a Balkanization of the schools. This experiment was implemented in three districts: Two Bridges (Lower East Side), I. S. 201 (Harlem), and Ocean Hill-Brownsville (Brooklyn), despite the opposition of the UFT. The subsequent transfer of nineteen faculty members from an Ocean Hill school on the grounds that they were attempting to undermine the experiment prompted a year-long teachers' strike, pitting parents and community leaders concerned with the welfare of their children against teachers who were resistant to this implementation of local autonomy. The UFT protested the transfers, claiming that they were in fact firings done in violation of due process and went on strike against the district, taking with them some 350 teachers. The Ocean Hill-Brownsville board, however, hired new replacement teachers for its unit. The UFT expanded its strike to all city schools, demanding the reinstatement of the transferred teachers and the 350 already out on strike. The UFT and the school board reached an agreement for the reinstatement of all teachers and a hearing for the transfers. While the Ocean Hill-Brownsville board claimed that it would not prevent the return of the teachers, residents of the communities barred their entry to the school on the following day, prompting the UFT to strike again. The Ocean Hill board was suspended for its actions and the UFT, as a condition of ending its strike, demanded that the decentralization project be deemed a failure. The community boards were suspended and the districts placed under state trusteeship pending the decision of the State Education Commissioner. In the following year, the experimental districts were dismantled and merged into 32 larger, newly created "community districts" under a new plan proposed by the central board and approved by the UFT.

The rhetoric of integration versus separatism quickly found its way into this conflict. Conservatives and parents arguing for decentralization and local community empowerment found themselves in opposition to liberal social democrats comfortable with the rhetoric of integration but unnerved by that of the new Black Power militancy. The fight for community control at Ocean Hill-Brownsville was essentially an outgrowth of the move by blacks to embrace traditional political cohesion. Although this move was not consistent with the civil rights leadership's views on education, the NAACP's official organ, *The Crisis*, offered the following statement in response to the events:

> [We demand that] the Board of Education of the City of New York reinstate the local board and its members and enjoin the City Board from interfering with the functioning of the local board in any manner which violates the Fourteenth Amendment. [*The Crisis*, p. 362]

Another NAACP representative made the point that

> [The UFT fight] is an extension of its successful fight in the state legislature . . . opposing decentralization . . . decentralization delegates authority to local governing boards . . . even though provisions for protection of teacher rights are included. The union is using the issue of teacher security in the Ocean Hill-Brownsville District as a smokescreen for its campaign of distortion. Its real objective is power to control the city's schools and to avoid teacher accountability for the failure to teach Negro and Puerto Rican children. [The Crisis, p. 363]

In many respects, this conflict is an extension of what had long existed between white paternalism and black self-determination with regards to education. From its earliest days, black access to education has been influenced, if not controlled, by the paternalistic "assistance" of whites, conservative and liberal alike. Operating from a position of power, whites determined not only the form but the content of black education (Anderson 1988; Franklin 1992; and Jones 1980). The paternalistic control that white liberals exercised over the education of minorities in New York was directly challenged by blacks and Puerto Ricans in Ocean Hill-Brownsville who sought control over the education of their own children. In this sense, the Ocean Hill-Brownsville conflict in New York of the 1960s was no different from those that occurred between black communities and white missionaries in the South during the 1860s (Anderson 1988). At both junctures the issues boiled down to who would set the agenda for African American education, whites or blacks themselves.

Many of the issues that the "community control of schools movement" sought to address remain unresolved. Schools located in predominately minority urban areas face many of the same conditions that were present 50 years ago—overcrowding, inadequate funding, poorly trained teachers, rundown facilities, mis-education and poor education of students, coupled with the more recent phenomena of economic dislocation, drugs, and violence. As a result, black students have yet to reach educational parity with whites, as measured on any standard scale of educational achievement. The integration movement, largely pushed forward by civil rights leadership, bears some of the responsibility for this situation. High-achieving students as well as their influential parents abandoned schools in black communities for schools in largely hostile white communities where they would have little or no influence on the education of their children (Webster, Stockard, and Henson 1981). Black community schools could have been maintained with full rather than partial funding from the state and controlled by black administrators, black teachers, and black parents. This did not happen, however, because community control of schools in African American communities was not addressed in *An American Dilemma*, was never an issue in *Brown*, and was not a priority of the liberal social science/civil rights leadership coalition. The issue therefore went unresolved but not forgotten in the communities most directly affected. Sizable numbers in black communities have periodically pressed for control over their children's educations. From the Reconstruction period to the Black Power era into the present, blacks have sought to assert their own agenda in the education of their young. Of late we see this recurrent sentiment expressed concretely in efforts to establish black male schools, Afrocentric curriculums, charter schools, and in efforts to ensure the survival of Historically Black Colleges and Universities.

Myrdal's study similarly failed to anticipate the intractability of American racial prejudice and discrimination. In his final analysis of the "American Dilemma" (Chapter 45), Myrdal asserted that he saw a gradual erosion of the American caste system. While this held true with regards to formal practices and laws, the emergence of white backlash in the late 1960s and early 1970s, coupled with the persistence of American racial beliefs, betray Myrdal's optimistic assimilationist view. Bobo and Kluegel (1993) argue that racial attitudes have improved, deteriorated, or remained unchanged depending on the measure selected due to the prevalence of white opposition to race-targeted policy in American society. White resistance to efforts to fundamentally alter the racial caste structure is more commonly attributed to group self-interest than to racial prejudice—but the end result is the same. Thus, despite educational gains made by African Americans since the publication of *An American Dilemma*, disproportionate black economic deprivation persists as does de facto racial segregation and negative, stereotypic racial beliefs about blacks (see Massey and Denton 1993; Jaynes and Williams 1989; Schumann, Steeh, and Bobo 1985; and Kirschenman and Neckerman 1989). In the 1970s, busing children to schools was seen as a way to correct the racial segregation in schools resulting from racial segregation in residence. But these attempts to integrate American schools failed miserably. Schools today are as segregated racially as they were four decades ago and, in some cases, segregation has actually worsened (Orfield 1993). Explanations for the failure of integration vary and encompass the following elements: racial hostility, economic restructuring, reprioritization by government, the American emphasis on personal freedom, shifting political moods, white backlash, urban violence, and declining funding for schools. A more fundamental explanation, however, goes to the heart of a socialized aversion of whites to sharing space and intimacy with blacks—especially as equals. Whites have been and are, albeit to a lesser extent, socialized from earliest memory to define blacks as inferior, deviant, and dangerous. From this negative imagery, emerge negative attitudes and negative actions that endure despite structural changes (Drake 1987 pp. 1–114).

That these manifestations were particularly virulent in the area of education points to the overarching optimism of Myrdal's evaluation. In fact, given his treatment of the social realm in the text, there is clear evidence that formal race relations have a tendency to improve without the underlying reality of conceptions of racial difference changing. Myrdal himself maintained that

> The important changes in the Negro problem do not consist of, or have close relations with, "social trends" in the narrower meaning of the term but are made up of changes in people's beliefs and valuations. [Myrdal, p. 998]

Where Myrdal's assimilationist stance saw black institutions and culture slowly becoming merged with those of white America, black education in fact remains a separate and problematic issue primarily due to the intractability of American racial beliefs. Du Bois's comments noted above ring particularly true in the face of Myrdal's failure to fully recognize the imbeddedness of the American racial order, to anticipate its impact on education, and to underestimate the role of education in its demise.

BLACK EDUCATIONAL INEQUITY: DILEMMA OR DESIGN?

Education has been and continues to be a key site of struggle in the African American quest for freedom, equality, dignity, and self-determination. As Myrdal correctly pointed out, this is understandable given the emphasis in the American Creed on the ideal of meritocracy and its concomitant assumption that upward mobility is available to all who desired and were willing to work hard to achieve. Schools were to be the great levelers in American democracy, providing equal opportunity for all without regard to race, gender, ethnicity, region, or class origins. On the level playing field of open, fair competition, merit would determine who won society's choicest prizes—prestigious jobs, high salaries, fine homes, the good life. But it has not worked out that way: the ideal has not become reality. As a highly valued resource, education has not been equally available to different groups in the society (Giroux 1992). Educational opportunities have been most available to the privileged and the powerful. Throughout their long history in this country, African Americans have been denied educational opportunity. During slavery it was forbidden to teach slaves, or for slaves to learn, to read and write, under threat of physical maiming or death (Webber 1978). It is therefore understandable that black Americans attached both symbolic and pragmatic significance to education as a key site of resistance and struggle.

In continuing the quest for educational parity which began with emancipation, African Americans had made advances towards closing the gap between themselves and whites at the time of *An American Dilemma*'s publication, although not without continued resistance and opposition. Myrdal's study documented the extreme educational disadvantages of African Americans. Concentrating on the South, where the overwhelming majority of blacks lived, he showed the systematic efforts of whites to limit black educational opportunities. Black schools were underfunded, black efforts at educational empowerment were thwarted, and black access to educational opportunity was denied as part of a larger strategy to prevent blacks from challenging the dominance of whites. Myrdal also showed how the dynamics of the black struggle for education were complicated by the competing motives and goals of northern whites, southern whites, and blacks themselves.

Over the half century since *An American Dilemma* was published, several significant events combined to change the face of black education. The study gave momentum to forces that were already in motion within the African American community, specifically a desire for and a push toward educational equality and full citizenship rights in the area of education. The most significant changes involved changes to the law of the land and ultimately led to broader changes in society. The NAACP Legal Defense Fund and a remarkable group of attorneys and social scientists pursued a successful strategy of court challenges. Attacking the principle of "separate but equal" on constitutional grounds, these legal challenges proved in a series of court cases focused mostly on higher education that blacks had been denied equal educational opportunities on the grounds of race. This successful legal campaign culminated in the 1954 Supreme Court *Brown* v. *Topeka Board of Education* decision, which outlawed segregation in the nation's public schools. In time, *Brown* would provide the basis for overturning Jim Crow segregation in all areas of the nation's public and private life (Chambers 1993).

After legal segregation was removed as a barrier to black educational opportunity, African Americans faced still other imposing barriers. De jure segregation was replaced by de facto segregation; denied the protection of law, whites simply improvised in order to continue their practices of excluding blacks and limiting their access to educational opportunity (Orfield 1993). Residential segregation continues to geographically separate blacks from whites, so much so that Massey and Denton speak of an "American Apartheid" system based on race and residential location. African Americans are more racially segregated than any other ethnic or racial group in America; moreover, the segregation rates for high-status blacks are essentially the same as those for their lower-status brethren (Farley and Frey 1994; and Farley and Allen 1989). Racial segregation is the engine that drives racial inequality in this society, thus black majority areas are characterized by poorer schools, lower school performance, more poverty, higher crime rates, fewer employment opportunities, and greater environmental deterioration (Baron 1969). Numerous schemes intended to achieve integrated schooling (e.g., busing, redistricting) have failed (see Bobo and Kluegel 1993), and where some modicum of school desegregation is achieved, black students are shown to suffer (i.e., lower achievement, higher dropout/suspension rates, lower aspirations). In short, the legacy of denied or thwarted black educational opportunity has continued under different arrangements. Absent an emphasis on the "quality of education" delivered, racial integration alone offers slim promise for African American educational improvement and eventual advancement out of the ranks of this society's despised, deprived, and degraded.

An unanticipated consequence of the outlawing of legal segregation in schools was the educational disempowerment of African Americans. Despite its obvious drawbacks, the system of separate schools allowed blacks greater control over the education of their young. Once the decision to merge schools was made, such mergers inevitably proceeded to the benefit of whites and to the detriment of blacks. Since blacks did not have equal power in the decision-making process, the tendency was for the numbers of black teachers and administrators to drop precipitously. And previously black-identified schools were more likely to be closed or to be merged under previously white-identified schools. At the same time, there was racially determined and differential allocation of human and physical resources: the better teachers and more innovative academic programs were assigned to schools that were previously white-identified. Moreover, the close connection that existed between the black community and segregated black schools—a connection that assured congruent values, shared commitments, and open lines of communication—was broken. Black children in desegregated schools now found themselves in environments and working with personnel who were at best indifferent to their culture and aspirations, but more often hostile. The effect was to trade the emotionally rich, supportive, encouraging environments of segregated black schools (albeit characterized by material deprivation) for the materially rich but alienating, discouraging environments of desegregated white schools. Black children were moved from one setting where teachers loved, understood, and cared for them to another where people resented them, failed to identify with them, and had no investment in their future. Black children also found themselves in schools where their parents' ability to exercise influence was greatly diminished. The end result was to greatly undercut the educational opportunities and performance of black students.

A review of the record of black educational progress since *An American Dilemma* gives cause for both celebration and concern. By all important indicators, African Americans have made tremendous educational process. In terms of illiteracy rates, school enrollment rates, and median years of schooling completed, blacks have achieved near parity with whites. However, several other measures highlight the vast differences that persist between black and white educational attainment in America. Blacks are significantly less likely to graduate high school and to enroll in and graduate from college. By the same token, blacks are much more restricted in their ability to receive the expected returns for years of schooling completed. Thus, blacks of equal educational attainment earn less than whites. It is interesting to note that Historically Black Colleges and Universities, institutions of higher learning where blacks exercise perhaps their strongest remaining influence over the content and direction of black education, contribute disproportionately to the production of black degree holders.

The dilemma of which Myrdal spoke is very much still with us in the area of black educational opportunity and achievement. This dilemma is manifested in the continued failure of this society to deliver on its promise of equal opportunity. African Americans are disadvantaged in the quantity and quality of education that is made available to them over the span of their lives. At the same time, their hopes for progress in a society that places a premium on educational attainment are thwarted, resulting in the continued subordination of black people in American society.

Gunnar Myrdal concluded that African Americans presented this nation with a moral dilemma, since legal segregation and the racial caste system were inconsistent with the American Creed and its embrace of freedom, equality, and democracy. Optimistically, he believed that the inherent tension between a reality that consigned blacks to second-class citizenship and the ideals defining America as the land of opportunity for all would eventually be reconciled in the acceptance of African Americans as full members of this society. The half century since publication of this study has proven Myrdal wrong. Racism, racial discrimination, racial prejudice, and racial stereotypes have been shown to be intractable. To be sure, there has been substantial progress and there have been many victories; nevertheless, the empirical record demonstrates unequivocally that blacks continue to be dominated and discriminated against in the land of their birth (Farley and Allen 1987; and U. S. Census 1993).

White America believes in and is firmly committed to maintaining the subordinate position of blacks. Deeply seated in the American psyche, in the institutional life of this country, are beliefs and practices that presume whites to be innately superior to blacks and to be entitled to privilege and dominion over this "lesser race." This fact is not erased by the ascension of token blacks into the positions of entertainment superstar, corporate board president, state governor, university professor, or four-star general. On the whole, African Americans continue to be mired in the lowest reaches of society, consigned to this subordinate, degraded position by the historical and contemporary forces of racism (both personal and institutional). Blacks have been at the bottom in America for nearly four centuries, and white America largely believes that this is as it should be, that it is the natural order of things.

Myrdal was correct in pointing to an American dilemma; however, he misconstrued this as a moral dilemma. Rather, the dilemma with which America wrestles—and has wrestled for centuries—is how best "to reconcile the practical morality of American capitalism with the ideal morality of the American Creed" (Ellison 1973, p. 83). How can a system that is inherently exploitative be accommodated within the rhetoric of equality? The country's racial climate remains in many ways unchanged from the years of Myrdal's research, giving a new urgency to the questions that many felt had been answered by the immense undertaking of *An American Dilemma* and the period of social change that followed. Our assertion here is straightforward: The historic and continuing subjugation of blacks in America results from conscious, willful, determined actions designed to achieve this end. The challenge before the country now, as was the case 50 years ago, is whether white America can commit to change and to a new, more democratic future or will the country continue to cling to its heritage of racial exploitation and oppression. How America answers this question will ultimately be the true measure of the nobleness of this unique experiment with democracy and of this country's hope for survival and prosperity.

Obie Clayton, Jr.

The Church and Social Change:
Accommodation, Moderation, or Protest

WHEN I BEGAN my work on this chapter, I considered revisiting Chapter 40 of *An American Dilemma* and simply giving an updating on the "Negro Church." However, this would not have done justice to Gunnar Myrdal, and I found myself examining the social conditions surrounding the black church since Myrdal's writings. Readers should not expect to find anything here resembling Myrdal's original study, but rather an attempt to analyze the contributions of organized religion and especially the black church in the area of social change and race relations from the 1940s to the present.

We will not examine the cultural contributions of the church outside of power relationships as manifested through calls for change and racial moderation. In other words, did the church, particularly the black church, provide leadership during the move toward racial equality during the civil rights movement? Most of the discussion will revolve around the church and its leaders in the South; even though northern churches assisted in the civil rights Movement, it was fundamentally a southern event.

Many scholars have argued that, aside from the family, the black church is incontestably the most important social institution within the black community. Gunnar Myrdal, writing in the 1940s, stated that the black church and press were unique to the black community because they were exclusively controlled by blacks with little outside interference from whites. Myrdal argued that these institutions, especially the church, served as a forum for blacks' self-expression:

> They bring Negroes together for a common cause. They train them for concerted action. They provide an organized followership for Negro leaders. In these institutions, theories of . . . accommodation and protest become formulated and spread. These institutions sometimes take action themselves in the power field, attempting to improve the Negro's lot or voicing the Negro protest. Even more often they provide the means by which Negro leaders and organizations, which are more directly concerned with power problems, can reach the Negro people.[1]

191

Myrdal was on target in arguing that the church served many functions aside from the merely spiritual. Throughout the periods of slavery, Reconstruction, and post-Reconstruction, the black church was a buffer against the harshness of a segregated and prejudicial society. It filled a basic social void for the black population. According to Myrdal and W.E.B. Du Bois,[2] it served all of the basic needs of the black community, providing an outlet for creative performances in the arts, politics, and sports, always trying to make life more livable for the individual. Even though the makeup and ritual of the black church were similar to that of the white church, the differences were many. The white church served a purely religious function; the black church served social, political, and economic needs.

The myriad functions of the black church have probably generated the majority of the criticisms leveled against Myrdal—that he failed to see the uniqueness of the black church and referred to it as an attempt to imitate the white religious order.[3] These criticisms are not entirely accurate because Myrdal was primarily interested in the role of the black church as a power-altering mechanism. Myrdal's critique of the black church was not wholly concerned with the contributions of this institution in other areas. Again, to quote Myrdal: "The religious, educational, and cultural aspects of their activity (churches) will be almost entirely neglected."[4]

Myrdal was also accurate in describing the black church as a unique institution created and maintained with little outside interference. Moreover, Myrdal argued effectively that "the Negro church fundamentally is an expression of the Negro community itself."[5] We in contemporary America must remember, as did Myrdal, that the black church has operated and still operates within the dominant community and shares a theological history that cannot be studied apart from mainstream white society and its theology. In the South, during the pre-civil rights movement, the church was the only forum available in which blacks could express themselves or hold positions of power. In the areas of race relations and social change, the black church sought the assistance of white religious leaders, hoping that the Christian belief of the "brotherhood of man" would aid them in their fight for equality. However, for the most part, this plea for assistance was ignored.

In many ways, the church (both black and white) offered the most effective vehicle for change in race relations and for racial accommodation and moderation. Americans, and southerners in particular, have always maintained a deep commitment to religion. Southern church attendance rates among the highest in the nation, and the organized church has traditionally held considerable influence. For example, in 1957, Mississippi had the highest rate of churches per capita in the nation. Approximately 78 percent of the white population aged 14 and over were counted as church members, constituting the fourth highest such figure in the United States: the black rate was slightly higher.[6] Despite its normal institutional tendency to support the societal status quo, the church had an ethical commitment to the Judeo-Christian legacy of the "Fatherhood of God and the Brotherhood of Man," which could be interpreted as dictating opposition to the extremism employed in the South to delegate blacks to inferior status. More than any other institution, the church could cite moral justification in its pleas for moderation, thereby giving such pleas more credence with the South's segregation-oriented populace. Moreover, the civil rights movement and black ministers looked to the white church for assistance. A noted civil rights activist, the Reverend Ed King, described the goal in these words:

> [The Movement was] pleading that Black and White Christians come together, pray together, admit the problems of society, and begin to change them. This approach tried to reach the white man at his best— or at least the place where he could offer the least resistance, the poorest defense of racism.[7]

The church had the responsibility more than any other institution—to provide guidance that would minimize violence and social turmoil. If there was any place where whites would listen to such moderate guidance, it seemed to be in the church. As Will Campbell of the Southern Regional Council said, "The South is a violent place. It is not prepared to listen to talk of law, order, the Constitution. But it will hear and understand words which only the Church can speak: grace, redemption, reconciliation."[8]

Despite its potential for effectiveness, the church in the South generally responded to the civil rights movement with silence. Although partially attributable to other nonpolitical factors, this response was largely the result of political pressure applied by extremist elements in a successful effort to force the church to maintain conformity with the established orthodoxy. Such intimidation constituted standard operating procedure for the southern political system, whose extremist fervor tended toward elimination of all opposition. From exercising economic and social pressure through the well-organized citizens councils, to passing legislative enactments designed to penalize enemies of segregation, to sending police to follow and harass nonconformists, the system constantly and effectively intimidated black ministers and parishioners and white moderates and would-be moderates who offered any threat to the right-wing status quo or the established orthodoxy.

THE WHITE CHURCH IN THE SOUTH: CHANGE OR STATUS QUO

In the summer immediately following the *Brown* v. *Board of Education* decision, southern right-wing forces organized for the inevitable battle against integration. The atmosphere of intolerance grew rapidly in the South, and extremist political forces began a movement to defend segregation. As James Silver, author of *Mississippi: The Closed Society* stated:

> For whatever reason, the community sets up the orthodox view. Its people are constantly indoctrinated—not a difficult task, since they are inclined to accept the creed by circumstance. When there is no effective challenge to the code, a mild toleration of dissent is evident, provided the non-conformist is tactful and does not go far. But with a substantial challenge from the outside—to slavery in the 1850's and to segregation in the 1950's—the society tightly closes its ranks, becomes inflexible and stubborn, and lets no scruple, legal or ethical, stand in the way of the enforcement of the orthodoxy. The voice of reason is stilled and the moderate either goes along or is eliminated. Those in control during such times of crisis are certain to be extremists whose decisions are determined by their conformity to the orthodoxy.[9]

This quotation captures the essence of the precarious situation in which the church found itself during the civil rights movement. Myrdal argued that the Negro church, school, and press were not to be misconstrued as agencies of power for the "Negro caste." The black church conformed, for the most part, to the orthodoxy of separatism. And many white southern religious leaders used the church as a platform to spread segregation and racism. As Silver suggested, society, especially southern society, tried to use religion as a mechanism to enforce tradition or orthodoxy. Those who spoke out for change found themselves subject to violence—a violence that became institutionalized.

The primary tool of the South in enforcing the orthodoxy of segregation was its political system—an amalgamation of the executive, legislative, judicial, and police power of the state, county, and city governments. These units joined in an ideological alliance with the quasi-governmental mouthpiece of white supremacy, the White Citizens Council.[10] During the early period of the civil rights movement, the system's most distinguishing feature was the extremism it exhibited in implementing this enforcement task. For the most part, the South's politicians readily followed the advice of Congressman (later Governor of Mississippi) John Bell Williams that Mississippians could not "afford the luxury of moderation, complacency or timidity."[11]

The campaigns of intimidation, which occurred in the South during the 1950s were aimed primarily at black churches, which were perceived as leaders in the movement towards integration. But sympathetic white churches were not spared: the political powers seemed to be wary of organized religion's influence. For example, in 1960 Mississippi passed the

Church Property Bill, which rescinded the tax-exempt status of integrated churches. This singular piece of legislation served two purposes: (1) to warn and punish state and national denominations advocating integration, and (2) to provide support for churches totally committed to segregation.[12]

Further, the political system went beyond legislative enactments to intrude into the lives of churches and churchmen who posed a threat to the racial orthodoxy. It also employed a more direct and immediate tactic—police harassment. In Birmingham, Alabama; Jackson, Mississippi; and in scores of other Deep South cities, police officials arrested and threatened church officials who opened their doors to blacks. Integration teams from the North were often the victims of these threats. So it was that the southern political system exercised its brand of societal control on the church. All of the branches and offshoots of that system were welded together by one common purpose—enforcement of the orthodoxy—and they executed that purpose by systematic harassment and intimidation of all potential moderates, particularly those in the church.

Many churches, especially small rural churches, remained silent on the civil rights issue, and this silence constituted acquiescence to and support for the right-wing defense of segregation then perpetrated by the extremist leaders of the region. This failure of the religious leaders to take active concerted stances in civil matters portrayed support for segregation and supplemented the silent acquiescence of the general church to collectively present organized religion's tacit approval of the South's brand of political extremism.

Following the Birmingham church bombing in September 1963 and the resultant death of four little girls, a few of the larger urban churches in the South began to take a more moderate stance towards integration. Several churches even opened their doors to blacks. Sensing this liberal trend in the churches, the Citizens Councils, especially those in Mississippi and Alabama, immediately began a campaign to resegregate the churches announcing their availability to assist any lay group that wished to maintain segregation. In a newsletter in September 1963, the Council stated: "We feel that it is time to come forward with a positive plan of action to save these churches from integration." It planned to have "experienced lay leaders" conduct a series of meetings to formulate "an overall plan designed to eliminate church integration entirely."[13]

However, southern churches were not uniform in their submission to the status quo. Many individual churchmen and segments of the church became active in cautioning moderation and aiding the movement for integration and equality in the South. The church was probably the source of more native white support for the civil rights cause than any other segment of southern society, and many of the black churches provided leaders and permitted their buildings to be used as rallying points at the risk of physical violence, which was all too often the case.[14]

It is tempting to recognize the numerous instances of political support for civil rights coming from certain elements of the church, as well as to note that these elements of the church offered more of this support than elements of any other social institution, and to conclude therefore that organized religion fulfilled the much-needed mission of moderation and leadership in the South during the civil rights crisis. However, three factors mitigate against such a conclusion:

1. A closer analysis of these instances of support verifies James Silver's contention that "many individual preachers and a few ministerial groups have made courageous stands, but the church as a whole had placed its banner with the status quo." Most of the white church aid for the movement came from maverick ministers acting on their own without the backing of their congregations or state church leaders. When top church leaders were willing to speak out, they rarely did so in concert. The occasions when they did do so were extremely rare and therefore unrepresentative of the general church position during the civil rights crisis. All in all, the church's attempts at forwarding the cause of civil rights were very fragmented.

2. The contention that some elements of the church offered more political support for civil rights than the elements of any other native white institution does not necessarily indicate accomplishment of the mission of moderation or change. Within the intolerant framework of the South's closed society, very few institutions could support any individuals willing to take a moderate public position. The fact that the church was the source of more of these individuals than any other institution says very little in light of the consideration that all of the institutions together produced very few persons willing to stand up for moderation and social change.

3. These acts of support by the church for racial progress must be viewed in the light of the more numerous, yet not so easily countable, instances of acquiescence. The two sets of actions form a paradox, which renders the church's response to the South's civil rights as very ambiguous.

For the white church in the South, the response to political pressure was one of submission, constituting an acquiescence to the extremists' defense of segregation. This acquiescence came in two forms. The most general, and the most profound in terms of the church's mentality at this time, was a response of silence to the racial troubles that saturated the South. The other form was one of overt action in support of the dictates of southern racism. This form of action was not so surprising. In the deep southern states, where the governments were run by extremists, it could be expected that a few right-wing radicals would be lodged in the other institutions of society, including the church. These radicals, although certainly more numerous than the vocal supporters of racial progress, did not represent the rank-and-file of the southern religious community. They were largely ministers and high-ranking laymen with ties to the Citizens Councils.

It was the silent response of the church to political pressure that was most surprising, for it represented the collapse of the moderates in the South. Although most religious individuals did not vehemently declare that God is a segregationist, they gave their implicit support to the extremist brand of southern racism. They were in the position to use the moral teachings of the Judeo-Christian heritage to provide some moderate guidance for change in race relations. Yet they refused to do so, and, as a consequence, the church in general quietly professed an unwillingness to help resolve the racial problems that beset the nation. Indeed a moral, ethical, and American Dilemma.

Another important cause of organized religion's posture of passivity is the belief that the church should not be involved in political and social matters, such as race relations. But this did not inhibit many southern denominations from maintaining their societal crusades against the traditional vices of drinking and gambling.

The final factor explaining the church's acquiescence to the southern racial mentality is a kind of cultural identification which American churches have always had. In *The Burden of Southern History*, C. Vann Woodward said, "The conformist is not required nor expected to abandon his distinctive religion. But whether he remains a Protestant, a Catholic, or a Jew, his religion typically becomes subordinate or secondary to a national faith."[15] In other words, the goals and values of the various religions so closely follow those of the surrounding American culture that they are scarcely distinguishable. This is evidenced by the fact that the dominant American denominations rarely lead peace movements during times of war—a phenomenon sometimes seen in foreign nations. As American churches identify with the American culture, so do southern churches identify with the southern culture. The church so closely follows the prevalent way of life, that it cannot go against that way of life. Practically speaking, most southern churchmen were traditional southerners with traditional southern viewpoints, including the viewpoint that segregation was right.

Whatever their merits, these latter two explanations fall short of accounting for much of the church's intolerance of liberal ministers; of its silent support for governmental leaders who brazenly precipitated violence in the name of segregation; of its timid acceptance of police at the church door and of open political control of church policies; and of its pronounced indifference to the lives and rights of blacks. The only other explanation for these injustices is pressure, particularly political pressure. Because of the actions of the extremists who held governmental or quasi-governmental power in the South, the churches of the South acquiesced to racist extremism and to the intolerant atmosphere of what James Silver termed "The Closed Society."

It can be reasonably said that the attempts by elements of the white church in the South to forward the cause of moderation were significant and noteworthy; however, they represent no clear-cut institutional call of organized religion. The church as a whole did not come close to fulfilling its potential as a voice for moderation and social change. Considering that the church was the source of the most frequent cries for racial progress, society as a whole failed drastically. The frustration that many blacks felt in the face of this religious and moral dilemma may best be expressed by a quotation from Dr. Martin Luther King, Jr., in his "Letter from a Birmingham Jail":

> I must make two honest confessions to you, my Christian and Jewish brothers. First I must confess that over the past few years I have been gravely disappointed with the white moderate. I have almost reached the regrettable conclusion that the Negro's great stumbling block in his stride toward freedom is not the White Citizen's Councilor or the Ku Klux Klanner, but the white moderate, who is more devoted to "order" than to justice. . . . I have just received a letter from a white brother in Texas. He writes: "All Christians know that the colored people will receive equal rights eventually, but is it possible that you are in too great a religious hurry. . . . "Let me take note of my other major disappointment. I have been so greatly disappointed with the white church and its leadership. . . . I felt the white ministers, priests and rabbis of the South would be among our strongest allies. Instead some have been outright opponents.[16]

It was within this often hostile social context that the black church had to operate—conditions that were similar to the ones that had generated the first black churches in this country over a hundred years earlier.

THE BLACK CHURCH'S REACTION TO
SOUTHERN WHITE ACQUIESCENCE

Conditions in the South during the 1940s and 1950s were less than ideal for the majority of blacks. True, there were havens of social and economic activity—as Atlanta, Georgia, and Durham, North Carolina—but for the most part blacks were relegated to menial jobs and lived in substandard conditions. Legalized discrimination, persistent prejudice, and frequent violence were just as common in the post–World War II South as they had been during the period shortly after Reconstruction. These social and economic conditions are frequently cited as the major causes of the mass migration of blacks out of the South during the early 1900s. The migration was so pronounced that by the mid-1960s, 50 percent of blacks resided in northern cities; in 1900 more than 90 percent of all blacks had resided in the South.

Many of the blacks who moved to the North had simply given up on the idea of seeing any real change in the Deep South, and they ignored the advice of Booker T. Washington to "cast down your buckets where you are." These individuals saw a South that was basically unchanged from the 1870s. Change was quite often greeted with violence, as evidenced by the terrorism levied against the Southern Tenant Farmers Union, which was formed to improve the conditions of the black sharecroppers who dominated the southern agricultural scene. The consensus was that things had to be better in the North.[17] Many of the blacks who did not migrate northward sought to improve their conditions by working through the existing institutions, especially the church.

Prior to 1954 there were some signs of racial cooperation between blacks and whites, and the church was somewhat instrumental in encouraging racial moderation. However, after the 1954 *Brown* v. *Board of Education* decision, positive relationships between black and white religious leaders waned for reasons cited earlier. Moreover, younger blacks and the educated saw organized religion as too conservative in its stances and the black church as identifying too closely with the dominant white religious leaders, who were not advocating rapid social change but accommodation. These blacks, dissastsfied with the pace of change, began abandoning the church in large numbers, lessening the church's ability to provide a unified front in the civil rights movement.

Despite its shortcomings, the black church in the South served as a much needed forum for the emotional release of feelings against the dominant white ruling class that could not be expressed elsewhere without risk of punitive reprisals. It capitalized upon the particularly strong belief among southern blacks in the Christian tenet that the "sufferings of this world" would inevitably result in rich rewards promised by God during an "afterlife." This fundamental Christian belief led many critics of the black church to suggest that its primary goal centered on the afterlife or fostered a pie-in-the-sky attitude. Given the Jim Crow social system, black southern churches had to teach an ontology that stressed a better life, thus adding to the social cohesion of the community.

The black church in southern society, both historically and contem-
porarily, has always been somewhat of a religious anomaly: a body that is
equally directed towards alterations in power relations between blacks and
whites while maintaining a conservative theology which, in essence, reflects the broad needs of the black community. For example, from the post-
Reconstruction period until the early 1950s the black church worked
primarily behind the scenes to improve the conditions of black Americans,
thus altering the power inequities. However, the years immediately following *Brown* changed the way black ministers and black people pushed
for change. It was this Supreme Court decision that opened the nationwide
discussion about the rightness of segregation and gave clergymen the opportunity to speak to the matter. However, those clergymen who chose to
voice their opinion and beliefs did so at the risk of provoking right-wing
hysteria, and again blacks became frustrated at the pace of change and the
inability of religious leaders to effectively voice their opinion.

Armed with the *Brown* decision, blacks in Montgomery and Birmingham,
Alabama, and Tallahassee, Florida, began a series of boycotts of local mer-
chants in reaction to legislative gerrymandering which effectively destroyed their voting strength. The success of these boycotts ushered in a
new era of direct action as a mechanism for effecting social change. As Meier
and Rudwick stated in *From Plantation to Ghetto*, a new South had emerged
and it had a new spokesman, Dr. Martin Luther King, Jr.[18]

THE BLACK CHURCH IN THE 1960s AND BEYOND

Two important and historic changes had occurred in America between 1910
and 1960 which allowed for the rise of Dr. Martin Luther King, Jr. and led
to the protests, riots, and other social movements of the period. First,
America had become an urban society. Migrating black populations, moving north in search of better work opportunities, often found that they
lacked the resources and the education that employers demanded. There
was no work for them, and they settled in large urban ghettos where there
were few social institutions in place to handle their special needs.

Robert Franklin believed that the churches were the only established social institutions able to care for these new arrivals. The urban churches "as
the institutional center of the black community constituted the stasis of pre-
migration life. It became an extended family away from home (communi-
tas) for thousands of unemployed, hungry and new arrivals."[19] Franklin
and other scholars recognized that though the black churches in the North
tried to help this large influx of migrants, many were ill-equipped to do so.
Their small size and very limited budgets made any extensive outreach program impossible.

Second, in the new urban America, large numbers of blacks abandoned the churches altogether. Many sought to "redefine themselves in more secular terms,"[20] more militant, more politically active terms. Taking confidence from their success with direct action, protest, and activism, they began to demand more in respect to civil liberties, not only from the dominant white society but also from their own leaders. Myrdal had predicted this change:

> When the Negro community changes, the church will also change. It is true that the church has not given much to reforms but has rather lagged when viewed from the advanced positions of Negro youth and Negro intellectuals. But few Christian churches have ever been, whether in America or elsewhere, the spearheads of reform.[21]

While the mass migration of blacks to the North caught most religious denominations off guard, in the 1960s the churches made great efforts to develop outreach programs. These urban ministries, seeking to help new arrivals, mostly the poor, lacked the resources to deal with the grave economic and social problems for which there were no easy solutions.

Although many historians refer to the 1960s as a time of building, indeed of great creativity, the decade witnessed also the rise of a large black underclass. This coincided with an awareness of a host of new urban social problems created by white flight, the construction of highways which interrupted or destroyed neighborhoods, the migration of jobs out of the central city, and increases in crime, delinquency, and school dropout rates. To help cope with some of these problems, the Johnson administration launched its "War on Poverty," largely an appeal for racial cooperation.[22] While many blacks benefited from the social and economic programs of the early and mid-1960s, the vast majority did not. The proportion of black families living in poverty almost doubled between 1970 and 1990.[23] Growing poverty, increased unemployment, and a high crime rate were the most conspicuous social characteristics of the period. The new patterns of migration, which brought many blacks, manifestly ill-suited to city life, whose skills were principally in agriculture, could not fail to create problems in an urban economy dominated by manufacturing.

The percentage of black families earning less than $10,000 increased from 20.9 percent in 1970 to 26 percent in 1990. Black Americans suffered losses in all income brackets, with the exception of those earning over $35,000. One of the reasons for these grim statistics was the decline of the two-parent family within the black community. Beginning in the 1960s, black families were increasingly headed by single females. Children in such families, lacking positive role models, were less likely to attend church and to participate in other social and communal activities.

As social and economic conditions deteriorated, African American youths, particularly young men, abandoned the churches in record numbers. The churches, which had historically attracted significant numbers of men, were now filled principally with women.[24] Secular concerns and politics replaced religion and theology: "black power" became the rallying cry for a new generation of urban African Americans. The liberation message spread by leaders such as Stokley Carmichael and Eldridge Cleaver attracted a large following in urban areas, though it did not have great appeal to black ministers and older churchgoers who hesitated to become too involved in direct action and confrontation. One of the most notable radical developments of the period was the founding of the Black Methodists for Church Renewal (BMCR).[25]

James H. Cone described the BMCR as one of the earliest attempts by black clergy to become active in power-altering activities; the term black power took on new significance. Cone wrote:

> BMCR represented one of the creative examples of what the Black church was called to be and to do in the 1960s. . . . All Black caucuses in white denominations seemed to be enthusiastic in their support of an emerging Black consciousness, politically expressed in Black Power and theologically expressed in Black theology.[26]

A few black ministers went so far as to challenge the white churches for their inability or unwillingness to advance the cause of civil rights, especially in the North.[27] With black caucuses within predominantly white religious bodies calling for change, some religious leaders who had remained silent on the civil rights issues in the 1950s began to speak out. Something of a new ecumenical movement within the churches began to take shape.

The churches, especially the Methodist Church, began to take a more activist stance, lobbying for legislation in the area of civil rights and racial justice. Unfortunately, the activism proved to be short-lived. Given the enormity of the problems confronting America's cities in the 1960s, many whites and middle-class blacks abandoned the urban churches in the 1960s, resulting in a loss not only in membership but in revenue as well. Community outreach programs went unfunded; the number of voices calling for change declined; optimism gave way to hopelessness. The failure of the black churches to react to the crises of the cities caused them to lose respect, especially among the poor.

The failure of the majority of the black churches to foresee the problems associated with the urbanization of black Americans, and to formulate policies and procedures adequate to the situation, was due in part to their history and theology. Though urban black churches in the East and the North had long existed, the traditional black denominations (e.g., Baptists and Methodists) were primarily rural in philosophy if not in origin. They were unprepared to deal with an increasingly militant urban population, and compounding their problem was a bleak financial picture which saw most of them close to bankruptcy.[28] They were incapable of strategic planning; they could not provide aid to the needy.

Some churches—indeed religions—positioned themselves to do precisely those things. The Church of God in Christ (COGIC), founded in the late 1880s and firmly entrenched in Northern cities by the early 1900s, had as one of its basic tenets the caring for the spiritual and economic needs of poor blacks, especially those who were migrating to the cities. In many ways COGIC reflected a radical shift in black religious thought. It welcomed women into its leadership ranks to fill the void created by a lack of male members. Women brought the ministry to urban centers, operating day-care centers and food banks, preaching, working to educate those who came to them. While they could not be ordained, this did not preclude their service.[29]

Committed to social change, COGIC stressed the message of the "brotherhood of man" and insisted that all Christians must develop mutual respect. The theme of self-respect was emphasized in their music and ritual: drums, dancing, and spontaneous speaking hearkened back to African traditions. The Church of God in Christ, committed to empowerment, saw its ministers work to achieve civil rights goals through antipoverty programs, with self-improvement achieved through economic growth.

Some of the same messages made their way into another religion, Islam, increasingly popular with blacks. The Nation of Islam, like COGIC, came to life in the United States in the 1930s; its founder, Master Farad Muhammad, stressed the concept of "self-help." The self-help message of the Muslims, enunciated by its two most vocal proponents, Elijah Muhammad and Malcolm X, had great appeal for those who had lost faith in mainstream religion.

From a historical perspective, the timing of the introduction of Islam into the black community could not have been better. The Nation of Islam made its major strides during the 1960s and 1970s, when optimism, vision, and social activism were still possible. The teachings of Malcolm X in particular brought many black Americans back to religion, helping them to find a place for themselves in society. It had a unique recruitment strategy. Whereas traditionally the churches had served primarily the middle and working classes, the Muslims sought the poor, the young, and, most importantly, those with criminal records. The Muslims reached out to groups in greatest need, for the most part neglected by the mainstream Protestant denominations.

Probably the single greatest contribution of Islam to black America was the ideology of black pride and black power.[30] Muslim leaders, like the leaders of COGIC, were concerned above all with empowerment. Unlike many other religious leaders, the Muslim leaders did not steer clear of the civil rights issue. Attempting to reverse the extremist tide of resistance to human rights by cautioning black leaders and challenging them to take proactive stances, they spoke out against the flagrant atrocities which were attributable to "Christians," calling on all whites to share collectively the burden of guilt for the racial turmoil in the United States. They gave positive support to organizations concerned with self-help.

Islam, a growing religion within the black community, is especially popular among young black males. Lincoln and Mamiya argue that a great deal of that popularity may be attributed to the macho image projected by Malcolm X who "was viewed by many as the uncompromising critic of American society."[31] Malcolm X, believing that American society was reluctant to change, especially in the area of race relations and power distribution, argued that black Americans had to take the initiative in altering race relations. Many who criticized the black Muslims argued that their principal message was one of hate, which rendered all whites and Jews as the ultimate enemy.

Black nationalism, as advocated by Malcolm X and other Muslim leaders, is viewed today by many as reverse discrimination and prejudice. There may be some justification for this sentiment, all the more unfortunate because of the good work which has been done by Muslims in the black communities, specifically their work with the poor. It would indeed be tragic if the racial extremism and cultural elitism which the Muslims argued against became their own most distinctive feature.

CONCLUSION

All we preachers is [sic] supposed to do is to preach the Lord and Savior Jesus Christ and Him Crucified, and that's all.[32]

As the preceding quote from Myrdal's study suggests, it was the view of most religious leaders, especially Southerners, that the churches had no business becoming involved in political and social matters such as race relations. By harassing moderate ministers, the extremist political elements in the South created a climate of fear which deterred great numbers of churchmen from speaking out. Even when the racial situation became overtly violent, when the churches had the opportunity to exert their influence, they rarely made their voices heard. Many blacks, disillusioned with the churches, saw their silence on civil rights issues as evidence of an unwillingness to help.

The failure of the churches to meet the needs of urban blacks led to dramatic increases in membership in COGIC and the Nation of Islam. These religious bodies, unlike the mainstream Christian denominations. were socially concerned, intent on being proactive. The black community, having changed, looked to a new set of institutions for help. Black churches, if they are to remain viable, will have to adapt to the changing demands of a population which is now more diverse than at any time in the past. Still, it must be said that Myrdal saw the significance of the Islamic "cults" more than fifty years ago. If the movement was smaller then, it was already antiwhite. As Myrdal explained, the Black Muslims "look to the brown peoples of Asia Minor and North Africa to save them from the whites."[33] When he wrote, the Muslims were few in number. Far more important was another antiwhite group, the African Orthodox Church, which owed its origins to the Garvey movement of the 1920s. Affiliated with the Greek Orthodox Church, it had, according to Myrdal, somewhat abated its antiwhite stance, but it was still a church of protest.[34] So, also, was the Abyssinian Baptist Church in Harlem, led by the Rev. A. Clayton Powell, which boasted eight thousand members in 1939, the largest black congregation in the city.[35] Powell was active in sponsoring community welfare work, but also in finding employ for blacks. Myrdal, half a century ago, saw that black youths were "abandoning" the churches in numbers greater than was common among whites, except, interestingly, for young Jews. He attributed the trend to "increased education and sophistication among blacks," but also to the "backwardness" of their churches, as evidenced in their "emotionalism and puritanism."[36] If, as in white America, church membership conferred respectability, blacks, on marrying, Myrdal wrote, could be expected to join a church, though not necessarily that of their parents.[37]

If black Americans were predominantly Protestant in Myrdal's day, their church affiliations, as with whites, reflected their social standing. The greatest number attended churches that resembled "any lower class Protestant church."[38] Except for the emotionalism characteristic of the service, there were no theological innovations worthy of mention.[39] While "race" might figure in the sermon, particularly in Northern churches, there was little in the service itself to suggest that it was a black church. Still, the Negro spirituals would not be heard in a white church, and the preacher's manner—his way of speaking and his body language—like the responses of the congregation suggested a difference. Myrdal thought the difference with "lower class white churches in isolated regions" was not very great.[40] There were the same Sunday schools, the same voluntary organizations, even the same hymns, with an even more urgent need to collect money from the small congregations, to avert bankruptcy.[41]

If there was little "inter-racial cooperation" between white and black churches in Myrdal's day, the situation today has not changed dramatically. The "insincerity of white people" was constantly alluded to.[42] Myrdal put the matter very succinctly when he wrote: "The great majority of white churches, in the North as well as in the South, thus do not want to have a substantial Negro membership. The great majority of Negroes do not seem to want to join white churches, even if they are allowed."[43] Has very much changed in half a century?

Poverty and cultural isolation were wreaking havoc then. They still do. The conditions that made the black ministry less attractive in Myrdal's day have become even more powerful since. The brightest and the most ambitious have no thought to become preachers and the consequences for the black churches have been what Myrdal most feared—a loss of influence in the black communities.[44] If few Christian churches had been "the spearheads of reform,"[45] Myrdal was not without hope. He looked particularly to the young, to the better educated, even to the "new cults," hoping that "emotionalism" would diminish, that the "professional evangelist" would disappear, that the sermons would be "more thought-provoking," that all this would advance the "general process of acculturation."[46] It is precisely that process which is today in question. The mixing of the races that Myrdal had so much hoped for is today being questioned, not only by these academics who speak in the name of "multiculturalism" but by those preachers and religious leaders more generally who imagine that the condition of millions of blacks will not be "ameliorated" by such means. They, in their longstanding and continuing disappointments with the white record, seek other solutions for the problems of the black people in the United States. This cannot fail to affect those religious bodies which aspire to be agencies of change, indeed agencies of power.

NOTES

I would like to give special thanks to my graduate assistant, Rustin Lewis, and my colleague Robert McDuff for all of their research on this paper.

1. Gunnar Myrdal. *An American Dilemma: The Negro Problem and Modern Democracy* (New York: Harper & Brothers, 1944), p. 858.
2. Ibid., p. 867; and W.E.B. Du Bois. *The Negro Church* (Atlanta: Atlanta University Press, 1980).
3. C. Eric Lincoln and Lawrence H. Mamiya. *The Black Church In the African American Experience* (Durham, N.C.: Duke University Press, 1993), pp. 11, 209.

4. Myrdal, p. 859

5. Ibid., p. 877.

6. Harold F. Kaufman. *Mississippi Churches: A Half Century of Change* (Social Science Research Center—Mississippi State University, 1959), pp. 10–11.

7. Ed King. "White Churches." Unpublished manuscript, Jackson, Miss., 1969), Chap. 1, p. 5.

8. "The Concerned." *Newsweek* (November 5, 1962), p. 99.

9. James Silver. *Mississippi: The Closed Society*, 2nd ed. (New York: Harcourt, Brace, & World, 1966), p. 6.

10. Neil McMillen. *The Citizens Council* (Urbana: University of Illinois Press, 1971), p. 11.

11. Silver, p. 45.

12. Hearing Before the United States Commission on Civil Rights, Vol. II (Jackson, Miss.: Administration of Justice, February 16–20, 1965).

13. *Jackson Daily News*, September 28, 1963.

14. *New Orleans Times-Picayune*, October 7, 1963, and King, Chap. 1, p. 30.

15. C. Vann Woodward. *The Burden of Southern History* (Baton Rouge: L.S.S. Press, 1960), p. 14.

16. Martin Luther King, Jr. *Why We Can't Wait* (New York: Harper & Row, 1964, 1965), pp. 87–90.

17. August Meier and Elliott Rudwick. *From Plantation to Ghetto* (New York: Hill and Wang, 1970), p. 241.

18. Meier and Rudwick, op. cit.

19. Robert M. Franklin. "'My Soul Says Yes': The Urban Ministry of the Church of God in Christ." Unpublished manuscript.

20. Cornel West. *Prophsey, Deliverance* (Philadelphia: Westminister Press, 1982).

21. Myrdal, p. 877.

22. West, pp. 280–295.

23. Ibid.

24. James H. Cone. *My Soul Looks Back* (Nashville, Tenn.: Abingdon, 1982), p. 91.

25. Ibid., pp. 76–80.

26. Ibid., p. 78.

27. Ibid., p. 79.

28. Benjamin Mays and Joseph Nicholson. *The Negro Church* (New York: Russel and Russel, 1969).

29. Franklin, op. cit.

30. Lincoln and Memiya, op. cit.

31. Ibid.

32. Myrdal, p. 876.

33. Ibid., p. 862

34. Ibid.

35. Ibid., p. 863

36. Ibid.

37. Ibid.

38. Ibid., p. 866.

39. Ibid.
40. Ibid.
41. Ibid., p. 867.
42. Ibid., p. 868.
43. Ibid., p. 871.
44. Ibid., p. 876.
45. Ibid., p. 877.
46. Ibid., p. 878.

Susan Welch · Michael W. Combs
Lee Sigelman · Timothy Bledsoe

Justice for All:
Still An American Dilemma

GUNNAR MYRDAL'S analysis of "an American dilemma" focused on the so-called American Creed, a set of values that emphasize individual worth and liberty. In powerful language and with hundreds of chilling examples, Myrdal depicted the conflict between these values and the actual treatment of African Americans over the course of American history.[1]

In his chapters on justice, Myrdal highlighted a corollary to the American Creed, the idea that "Negroes are entitled to justice equally with all other people."[2] This corollary was far from being universally accepted in 1944. Today it is far more widely accepted in principle, though far from always in practice. In this chapter we examine Myrdal's arguments about the inequality of justice based on race,[3] describe changes that have occurred in the half century since Myrdal wrote, and focus on some contemporary issues surrounding racial justice in America, spotlighting data over a 25-year period drawn from surveys of black and white respondents in Detroit as well as national data from an 11-year period.[4]

BLACKS, WHITES, AND JUSTICE: THE PAST HALF CENTURY

Racial Justice in the 1940s

Myrdal argued that the quality of justice received by blacks is tied to the racial attitudes prevalent in a community, the historical traditions that govern the administration of justice in a community, and the degree to which blacks share political power. These three factors, he believed, explained why justice was administered quite differently in the North and the South.

Myrdal thought that white northerners had, for the most part, incorporated blacks within the American Creed and wanted justice to be impartial "regardless of race, creed, or color (p. 529)." He argued, optimistically, that in the North, blacks could generally get justice, although he also saw that blacks' disproportionately lower incomes and levels of education were barriers to the kind of treatment that middle-class individuals received. Why were blacks treated more fairly in the North? Myrdal contended that northerners were further removed from the traditions of slavery; that blacks constituted a small minority in most northern localities, and that blacks in the North tended to have more education, income, and greater organizational strength than their southern counterparts.[5]

In the South, racial injustice was more prevalent, reflecting the more pronounced power differential between blacks and whites. Historical circumstances shaped a political climate of injustice. The South had a relatively recent tradition of slavery, whose legal foundations had given slave owners life-and-death power over slaves. Although some laws during the antebellum period did attempt to regulate arbitrary powers over slaves, these laws were not enforced. This history also led directly to the political disfranchisement and hence the political powerlessness of blacks, which in turn meant that white officials were not accountable to the black public. "The extreme democracy in the American system of justice turns out . . . to be the greatest menace to legal democracy when it is based on restricted political participation and an ingrained tradition of caste suppression" (p. 524), was Myrdal's summary of what was wrong with southern "justice." Except for a few large cities, blacks possessed no influence over the legal system and had no voice in government. The imperatives of election meant that sheriffs, prosecutors, and even judges were responsive to the attitudes of whites, not blacks.

The culture emanating from these historical patterns of race relations influenced the informal socialization as well as the formal education of officials of the justice system. Local justice officials reflected their upbringing in communities where the American Creed did not apply to black citizens.[6]

Yet judges and other highly educated justice officials were susceptible to cross-pressures derived from their legal training and their familiarity with public and legal opinion from outside their community. Indeed, Myrdal believed that better professional training and greater exposure to other norms could improve the quality of justice:

> Lingering inequality in justice in the South is probably due more to low and lagging professional standards—certainly among the police, and in many regions even among the lawyers who are willing to enter into court service—than it is to opinion in favor of legal inequality. [p.534]

Finally, Myrdal believed that inequality in the justice system was aggravated by the low level of education, political weakness, and poverty of most southern blacks. These problems meant that class as well as racial barriers stood in the way of fair treatment.

Because of the injustice of the "justice" system, blacks' trust in government was low. This was particularly true of their attitudes toward the police, whom they perceived as protectors of an oppressive racist system rather than as enforcers of an impartial law. Injustice also enhanced solidarity among blacks in their stance toward the justice system. Police often beat black suspects on the way to jail or once they were there and, in general, many police officers believed that black suspects or any black who showed signs of insubordination should be punished bodily. This tradition of police brutality shaped blacks' attitudes toward the police and the system of "justice" they enforced. Myrdal pointed out:

> The arrested Negro often acquires the prestige of a victim, a martyr, or a hero, even when he is simply a criminal. It becomes part of race pride in the protective Negro community not to give up a fellow Negro who is hunted by the police. Negroes who collaborate with the police [are] looked upon as stool pigeons. [p. 525]

Racial Justice and the Kerner Commission

The South that Myrdal described was slowly changing even as he wrote. The pace of change accelerated dramatically during the 1950s as the civil rights movement gathered momentum and as the Supreme Court began to chip away at the legal foundations of segregation. Those foundations were cast aside with the passage of the Civil Rights Act of 1964 and the Voting Rights Act of 1965. No longer would elected officials in the South be responsive only to their white constituents.

Yet Americans quickly learned that the demise of legal segregation did not usher in a new era of racial harmony. Old patterns of race relations and the impact of centuries of subordination and injustice could not be eradicated in a day, a month, or a year. Nowhere did the old patterns seem to persist more than in the justice system, especially in the relations between blacks and the police. Nor were these problems restricted to the South, for race relations appeared to be almost as tense in large northern metropolitan areas as in rural communities of the South. No longer small minorities in the great northern cities, black communities grew ever larger, and to whites in these cities ever more threatening in their potential political and economic power.

Along with unemployment, poor housing, and other conditions linked to poverty, the justice system continued to be a focus of racial tensions. In the late 1960s these tensions exploded into violence in major cities across the nation. In Detroit in 1967 a police raid on an after-hours black nightclub sparked several days of death and destruction. In Newark that same summer, and in other cities after the assassination of Dr. Martin Luther King, Jr., the following summer, more death and destruction ensued. As a consequence, President Lyndon Johnson appointed the National Advisory Commission on Civil Disorders, chaired by Illinois Governor Otto Kerner, to investigate the causes of the riots. The Commission declared that the nation was moving toward "two separate societies, one black, one white . . . separate and unequal." Its intensive review of both the deep-rooted and the proximate causes of the disorder characterized bitterness toward police behavior in black neighborhoods as the deepest source of resentment sparking the riots. Blacks resented the police for their frequent brutality, harassment, and enforcement of two standards of justice.

Surveys by the Commission found that black grievances against police practices, including verbal and physical abuse of blacks by police, discrimination against blacks who applied for jobs as police officers, lack of respect shown to blacks, and the failure of the police to protect black citizens from crime in their neighborhoods, were rivaled in seriousness only by grievances about unemployment and inadequate housing.[7] Most blacks believed that police harassed black suspects, and most officers did hold prejudiced attitudes. Indeed, only 1 percent of the officers employed in predominantly black districts had attitudes "which could be described as sympathetic toward Negroes. . . . Close to half showed extreme prejudice" (p. 306).[8]

In white communities rigorous standards of law enforcement were implemented, but in black communities a less demanding standard allowed drug addiction, prostitution, and street violence to flourish. Response to black complaints was slow, and the responding police were overwhelmingly white. The small numbers of black police officers and the even smaller numbers of black higher officials within the police force reinforced the perception of many blacks that the police were agents of the dominant white community.

Discrimination in the rest of the justice system was another grievance, though generally of lower intensity. Respondents in the Kerner Commission surveys were as likely to complain about the inadequacy of federal programs, municipal services, and welfare programs, for example, as they were to complain about discrimination in the justice system.

Based on its findings, the Commission offered a number of recommendations for change. It emphasized the recruitment and promotion of black officers, the training of white officers in professional behavior and sensitivity to blacks, and the provision of mechanisms by which citizens could voice complaints about poor treatment.

Race and Justice Today

In some ways, the United States has come a long way from the world of Gunnar Myrdal, and even from the world of the Kerner Commission. Blacks have won the right to vote, and in many communities their votes determine who wins and who loses. In some communities, the majority of elected officials are blacks. In most communities, especially in big cities, police forces reflect the racial composition of the community much more closely than they did 25 years ago. Between 1970 and 1990, the number of black police officers nearly tripled.[9]

Yet racial distrust has lingered, and, some would say, even intensified. The "two separate societies, one black, one white" remain. Tensions between police and blacks remain the focus of headlines. Blacks are disproportionately the victims when police kill civilians, though analysts disagree about the extent to which racism is responsible.[10] Rodney King became a household word, and many feel that his beating was unique only because it was captured on videotape.[11] The original acquittal of the officers charged with the King beating seemed to confirm the verdict that little had changed.

But at another level, some changes have occurred. Most Americans were outraged by the King beatings. Nearly two-thirds of whites and 92 percent of blacks thought the officers should have been convicted, as two of them later were. Yet, while 78 percent of blacks agreed with the assessment that the original acquittal meant that "blacks cannot get justice in this country," 66 percent of the white public disagreed (Edsall 1992). The racial divide persists.

In the rest of this chapter, we explore how blacks and whites see justice in America, and how these views have changed. Unfortunately, national longitudinal data on these topics are scarce. But we have two sources for our exploration. First, we examine some longitudinal General Social Survey data to determine racial differences in opinions about appropriate police behavior. These data span 1973 to 1993. We then take a more detailed look at attitudes about the police and the quality of policing in communities. The analysis is based on a variety of surveys done in Detroit during 1959 to 1992. Detroit is an especially appropriate site in that Myrdal considered it notable for its inhospitality to blacks, and its racial disturbances in 1967 were instrumental in the appointment of the Kerner Commission.

PUBLIC ATTITUDES TOWARD APPROPRIATE POLICE BEHAVIOR

The General Social Survey, conducted by the National Opinion Research Center, provides social scientists and the public with a view of changing public attitudes on a variety of issues. Although the survey has tapped an extensive variety of opinions about race, it has not traced many opinions about the police or their behavior. Still, one important set of questions asked respondents about their view of possible times when it would be appropriate for a police officer to strike an adult male. These questions were asked in most years from 1973 through 1993.

First, respondents were asked: "Are there any situations you can imagine in which you would approve of a policeman striking an adult male citizen?" Averaging all years, we find significant racial differences in responses to these questions. Blacks are much less likely than whites to agree that it would be appropriate for police to hit an adult male. Still, slightly over half of all blacks (54 percent) do say they can think of such circumstances, compared to 79 percent of all whites. Undoubtedly, the greater reluctance of blacks to endorse such conduct reflects the greater likelihood of blacks' being victims of police homicide and other brutality, and the general distrust of the police.

Given our interest in longitudinal trends, Figure 9.1 is interesting in its portrayal of rather static opinions. Over this 21-year period, neither black

Figure 9.1

Attitudes toward police use of force, by race.

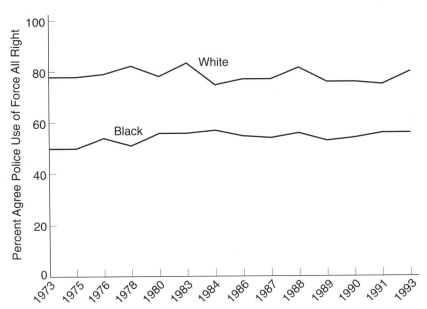

Source: General Social Survey data: Data for blacks averaged over three years to smooth the curve.

nor white opinions have varied much. Blacks have ranged from 50–57 percent support, while whites ranged from 75–82 percent. Because of the small number of blacks sampled in most years of the GSS, we have averaged black responses over a 3-year period in order to eliminate sharp variations due mostly to small sample sizes. With that caveat, we can see that the differences between blacks and whites have averaged between 20–30 percent during the entire period, with perhaps a slight tendency for the gap to be narrower toward the end of the series.[12]

Figure 9.1 illustrates that black (and white) opinions about appropriate police behavior have varied little over the last two decades. We might expect that racial differences in attitudes toward the police would diminish if the question was more specific; the general nature of the question asked by the GSS allows each individual to imagine the conditions under which the policeman is striking the citizen. Blacks might be more likely than whites to visualize an innocent person being harassed by the police.

We can test this expectation, by analyzing some more specific questions that the GSS poses following this general question:

Would you approve of a policeman striking a citizen who was being questioned as a suspect in a murder case?

> Who had said vulgar and obscene things to the policeman?
>
> Who was attempting to escape from custody?
>
> Who was attacking the policeman with his fists?

Figure 9.2 shows racial differences in responses to these items. On three of the four items, providing specific contexts causes racial differences to shrink dramatically. Neither whites nor blacks approve of police violence when the person is being questioned for murder or when the suspect verbally abuses the police. Both blacks and whites approve of police use of force when the suspect attacks the police with his fists. The largest difference between blacks and whites is when a police officer is subduing a suspect who is attempting to escape from custody. In that circumstance, racial differences are significant, with 83 percent of whites but only 59 percent of blacks agreeing that force is appropriate. Here again, this racial difference might reflect the fact that whites are more likely to believe that suspects are guilty, but blacks that suspects may be victims of police harassment rather than perpetrators of crimes.

Given the striking regional differences that underlay race relations in Myrdal's time, we examined these attitudes to determine if blacks in the South were similar to northern blacks in their views of the police. Perhaps surprisingly, we found no regional differences. Black and white differences, and similarities, were the same in the South as in the North.

Figure 9.2

Approval of police use of force under various circumstances, by race.

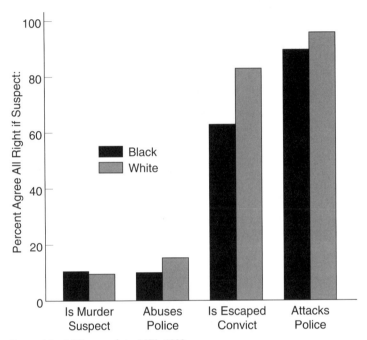

Source: General Social Survey data: 1973–1993.

CHANGING VIEWS OF JUSTICE IN DETROIT

The limitations of the GSS led us to turn to a series of studies of Detroit for a closer look at racial differences in attitudes toward the police. Detroit is an old industrial city of the Frostbelt whose population peaked at about two and a half million residents in the mid-1950s. During the 1950s many people began to leave the city for its suburbs, and many new residents of the area settled immediately in the suburbs. Today, Detroit's population barely tops one million, but its suburbs hold more than three million residents in the immediate three-county area.

At the time of the Kerner Commission report, Detroit was controlled by whites. It had a white mayor, a white city council, and a white police force. In a community where 39 percent of the population was black, only 5 percent of police officers were black.[13] Today, blacks control the mayor's office and the city council and comprise fully 55 percent of the police force. But two decades after the first African American was elected mayor, Detroit's metropolitan area is still regarded as one of the most highly segregated in the nation (Massey and Denton 1993).

Detroit thus offers an appropriate site to examine changing views about race and justice. It is also a useful site because of the availability of survey data extending over 30 years. The major part of our analyses is based primarily on two surveys, one conducted in 1968 as part of the Kerner Commission study of the urban riots,[14] and a second conducted in 1992.[15] We also examine other survey data stretching back to 1959.

Evaluations of the Police

One measure of how black citizens assess the justice system is their level of satisfaction with their local police. Does the fact that Detroit now is controlled by an African American local government positively influence the reaction of black Detroiters to the police? Of course, any assessment of the effectiveness of police services depends not only on the services themselves but also on the seriousness of crime in the neighborhood. Even so, evaluations of police effectiveness reflect a perception of fair treatment and responsiveness as well as crime-solving.

Figure 9.3 reports some black and white evaluations of the police in 1992. Respondents were asked whether they believed that the police would respond as quickly to their call as to the call of a person for the other race; whether the police provide enough protection in their neighborhood; and whether police officers, if given a right to stop and search people who look suspicious, would use this against blacks.

In each case, blacks voiced considerably greater distrust of the police than did whites. In 1992, three times as many whites as blacks (61–19 percent) said that the police provide enough protection in their neighborhood. Only a bare majority (52 percent) of blacks believed that the police would respond as quickly to their call for help as they would to a white person's call. And nearly all blacks (89 percent) agreed that police officers would use the right of stop and search against blacks (61 percent of whites believed the same).

Another piece of evidence on how blacks view the police stems from Detroit's own version of the Rodney King incident. In November 1992 several members of the Detroit Police Department repeatedly kicked, punched, and bludgeoned Malice Green, a black Detroit resident, who subsequently died from "blunt force trauma to the head." Seven officers (six whites and their black supervisor) were suspended for their roles in the beating. This incident occurred while our survey was being conducted. Although 90 percent of our respondents had already been interviewed, nearly one hundred interviews were carried out afterwards, allowing for an examination of the impact of that beating on respondents' views of the police.

Figure 9.3

Positive attitudes toward the Detroit police, by race.

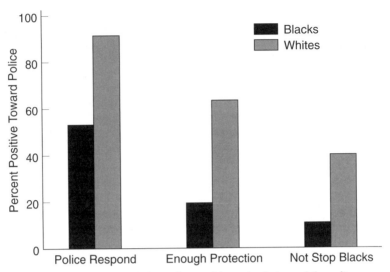

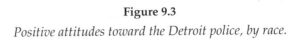

Source: Authors' survey. Items coded to reflect positive attitude toward the police.

Before the incident occurred, 80 percent of the blacks in our sample stated that a "Rodney King–like incident could happen here," reflecting a deep distrust of the police and the justice system. After the Malice Green beating, nearly every black (99 percent) agreed with this statement, and the proportion of whites who agreed rose dramatically, from 24–63 percent. Thus, even before the Green incident, black Detroiters distrust in their police was quite deep; afterwards it was nearly universal.

It is useful to situate black assessments of the police today in light of their past assessments. To trace longitudinal changes, we have results from surveys done in Detroit in 1959, 1971, and 1992 (Bledsoe 1990). Blacks' satisfaction with police service actually *dropped* dramatically from 1959 through 1990.[16] In 1959 about 20 percent more blacks were likely to say they were very satisfied with police service than said they were dissatisfied (Figure 9.4). By 1971 about 20 percent more were dissatisfied than very satisfied; and by 1990 about 25 percent more were dissatisfied. Thus, most of the decrease in satisfaction occurred between 1959 and 1971, when the police department was still dominated by whites. The election of a black mayor and the transformation of the police into a majority black unit slowed but did not reverse the downward trend.

We can contrast this with trends in white opinion toward the police. In 1959, as one might predict from Myrdal's and Kerner's analysis of the re-

Figure 9.4

Satisfaction with police service in Detroit, by race.

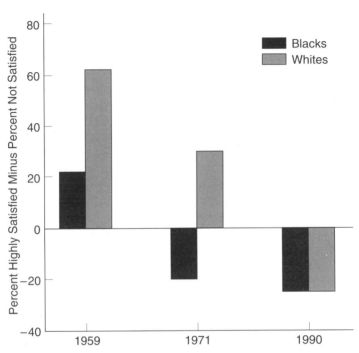

Source: Bledsoe, 1990.

lationship of the police to the white-dominated society, whites were much more satisfied with the police than were blacks. The excess of positive over negative views was extremely high, over 60 percent. Satisfaction waned somewhat over the next 12 years, but whites' views were still very positive, and the racial difference in satisfaction with the police remained rather constant. However, between 1971 and 1990, white satisfaction with the police plummeted—white dissatisfaction with the police now equals black dissatisfaction. Thus, having the membership of the police more closely reflect the racial makeup of the community has not improved black satisfaction, and it may have reduced white satisfaction. Racial equality has been achieved in public assessments of this key government service, but certainly not in the way that Myrdal and the Kerner Commission would have hoped.

We can compare responses to similar (though not identical) questions asked in the 1968 and 1992 surveys about satisfaction with police protection in the respondents' neighborhoods (Figure 9.5).[17] Blacks have become

Figure 9.5

Satisfaction with police protection: 1968 and 1992, by race.

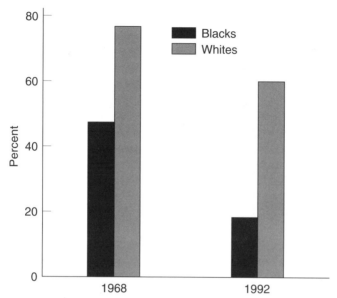

Source: Authors' survey and 1968 Kerner Commission Survey.

significantly less satisfied with the police protection provided their neighborhoods, while whites have become somewhat less satisfied. As a result, the racial divide between blacks and whites in the perceived safety afforded by police has increased. Compared to the average white living in the Detroit area, the average black feels even less secure than he or she did a quarter century ago.

What is not apparent from this simple comparison of blacks and whites is the dramatic importance of location on evaluations of police protection. Assessments of police protection among black Detroit residents have dropped noticeably, but evaluations of police protection among white Detroit residents have dropped more than twice as much. Indeed, in sharp contrast to the situation of 1968, today there is no racial difference in Detroit residents' evaluations of the police—blacks and whites offer identical and extremely negative evaluations of the police.

Far more whites live in the suburbs today than did then, and suburban whites are about as content with police protection in their neighborhoods as they were 25 years ago. The suburbanization of whites, then, explains the overall higher ratings that whites give the police.

We take a closer look at these relationships in Figure 9.6, which shows the percentage of blacks and whites who are well satisfied with the protection afforded their neighborhoods by the police. If by equal justice we mean equal protection under the law, it is clear that blacks and whites do not enjoy equal justice in metropolitan Detroit.

If we compare blacks and whites residing in the same mixed-race neighborhoods of the city, we see little difference in views of police protection. Nor is there much difference between the way whites in white city neighborhoods and blacks in black city neighborhoods view police protection. The vast majority of every group living in the city have negative views toward the quality of police protection, and blacks are slightly more positive than whites.

Black and white suburbanites living in mixed-race neighborhoods have similar views of police protection. Both groups are much more positive than any group living in the city. It is only when we turn to blacks and whites living in the suburbs that we find significantly different levels of satisfaction with police services. Whites living in white neighborhoods are over twice as likely to be satisfied than blacks living in black neighborhoods (59–25 per-

Figure 9.6

Satisfaction with police protection: 1992, by race and place of residence.

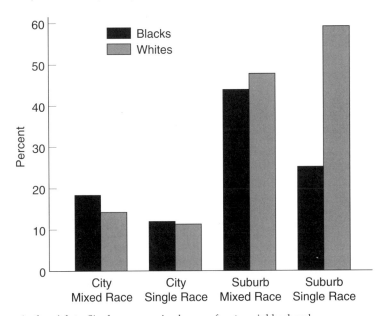

Source: Authors' data. Single race or mixed race refers to neighborhood.

cent). This discrepancy reflects the fact that black and white suburbanites in single-race neighborhoods are likely to live in different suburbs.

In general then, when we control for location, race differences in satisfaction with police service are negligible, with the exception being single-race suburban neighborhoods. However, this conclusion overstates the equality in police protection because it does not reflect the proportion of blacks and whites living in each type of location. For example, while it is true that whites living in white Detroit neighborhoods are as unhappy with police protection as are blacks living in black Detroit neighborhoods, it is also true that whites in this living condition are only 3 percent of the metropolitan white population, but blacks living in this condition are 54 percent of all metropolitan blacks. And while suburban blacks in mixed-race neighborhoods are relatively pleased with their police protection, only 10 percent of metropolitan blacks are in these neighborhoods.

The stark racial contrast in satisfaction with police services is best illustrated by the fact that those whites with the highest levels of satisfaction, those living in white suburban neighborhoods, are 84 percent of all whites in the Detroit metropolitan area. Those blacks in the least satisfied group, central-city blacks in black neighborhoods, are 54 percent of all metropolitan blacks. Controls for location, then, reveal the source of frustration with police services, but they conceal the real differences in attitudes between most blacks and most whites in the metropolitan area.

The complexity of these patterns becomes even more obvious when we relate these satisfaction levels to the control of government. For it is in the black-controlled city where blacks are least satisfied with police protection, and in the white-controlled suburbs where they are much more satisfied. Thus, unlike in Myrdal's era, and even that of Kerner, when one could attribute police brutality and neglect of African American needs to the absence of black control over government, today the relationship is not that simple. The social ills bred by poverty and leading to a miasma of crime and violence must bear a major responsibility for the dissatisfaction of city residents with the police.

DISCUSSION

Myrdal argued that the quality of justice received by blacks is tied to the racial attitudes of the community, the historical traditions that governed the administration of justice, and the amount of political power that blacks possess in a community.

Today, blacks possess considerably more political power than they did in 1944. Their power is particularly great in many large communities, like Detroit, where they control the apparatus of local government. Yet even in those cities, satisfaction with the justice system is low. Indeed, in Detroit, satisfaction with police service has continued to decline even under a black mayor. Thus, while political power has eroded the most blatant injustices of the justice system, it alone has proven not sufficient to provide an adequate system of justice that protects black citizens as well as treating them fairly.

The historical traditions shaping the justice system will take decades to erode. In the South, the role of the police and other law enforcement officials has been shaped by decades of slavery and then legalized discrimination. In most of the North, there is no tradition of slavery, but there is a strong tradition of discrimination, some legal, some extralegal.

In the era of legal segregation, police discrimination against blacks was legal and expected. Although the laws and police behavior have changed, the residues of segregation and discrimination remain. These residues remain in the actions of police who sometimes violate the rights of African Americans, as well as in residual influence on the attitudes of blacks. More directly, the data suggest that blacks are distrustful of the police, even when the uniform is worn by a black person. Blacks, like whites, are not supportive of police when their homes and neighborhoods are not safe. This suggests the limitations of the acquisition of political power in eradicating historical patterns that are ever more remotely grounded in present political realities. As we saw in the national surveys, when asked a general question about appropriate police behavior, black Americans are far more likely than whites to want to limit police discretion. When more details of the context for police action are provided, black attitudes become much closer to those of whites, suggesting that blacks probably expect the same sort of law enforcement as do whites, but that, in theory, the police are viewed as symbols of oppression.

An important finding from our Detroit survey data is that place of residence shapes the responses of blacks to the police. Blacks in the suburbs feel differently about the police than do those in the city, no doubt reflecting their different experiences of neighborhood crime and safety. Indeed, within the city, blacks and whites have similar views about the police, and the same is true in suburban mixed-race neighborhoods. Only in suburban single-race communities do blacks and whites differ in their evaluation of the police. Nonetheless, despite the fact that in similar circumstances, blacks and whites have similar evaluations of the police, relatively few metropolitan Detroit blacks are in the kinds of circumstances that lead to more positive views of the police. Thus, the segregation of African Americans into central-city locations reinforces the differential quality of justice that blacks and whites receive, even though the control of the police in the city is in the hands of African Americans.

In sum, we have come a long way from the America of Gunnar Myrdal. Attitudes have changed and continue to change. Blacks have gained substantial political power. And the historical traditions of slavery and legal discrimination are fading into the past. But differential patterns of justice remain. Bringing about a justice system that is truly just remains an American dilemma.

NOTES

1. Except where quoting from the original text, we use the terms *black* or *African American* in this chapter even though Myrdal's references were to Negroes.
2. Gunnar Myrdal. *An American Dilemma* (New York: McGraw-Hill, 1964), p. 526.
3. Ibid., Chap. 24.
4. We touch only briefly on two other important aspects of justice in America, police behavior and sentencing, because these are examined in other papers.
5. Myrdal did remark that blacks fared worse in the border states, and in certain northern cities, such as Detroit, with large numbers of southern immigrants.
6. Later events showed that during the civil rights era, southern federal judges were largely representative of their communities in supporting segregation. Only southern judges who had been educated outside the south and were less connected to their communities supported a more integrationist policy (Peltason 1961).
7. The Commission sponsored surveys in fifteen cities and four suburbs to ascertain the attitudes of blacks and whites about race relations. See U.S. Kerner Commission. *Report of the National Advisory Commission on Civil Disorders* (New York: E.P. Dutton, 1968), pp. 143–150.
8. The study cited is that of Albert Reiss.
9. Blacks filled over 40 percent of new police officer positions created during that time (Hacker 1992, p. 130).
10. Jaynes and Williams 1989, pp. 478–479. Some research suggests that police are more likely to shoot blacks because blacks are more likely to be armed with guns or be involved in criminal activities (Milton 1977; Fyfe 1981), but also that the rate of police shootings of blacks is much less when police departments have stringent policies on use of firearms and stringent reviews when they are used (Fyfe 1982; Sherman 1980).
11. Representative John Conyers called this "the most heinous, vicious, brutal police brutality case that has been recorded for all time" (Edmonds, March 13, 1991), but he was obviously temporarily forgetting the history of blacks in America during most of the nineteenth and twentieth centuries.
12. Our 3-year averages (except at the ends of the time series, when 2 years were averaged) does hide the 1991 dip in black support for police striking an adult male. This dip was undoubtedly due to the Rodney King incident. Interestingly, while black support was 59 percent and 60 percent in the 2 years

preceding 1992, it shot up to 69 percent in 1993, the next GSS after the incident. Of course, the sample sizes are small in each of these years.

13. Black police were more representative of the community population in several cities with large black populations, though none approached proportionality. Philadelphia, for example, had 29 percent black population and 20 percent black police force; St Louis, 37 percent and 11 percent respectively, Atlanta, 38 percent and 10 percent, Chicago 27 percent and 17 percent. Detroit was more similar to Baltimore (41 percent and 7 percent), Cleveland (34 percent and 7 percent), Memphis (38 percent and 5 percent), and New Orleans (41 percent, 4 percent).

14. Under the direction of Angus Campell and Howard Schuman, this 15-city survey included Detroit. About 200 black and 200 white residents of Detroit and 200 white suburban residents were interviewed. The roughly equal number of white city and suburban respondents conveniently approximates the population split between city and suburbs at the time.

15. This survey was conducted by Wayne State University's Center for Urban Studies with support from the National Science Foundation. Also like the first, the second sample strictly matched race of interviewer to race of respondent. This sample included about 300 blacks and 230 whites in Detroit, and about 230 whites and 350 blacks in the suburbs. The data are weighted to reflect the true population parameters in adjusting for this disproportionate stratified sample.

16. "Are you well satisfied, more or less satisfied, or not at all satisfied with the protection provided for your neighborhood by the police?"

17. The 1968 Kerner study question reads: "I'd like to ask you how satisfied you are with some of the main services the city is supposed to provide for your neighborhood. What about the quality of police protection in this neighborhood—are you generally satisfied, somewhat dissatisfied, or very dissatisfied?" The similar item drawn from our 1992 study read: "Are you [well satisfied, more or less satisfied, or not satisfied at all] with the police protection provided for your neighborhood?"

Samuel Walker

10

"A Strange Atmosphere of Consistent Illegality": Myrdal on "The Police and Other Public Contacts"

POLICING IN THE SOUTH, concluded Gunnar Myrdal, was marked by "a strange atmosphere of consistent illegality." He found a pattern of systematic police lawlessness directed against African Americans.[1] The abuses included physical brutality, unjustified shootings, arrests without legal pretext, and failure to arrest whites who committed crimes against African Americans.

Fifty years later some observers might argue that little has changed. Police misconduct, particularly the excessive use of force against racial minorities, remains a serious national problem. The widely broadcast videotape of Los Angeles police officers beating Rodney King on March 3, 1991, made visible what many African Americans believe to be a common occurrence in the big cities of the United States. An investigation of corruption in the New York City police department found a complete failure to punish rampant violence directed against racial minority citizens.[2]

Many observers regarded the riots that followed the acquittal of four Los Angeles police officers involved in the beating as an expression of pent-up rage over the failure of the entire justice system to respond to the interests of minority communities.[3] Public opinion polls over the past quarter-century have consistently found that African Americans have less confidence in the criminal justice system, and the police in particular, than do white Americans. The Gallup Poll reported in 1993 that 74 percent of blacks (as compared with 35 percent of whites) felt that blacks were "treated more harshly in this country's criminal justice system."[4]

It would be a mistake, however, to think that nothing has changed in police–race relations since the 1940s. Even a cursory reading of Chapter 25 of *An American Dilemma* reveals that a genuine revolution in southern policing has occurred.[5]

The most important change has been the demise of Jim Crow, the system of institutionalized segregation. Myrdal's basic thesis in Chapter 25 was that the primary role of the police in the South was to maintain the racial caste system. That role defined routine police activity and explained nearly all of the observed problems. Today, the racial caste system is gone, swept away by the civil rights movement between the mid-1950s and mid-1960s. Supreme Court decisions and federal legislation have ended de jure segregation. Although racial discrimination continues to be a national problem, police problems in the southeastern states do not differ in any fundamental way from those in the rest of the country: policing in Atlanta and New Orleans is not fundamentally different from policing in Boston and Seattle.[6] The revolution in southern policing, in short, involves the integration of the region into the broader patterns of American society.

MYRDAL ON THE POLICE: CONTRIBUTIONS AND LIMITATIONS

A Valuable Historical Document

Chapter 25 of *An American Dilemma* offers an extremely useful benchmark for analyzing the degree of change in policing in the south.[7] A richly anecdotal account, it is a valuable historical document, describing the special character of policing in the Jim Crow era. As this era in American history recedes further into the past and the number of people with first-hand experience of it steadily diminishes, memories steadily vanish.

Published accounts of southern policing in the Jim Crow era are rare. Prior to 1944 there were numerous reports on American policing, including investigations by federal, state, and local crime commissions,[8] along with national surveys by Raymond Fosdick[9] and Bruce Smith.[10] None of these reports examined the role of southern police in maintaining the racial caste system as did Myrdal. The 1931 *Report on Lawlessness in Law Enforcement* by the federal Wickersham Commission was a landmark in documenting the problem of police abuse. It contained detailed reports on fifteen cities, but only Dallas and El Paso could be considered southern, and there was no discussion of the Deep South states of Mississippi, Alabama, Georgia, or South Carolina.[11]

In short, Myrdal's chapter stands as the most detailed contemporary account of this special part of American police history.

Limited Geographical Focus

Unfortunately, Myrdal's study suffers from several serious limitations. Most serious is its limited geographic focus. Despite the fact that *An American Dilemma* purports to be a national study of American race relations, it concentrated exclusively on the thirteen states of the old Confederacy. Consequently, it is not a national survey of the relations between African Americans and the police.

Myrdal's failure to conduct a national survey limits the value of his observations in several important respects. His description of police–race problems offers no perspective on the extent to which southern patterns were similar to or different from those in the rest of the country. Had Myrdal's team broadened its focus, it would have found abundant evidence that severe police–community relations problems did exist outside of the South at that time. The year before *An American Dilemma* was published there were major urban racial disorders in several cities outside the South, all of which involved police misconduct. NAACP legal counsel Thurgood Marshall, for example, condemned the Detroit police as "the Gestapo"—strong words in the middle of World War II.[12] The 1943 riots, in fact, gave birth to the modern police–community relations movement, defined as a interracial effort to improve policing with respect to the African American community.[13] A national survey of policing would have given Myrdal's observations about the South a much richer context.

From other sources, there is considerable evidence that, independent of race, many of the forms of police misconduct that Myrdal identified in the South were not unique to that region. The Wickersham Commission report on *Lawlessness in Law Enforcement*, although not focusing on racism per se, found systematic police abuse of citizens across the country.[14] The companion Wickersham report on police administrative practices, found low personnel standards in all police departments.[15] A national survey of police practices would have put Myrdal's observations about southern policing in broader perspective and would have helped to identify those features that were unique to that region.

Methodological Problems

Myrdal's description of southern policing is also flawed by the methodology used by his research team. Two aspects are especially problematic. First, the data are almost entirely anecdotal. While Myrdal's account of police mistreatment of African Americans is detailed and evocative, we have no idea how frequently particular acts of lawlessness occurred. Only with respect to employment practices does he rely on survey data. In fairness, it should be noted that the systematic observation of the police in the United States did not begin until many years later.[16]

The second problem, to which we have already alluded, is that Myrdal's team completely ignored the existing literature on the police. A substantial body of federal, state, and local crime commission reports, along with the surveys of such national experts as Raymond B. Fosdick and Bruce Smith were readily available.[17] The most significant sources were two 1931 Wickersham Commission reports, one on police administration and the other on police misconduct.[18] It is astonishing that Myrdal, a social scientist of high repute, did not conduct even the most cursory literature review.[19] The literature would have alerted him and his research team to the national aspects of police problems and helped to give his observations a fuller context.

Despite these serious limitations, however, Chapter 25 remains a valuable report on the unique features of southern policing during an important time and place in American history.

THE POLICE ROLE IN THE RACIAL CASTE SYSTEM

Myrdal's central argument was that southern policing was defined by its role in maintaining the prevailing system of institutionalized segregation. Each individual law enforcement official stood "for `white supremacy' and the whole set of social customs associated with this concept."[20] Directly or indirectly, this special role shaped virtually all aspects of southern policing.

Experts on the police agree that this social institution is invested with the unique role of being the symbol of established authority.[21] For many people the officer on the street is the most tangible personification of the authority of the state. The deployment of police officers throughout the community in highly visible uniforms and patrol cars enhances the symbolic aspect of their role. In the Jim Crow era, the "law" and the "order" that the police represented was the racial caste system. The police did *not* represent the law in the sense of the Anglo-American principles of equal treatment and due process.

SOUTHERN POLICE LAWLESSNESS

General Considerations

The police role in maintaining the racial caste system tolerated, and even encouraged, a form of police lawlessness that appears qualitatively different from that found in the rest of the United States. The evidence is fairly strong on this point but, as we have already suggested, it is anecdotal, and our conclusions must be somewhat tentative. Police lawlessness was a pervasive national problem at the time. The Wickersham Commission report of 1931 found widespread physical brutality, torture, and prolonged detention of arrested persons.[22] Myrdal documented similar practices in the South, but he clearly indicates that they had a distinct purpose related to the caste system.

In a dry and understated style, Myrdal observed: "to enable the policeman to carry out this function [of maintaining the caste system], the courts
are supposed to back him even when he proceeds far outside normal police activity." The phrase "outside normal police activity" was a polite eu-
phemism for the most egregious forms of lawlessness, completely free of
any meaningful accountability.

At the level of the basic encounter between police officer and citizen, the
white police officer's "word must be taken against Negroes without regard
for formal rules of evidence."[23] On this crucial point, southern police lawlessness diverged from national patterns. The Wickersham report, for example, clearly suggests that police officers knew that certain practices were
illegal, and they made at least some effort to conceal them.[24] The report also
indicates that in some instances there was a limited measure of accountability. An extreme case of police abuse might be exposed by a crusading
journalist; there were occasional special investigating commissions; and
some criminal convictions were overturned because of police misconduct.
Thus, there was some recognition of the idea of the rule of law and that
there were limits on what a police officer could do to a citizen. Myrdal, however, found that police mistreatment of African Americans was quite open.
He reported that the worst violations were "freely admitted" by judges and
police officers.[25]

Discrimination in Arrests

Myrdal reported frequent arrests of African Americans even where "it is
clear that their only offense was to resist a white person's unlawful ag-
gression."[26] Many arrests reportedly occurred on buses or streetcars where
the alleged "offense" involved an African American demanding correct
change or failing to yield a seat in the "colored section" to a white person.
African Americans were also often arrested merely for being in a white
neighborhood after dark.[27]

Since Myrdal's evidence is anecdotal, there is no way of knowing exactly
how frequently such blatant incidents of racial injustice occurred. But precise measurement of the frequency of such incidents may not be the most
important consideration. The purpose of such arrests was to maintain the
racial caste system. There may have been only occasional challenges to that
system, and it may have required only occasional arrests to reinforce public awareness of it. More systematic observation of police practices by
Myrdal might have provided us with a better sense of the frequency of such
challenges and the law enforcement requirements of maintaining a caste
system.

The blatant racial discrimination in law enforcement that Myrdal reported continued through the mid-1960s. A 1965 report by the U.S. Civil Rights Commission found a systematic pattern of failure by local law enforcement officials in Mississippi, Alabama, Georgia, and Florida to investigate, arrest, and prosecute in cases of violence against civil rights activists.[28]

Southern arrest practices were different in kind, rather than degree, from those in the rest of the country. Questionable arrest practices were common in other parts of the country, as documented by the 1931 Wickersham Commission report. The first direct observation of police arrest practices, conducted in 1940, found that a significant proportion of arrests were illegal.[29] The first systematic observation of police work, conducted in Kansas, Wisconsin, and Michigan by the American Bar Foundation in the mid-1950s, found that police officers routinely did not arrest suspects even when they had probable cause while arresting other people for purposes of harassment.[30] The question of whether arrest practices outside the South represented a clear pattern of race discrimination has been the subject of much debate and continuing research.[31] Whatever the extent of race discrimination, however, it is clear that in other parts of the country the practice did not have the purpose of maintaining a racial caste system.[32]

The sanctioning of white criminal violence against African Americans blurred the distinction between private and public authority. Myrdal noted that in rural areas, plantation owners "tenaciously held to the old pattern of executing actual police power themselves over their Negro labor."[33] In this respect, 80 years after the abolition of slavery, southern policing perpetuated one of the traditional customs of the old slave system.

Excessive Use of Physical Force

Myrdal found pervasive and racially discriminatory physical brutality. He reported that southern police officers took it for granted that "any Negro who shows signs of insubordination should be punished bodily."[34] Thus, police brutality was a key element in maintaining the racial caste system. The absence of any meaningful form of accountability was nearly total: "There are practically no curbs to the policeman's aggressiveness when he is dealing with Negroes whom he conceives of as dangerous or as 'getting out of their place.'"[35] Southern African Americans complained "indignantly" about "police brutality" to Myrdal and his staff.[36] These informants, however, knew that complaining to the authorities was useless and often likely to provoke retaliation, even in cases where the complaint was valid.

Police brutality was pervasive in the rest of the country, according to the 1931 Wickersham Commission, but qualitatively different than in the South. Elsewhere, there were few avenues for redress of legitimate grievances, but at least there were a few. The Wickersham Commission cited a number of cases where courts, invoking the Fifth Amendment, reversed criminal convictions because the suspect had been beaten or otherwise abused.[37] Myrdal's account does not indicate any hope of redress for the southern African American citizen who had been mistreated by the police.

Much of the southern police brutality was openly delegated to police officers on the street by other criminal justice officials. According to Myrdal, southern police officers assumed the duty of not just arresting "but also of sentencing and punishing the culprit." He reported that judges were "grateful" for being "spared" the work of handling many criminal cases.[38] Thus, the racial caste system permitted an informal and inexpensive form of "justice." "Curbside justice" existed in other parts of the country as well. Studies of police–community relations in the 1960s found that officers physically beat suspects they felt "deserved" some form of punishment. None of these reports, however, suggested that it was done with the open encouragement of judges and other responsible officials.[39]

Police Shootings

With respect to the police use of deadly force, Myrdal concluded that the "majority" of police killings of African Americans were "unnecessary when measured by a decent standard of policemanship."[40] The data indicated that half of all blacks killed by whites were killed by police officers. There is good reason to believe, however, that the pattern of police shootings in the South was not all that different from that in the North. Police use of deadly force has been one of the most serious police–community relations issues across the country. In 1978 James J. Fyfe, one of the leading authorities on the subject, concluded that, nationally, the police appeared to have "two trigger fingers," one for whites and another for African Americans.[41]

On the issue of police shootings, Myrdal's sympathies seemed to shift toward the white police officer. He noted the high number of officers killed by African American citizens and suggested a pattern of reciprocity in police-citizen killings.[42] Many police shootings of African Americans, he argued, were the result of legitimate fears by the police officer about being attacked or killed by African American assailants. Myrdal cited the figures on deaths of officers to suggest that these fears might be justified.[43] On no other subject in Chapter 25 did Myrdal even begin to justify police practices in the slightest way.

Other Issues

Although the racial caste system was common to the entire South, Myrdal found some notable variations within the region. African Americans tended to be "treated more justly and courteously [by the police] in the Upper South than in the Deep South."[44] Subsequent studies of police employment practices found a similar regional variation.[45]

Even though the racial caste system dominated police practices, Myrdal found that many whites were also the victims of police lawlessness. The "undesirable" elements included the so-called outside agitators, Communists, and subversive influences.[46] On this point, southern policing closely resembled the rest of the country. Radical political activists were routinely denied basic civil liberties by the police everywhere. Many police departments maintained special Red Squads, which spied on alleged radicals, broke up meetings, and made blatantly illegal arrests. The Los Angeles police Red Squad was the most notorious of them all.[47] In New York City, Mayor Fiorello LaGuardia responded to Communist-led demonstrations in the 1930s by ordering his police officers to "muss em up."[48]

Myrdal's failure to explore the class bias of southern policing leaves an incomplete picture of the role of the police in maintaining the racial caste system. Historians have argued that institutionalized racial segregation arose in the 1890s as a means of dividing poor whites and poor blacks. The early Populist movement indicated that an interracial political movement was a distinct possibility.[49] Myrdal offers us a vivid, if anecdotal picture of the role of the police with respect to blacks. Missing from this picture, however, is any similar detail on the role of the police in suppressing any potential white challenges to the status quo, which might have formed the basis of an interracial political movement. We are left with no sense of how frequent were incidents directed against whites or the extent to which the police themselves were conscious of the political implications of their actions.

The caste system also blurred the distinction between the police and other public officials (hence the title of Chapter 25: "The Police and Other Public Contacts"). Numerous petty officials were given very broad law enforcement powers. Myrdal cited the example of the African American boarding a train or a bus. Conductors and other transit officials were "legally empowered to carry out their duties" in enforcing the system of segregation public facilities. Thus, the streetcar conductor had essentially the same power as the police officer, and a large number of arrests occurred on public transportation.[50]

POLICE ACCOUNTABILITY AND THE RACIAL CASTE SYSTEM

To use contemporary terminology, the system of policing that Myrdal described involved a near total absence of accountability. The police officer who savagely beat an African American citizen or arrested that person without any objective pretext, feared no consequences. There was no chance that the officer guilty of the worst misconduct would be disciplined by the department, or that an arrest would be dismissed or a conviction overturned, or that the media would expose the incident. Myrdal's evidence, in fact, suggests that the officer was likely to be praised for a job well done.

Although Myrdal did not use the term, his evidence clearly suggests that southern policing, and the entire southern criminal justice system for that matter, represented a totalitarian regime. For the African American citizen, there was no "law" in the sense of a universalistic set of standards that were applied equally and fairly. The region might be compared to the former Soviet Union where the law-on-the-books enunciated glittering political and civil rights, including standards of due process, while the law-in-action systematically violated all of those principles.

One of the distinguishing features of the American criminal justice system is the direct and indirect control of justice agencies through the ballot. Sheriffs and county prosecutors are directly elected in almost all states; judges are directly elected in many jurisdictions and subject to reappointment by referendum in others; police chiefs are appointed (and regularly fired) by mayors who are in turn directly elected; and grand and petit juries are traditionally selected from the list of registered voters. Disenfranchisement ensured that the entire criminal justice system served the racial caste system and denied to African Americans mechanisms of accountability through the political processes that were available outside the South. Although Myrdal did not address the issue directly in Chapter 25, it is nonetheless clear that the lack of accountability in law enforcement was a direct consequence of the disenfranchisement of African American voters.[51]

THE SOUTHERN POLICE OFFICER

Employment Discrimination

Not surprisingly, given the system of institutionalized segregation, African Americans were almost completely barred from employment in southern policing. Myrdal began Chapter 25 with the comment that "Practically all public officials in the South are white."[52] He cited a 1930 survey which found only 1,297 African American law enforcement officials in the entire country (this figure included probation and truant officers who are not normally classified as "police" officers even though they have arrest powers in some states). Only 7 percent, or about 90, were in the Deep South. In 1940 there was not a single African American police officer in any city in Mississippi, South Carolina, Louisiana, Georgia, or Alabama, where 40 percent of the entire African American population then lived.[53]

Employment practices were a bit more open in the Upper South. Myrdal found 39 African American city police officers in Maryland, Delaware, Tennessee, and Texas, with another 34 in the District of Columbia. The differences between the Upper South and the Deep South continued over the next decade and a half. Elliott Rudwick's 1961 survey for the Southern Regional Council found many more African American officers in the Upper South and very few in the Deep South. Even in the Upper South, however, progress in the employment of African American police officers was very limited prior to 1961.[54]

Employment discrimination in policing was not confined to the South, however. The 1930 data indicated at most about 1,000 African American police officers outside the South. Although there were no systematic studies of employment practices by race, the available data suggest a pattern of tokenism similar to that found in the Upper South.

Progress in the employment of African American officers was extremely slow and occurred largely in response to protests by local civil rights activists. In 1967 the President's Crime Commission reported serious underrepresentation of African American officers in the big city police departments of the North and West.[55] In no American city could their presence be described as even adequate until the early 1980s—and that was only a result of substantial litigation under the 1964 Civil Rights Act. It might also be noted that by 1992 some of the cities with the best records on racial minority employment were in the Deep South.[56]

The Special Role of the African American Officer

The few African Americans who were nominally police officers were severely restricted in terms of their powers. Indeed, they were not full-fledged police officers at all. They were confined to duty within African American communities and did not have the power to arrest white persons, no matter how blatant the offense. As late as 1961, Rudwick found that African American officers could arrest any citizen regardless of race in only one-third of the southern cities he surveyed.[57]

Discriminatory assignment of officers persisted in northern cities, at least through the mid-1960s. Black officers were generally confined to black neighborhoods, where they were joined by incompetent white officers. Researchers employed by the President's Crime Commission found several northern police departments that deliberately "dumped" incompetent white officers on racial minority communities.[58]

Despite his commitment to racial equality, Myrdal endorsed the practice of racially segregated police assignments. While calling for better training of white police officers, he asserted that "The use of equally well-trained

Negro policemen, particularly for patrolling the Negro communities, would be an especially wholesome reform."[59] He confidently predicted that whites in at least some cities "would tolerate such a reform." His believed that qualified African American officers would be more likely to take seriously crimes by "Negro offenders against other Negroes" than would white officers.[60] Myrdal noted widespread complaints by law-abiding African Americans that they were "left practically without police protection."[61]

On this issue, Myrdal accommodated his recommendations to the prevailing racial caste system. He did not confront the issue of racism directly, offering no suggestion that white officers be directed to seriously consider crimes against African Americans, whether by whites or by other African Americans. Nor did he contemplate the assignment of African American officers to white neighborhoods.

The White Police Officer

Myrdal found that personnel standards in southern police departments were utterly abysmal, characterizing sheriffs and their deputies as "petty politicians with no police training at all."[62] He quoted Arthur Raper's devastating comment that the job was open to "almost anyone on the outside of the penitentiary who weighs enough and is not blind or crippled."[63] Of the 112 southern cities surveyed by Raper, 30 had no educational requirements at all, and only 33 provided any formal pre-service training. A person could acquire the awesome powers of a police officer overnight: "One day he is a barber, textile worker, truck driver . . . the next day . . . he is a full-fledged police officer."[64]

Because he did not examine the available literature on the police, Myrdal was not aware that personnel standards in southern police practices were not that different from the rest of the country. The Wickersham Commission found that in 1931 over 60 percent of all sworn officers in the country had never even enrolled in high school.[65] And with the exception of a few cities, standards did not improve much over the next decade. In 1961, 24 percent of all police departments across the country had no minimum educational requirements. Standards in New England were as low as those in the south.[66] Until the early 1970s, by which time every state required formal training and certification of all sworn police officers, it was possible in most states to become a police officer overnight.

Myrdal found that politics played a major role in the appointment of southern police officers, even where a nominal civil service system existed.[67] Here again, the South was not different that the rest of the country. Politics had always been the primary influence on hiring practices in American policing which continued well into the 1960s.[68]

THE REFORM OF SOUTHERN POLICING

In response to the deplorable state of southern policing, Myrdal outlined a reform agenda emphasizing higher educational standards for police officers. There are several notable aspects of Myrdal's approach to reform. First, his recommendations were unrelated to the very conditions he described. Second, he gave no attention to the constitutional and legislative attack on segregation that ultimately ended Jim Crow and revolutionized southern policing.

Myrdal argued that the police represented "a crucial and strategic factor in [southern] race relations," and that improved personnel standards would significantly reduce "some of the most morbid tensions" in the region. This included college education for officers, specialized training, freedom from political influence, and better salaries. To that end, he suggested that "few strategic moves to improve the Southern interracial situation would be more potent than the opening of a pioneering modern police college in the South."[69] This goal was realized a few years later with the creation of the Southern Police Institute at the University of Louisville, funded in part by the Carnegie Corporation, which had sponsored *An American Dilemma*.

Police reformers at the national level had also put considerable emphasis on education. August Vollmer had been recommending college-level education for police officers for nearly three decades. Vollmer and other reformers, however, had a far more comprehensive agenda for police professionalization, one that included many organizational and administrative improvements. Myrdal ignored these other recommendations and concentrated almost solely on education.[70]

The most notable aspect of Myrdal's emphasis on education for police officers is that it was essentially irrelevant in light of his own evidence. His basic thesis, we should recall, is that the dominant features of southern policing, including its worst elements, are related to the racial caste system. Raising the educational levels of police officers would hardly challenge that system. At best, he seemed to hope that the more educated officer would be less brutal than the poorly educated officer.

In fact, at no point in Chapter 25 does Myrdal suggest a direct challenge to either the racial caste system or the worst forms of police misconduct. He suggested that hiring African American police officers would serve to protect African American crime victims, and he quietly ignored the question of directing white officers to enforce the law equally. The failure to connect his reform proposals to his own evidence reveals a serious intellectual and political failure on Myrdal's part.

Implicit in Myrdal's emphasis on education was the reformist notion of "uplifting" African Americans. Two sections of the chapter are particularly revealing on this point. First, he suggested that the experience of dealing with educated and fair-minded whites would encourage African Americans to pursue their own education. He expressed much alarm that the brutality and lawlessness of southern policing were "*undoing much of what Northern philanthropy and Southern state governments are trying to accomplish through education and by other means*" [italics in original].[71] Thus, the better-educated police officer would be a role model for the African American community.

Second, Chapter 25 closed with a brief discussion of the work of various federal agencies. Many of these agencies had curbed discrimination in their own operations. Dealing with fair-minded federal officials, Myrdal argued, "has given the Negroes a new type of contact with public authority." These officials sought not to keep African Americans in the place, but "to advise them and help them to a better life." In a clear statement of its agenda for social change, the chapter ended with the declaration that such experiences "will, in time, stand out as a social and spiritual revolution."[72] In other words, a few good white officials would inspire and uplift African Americans. Eventually, if there were enough of these inspiring examples, society as a whole would be transformed.

Myrdal's vision of social change was gradualist and nonconfrontational. The reference to a "spiritual revolution" was consistent with the emphasis on moral values that pervades all of *An American Dilemma*. Progress toward racial equality would come slowly, as a result of education and urbanization, and depended on a change in the moral perspective of white Americans. Through education, this would come about gradually, without great social conflict. As other critics have noted, *An American Dilemma* embodied an unwarranted optimism about progress in race relations.[73]

THE CIVIL RIGHTS MOVEMENT
AND THE REFORM OF SOUTHERN POLICING

Almost completely absent from Myrdal's vision of social change was the potential role of litigation in reforming police and ending the entire racial caste system. *An American Dilemma* contains almost no references to litigation as a strategy for ending institutionalized segregation. Yet, the Supreme Court had already signaled its willingness to entertain constitutional challenges to segregation. The NAACP, correctly reading those signals, had organized a separate Legal Defense Fund in 1938 and stepped up its litigation program. The road to *Brown* v. *Board of Education* (1954) was, in effect, already clearly marked.[74]

Myrdal could not have been unaware of these developments. The civil rights community was extremely small in the late 1930s and early 1940s when he worked on *An American Dilemma*. All of the people who contributed, directly and indirectly, to this monumental study—foundation leaders, scholars, advisers, and the like—must have been aware of new opportunity for legal challenges to segregation. Yet, *An American Dilemma* scarcely mentions it.

Ultimately, the system of southern policing that Myrdal described was demolished by the revolution in American law produced by the civil rights movement. The U.S. Supreme Court led this revolution through a concerted attack on the institutionalized, de jure segregation. The 1964 Civil Rights Act, meanwhile, established equality as national policy with respect to public accommodations, employment, and other aspects of American life. Among other things, Title VII of the 1964 Civil Rights Act outlawed the employment discrimination that had characterized southern police departments.

This legal revolution destroyed the old southern caste system that was at the heart of southern policing. The civil rights movement, not more education for police officers as Myrdal had hoped, put an end to the special and blatantly racist form of southern policing.

The Supreme Court's "due process revolution," meanwhile, was also instrumental in reforming the police at the national level. While the major Court decisions on police practices were racially neutral—*Miranda*, for example, is not a civil rights decision—there can be little doubt that racial minorities have been the primary beneficiaries. The introduction of constitutional standards for routine police practices helped to establish some of the mechanisms of accountability that were totally lacking in southern policing. Archibald Cox argued that the Justices of the Warren Court were well aware of the civil rights implications of due process decisions. "Many purely procedural questions," he wrote, "were influenced by the realization that in another case they might affect the posture of a Negro in a hostile southern court."[75] As virtually all the historical and contemporary evidence suggests, racial minorities are far more likely to come into contact with the police, to be subject to arrest, and to be the victims of police misconduct.[76] Any reform in police practices, therefore, tended to benefit African Americans more than any other group.

In fairness to Myrdal, we should note that the modern "due process revolution" still lay in the future at the time he worked on *An American Dilemma*. He could not have foreseen how important it would become in the reform of American criminal justice; few, if any, experts did. Nonetheless, as he was preparing *An American Dilemma*, the Supreme Court had taken the first tentative steps in the direction of imposing constitutional standards on criminal justice agencies. Significantly, the initial cases had come from the South and involved the mistreatment of African Americans.[77] As is the case with the constitutional challenges to segregation, Myrdal could not have been unaware of these developments. His failure to discuss them, if only to argue against them, represents a striking intellectual failure.

One other legal change, not related to the civil rights movement, also deserves comment here because of its impact on traditional southern police practices. A major development in policing over the past 25 years has been the emergence of strong police unions with the legally recognized right to engage in collective bargaining. Police union contracts generally contain formal, seniority-based provisions governing the assignment of police officers. These provisions have eliminated the traditional pattern of racist assignments in which the worst officers were deliberately "dumped" on racial minority communities.[78]

In the end, then, none of the forces that have revolutionized southern policing since the publication of *An American Dilemma* were anticipated by Myrdal. Committed to a brand of liberal reform that emphasized gradual change through education, he failed to appreciate the special role that the law as a coercive instrument of social control could play in bringing about social change, including both a revolution in southern policing and a fundamental change in American race relations.

REGIONAL DIFFERENCES IN AMERICAN POLICING TODAY

There can be no question that the combined impact of the civil rights movement and the due process revolution swept away the racial caste system and with it the distinctive features of southern policing described by Myrdal in *An American Dilemma*. Left unanswered is the question of whether distinct regional differences in American policing persist today. Does the legacy of the Jim Crow era continue to give southern policing a special dimension with respect to race relations?

At the outset of this chapter we answered that question in the negative. Our argument is that the police in the southeastern United States have been "integrated" into a national system to the extent that police problems in Atlanta are not fundamentally different from those in, say, Seattle. In truth, however, this interpretation is based on inferences from the existing literature on policing rather than on any direct investigation of the question.

The last three decades have witnessed a revolution in research on policing coupled with a reform movement that has transformed many aspects of American policing.[79] The literature on many specific subjects is voluminous. Although no studies sought to investigate regional differences directly, none has found any such differences.

The most systematic recent study of policing is the Police Services Study (PSS) conducted in the mid-1970s. The PSS included direct observations of police work and community surveys in three metropolitan areas: Rochester, New York; St. Louis, Missouri; and Tampa-St. Petersburg, Florida. None of the published studies using the PSS data have identified any distinct patterns in policing in the southern community compared with the other two.[80] In particular, the studies of arrest discretion based on the PSS data did not identify any regional pattern with respect to race discrimination in arrest.[81]

Along the same lines, the voluminous literature on police use of deadly force has failed to identify any regional patterns. That is to say, police officers in southeastern cities are not more likely to use deadly force or to shoot and kill racial minorities than are police in other parts of the country. The reforms that have reduced police shootings over the past 20 years appear to have affected departments irrespective of region.[82]

The question of race discrimination in the employment of police officers remains a contentious issue across the country. Surveys of the employment of African Americans and Hispanics between 1983 and 1992, however, have not found any distinct racial pattern in the persistence of discrimination. Cities that have made considerable progress in equal employment opportunity are found in all regions, while many of those that have made the least progress are found outside the southeast.[83]

The issues that have dominated police administration in recent years do not reflect any regional pattern. Most important, the move toward community policing has been a national movement, with departments from all regions participating.[84] Southern police departments, meanwhile, have been equally engaged in the movement to reform police response to domestic violence.[85] Finally, the career of Lee P. Brown suggests the absence of any distinct regional differences in American policing. Brown, who is black, has served as the chief law enforcement officer in Multnomah County, Oregon; Atlanta, Georgia; Houston, Texas; and New York City.

In short, all of the evidence supports the conclusion that the police in the southeastern United States have been "integrated" into a national system of policing that has no distinct regional differences.

CONCLUSION

Chapter 25 of *An American Dilemma* provides a valuable description of police–race relations in the era of segregation. It is perhaps the only detailed analysis of that special chapter of the history of American policing. Although richly detailed, Myrdal's analysis is flawed by several weaknesses. It is almost entirely anecdotal and limited to the thirteen states of the Old Confederacy. Myrdal made no effort to examine police–race relations in the rest of the country, and he ignored the available literature on the police that would have placed his observations in a broader context.

Myrdal's prescription for the reform of southern policing represents another serious weakness, as his recommendations were unrelated to the reality he had just described. He placed virtually all of his faith in raising the educational levels of white police officers. At no point did he consider any direct challenge to the blatant racism and lawlessness that, by his own account, dominated southern policing. Ultimately, the special form of policing he described was swept away by the civil rights movement. Yet, his survey of American race relations completely failed to take into account the early stirrings of that movement and its potential for reforming race relations.

In the end, the treatment of the police in *An American Dilemma* is an extremely ambiguous achievement: invaluable today as a historical document of an important but now bygone era, but deeply flawed in several important respects. Myrdal described a profoundly racist system of law enforcement. The racial caste system of which it was a part has been abolished. And yet racial discrimination in policing remains. The problems that exist today are far more subtle and intractable that those described by Gunnar Myrdal 50 years ago.

NOTES

1. Gunnar Myrdal. *An American Dilemma: The Negro Problem and Modern Democracy* (New York: Harper & Brothers, 1944), p. 536.
2. City of New York, Commission to Investigate Allegations of Police Corruption (Mollen Commission). *Commission Report* (New York City, 1994).
3. Samuel Walker, Cassia Spohn, and Miriam DeLone. *The Color of Justice* (Belmont, Cal.: Wadsworth, forthcoming); National Research Council, *A Common Destiny: Blacks and American Society* (Washington, D.C.: National Academy Press, 1989), Chap. 9; National Minority Advisory Council on Criminal Justice. *The Inequality of Justice* (Washington, D.C.: U.S. Government Printing Office, 1982).
4. Bureau of Justice Statistics. *Sourcebook of Criminal Justice Statistics–1993* (Washington, D.C.: U.S. Government Printing Office, 1994), pp. 165–171.
5. Myrdal, pp. 535–546.
6. For a general overview, see Samuel Walker. *The Police in America: An Introduction*, 2nd ed. (New York: McGraw-Hill, 1992); Michael Tonry and Norval Morris, eds. *Modern Policing*, Vol. 15, *Crime and Justice: A Review of Research* (Chicago: University of Chicago Press, 1992). On the criminal justice system, see Walker, Spohn, and DeLone. *The Color of Justice*.
7. An extremely valuable survey, following up on many of the issues covered by Myrdal, is Elliott M. Rudwick. *The Unequal Badge: Negro Policemen in the South* (Atlanta, Ga.: Southern Regional Council, 1962).

8. Samuel Walker. *Popular Justice: A History of American Criminal Justice* (New York: Oxford University Press, 1980), pp. 169–175.

9. Raymond B. Fosdick. *American Police Systems* (New York: Century Co., 1920).

10. Bruce Smith. *Police Systems in the United States* (New York: Harper & Brothers, 1940).

11. National Commission on Law Observance and Enforcement. *Lawlessness in Law Enforcement* (Washington, D.C.: U.S. Government Printing Office, 1931).

12. Thurgood Marshall. "The Gestapo in Detroit." *Crisis* (1943): 232–233.

13. Samuel Walker. "Origins of the American Police-Community Relations Movement: The 1940s." *Criminal Justice History: An International Annual*, Vol. I (New York: John Jay Press, 1980). Two useful collections on the history of urban racial disturbances are Anthony M. Platt, ed. *The Politics of Riot Commissions* (New York: Collier Books, 1971); and Allen D. Grimshaw, ed. *Racial Violence in the United States* (Chicago: Aldine, 1969).

14. National Commission. *Lawlessness in Law Enforcement*.

15. National Commission on Law Observance and Enforcement. *Report on Police* (Washington, D.C.: U.S. Government Printing Office, 1931).

16. The first significant qualitative research was done by the American Bar Foundation and is reported in Wayne LaFave. *Arrest* (Boston: Little, Brown, 1965). The first systematic quantitative research was done for the President's Crime Commission in 1966 and is in Albert Reiss. *The Police and the Public* (New Haven, Conn. Yale University Press, 1971).

17. Samuel Walker. "The Era of the Crime Commission." In *Popular Justice: A History of American Criminal Justice* (New York: Oxford University Press, 1980), pp. 169–180.

18. National Commission on Law Observance and Enforcement. *Lawlessness in Law Enforcement*. National Commission on Law Observance and Enforcement. *Report on Police*.

19. The only reference to any of the police literature is a passing reference to August Vollmer's *The Police and Modern Society* (Berkeley, Cal.: University of California, 1936).

20. Myrdal, p. 535.

21. Peter Manning. *Police Work: The Social Organization of Policing* (Cambridge, MA: MIT Press, 1977).

22. National Commission. *Lawlessness in Law Enforcement*.

23. Myrdal, p. 535.

24. National Commission. *Lawlessness in Law Enforcement*.

25. Ibid., p. 535.

26. Ibid., p. 536.

27. Ibid., p. 1339, fn. 2.

28. U.S. Commission on Civil Rights. *Law Enforcement: A Report on Equal Protection in the South* (Washington, D.C.: U.S. Government Printing Office, 1965).

29. Sam Bass Warner. "Investigating the Law of Arrest." *ABA Journal* 26 (1940): 151–155.

30. LaFave. *Arrest*; Samuel Walker. "Origins of the Contemporary Criminal Justice Paradigm: The American Bar Foundation Survey, 1953–1969." *Justice Quarterly* 9 (March 1992): 47–76.

31. For a review, see Chap. 4 of Walker, Spohn, and DeLone, op. cit.
32. On race discrimination in arrests, see Reiss. *The Police and the Public;* and Donald Black. *The Manners and Customs of the Police* (New York: Academic Press, 1980). Both used the data from the President's Crime Commission field studies in 1966.
33. Myrdal, p. 536.
34. Ibid., p. 541.
35. Ibid., p. 540.
36. Ibid., p. 541.
37. National Commission. *Lawlessness in Law Enforcement.*
38. Myrdal, p. 536.
39. Reiss. *The Police and the Public.*
40. Myrdal, p. 542.
41. James J. Fyfe. "Reducing the Use of Deadly Force: The New York Experience." In U.S. Department of Justice. *Police Use of Deadly Force* (Washington, D.C.: U.S. Government Printing Office, 1978), p. 29. The most thorough recent study is William Geller and Michael S. Scott. *Deadly Force: What We Know* (Washington, D.C.: Police Executive Research Forum, 1993).
42. The more systematic studies of police–citizen shootings that began in the 1960s and blossomed in the 1970s confirmed Myrdal's point about reciprocity. Indeed, the decline in the number of both citizens and police officers shot and killed beginning in the mid-1970s suggests that the new legal restrictions on police shootings reduced the number of retaliatory shootings—and, hence, fewer officers shot and killed. Lawrence W. Sherman and Ellen G. Cohn. *Citizens Killed by Big-City Police, 1970–1984* (Washington, D.C.: Crime Control Institute, 1986); Geller and Scott. *Deadly Force.*
43. Myrdal, p. 542.
44. Ibid., pp. 537–538.
45. Rudwick. *Unequal Badge.*
46. Myrdal, p. 540.
47. Frank Donner. *Protectors of Privilege: Red Squads and Police Repression in Urban America* (Berkeley: University of California Press, 1990).
48. Quoted in Samuel Walker. *In Defense of American Liberties: A History of the ACLU* (New York: Oxford University Press, 1990), p. 97.
49. C. Vann Woodward. *The Strange Career of Jim Crow* (New York: Oxford University Press, 1955).
50. Myrdal, p. 537.
51. The point was made in 1965 by the U.S. Commission on Civil Rights. *Law Enforcement: A Report on Equal Protection in the South.*
52. Myrdal, p. 535.
53. Ibid., p. 543, especially note a. Rudwick. *The Unequal Badge* contains valuable data on the period from 1945 through 1961.
54. Rudwick. *Unequal Badge,* p. 4.
55. President's Commission on Law Enforcement and Administration of Justice. *Task Force Report: The Police,* pp. 167–174.
56. Samuel Walker and K.B. Turner. *A Decade of Modest Progress: Employment of Black and Hispanic Police Officers, 1983–1992* (Omaha: University of Nebraska, 1992).

57. Rudwick. *Unequal Badge*, pp. 9–10, especially Table 2, pp. 13–14.
58. Reiss. *The Police and the Public*, p. 168. President's Commission on Law Enforcement. *Task Force Report: The Police*, p. 165.
59. Myrdal, p. 545.
60. Ibid., p. 542.
61. Ibid., p. 542.
62. Ibid., p. 538.
63. Ibid., pp. 538–539.
64. Ibid., p. 539, note a.
65. National Commission on Law Observance. *Report on the Police*, p. 58.
66. President's Commission on Law Enforcement. *Task Force Report: The Police*, pp. 126–127.
67. Myrdal, p. 539.
68. Samuel Walker. *A Critical History of Police Reform* (Lexington, Mass.: Lexington Books, 1977); National Commission on Law Observance. *Report on Police*, p. 53.
69. Ibid., pp. 544–545.
70. Myrdal cited Vollmer's 1936 book, *The Police and Modern Society*. See also National Commission on Law Observance. *Report on the Police*, written largely by Vollmer. On the agenda of the professionalization movement, see Walker. *A Critical History of Police Reform*.
71. Myrdal, p. 540.
72. Ibid., p. 546.
73. David W. Southern. *Gunnar Myrdal and Black-White Relations: The Use and Abuse of An American Dilemma, 1944–1969* (Baton Rouge: Louisiana State University Press, 1987).
74. Richard Kluger. *Simple Justice* (New York: Vintage Books, 1977).
75. Archibald Cox. *The Warren Court* (Cambridge, MA: Harvard University Press, 1968), p. 6.
76. Walker, Spohn, and DeLone. *The Color of Justice*, Chap. 4.
77. The first important police abuse case was *Brown* v. *Mississippi*, 297 U.S. 278 (1936). The first major due process case emerged from the famous Scottsboro case: *Powell* v. *Alabama*, 287 U.S. 45 (1932). The best treatment of the early years, which he describes as the "stone age" of constitutional standards of due process, is Yale Kamisar. *Police Interrogations and Confessions* (Ann Arbor: University of Michigan Press, 1980).
78. Reiss. *The Police and the Public*, p. 168.
79. Walker. *The Police in America*.
80. Gordon P. Whitaker, ed. *Understanding Police Agency Performance* (Washington, D.C.: U.S. Government Printing Office, 1984).
81. Douglas A. Smith and Christy A. Visher. "Street-Level Justice: Situational Determinants of Police Arrest Decisions." *Social Problems* 29 (December 1981): 167–177; Douglas A. Smith, Christy A. Visher, and Laura A. Davidson. "Equity and Discretionary Justice: The Influence of Race on Police Arrest Decisions." *Journal of Criminal Law and Criminology* 75 (Spring 1984): 234–249.
82. Geller and Scott. *Deadly Force: What We Know*.

83. Samuel Walker and K. B. Turner. *A Decade of Modest Progress: The Employment of Black and Hispanic Police Officers, 1983–1992* (Omaha: University of Nebraska, 1992).
84. Jack R. Greene and Stephen D. Mastrofski, eds. *Community Policing: Rhetoric or Reality?* (New York: Praeger, 1988).
85. Lawrence W. Sherman. *Policing Domestic Violence* (New York: The Free Press, 1992).

Cassia C. Spohn

11

Courts, Sentences, and Prisons

"The whole judicial system of courts, sentences and prisons in the South is overripe for fundamental reforms," concluded Gunnar Myrdal in *An American Dilemma*.[1] Relying primarily on anecdotal accounts of differential treatment of African Americans and whites in southern court systems, Myrdal documented widespread discrimination in assignment of counsel, bail setting, jury selection, court processing, and sentencing. Myrdal noted that although the danger of discrimination was greatest in lower state courts, where judges with limited education were more susceptible to the pressures of public opinion, it was found to some extent in all state courts in the South. He stated, "In a court system of this structure, operating within a deeply prejudiced region, discrimination is to be expected."[2]

Although Myrdal was dismayed by the racial inequities he observed, he was optimistic that southern courts would become more impartial, and he saw numerous signs of change. He noted that the U.S. Supreme Court and lower federal courts were increasingly willing to censor state courts for violating the rights of criminal defendants, and that it was becoming easier for African Americans to obtain the services of competent attorneys. He also predicted that socioeconomic changes in the South, coupled with the growing activism of civil rights groups and the increasingly important "Negro vote,"[3] would lead to reform. As he stated, "It is the author's observation that, *in principle, the average white Southerner is no longer prepared to defend racial inequality of justice.*"[4]

Some observers might contend that Myrdal's predictions were overly optimistic and that the reforms he envisioned have not produced the results he anticipated. It is certainly true that the past 50 years have witnessed significant changes. The U.S. Supreme Court has handed down decisions designed to protect the rights of criminal defendants and to prohibit racial discrimination in selection of the jury pool, use of peremptory challenges, and imposition of the death penalty. States likewise have enacted legislation and adopted policies designed to decrease the likelihood of overt class and race discrimination in the processing of criminal defendants.

Despite these reforms, inequalities persist. African Americans continue to suffer direct and indirect discrimination in decisions regarding bail, charging, jury selection, and sentencing. As Mauer recently concluded, "The extended reach of the criminal justice system has been far from uniform in its effects upon different segments of the population. . . . as has been true historically, but even more so now, the criminal justice system disproportionately engages minorities and the poor."[5]

In the sections that follow, we evaluate Mydral's findings concerning the inequities inherent in the southern criminal justice system. We also discuss reforms designed to eliminate these inequities and review recent research on the effect of race on court processing decisions. We conclude that while the reforms Myrdal envisioned may have eliminated "the more blatant forms of deviation from fair trial in the lower courts,"[6] they have not produced equality of justice.

DECISIONS REGARDING COUNSEL AND BAIL

Myrdal found that southern blacks suffered both class and race discrimination in decisions regarding appointment of counsel and bail. Although he cited no statistics or empirical evidence in support of his claims (a problem found throughout the chapter), he concluded that African Americans charged with crimes frequently were unable to obtain competent counsel or pretrial release. Myrdal admitted that poor whites faced similar problems, but he argued that African Americans were at a greater disadvantage because of their race. He noted that white lawyers were reluctant to take cases with African American defendants, and that bail "was most often refused or made prohibitively high to accused Negroes, particularly when the alleged crime is against whites."[7]

Right to Counsel

Myrdally regarded lack of access to competent counsel as a serious problem. He concluded that success in reforming the southern court system hinged on the establishment of "legal aid agencies . . . to assist poor whites and Negroes to enforce their rights under existing laws in civil and criminal cases."[8] Myrdal argued that use of court-appointed attorneys, who he suggested were often young and inexperienced, was not sufficient. He recommended that southern jurisdictions establish independent agencies staffed by professional lawyers who would not only defend those charged with crimes but who would also monitor the treatment of racial minorities in courts and prisons.

In discussing the right to counsel, Myrdal stated, incorrectly, that in criminal cases courts will "appoint a lawyer for anybody who cannot afford to provide himself with proper legal aid."[9] In fact, until the early 1960s, several southern states, in compliance with the Supreme Court's decision in *Powell* v. *Alabama*,[10] guaranteed the right to counsel only to defendants in capital cases. The Court's decision in a 1938 case, *Johnson* v. *Zerbst*,[11] required the appointment of counsel for all indigent defendants in federal criminal cases, but the requirement was not extended to the states until *Gideon* v. *Wainwright*[12] was decided in 1963.[13] In subsequent decisions the Court ruled that "no person may be imprisoned, for any offense, whether classified as petty, misdemeanor, or felony, unless he was represented by counsel,"[14] and that the right to counsel is not limited to trial, but that it applies to all "critical stages" in the criminal justice process.[15]

At the time the *Gideon* decision was handed down, thirteen states, including five in the South, had no statewide requirement for appointment of counsel except in capital cases.[16] Other states relied on members of local bar associations to defend indigents, often on a pro bono basis. Following *Gideon*, it became obvious that other procedures would be required if all felony defendants were to be provided attorneys.

States moved swiftly to implement the constitutional requirements articulated in *Gideon* and the cases that followed, either by establishing public defender systems or by appropriating money for court-appointed attorneys. The number of public defender systems grew rapidly. In 1951 there were only 7 public defender organizations in the United States; in 1964 there were 136 and by 1973 the total had risen to 573.[17] A 1981 survey of indigent defense services found that 66 percent of U.S. counties used assigned counsel or contract attorneys and that 34 percent used public defender systems; the survey also revealed that over half of the case assignments were made within 48 hours of arrest.[18]

In sum, while Myrdal's recommendations regarding the establishment of independent legal aid agencies have not been implemented, significant changes have occurred. As a result of Supreme Court decisions expanding the right to counsel and the development of policies implementing these decisions, African American defendants are no longer denied legal representation at trial or at any of the other "critical stages" in the criminal justice process.[19] Although questions have been raised about the quality of legal representation provided to indigent defendants,[20] it is no longer true that "Negroes are without a voice"[21] in southern courts.

Bail Decision-Making

Myrdal's examination of the bond and bail system was extremely brief. He noted that the system "works automatically against the poor classes."[22] He added that African American defendants, particularly those accused of crimes against whites, were more likely than white defendants to be detained prior to trial, either because the judge refused bail or because the judge set bail at an unaffordable level. Myrdal did not discuss the consequences of pretrial detention and made no specific recommendations for reforming the bail system.

The issue of bail reform did not reach the national political agenda until nearly 20 years after the publication of *An American Dilemma*. Concerns about the rights of poor defendants led to the first bail reform movement, which emerged in the early 1960s and emphasized reducing pretrial detention. Those who lobbied for reform argued that the purpose of bail was to ensure the defendant's appearance in court and that the amount of bail therefore should not exceed the amount necessary to guarantee that the defendant would show up for all court proceedings. Proponents of this view asserted that whether a defendant was released or detained prior to trial should not depend upon his or her race or economic status. They also cited research demonstrating that the type and amount of bail imposed upon the defendant and the time spent by the defendant in pretrial detention affected the likelihood of a guilty plea, the likelihood of conviction at trial, and the severity of the sentence.[23]

Arguments such as these prompted state and federal reforms designed to reduce pretrial detention. Encouraged by the results of the Manhattan Bail Project, which found that the majority of indigent defendants released on their own recognizance did appear for trial,[24] local jurisdictions moved quickly to reduce reliance on money bail and to institute programs modeled after the Manhattan Bail Project. Many states revised their bail laws and in 1966 Congress passed the Bail Reform Act, which proclaimed release on recognizance the presumptive bail decision in federal criminal cases.

Then, as Walker has noted, "the political winds shifted."[25] The rising crime rate of the 1970s generated a concern for crime control and led to a reassessment of bail policies. Critics challenged the traditional position that the only function of bail was to ensure the defendant's appearance at trial. They argued that guaranteeing public safety was also a valid function of bail and that pretrial detention should be used to protect the community from "dangerous" offenders.

These arguments fueled the second bail reform movement, which emerged in the 1970s and emphasized preventive detention. Conservative legislators and policymakers lobbied for reforms allowing judges to consider "public safety" when making decisions concerning the type and amount of bail.[26] By 1984, 34 states had enacted legislation giving judges the right to deny bail to defendants deemed dangerous.[27] Also in 1984, Congress passed a law authorizing preventive detention of dangerous defendants in federal criminal cases.[28]

The effect of race on bail decision-making.   Proponents of bail reform argued that bail decisions should rest either upon assessments of the likelihood that the defendant would appear in court or upon predictions of the defendant's dangerousness. But there is no way to guarantee that race will not influence these assessments and predictions. As Mann has asserted, even the seemingly objective criteria used in making release on recognizance decisions and in determining dangerousness "may still be discriminatory on the basis of economic status or skin color."[29]

Studies examining the effect of race on bail decisions have yielded contradictory findings. Some researchers have concluded that bail decisions are determined primarily by legal variables, such as prior record and offense seriousness, and that race has no effect once controls for these legal variables are taken into consideration.[30] Other researchers contend that it is the defendant's economic status, rather than the defendant's race, that determines the likelihood of pretrial release.[31] If this is the case, one could argue that bail decision-making reflects *indirect* racial discrimination, since African American defendants are more likely than white defendants to be poor.

There are several studies that conclude either that defendant race directly affects bail outcomes[32] or that defendant race interacts with other variables that are themselves related to bail severity.[33] One study, for example, found that African Americans and Native Americans were less likely than whites to be released on their own recognizance.[34] Another study of bail decision-making in ten federal district courts found that race did not have a direct effect on bail outcomes, but that it did interact with a number of other variables to produce harsher bail outcomes for some types of African American defendants.[35] More specifically, the authors found that having a prior felony conviction had a greater negative effect on bail severity for African American defendants than for white defendants, while having more education or a higher income had a greater positive effect for whites than for African Americans.

Although the findings are contradictory, it appears that the reforms instituted since the 1960s have not produced racial equality in bail decision-making. There is evidence that judges in some jurisdictions continue to take race into account in deciding on the type and amount of bail. There is also evidence that race interacts with other factors to produce higher pretrial detention rates for African American defendants than for white defendants. Given the serious negative consequences of pretrial detention, these findings are an obvious cause for concern.

JURY SELECTION

Myrdal's examination of the southern court system revealed that the typical jury was an all-white jury.[36] Myrdal noted that some courts, in response to a 1935 Supreme Court decision[37] stating that African Americans could not be systematically excluded from the jury pool, had taken steps "to have Negroes on the jury list and call them in occasionally for service."[38] He added, however, that many southern courts, particularly those in rural areas, had either ignored the constitutional requirement or had developed techniques "to fulfill legal requirements without using Negro jurors."[39]

Since 1943 the Supreme Court has made it increasingly difficult for court systems to exclude African Americans from the jury pool. The Court has consistently struck down the "techniques" used by southern jurisdictions to circumvent the requirement of racial neutrality in the selection of the venire. The Court, for example, ruled that it was unconstitutional for a Georgia county to put the names of white potential jurors on white cards, the names of African American potential jurors on yellow cards, and then "randomly" draw cards to determine who would be summoned.[40] Similarly, the Court struck down the "random" selection of jurors from tax books where the names of white taxpayers were in one section and the names of African American taxpayers in another.[41] As the Court stated in *Avery* v. *Georgia*, "the State may not draw up its jury lists pursuant to neutral procedures but then resort to discrimination at other stages in the selection process."[42]

Myrdal's analysis of the jury selection process did not address the use of peremptory challenges to exclude African Americans from the jury. This oversight is understandable. Historically, attorneys "enjoyed carte blanche freedom in exercising peremptory challenges."[43] The assumption was that these challenges were being used to achieve a fair and impartial jury. In reality, of course, peremptory challenges often were used to strike African American jurors from cases with African American defendants. Critics charged that this practice "both reduces minority participation on criminal juries and frustrates the interest of minority defendants in a jury of peers."[44]

The Supreme Court initially was reluctant to restrict the prosecutor's right to use peremptory challenges to excuse jurors on the basis of race. In the 1965 *Swain* v. *Alabama*, the Court ruled that the prosecutor's use of peremptory challenges to strike all six African Americans in the jury pool did not violate the equal protection clause of the Constitution. The Court reasoned:

> The presumption in any particular case must be that the prosecutor is using the State's challenges to obtain a fair and impartial jury . . . The presumption is not overcome and the prosecutor therefore subjected to examination by allegations that in the case at hand all Negroes were removed from the jury or that they were removed because they were Negroes.[45]

The Court went on to observe that the Constitution did place some limits on the use of the peremptory challenge. The Justices stated that a defendant could establish a prima facie case of purposeful racial discrimination by showing that the elimination of African Americans from a particular jury was part of a pattern of discrimination in that jurisdiction.

The problem was that the defendants in *Swain* and the cases that followed could not meet this stringent test. As Wishman observed, "A defense lawyer almost never has the statistics to prove a pattern of discrimination, and the state under the *Swain* decision is not required to keep them."[46] The ruling, therefore, provided no protection to the individual African American defendant deprived of a jury of his peers by the prosecutor's use of racially discriminatory strikes.

Despite harsh criticism from legal scholars and civil libertarians,[47] who argued that *Swain* imposed a "crushing burden . . . on defendants alleging racially discriminatory jury selection,"[48] the decision stood for 21 years. It was not until 1986 that the Court, in *Batson* v. *Kentucky*,[49] rejected *Swain*'s systematic exclusion requirement and ruled "that a defendant may establish a prima facie case of purposeful discrimination in selection of the petit jury solely on evidence concerning the prosecutor's exercise of peremptory challenges at the defendant's trial."[50] The Justices added that once the defendant makes a prima facie case of racial discrimination, the burden shifts to the state to provide a racially neutral explanation for excluding African American jurors.

Although *Batson* seemed to offer hope that the goal of a representative jury was attainable, an examination of cases decided since 1986 suggests otherwise. State and federal appellate courts have ruled, for example, that leaving one or two African Americans on the jury precludes any inference of purposeful racial discrimination on the part of the prosecutor,[51] and that striking only one or two jurors of the defendant's race does not constitute a "pattern" of strikes.[52] Trial and appellate courts have also been willing to accept virtually any explanation offered by the prosecutor to rebut the defendant's inference of purposeful discrimination.[53] Thus, "The cost of forfeiting truly peremptory challenges has yielded little corresponding benefit, as a myriad of `acceptable' explanations and excuses cloud any hope of detecting racially based motivations."[54]

Although it is no longer true that "the vast majority of the rural courts in the Deep South have made no pretense of putting Negroes on jury lists, much less calling or using them in trials,"[55] the jury selection process remains racially biased. Prosecutors continue to use the peremptory challenge to exclude African American jurors from cases with African American defendants,[56] and appellate courts continue to rule that their "racially neutral" explanations adequately meet the standards articulated in *Batson*.

Supreme Court decisions notwithstanding, the peremptory challenge remains an obstacle to impartiality.

COURT PROCESSING AND SENTENCING

Myrdal's examination of the southern court system uncovered widespread racial discrimination in case processing and sentencing. Myrdal observed that cases involving African American defendants were handled informally and with a lack of dignity, and that convictions often were obtained upon presentation of "scanty evidence." He noted that grand juries routinely refused to indict whites for crimes against African Americans, and added: "It is notorious that practically never have white lynching mobs been brought to court in the South, even when the killers are known to all in the community and are mentioned by name in the local press."[57]

A common theme in Myrdal's analysis of court processing and sentencing is the differential treatment of interracial and intraracial crimes. Noting that "it is part of the Southern tradition to assume that Negroes are disorderly and lack elementary morals,"[58] Myrdal concluded that African American defendants who victimized other African Americans were treated with great leniency. He observed that white southerners viewed the more lenient treatment of black-on-black crime "as evidence of the friendliness of Southern courts toward Negroes," but that "the Southern Negro community is not at all happy about this double standard of justice."[59]

According to Myrdal, interracial crimes evoked very different responses from southern courts, depending on the race of the offender. Whites who committed crimes, even very serious crimes, against African Americans were rarely convicted; those who were convicted received only the mildest punishment. African Americans charged with (or even suspected of) offenses against whites, on the other hand, were treated very harshly. Myrdal noted that African Americans charged with serious crimes against whites often faced a white lynching mob. He stated that in situations like this, "the court makes no pretense at justice; the Negro must be condemned, and usually condemned to death, before the crowd gets him."[60]

RACE AND PRETRIAL DECISION-MAKING

Since 1943 there has been a virtual explosion of research investigating the relationship between the defendant's race and court processing decisions. Although most of this research has focused on the effect of race on sentencing, there are a number of studies that examine decisions made prior to trial for evidence of racial discrimination. As noted earlier, several stud-

ies have analyzed the relationship between defendant race and bail decision-making. The results of these studies are contradictory, but some do
conclude that race affects the type and amount of bail imposed by the judge.

There also is evidence that prosecutors' charging decisions are affected
by race. An analysis of the prosecutor's decision to reject or dismiss charges
against defendants in Los Angeles County, for example, revealed a pattern
of discrimination in favor of female defendants and against African
American and Hispanic defendants.[61] A study by Petersilia,[62] on the other
hand, found that white suspects were *more* likely than African American or
Hispanic suspects to be formally charged. Her analysis of the reasons given
for charge rejection led her to conclude that the higher dismissal rates for
nonwhite suspects reflected the fact that "blacks and Hispanics in California
are more likely than whites to be arrested under circumstances that provide insufficient evidence to support criminal charges."[63]

Two studies concluded that both the race of the defendant and the race
of the victim are significant factors. LaFree[64] found that African Americans
arrested for raping white women were more likely to be charged with
felonies than were either African Americans arrested for raping African
American women or whites arrested for raping white women. Another
study found that defendants arrested for murdering whites in Florida were
more likely to be indicted for first-degree murder than those arrested for
murdering blacks.[65]

THE EFFECT OF RACE ON SENTENCING

Fifty years after publication of *An American Dilemma*, the issue of racial discrimination in sentencing continues to evoke controversy and spark debate.
Citing statistics showing that African American males account for one-half
of all state and federal prisoners,[66] critics charge that African American criminal defendants are more likely to be incarcerated and for longer periods of
time than are white defendants. They argue that judges' sentencing decisions are racially biased. Other researchers suggest that the harsher sentences imposed on African American defendants reflect, not racial
discrimination on the part of judges, but the fact that African American defendants commit more serious crimes and have more serious prior criminal
records than white defendants. They argue that racial disparities in sentencing will disappear once these legal factors are taken into consideration.

There is now a substantial body of research examining the relationship
between defendant race and sentence severity.[67] Early studies consistently
documented overt bias against African Americans,[68] but more recent studies have produced contradictory findings. These more methodologically
rigorous studies have not always supported the proposition that "blacks or

other nonwhites will receive more severe punishment than whites for all crimes, under all conditions, and at similar levels of disproportion over time."[69] Although a number of studies have found that African Americans are sentenced more harshly than whites,[70] others have found either that there are no significant racial differences[71] or that African Americans are sentenced more leniently than whites.[72]

The failure of research to produce uniform findings of racial discrimination in sentencing has led to conflicting conclusions. Some researchers[73] assert that racial discrimination in sentencing has declined over time and contend that the predictive power of race, once relevant legal factors are taken into account, is quite low. Others[74] claim that discrimination has not declined or disappeared but simply has become more subtle and difficult to detect. These researchers argue that race affects sentence severity *indirectly* through its effect on variables such as bail status,[75] type of attorney,[76] or type of disposition,[77] or that race *interacts* with other variables and affects sentence severity only in some types of cases,[78] in some types of settings,[79] or for some types of defendants.[80]

Differential Treatment of Interracial and Intraracial Crime

Myrdal emphasized differences in the treatment of interracial and intraracial crime in southern courts. He observed that African Americans who victimized whites received the harshest punishment, while African Americans who offended against other African Americans were often "acquitted or given a ridiculously mild sentence.[81] Myrdal also noted that "it is quite common for a white criminal to be set free if his crime was against a Negro."[82]

Race and sentences imposed for sexual assault. Recent empirical research confirms these conclusions. There have been a number of studies comparing the processing of interracial and intraracial sexual assaults. LaFree,[83] for example, examined the impact of offender/victim race on the disposition of sexual assault cases in Indianapolis. He found that African American men who sexually assaulted white women were sentenced more severely than were other defendants, while African American men who assaulted African American women were sentenced more leniently than were other defendants. Walsh[84] reached a similar conclusion. When he examined the sentences imposed on African American and on white defendants convicted of sexual assault in a metropolitan Ohio county, he found that neither the defendant's race nor the victim's race affected sentence severity. Further analysis, however, revealed that black-on-white sexual assaults received more severe sentences than black-on-black sexual assaults.

Spohn's[85] study of sentences imposed on defendants convicted of violent felonies in Detroit also highlighted the importance of testing for race-of-victim and type-of-crime effects. When the author examined the sentences imposed on all felony defendants, she found that offender/victim race did not affect sentence severity in the predicted manner. When she analyzed the effect of offender/victim race on sentence severity *separately* for the various types of crimes, on the other hand, she found that offender/victim race did influence judges' sentencing decisions in sexual assault and murder cases. African Americans who sexually assaulted whites faced a greater risk of incarceration than either African Americans who sexually assaulted African Americans or whites who sexually assaulted whites; similarly, African Americans who murdered whites received longer sentences than did offenders in the other two categories. For these two crimes, then, the author found discrimination based on the race of the offender *and* the race of the victim.

Race and the death penalty.   Myrdal devoted surprisingly little attention to the issue of racial discrimination in the application of the death penalty. Citing statistics on the numbers of African Americans and whites sentenced to death, he simply noted that "The South makes the widest application of the death penalty, and Negro criminals come in for much more than their share of the executions."[86]

Statistics collected since the early 1940s suggest that little has changed, in the South or elsewhere. African Americans continue to be executed at a disproportionately high rate. Over 50 percent of the prisoners executed between 1930 and 1977 were African Americans; indeed, nearly 90 percent of those executed for rape from 1930 to 1977[87] were African Americans, and most were African Americans convicted of raping white women.[88] Between 1977 and 1992, 157 persons were executed by 16 states; of these, 94 (60 percent) were white and 63 (40 percent) were black.[89]

African Americans also are overrepresented among those sentenced to death. Data collected by the NAACP Legal Defense and Educational Fund (NAACPLDF) indicate that nearly 40 percent of the current death row inmates in the United States are African Americans; the data also reveal that there is a disproportionate number of minorities awaiting death in most of the 35 states with capital punishment statutes.[90] In 1992, for example, the percentage of African Americans on death row was 64 percent (84/132) in Illinois, 60 percent (82/137) in Pennsylvania, 59 percent (30/51) in Mississippi, 54 percent (20/37) in Louisiana, and 53 percent (59/111) in Ohio.[91]

Although these statistics indicate racial disparity in the application of the death penalty, they do not prove that states impose the death sentence in a racially discriminatory manner. Recent studies of the imposition of the death penalty, however, suggest that the disparities do reflect discrimination. There is a substantial body of research demonstrating that African Americans who murder whites are much more likely to be sentenced to death than African Americans who murder other African Americans, or whites who murder African Americans or whites.[92] The most widely cited of these studies[93] found that defendants convicted of killing whites were over four times as likely to receive a death sentence as defendants convicted of killing blacks. Baldus and his colleagues also found that African Americans who killed whites had the greatest likelihood of receiving the death penalty.

Some commentators have questioned the national significance of findings of victim-based racial discrimination in the capital sentencing process, noting that almost all of the studies address capital sentencing in southern states. Recent research by Gross and Mauro,[94] however, demonstrates that discrimination based on the race of the victim is not confined to the South. Gross and Mauro found capital sentencing disparities by the race of the victim in each of the eight states—Florida, Georgia, Illinois, Oklahoma, North Carolina, Mississippi, Virginia, and Arkansas—included in their study. They concluded that their data showed "a clear pattern" of victim-based discrimination "unexplainable on grounds other than race."[95]

Evidence such as that cited above has been used to mount constitutional challenges to the imposition of the death penalty. African American defendants convicted of raping or murdering whites have claimed that the death penalty is applied in a racially discriminatory manner in violation of both the equal protection clause of the Fourteenth Amendment and the cruel and unusual punishment clause of the Eighth Amendment. These claims have been consistently rejected by federal appellate courts. In a series of decisions, the Courts of Appeals ruled, first, that the empirical studies used to document systematic racial discrimination did not take every variable related to capital sentencing into account and, second, that the evidence presented did not demonstrate that the appellant's *own* sentence was the product of discrimination.[96]

The Supreme Court addressed the issue of victim-based racial discrimination in the application of the death penalty in the case of *McCleskey* v. *Kemp*[97] Warren McCleskey, an African American, was convicted and sentenced to death in Georgia for killing a white police officer during the course of an armed robbery. McCleskey claimed that the Georgia capital sentencing process was administered in a racially discriminatory manner. In support of his claim, he offered the results of the study conducted by Baldus and his colleagues.[98] As noted above, this study found that African Americans who were convicted of murdering whites had the greatest likelihood of receiving the death penalty.

The Supreme Court rejected McCleskey's Fourteenth and Eighth Amendment claims. Although the majority accepted the validity of the Baldus study, they nonetheless refused to accept McCleskey's argument that the disparities documented by Baldus signaled the presence of unconstitutional racial discrimination. The Court argued that the disparities were "unexplained" and stated, "At most, the Baldus study indicates a discrepancy that appears to correlate with race."[99] The Court also ruled that the Baldus study was "clearly insufficient to support an inference that any of the decision-makers in McCleskey's case acted with discriminatory purpose."[100]

Legal scholars and civil libertarians have questioned the Supreme Court's reasoning in *McCleskey*. Citing the inconsistency inherent in assuming the validity of the Baldus study but then refusing to acknowledge the existence of racial discrimination, Gross and Mauro conclude, "The central message of the *McCleskey* case is all too plain; de facto racial discrimination in capital sentencing is legal in the United States."[101]

Racial Discrimination in Sentencing: Summary and Analysis

Research conducted since the publication of *An American Dilemma* suggests that racial discrimination in sentencing persists in the South and elsewhere. It is no longer true that whites accused of crimes against African Americans are routinely "set free" or that African Americans suspected of raping or murdering whites are routinely threatened by white lynching mobs bent on vengeance. Although these types of overt racism have been eliminated, discrimination in sentencing has not. African Americans convicted of crimes against whites, and particularly those convicted of sexual assault or murder, continue to be punished more harshly than other offenders. They are more likely than other offenders, particularly African Americans who victimize other African Americans, to be sentenced to prison or to be sentenced to death.

Researchers have advanced two interrelated explanations for the harsher treatment of crimes involving African American offenders and white victims—the more lenient treatment of crimes involving African American offenders and African American victims. The first explanation builds on conflict theory's premise that the law is applied to maintain the power of the dominant group and to control the behavior of individuals who threaten that power.[102] It suggests that crimes involving black offenders and white victims are punished most harshly because they pose the greatest threat to "the system of racially stratified state authority."[103]

Researchers have advanced a similar explanation for the harsher treatment of African Americans who sexually assault whites. Using the concept of sexual stratification, LaFree[104] argues that one measure of the dominant group's power is its ability to control sexual access to women in the dominant group, who are regarded as the scarce and valuable sexual property of men of their own race. The sexual assault of a white woman by an African American man, then, threatens the power of the dominant group by violating the group's sexual property rights. This, according to Walsh, "accounts for the strength of the taboo attached to inter-racial sexual assault."[105] It also explains why sexual assaults of African American women, who are seen as less valuable sexual "commodities," are perceived as less serious crimes.

The second explanation for the harsher penalties imposed on those who victimize whites emphasizes the race of the victim rather than the racial composition of the victim/offender dyad. This explanation suggests that crimes involving African American victims are not taken seriously or that crimes involving white victims are taken very seriously; it suggests that the lives of African American victims are devalued relative to the lives of white victims. Thus, crimes against whites will be punished more severely than crimes against African Americans regardless of the race of the offender.

Most researchers have failed to explain adequately *why* those who victimize whites are treated more harshly than those who victimize African Americans. Gross and Mauro suggest that the explanation, at least in capital cases, may hinge on the degree to which jurors are able to identify with the victim.[106] The authors argue that jurors take the life-or-death decision in a capital case very seriously. To condemn a murderer to death thus requires something more than sympathy for the victim. Jurors will not sentence the defendant to death unless they are particularly horrified by the crime, and they will not be particularly horrified by the crime unless they can identify or empathize with the victim. According to the authors,

> In a society that remains segregated socially if not legally, and in which the great majority of jurors are white, jurors are not likely to identify with black victims or to see them as family or friends. Thus jurors are more likely to be horrified by the killing of a white than of a black, and more likely to act against the killer of a white than the killer of a black.[107]

The same reasoning could be applied to judicial sentencing decisions. One might argue that judges, the majority of whom are white, will identify more readily with white victims and thus will be more horrified by crimes against whites. As a consequence, they will be more willing to impose harsh penalties on those who victimize whites.

CONCLUSION

The court system described by Myrdal in *An American Dilemma* no longer exists, in the South or elsewhere. Reforms mandated by the U.S. Supreme Court or adopted voluntarily by the states have eliminated much of the overt racism against African American criminal defendants documented by Myrdal. Implementation of these reforms, however, has not produced equality of justice. African Americans who find themselves in the arms of the law continue to suffer discrimination in court processing and sentencing.

Myrdal described a court system characterized by flagrant racism against African American criminal defendants. Most of these blatant injustices have been eliminated. In the 1990s whites who commit crimes against African Americans are not beyond the reach of the criminal justice system, African Americans suspected of crimes against whites do not receive "justice" at the hands of white lynching mobs, and African Americans who offend against other African Americans are not immune from punishment. As a result of reforms instituted during the past 50 years, African American criminal defendants are no longer routinely denied bail and then tried by all-white juries without attorneys to assist them in their defense.

Despite these significant changes, discrimination persists. Social scientists and legal scholars have shown that defendant race continues to affect decisions regarding bail, charging, jury selection, and sentencing. Some researchers conclude that race has a direct and obvious effect on these decisions; they contend that African Americans are more likely than whites to be detained, charged, sentenced to prison, or sentenced to death.

Other researchers conclude that discrimination in court processing and sentencing has become more subtle and difficult to detect. They assert that discrimination against African Americans is not universal but is confined to certain types of cases, certain types of settings, and certain types of defendants. These researchers argue, for example, that African American defendants who murder or rape whites will be punished more harshly than other defendants. They also suggest that being unemployed, having a prior criminal record, or being detained prior to trial have more negative effects on court outcomes for African Americans than for whites.

In sum, while the reforms envisioned by Myrdal may have eliminated the more obvious examples of racial discrimination in the criminal justice system, they have not produced an equitable, or color blind, system of justice. Fifty years after the publication of *An American Dilemma*, African Americans continue to suffer discrimination at the hands of criminal justice officials in the United States.

NOTES

1. Gunnar Myrdal. *An American Dilemma: The Negro Problem and Modern Democracy* (New York: Harper & Brothers, 1944), p. 555.
2. Ibid., p. 550.
3. Ibid., p. 556.
4. Ibid., p. 556.
5. Mark Mauer. *Young Black Men and the Criminal Justice System: A Growing National Problem* (Washington, D.C.: The Sentencing Project, 1990).
6. Myrdal, p. 555.
7. Ibid., p. 548.
8. Ibid., p. 556
9. Ibid., p. 548.
10. *Powell* v. *Alabama*, 287 U.S. 45 (1932).
11. *Johnson* v. *Zerbst,* 304 U.S. 458 (1938).
12. *Gideon* v. *Wainwright*, 372 U.S. 335 (1963).
13. *Gideon* v. *Wainwright* required the states to provide counsel for indigent defendants charged with felonies. In 1972 the Supreme Court ruled that "no person may be imprisoned for any offense, whether classified as petty, misdemeanor, or felony, unless he was represented by counsel [*Argersinger* v. *Hamlin,* 407 U.S. 25 (1972)].
14. *Argersinger* v. *Hamlin*, 407 U.S. 25 (1972).
15. A defendant is entitled to counsel at every stage "where substantial rights of the accused may be affected" that require the "guiding hand of counsel" (*Mempa* v. *Rhay*, 389 U.S. 128, 1967). These critical stages include arraignment, preliminary hearing, entry of a plea, trial, sentencing, and the first appeal.
16. Anthony Lewis. *Gideon's Trumpet* (New York: Vintage Books, 1964).
17. Lisa J. McIntyre. *The Public Defender: The Practice of Law in the Shadows of Repute* (Chicago: University of Chicago Press, 1987).
18. Bureau of Justice Statistics. *Criminal Defense Systems: A National Survey* (Washington, D.C.: U.S. Government Printing Office, 1984).
19. In a series of cases, the U.S. Supreme Court decided that the right to counsel is not limited to the trial, but applies to all critical stages in the process. A defendant is entitled to counsel at every stage "where substantial rights of the accused may be affected" that require the "guiding hand of counsel" (*Mempa* v. *Rhay*, 389 U.S. 128, 1967). These critical stages include arraignment, preliminary hearing, entry of a plea, trial, sentencing, and the first appeal.
20. Studies comparing the quality of legal services provided by private attorneys and public defenders are inconclusive. A study in Cook County, Illinois, found that clients represented by public defenders were more likely than those represented by private attorneys or assigned counsel to plead guilty (Dallin H. Oaks and Warren Lehman. *A Criminal Justice System and the Indigent*. (Chicago: University of Chicago Press, 1968)). Other studies found no differences. See Jean Taylor, Thomas Stanley, Barbara Deflorio, and Lyne Seekamp. "An Analysis of Defense Counsel in the Processing of Felony Defendants in

Denver, Colorado." *Denver Law Journal* 50 (1973): 9–44; Paul Wice. *Criminal Lawyers: An Endangered Species* (Beverly Hills, Cal.: Sage Publications, 1978).

21. Myrdal, p. 547.
22. Ibid., p. 548.
23. Celesta A. Albonetti. "An Integration of Theories to Explain Judicial Discretion." *Social Problems* 38 (1991): 247–266; Ronald A. Farrell and Victoria L. Swigert. "Prior Offense Record as a Self-Fulfilling Prophecy." *Law and Society Review* 12 (1978): 437–453; C. Foote. "Compelling Appearance in Court: Administration of Bail in Philadelphia." *University of Pennsylvania Law Review* 102 (1954): 1031–1079; Joan Petersilia. *Racial Disparities in the Criminal Justice System* (Santa Monica, CA: Rand Corporation, 1978); G. R. Wheeler and C. L. Wheeler. "Reflections on Legal Representation of the Economically Disadvantaged: Beyond Assembly Line Justice." *Crime and Delinquency* 26 (1980): 319–332.
24. Wayne Thomas. *Bail Reform in America* (Berkeley: University of California Press, 1976).
25. Samuel Walker. *Taming the System: The Control of Discretion in Criminal Justice, 1950–1990* (New York: Oxford University Press, 1993), p. 54.
26. J. Austin, B. Krisberg, and P. Litsky. "The Effectiveness of Supervised Pretrial Release." *Crime and Delinquency* 31 (1985): 519–537; John S. Goldkamp. "Danger and Detention: A Second Generation of Bail Reform." *The Journal of Criminal Law and Criminology* 76 (1985): 1–74; Samuel Walker. *Taming the System.*
27. Goldkamp. "Danger and Detention."
28. This law was upheld by the U.S. Supreme Court in *United States* v. *Salerno*, 481 U.S. 739 (1987).
29. Coramae Richey Mann. *Unequal Justice: A Question of Color* (Bloomington and Indianapolis: Indiana University Press, 1993), p. 168.
30. Celesta A. Albonetti. "Bail and Judicial Discretion in the District of Columbia." *Sociology and Social Research* 74 (1989): 40–47; C. E. Frazier, E.W. Bock, and J.C. Henretta. "Pretrial Release and Bail Decisions: The Effects of Legal, Community, and Personal Variables." *Criminology* 18 (1980): 162–181; John S. Goldkamp and Michael Gottfredson. "Bail Decision Making and Pretrial Detention: Surfacing Judicial Policy." *Law and Human Behavior* 3 (1979): 227–249; Ilene H. Nagel. The Legal/Extra-Legal Controversy: Judicial Decisions in Pretrial Release." *Law & Society Review* 17 (1983): 481–515; and R. Stryker, Ilene Nagel, and John Hagan. "Methodology Issues in Court Research: Pretrial Release Decisions for Federal Defendants." *Sociological Methods and Research* 11 (1983): 469–500.
31. S. H. Clarke and G. G. Koch. "The Influence of Income and Other Factors on Whether Criminal Defendants Go To Prison." *Law & Society Review* 11 (1976): 57–92; Ronald A. Farrell and Victoria L. Swigert. "Prior Offense Record as a Self-Fulfilling Prophecy." *Law & Society Review* 12 (1978): 437–453; and J. D. Unnever. "Direct and Organizational Discrimination in the Sentencing of Drug Offenders." *Social Problems* 30 (1982): 212–225.
32. E. Britt Patterson and Michael J. Lynch. "Biases in Formalized Bail Procedures." In Michael J. Lynch and E. Britt Patterson, eds. *Race and Criminal Justice* (New York: Harrow and Heston, 1991).

33. Margaret Farnworth and Patrick Horan. "Separate Justice: An Analysis of Race Differences in Court Processes." *Social Science Research* 9 (1980): 381–399.

34. Tim Bynum. "Release on Recognizance: Substantive or Superficial Reform?" *Criminology* 20 (1982): 67–82.

35. Celesta A. Albonetti, Robert M. Hauser, John Hagan, and Ilene H. Nagel. "Criminal Justice Decision Making as a Stratification Process: The Role of Race and Stratification Resources in Pretrial Release." *Journal of Quantitative Criminology* 5 (1989): 57–82.

36. Myrdal, p. 549.

37. *Norris* v. *Alabama*, 294 U.S. 587 (1935).

38. Myrdal, p. 549.

39. Ibid., p. 549.

40. *Avery* v. *Georgia*, 345 U.S. 559 (1953).

41. *Whitus* v. *Georgia*, 385 U.S. 545 (1967).

42. *Avery* v. *Georgia*, 345 U.S. 559 (1953) at 562.

43. David W. Neubauer. *America's Court & the Criminal Justice System*, 3rd ed. (Pacific Grove, Cal.: Brooks/Cole Publishing, 1988), p. 307.

44. Brian J. Serr and Mark Maney. "Racism, Peremptory Challenges, and the Democratic Jury: The Jurisprudence of a Delicate Balance." *The Journal of Criminal Law & Criminology* 79 (1988): 9.

45. *Swain* v. *Alabama*, 380 U.S. at 222.

46. Seymour Wishman. *Anatomy of a Jury: The System on Trial* (New York: Times Books, 1986).

47. See Comment, "*Swain* v. *Alabama*, A Constitutional Blueprint for the Perpetuation of the All-White Jury." Virginia Law Review 52 (1966): 1157; Note, "Rethinking Limitations on the Peremptory Challenge." *Columbia Law Review* 85 (1983): 1357.

48. Serr and Maney. "Racism, Peremptory Challenges, and the Democratic Jury." p. 13.

49. *Batson* v. *Kentucky*, 476 U.S. 79, 93–94 (1986).

50. Ibid., at 96.

51. *United States* v. *Montgomery*, 819 F.2d at 851. The Eleventh Circuit, however, rejected this line of reasoning in *Fleming* v. *Kemp* [794 F.2d 1478 (11th Cir. 1986)] and *United States* v. *David* [803 F.2d 1567 (11th Cir. 1986)].

52. *United States* v. *Vaccaro*, 816 F.2d 443, 457 (9th Cir. 1987); *Fields* v. *People*, 732 P.2d 1145, 1158 n.20 (Colo. 1987).

53. Serr and Maney. "Racism, Peremptory Challenges, and the Democratic Jury." pp. 43–47.

54. Ibid., p. 63.

55. Myrdal, pp. 547–548.

56. A study of peremptory challenges issued from 1976 to 1981 in Calcasieu Parish, Louisiana, for example, found that prosecutors excused African American jurors at a disproportionately high rate. See Billy M. Turner, Rickie D. Lovell, John C. Young, and William F. Denny. "Race and Peremptory Challenges During Voir Dire: Do Prosecution and Defense Agree?" *Journal of Criminal Justice* 14 (1986): 61–69.

57. Myrdal, pp. 552–553.

58. Ibid., p. 551.

59. Ibid., p. 551.

60. Ibid., p. 553.

61. Cassia Spohn, John Gruhl, and Susan Welch. "The Impact of the Ethnicity and Gender of Defendants on the Decision To Reject or Dismiss Felony Charges." *Criminology* 25 (1987): 175–191.

62. Joan Petersilia. *Racial Disparities in the Criminal Justice System* (Santa Monica, Cal.: RAND, 1983).

63. Ibid., p. 26.

64. Gary D. LaFree. "The Effect of Sexual Stratification by Race on Official Reactions to Rape." *American Sociological Review* 45 (1980): 842–854.

65. Michael L. Radelet. "Racial Characteristics and the Imposition of the Death Penalty." *American Sociological Review* 46 (1981): 918–927.

66. Patrick A. Langan. *Race and Prisoners Admitted to State and Federal Institutions, 1926–1986* (U.S. Department of Justice, Washington, D.C.: U.S. Government Printing Office, 1991).

67. For a review of these studies and for a discussion of the four waves of research on sentencing disparities, see Marjorie S. Zatz. "The Changing Forms of Racial/Ethnic Biases in Sentencing." *Journal of Research in Crime and Delinquency* 24 (1987): 69–92.

68. See, for example, Hugo A. Bedau. "Death Sentences in New Jersey." *Rutgers Law Review* 19 (1964): 1–2; E. H. Johnson. "Selective Factors in Capital Punishment." *Social Forces* 58 (1957): 165–169; E. M. Lemert and J. Rosberg. "The Administration of Justice to Minority Groups in L.A. County." *University of California Publications in Culture and Society* (1948): 1–27; and Thorsten Sellin. "Race Prejudice in the Administration of Justice." *American Journal of Sociology* 41 (1935): 212–217;

69. Hawkins. "Beyond Anomalies." p. 724.

70. Joan Petersilia. *Racial Disparities in the Criminal Justice System* (Santa Monica, Cal: RAND, 1983); Cassia Spohn, John Gruhl, and Susan Welch. "The Effect of Race on Sentencing: A Re-Examination of an Unsettled Question." *Law & Society Review* 16 (1981–82): 71–88; and Marjorie S. Zatz. "Race, Ethnicity, and Determinate Sentencing: A New Dimension to an Old Controversy." *Criminology* 22 (1984): 147–171.

71. Stephen Klein, Joan Petersilia, and Susan Turner. "Race and Imprisonment Decisions in California." *Science* 247 (1990): 812–816.

72. Ilene Nagel Bernstein, William R. Kelly, and Patricia A. Doyle. "Societal Reaction to Deviants: The Case of Criminal Defendants." *American Sociological Review* 42 (1977): 743–795; James L. Gibson. "Race as a Determinant of Criminal Sentences: A Methodological Critique and a Case Study." *Law & Society Review* 12 (1978): 455–478; and Martin A. Levin. "Urban Politics and Policy Outcomes: The Criminal Courts." In George F. Cole, ed. *Criminal Justice: Law and Politics* (Belmont, Cal.: Wadsworth, 1988).

73. John Hagan. "Extra-Legal Attributes and Criminal Sentencing: An Assessment of a Sociological Viewpoint." *Law & Society Review* 8 (1974):

357–383; Gary C. Kleck. "Racial Discrimination in Sentencing: A Critical Evaluation of the Evidence with Additional Evidence on the Death Penalty." *American Sociological Review* 43 (1981): 783–805; and Charles R. Pruitt and James Q. Wilson. "A Longitudinal Study of the Effect of Race on Sentencing." *Law & Society Review* 7 (1983): 613–635.

74. Steven Klepper, Daniel Nagin, and Luke-Jon Tierney. "Discrimination in the Criminal Justice System: A Critical Appraisal of the Literature." In Alfred Blumstein, Jacqueline Cohen, Susan E. Martin, and Michael H. Tonry, eds. *Research on Sentencing: A Search for Reform,* Vol. 2 (Washington, D.C.: National Academy Press, 1983, pp. 55–128); Marjorie S. Zatz. "The Changing Forms of Racial/Ethnic Biases in Sentencing." *Journal of Research in Crime and Delinquency* 24 (1987): 69–92.

75. Gary D. LaFree. "Official Reactions to Hispanic Defendants in the Southwest." *Journal of Research in Crime and Delinquency* 22 (1985): 213–23; Alan J. Lizotte. "Extra-legal factors in Chicago's Criminal Courts: Testing the Conflict Model of Criminal Justice." *Social Problems* 25 (1978): 564–580.

76. Spohn, Gruhl, and Welch. "The Effect of Race on Sentencing."

77. Gary D. LaFree. "Adversarial and Nonadversarial Justice: A Comparison of Guilty Pleas and Trials." *Criminology* 23 (1985): 289–312; Cassia Spohn. "An Analysis of the 'Jury Trial Penalty' and Its Effect on Black and White Offenders." *The Justice Professional* 7 (1992): 93–112; and Thomas M. Uhlman and J. Darlene Walker. "'He Takes Some of My Time, I Take Some of His': An Analysis of Sentencing Patterns in Jury Cases." *Law & Society Review* 14 (1980): 323–341.

78. Arnold Barnett. "Some Distribution Patterns for the Georgia Death Sentence." *U.C. Davis Law Review* 18 (1985): 1327–1374; Cassia Spohn and Jerry Cederblom. "Race and Disparities in Sentencing: A Test of the Liberation Hypothesis." *Justice Quarterly* 8 (1991): 305–327.

79. Darnell F. Hawkins. "Beyond Anomalies: Rethinking the Conflict Perspective on Race and Criminal Punishment." *Social Forces* 65 (1987): 719–745; Kleck. "Racial Discrimination in Sentencing"; and Martha A. Myers and Susette Talarico. "The Social Contexts of Racial Discrimination in Sentencing." *Social Problems* 33 (1986): 236–251.

80. Theodore G. Chiricos and William D. Bales. "Unemployment and Punishment: An Empirical Assessment." *Criminology* 29 (1991): 701–724; Gary D. LaFree. *Rape and Criminal Justice: The Social Construction of Sexual Assault* (Belmont, Cal.: Wadsworth, 1989); Ruth Peterson and John Hagan. "Changing Conceptions of Race: Toward an Account of Anomalous Findings in Sentencing Research." *American Sociological Review* 49 (1984): 56–70; Cassia Spohn. "Crime and the Social Control of Blacks: The Effect of Offender/ Victim Race on Sentences for Violent Felonies." In George Bridges and Martha Myers, eds. *Inequality, Crime and Social Control* (Boulder, Colo.: Westview Press, 1994); and Anthony Walsh, "The Sexual Stratification Hypothesis and Sexual Assault in Light of the Changing Conceptions of Race." *Criminology* 25 (1987): 153–173.

81. Myrdal, p. 551.

82. Ibid., p. 553.

83. LaFree. *Rape and Criminal Justice.*

84. Walsh. "The Sexual Stratification Hypothesis."

85. Spohn. "Crime and the Social Control of Blacks."

86. Myrdal, p. 554.

87. In 1977 the Supreme Court ruled that imposition of the death penalty for the rape of an adult woman was a violation of the Eighth and Fourteenth Amendments [*Coker* v. *Georgia*, 433 U.S. 584 (1977)].

88. Marvin E. Wolfgang and Marc Riedel. "Race, Judicial Discretion, and the Death Penalty. *The Annals* 407 (1973): 119–133.

89. Lawrence A. Greenfeld. *Capital Punishment 1991* (Washington, D.C.: U.S. Department of Justice, Bureau of Justice Statistics, 1992), p. 2.

90. National Association for the Advancement of Colored People—Legal Defense Fund (NAACP–LDF). *Death Row U.S.A.* (New York: NAACP–LDF, Inc., 1992).

91. Greenfield. *Capital Punishment 1991*, p. 8.

92. Steven D. Arkin. "Discriminations and Arbitrariness in Capital Punishment: An Analysis of Post-*Furman* Murder Cases in Dade County, Florida, 1973–1976." *Stanford Law Review* 33 (1980): 75–101; David C. Baldus, Charles Pulaski, and George Woodworth. "Comparative Review of Death Sentences: An Empirical Study of the Georgia Experience." *Journal of Criminal Law and Criminology* 74 (1983): 661–753; David C. Baldus, George Woodworth, and Charles Pulaski. "Monitoring and Evaluating Contemporary Death Sentencing Systems: Lessons From Georgia." *U.C. Davis Law Review* 18 (1985): 1375–1407; William J. Bowers and Glenn L. Pierce. "Arbitrariness and Discrimination under Post-*Furman* Capital Statutes." *Crime and Delinquency* 74 (1980): 1067–1100; Samuel R. Gross and Robert Mauro. *Death & Discrimination: Racial Disparities in Capital Sentencing* (Boston: Northeastern University Press, 1989); Thomas J. Keil and Gennaro F. Vito. "Race, Homicide Severity, and Application of the Death Penalty: A Consideration of the Barnett Scale." *Criminology* 27 (1989): 511–531; Peter B. Lewis, "Life on Death Row: A Post-*Furman* Profile of Florida's Condemned." In P.W. Lewis and K.D. Peoples, eds. *The Supreme Court and the Criminal Process—Cases and Comments* (Philadelphia: Saunders, 1978); Raymond Paternoster. "Prosecutorial Discretion in Requesting the Death Penalty: A Case of Victim-Based Racial Discrimination." *Law & Society Review* 18 (1984): 437–478; Michael L. Radelet. "Racial Characteristics and the Imposition of the Death Penalty." *American Sociological Review* 46 (1981): 918–927; and Paige H. Ralph, Jonathan R. Sorensen, and James W. Marquart. "A Comparison of Death-Sentenced and Incarcerated Murderers in Pre-*Furman* Texas." *Justice Quarterly* 9 (1992): 185–209.

93. Baldus, Woodworth, and Pulaski. "Monitoring and Evaluating Contemporary Death Penalty Systems."

94. Gross and Mauro. *Death and Discrimination.*

95. Ibid., p. 110.

96. See, e.g., *Maxwell* v. *Bishop*, F.2d 138 (8th Cir. 1968); *Spinkellink* v. *Wainwright*, 578 F.2d 582 (5th Cir. 1978); *Shaw* v. *Martin*, 733 F.2d 304 (4th Cir. 1984); and *Prejean* v. *Blackburn*, 743 F.2d 1091 (5th Cir. 1984).

97. *McCleskey* v. *Kemp*, 478 U.S. 279, 107 S. Ct. 1756 (1987).
98. Baldus et al. "Monitoring and Evaluating Contemporary Death Penalty Systems."
99. 107 S. Ct. at 1777.
100. 107 S. Ct. at 1769.
101. Gross and Mauro. *Death & Discrimination,* p. 212.
102. Quinney. *The Social Reality of Crime;* Austin Turk, *Criminality and Legal Order* (New York: Rand McNally, 1969).
103. Hawkins. "Beyond Anomalies," p. 726.
104. LaFree. *Rape and Criminal Justice.*
105. Walsh. "The Sexual Stratification Hypothesis," p. 155.
106. Gross and Mauro. *Death & Discrimination.*
107. Ibid., p. 113.

Antonio McDaniel

12

The Dynamic Racial Composition of the United States

A RACIALLY DIVIDED SOCIETY

In revisiting Myrdal's work it is appropriate that we reconsider the basis that underlies the theoretical orientation of his original work. For Myrdal and his collaborators, the "Negro problem" is reduced to a problem of assimilation or amalgamation. *An American Dilemma* presents the racial conflict in American society as a moral problem, a problem of the resistance to African amalgamation by European Americans.[1] The anti-amalgamation attitude of whites is seen as the obstacle to African Americans' assimilation. In *An American Dilemma* the problem is conceptualized in the context of amalgamation into white America. Race is viewed as a special case of ethnicity, and the problems of African Americans are considered in the same context as the problems of immigrants from Europe.[2] However, the book has little to say about the impact of immigration on the racial composition of the population.

Myrdal's approach conceives of the problem in terms that present the European American standard of behavior as that which African Americans and others should emulate. This view has its own built-in biases. For example, from this perspective it follows that European Americans set the standards of behavior in the United States, and that the Negro problem would be solved by African Americans adopting these standards. This view also dictates that the removal of barriers to assimilation would facilitate an improvement in the behavior of African Americans as well as provide them with access to the fruits of modern democracy. In addition, it is thought that the dropping of these barriers would eliminate the discrepancy between the ideal of American egalitarianism and the reality of racial discrimination. Thus, racism and discrimination are not problematic if assimilation is allowed.

Myrdal held that a group's racial problems are caused by that group being unassimilable. Such an approach assumes that racial discrimination is a contradiction rather than an integral part of the American system of

269

stratification, and it has lead to a kind of economic reductionism in the study of race relations in the United States. Herman Hoetink (1962) was one of the first to criticize this aspect of *An American Dilemma* in his work, *Caribbean Race Relations: A Study of Two Variants*.[3] "[I]f, in other words, the Negro group were spread over the higher and the whites on the lower rungs in proportion to their numbers, and the socio-economic gap separating whites and Negroes were to disappear—the race problem would cease to be a problem."[4]

Hoetink argued that populations show a proclivity for racial group attachments. There is a tendency for individuals to consider the interests of their group to be more important than those of other groups. Sociologists generally maintain that racial identity arises as a result of invidious intergroup distinctions and competition,[5] which result from individuals having a biosocial predisposition to consider members of their group to be more important than other people. Individuals seek to increase the position of their race at the expense of other races. When different populations come into contact, conflict will result. Resent research supports Hoetink's earlier formulation of the problem. Lawrence Bobo and James Kluegel suggest that in the United States, "the strongest aspect of group self-interest seems to be a straightforward calculation by whites that members of their own group will not benefit."[6] Even if we are not prepared to view racial problems as natural for human populations, we should consider the role of race in group conflict. This tendency may merit closer examination in our evaluation of the impact of a multiracial society, in which conflict between racial groups may be not only a result of the struggle over resources but also a struggle over standards of appropriate behavior and the legacy of difference. In the United States, behavioral differences have been connected to phenotypic differences. Race and behavior are thought to interact, thus racial classification is one of the ways that individuals are placed within the system of social stratification.

Generically, race refers to social relations among "distinct" peoples. Accordingly, a race may be defined as a group of people living competitively in a relationship of superordination or subordination with respect to some other group or groups of people within one state, country, or economic area. In societies in which migration plays a large role, the assimilability of individuals depends to a large degree on whether they are ethnically or racially different. For example, European immigrants to the United States are ethnically classified as foreign if they are born abroad of foreign-born parents. The descendants of these European immigrants, starting with the third generation, lose their foreign identity and merge into the mainstream, native-born white population. For immigrants from Africa and Asia in particular, a separate racial category has been maintained irrespective of how many generations lived in the United States. In this sense, race is distinct from ethnicity. The United States may have many ethnic groups, yet it is race not ethnicity that characterizes the divisions within this society. Particularly important in these divisions are physical differences, especially skin color.

Africans did not come to America as Africans, they came as Akan, Yoruba, Ibo, and Wolof. Europeans did not come as Europeans, they came as English, Scottish, French, and Irish. Likewise, Asians are not coming to the United States as Asians, they arrive as Chinese, Japanese, and Indians. Migrants from Latin America do not come to the United States as Hispanics or Latinos, they come as Mexicans and Cubans. Ethnicity and race are confounded in the United States by history and by the legacy of dichotomous somatic distinctions.

Furthermore, race is generally thought of in historical terms: a racial classification is usually applied based on a belief that different racial groups originate from different geographical locations. These geographical locations are thought to have given each racial group its dominant genetic pool. On the other hand, geographical locations are thought from the sociological point of view to have given each racial group its dominant culture origins, the source of its ethos. Our idea of race depends more on the supposed geographical origins of the population than on its biogenetic makeup. We are more concerned with the racial identity of the group associated with its historical origin as stated by the society and/or the members of the racial group. Thus, although Europeans originate from a variety of nations and cultures, their whiteness is what primarily identifies them in the United States. Likewise, the somatic distinction of blackness, or Africanness, identifies the African American.

As a concept, race requires that two or more distinct races be in existence. Thus, racial groups are always part of a system of race. Racial systems generally classify membership on the basis of culture and physical distinguishability. Though race may have a biological aspect, racial classification depends on social interaction. "Race relation" refers to the contact between different racial groups.

"Ethnic relations" are a special case of race relations. As in race relations, ethnic relations refer to the social interaction of two populations distinguishable on the basis of their somatic appearance and culture; however, the importance of somatic differences is not insurmountable. The contact between two distinct ethnic groups may initially be governed by race relations. Given time and favorable social conditions, the somatic differences are given decreasing significance, and the subordinate group's culture is assimilated into that of the dominant culture.

In the United States this process has been extremely important in the creation of the "white race." In the racial assimilation of an ethnic group, somatic distinctions are overshadowed by the myth of cultural and historical similarities. Assimilation requires that the subordinate group recognize myths of historical similarities and accept the dominant group's culture and historical predisposition. The classic case of this kind of assimilation is that of the Irish in the United States.[7] A similar form of assimilation occurred among the African immigrants to the United States. Although the African slaves were in no position to perpetuate their own national/tribal identity, they were forced by their social conditions within the Americas to accept their designation as blacks or Africans. However, unlike the Irish, the African population continues to be unassimilable within the United States. In fact, the unassimilability of the African-derived population continues to be a major element of racial classification within American society.

By insisting on the subclassification of humans into races, we have artificially imposed a formal nomenclature on the dynamic patterns of variability that we observe in American society. In this system of classification each race must be clearly defined. However, the boundaries of race are not fixed and definite because a member of one race can interbreed with members of any other race. Thus, racial classification is a tradition of convenience and is used because of the type of understanding of human variability we get by establishing discrete, geographically bounded packages within a species. However, in reality, the racial composition of the United States has been anything but stable, and immigrants show the absurdity of our concept of the racial classification of the population.

Not all racial heterogeneity is reducible to the problem of social integration. The symbols of social status should be considered as an independent factor in the creation of racial prejudice.[8] Every group has a complex of somatic (physical) characteristics that are accepted by the group as its norm.[9] Skin color is the most salient characteristic in the somatic norm image in the United States. The rejection of blackness by mainstream society is seen as a question of social power.[10] This rejection of blackness has had negative consequences for the African American population, especially those with darker skin tone. The African phenotype—blackness—has a significant negative effect on occupational status and income of African and Mexican Americans.[11] Thus, racial discrimination, racism, persists despite personal endowments and socioeconomic background.

The uncertainty and debate among Africans, Asians, and Hispanics (or Latinos) about their racial designation and/or identity in the United States stems from the ambiguity of racial classification. This ambiguity has had an impact on the collection of statistical data and the analysis of these data.

As the non-European-derived populations within the United States have gained some measure of political and academic power, they have led the fight in challenging how racial data are collected and analyzed in the United States.

THE DYNAMIC RACIAL COMPOSITION OF THE UNITED STATES

Changes in the racial composition of the United States result from a combination of differential fertility, differential mortality, and net immigration. In the United States all births, deaths, and migrations are racially classified. Racial classification and immigration have had a particularly direct impact on the social conceptualization of race in the United States. Figure 12.1 presents the changing racial composition of the United States from 1810 to 1990. Variations in fertility and mortality determine to a disproportionate degree the absolute size of past and future populations in the United States. The racial composition of the population of the United States has been dominated by immigration from Europe, Asia, and Africa. Historically, the most distinguishing feature of the changing racial composition of the United States was the growth of the African and European populations and the decline of the American Indian population. Equally important is the growth of the Asian and Hispanic populations from 1950 onwards. The sudden appearance of the Hispanic population results from a new classification, Hispanic, being accepted in contemporary debates about race and ethnic difference in the United States Census Bureau. Therefore, it is difficult, perhaps impossible, to estimate the actual size of the Hispanic population for the period before 1950[12] since the majority of them have been counted as white. Thus, they are found in the pre-1950 European population in Figure 12.1.

European immigrants and their descendants have dominated the racial makeup of the United States population since the eighteenth century. In 1810 the European population accounted for about 73 percent of the total population; by 1930, more than 88 percent; but by 1990, less than 80 percent. The early rise of the European population resulted from the extensive immigration from Europe during the period from 1810 to 1930, but it began to decline substantially following the Great Depression. The subsequent decline in the proportion of the European population was in large part caused by the increased migration of Asians and Hispanics (particularly Mexicans).

Figure 12.2 presents the changing racial composition of the African, Asian, American Indian, and Hispanic populations from 1810 to 1990. The American Indian and African proportion of the population declined until the 1940s. This decline is most notable for the American Indian population,

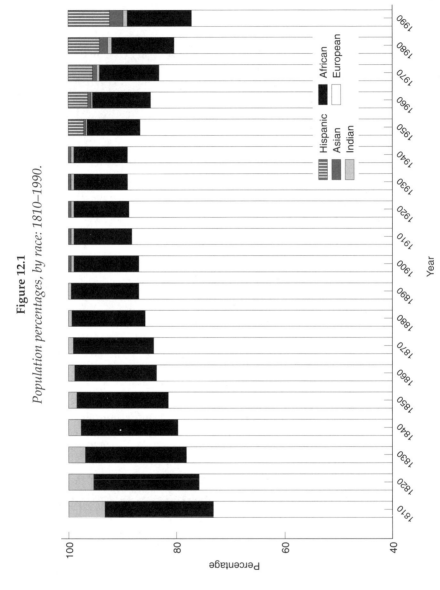

Figure 12.1

Population percentages, by race: 1810–1990.

Source: Appendix A of Antonio McDaniel, "The Dynamic Racial Composition of the United States," *Daedalus* 124 (1) (Winter 1995): 179–198.

Figure 12.2

Population percentages, by race (minus European): 1810–1990.

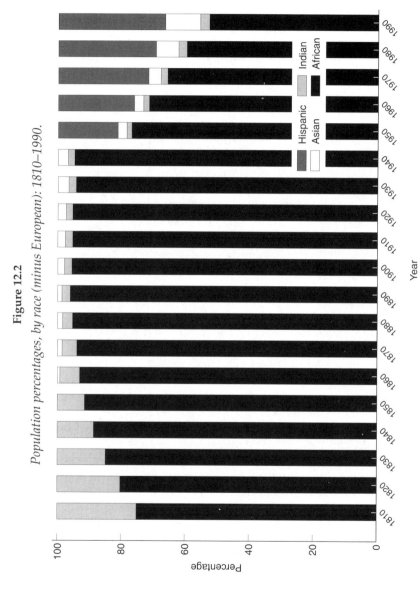

Source: Appendix A of Antonio McDaniel, "The Dynamic Racial Composition of the United States," *Daedalus* 124 (1) (Winter 1995): 179–198.

which did not begin to recover in its proportionate distribution until the 1970s, though its population decline ended around 1880. However, there is a clear decline in the African population as well, from a high of 20 percent in 1810 to a low of 10 percent in the 1920s through the 1960s.[13] For the most part, these declines in relative size were the results of European migration and exceptionally high rates of mortality within the American Indian and African populations. Another reason for the decline in the African population is that the legal slave trade to the United States ended in 1808 while the European rate of immigration was increasing. Around 1950 the Hispanic and Asian populations began to substantially increase their relative proportions of the population, with the Hispanic population experiencing the most proportionate growth.

From the fifteenth century to the beginning of the nineteenth century there was a massive transfer of populations from Africa and Europe to North America. In the nineteenth century and the first half of the twentieth century this transfer continued for European-derived population; however, the immigration of large numbers of Africans to North America was substantially reduced. In the last 50 years we have witnessed a massive new transfer of populations to North America, particularly the United States, from Asia, Latin America, and the Caribbean.

The diversity within the so-called minority population is complicated by the problems of racial classification. How racial groups are socially classified has a tremendous impact on the racial composition observed by any scholar. The Hispanic and Asian populations continue to confound the dominant conceptualization of race in United States society. In fact, Hispanics, Asians, and other immigrant groups are increasing in numbers and are not fitting into the traditional racial groups. In the 1990 census, close to 10 million people chose the "Other, Not Specified" race category rather than one of the specified categories. This makes racial classification of the population difficult and projections by race suspect.

The United States is often thought of as a refuge for immigrants, and the criteria by which immigrants are absorbed into United States society embody some of the society's essential values. But when immigrants arrive, they are subjected to the system of racial stratification within the United States. This process has had a tremendous impact on U.S. immigration policies.

Following the termination of the slave trade, Congress attempted to regulate the racial and ethnic composition of the immigrant population as part of its national immigration policy (Hutchinson 1981, pp. 478–491). Race, regional origin, and ethnicity have always been fundamental aspects of the selection of immigrants permitted to enter and settle in the United States. The major policy seems to have been to maintain the racial composition of the national population, or to maintain the white population's majority. This policy found its fullest expression in the national-origin system for the allocation of immigration quotas. It excluded certain populations on the basis of region of origin. For example, the Asiatic Barred Zone Act of 1917 excluded various national populations from Asia. This exclusion did not end until 1952, when quotas for Asians were established on the basis of race or ancestry rather than birthplace. Another less drastic example was the more selective policy used to curb Southern and Eastern European immigration.

The Hart-Celler Immigration Act of 1965 attempted to eliminate the racially preferential nature of immigration legislation. The stated purpose of the bill was "the elimination of the national-origins system as the basis for the selection of immigrants to the United States" (House of Representatives 1965, in Hutchinson 1981). The results of the national-origins system are most clearly reflected in the numbers and national origins of legal immigrants to the United States. Table 12.1 presents the percentage of legal immigrants to the United States between 1920 and 1992 by region of last residence.

Changes in the source of legal and illegal immigrants to the United States coincide with changes in immigration laws. Before the Hart-Celler Immigration Act, the vast majority of legal immigrants to the United States (over 80 percent) were from Europe. Since 1965 the proportion of immigrants from Europe has substantially declined, while the proportions from the Americas and Asia have substantially increased. Asians dominate the legal immigrant population; but the magnitude of undocumented immigration is substantial, and most illegal immigrants come to the United States primarily from Latin America. Thus, the picture of immigration may be substantially larger than that represented in Table 12.1. In addition, the proportion of the immigrant population from Latin America may be substantially higher.

RACIAL CLASSIFICATION OF THE FOREIGN-BORN

Immigrants from Asia, Latin America, and the Caribbean have a conceptualization of racial identity that is different from the bipolar racial categories of the United States.[14] For example, Mexicans have a racial continuum that runs from white to red, not from white to black as in Puerto Rico. Furthermore, the Puerto Rican continuum from white to black is different from the bipolar conceptualization in the United States. The Puerto Rican continuum may have more to do with culture than with skin color.[15] Racial identification for Asians may not be based on a color continuum and may have more to do with social and political exigencies than with color.[16] For immigrants from the non-Hispanic Caribbean, Africa, and Europe, racial identification within the United States is clearly rooted in the history of the United States and these other geographical areas. Black immigrants from

Table 12.1

Legal immigration to the United States, by region of last residence: 1820–1992.
(Percentage of total)

Intercensal Decade	Total Number	Europe	Asia	Africa	Caribbean[a]	Latin America[b]
1820–1830	151,824	70.1	—	—	2.6	3.6
1831–1840	599,125	82.7	—	—	2.1	1.3
1841–1850	1,713,251	93.2	—	—	0.8	0.4
1851–1860	2,598,214	94.4	1.6	—	0.4	0.2
1861–1870	2,314,824	89.2	2.8	—	0.4	0.2
1871–1880	2,812,191	80.8	4.4	—	0.5	0.2
1881–1890	5,246,613	90.3	1.3	—	0.6	0.1
1891–1900	3,687,564	96.4	2.0	—	0.9	0.1
1901–1910	8,795,386	91.6	3.7	0.1	1.2	0.8
1911–1920	5,735,811	75.3	4.3	0.1	2.2	4.8
1921–1930	4,107,209	60.0	2.7	0.2	1.8	12.6
1931–1940	528,431	65.8	3.0	0.3	2.9	6.8
1941–1950	1,035,039	60.0	3.1	0.7	4.8	10.1
1951–1960	2,515,479	52.7	6.1	0.6	1.4	20.9
1961–1970	3,321,677	33.8	12.9	0.9	5.1	33.5
1971–1980	4,493,314	17.8	35.3	1.8	7.3	33.0
1981–1990	7,338,062	10.4	37.3	2.4	6.6	40.6

Source: U.S. Immigration and Naturalization Service. 1992. *Statistical Yearbook of the Immigration and Naturalization Service, 1992*, Washington, D.C.: U.S. Government Printing Office, 1992.

[a] Data for Caribbean immigrants include Haiti, Jamaica, and other Caribbean countries.

[b] Data for Latin American immigrants include Mexico, Cuba, Dominican Republic, Central America, and South America.

the Caribbean and Africa enter the United States as African Americans and experience the United States as do other African Americans. Immigrants from Europe enter the United States as European Americans. But at the turn of the century they experienced a similar transformation in racial conceptualization. European ethnic groups were integrated into the European-derived white population of the United States, and they employ their ethnic identity as an option rather than an ascribed status, as it is for Africans, Asians, American Indians, and, to a lesser degree, for Hispanics.[17]

Immigrants must modify their actions to coincide with their host society's concept of racial stratification or face social isolation and dislocation. In the United States racial groups are power groups, which stand culturally or racially as potential or actual antagonists. A society that is characterized by racial antagonism is a racist society in which a group of individuals have their options to a large degree determined by some physical trait.

Racial polarization is accepted by the native-born population regardless of race and has been important in the identification of the new wave of immigrants. Immigrants from the Caribbean and Latin America have had to conform their notions of who is black and white to the racial conceptualizations prevalent in the United States.[18] Immigrants from the Asian and Latin American countries have been lumped together by the larger society as Asians and Hispanics, regardless of national origin, and they have used this social ascription as a basis for the formation of a community of interest.[19]

We may get a better picture of the racial classification of immigrants by examining the racial classification of the foreign-born. Table 12.2 presents a cross-tabulation of race by birth status for the period from 1960 to 1990. However, Table 12.2 confounds the reality of racial classification within the United States. The majority of Asians and a large percentage of Hispanics are foreign-born. And the racial taxonomy of the United States differs from that of other nations. In the United States races have traditional legally de-

Table 12.2

Percentage of the population, by race and nativity: 1960–1990.

Race	1960	1970	1980	1990
African American				
Foreign-born	1	1	3	4
Native-born	99	99	97	96
Hispanic				
Foreign-born	32	28	36	41
Native-born	69	72	64	60
European American				
Foreign-born	5	5	4	3
Native-born	95	95	96	97
Asian				
Foreign-born	32	37	61	63
Native-born	68	63	39	37
American Indian				
Foreign-Born	1	2	2	1
Native-born	99	98	98	99

Source: U.S. Bureau of the Census, PUS 1960–1990.

fined categories; however, in reality race has been a dynamic concept. Racially, each person is located on a continuum between white and black. The new wave of Asian and Latin America immigrants are challenging this definition. Figure 12.3 shows this dynamic character of the racial classification of immigrants from Latin America.

Most Asians classify themselves as Asian, but the racial classification of the Hispanic population is particularly problematic. The two principal problems in racially classifying Hispanics arise from the large percentage of the Hispanic population that are immigrants and the different racial classifications within their country of origin (see Table 12.2). Many Hispanics coming to the United States would be classified as whites in the their country of origin. In fact, most Hispanics classified themselves as racially white within the United States prior to 1980 (see Figure 12.3). In 1960 and 1970 over 95 percent of the immigrants from Latin America were classified as white. In 1980 the Census Bureau broadened its racial classifications to allow the Hispanic population to indicate their "Spanish" origin. In 1990 the

Figure 12.3

Racial classification of Latin American immigrants: 1960–1990.

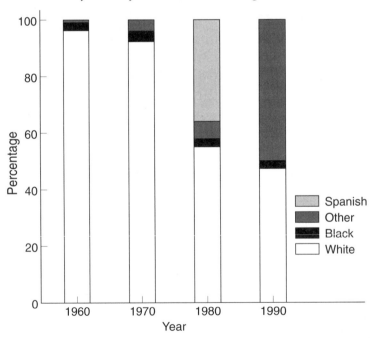

Sources: 1960–1990 Public Use Microdata files.

Census Bureau eliminated the "Spanish"-origin category, but the immigrants from Latin America continued to classify themselves as other than black or white.

THE LIMITS OF RACIAL ASSIMILATION

The classical model of assimilation is the melting pot,[20] which model assumes that immigrants arrive with a relative disadvantage vis-à-vis European Americans, and that they are culturally distant and distinct, lacking in communication and other skills. Thus, immigrants are initially clustered/segregated near the core of the city. However, the passage of time brings a withering of ethnic differences, and socioeconomic advancement translates into residential mobility/assimilation. This model assumes that the immigrant group will become like the majority population, that is, the white population. In the United States the three principal forms of assimilation are residential integration, intermarriage, and the racial classification of children. In each of these types of assimilation the African American has been uniquely excluded.

African Americans are by far the most segregated racial group within the United States.[21] Compared with Asians and Hispanics, among whom higher levels of education and income have been associated with lower levels of segregation, African Americans show a tendency to be residentially isolated regardless of level of income, education, or occupation. Thus, residential segregation may be more related to racial stratification than to class inequality; however, residential segregation may itself be an aspect of class inequality. Residential segregation is a reflection of the racial separation within the United States. The significance of this separation is rooted in how the society's members see themselves and what they want to see in the future. The saying goes "If you're white, well all right, if you're brown, stick around, but if you're black, get back."

Both ethnic and racial groups share putative ancestral origins. Thus, ethnic and racial ancestry are attributes that parents transmit to their children within the constraints of socially prescribed rules. European-descent populations have very high rates of intermarriage,[22] however, regardless of the type of ethnic intermarriage, they remain racially homogenous. These children could be classified as ethnically mixed, but they are racially white.[23]

The issue of racial heredity is complicated by the tendency for bipolar racial categorizing. Recent research suggests that in racially mixed marriages with African Americans the children are classified as African American.[24] However, Native Americans and Asians in mixed marriages with whites classified their children as white almost twice as often as did African American parents in mixed marriages. Asian women generally choose to categorize their children as the race of the white father more often than Asian men with white wives.

The tendency of interracial births to be classified as white by all but African Americans is further complicated by the patterns of interracial/interethnic marriage. African American intermarriage patterns are distinct in their gender preferences and exceptionally low.[25] Though, the rates of intermarriage of African Americans and whites increased over the last two decades. For example, about 40 percent of Japanese and more than 50 percent of Native American women are interracially married. Such behavior is still very rare among African Americans. Only about 1 percent of African American women and 3 percent of African American men are interracially married. Female outmarriage is higher for every racial and ethnic group except African Americans.

These patterns of intermarriage and the inclination to racially identify as white is a reflection of assimilation, American-style. American Indians and Asians are assimilating not only culturally but physically as well, via intermarriage and residential integration. African Americans are not being assimilated culturally, residentially or physically. African American children from mixed marriages are being classified as African American; as a group they are not intermarrying as often as other groups, and residential segregation may be increasing. Race continues to be a salient issue in American life.

DISCUSSION

Immigration is an important factor in accounting for the proportional differences in the racial composition of the population of the United States. The American Indian population experienced a dramatic decline in size as a result of the formation of the United States of America. The African and European populations increased in their size both because of this decline and because of their continued immigration as slaves, serfs, and colonizers. Immigration continues to be a central issue in race relations in the United States.

When people immigrate, assimilation is the social process by which they become part of the population in the host country. Racial conflict and competition have been hallmarks of American society from the moment the European settlers encountered established Native American populations in the fifteenth century. Thus, the reception of immigrants into the United States to a large degree reflects the interest of the racial groups that compose the population, especially the European descendant population.

In the first half of the twentieth century European immigrants to the northern United States "provided new supplies of cheap labor that competed with Negro labor for even the lower jobs such as domestics and common laborers."[26] Africans have historically felt that immigrants displaced African workers and contributed to their continued poverty.[27] Recently, however, African Americans have began to see their stance on immigration in racial/political terms. This new perspective is seen in their views about the different treatment given Haitian and Cuban immigrants to the United States. The older concern with displacement has not died, but it is becoming more politically motivated.

Following immigration, white ethnic groups intermarried and reduced their own racial classification to a social option. And given the recent rise in levels of intermarriage among Asians, Hispanics, and American Indians, the importance of homogamy as a factor in racial classification is being called into question. The majority of children produced by these interracial marriages are classified by their parents as whites, which reinforces the polarized definition of race. Even the high numbers of Hispanics who have racially classified themselves as "other" in the decennial censuses has led some scholars to argue that these Hispanics are racially intermediate between white and black.[28] Others have argued that groups like Puerto Ricans view race as culture regardless of the physical types within the culture.

Recently, both Asians and Hispanics have sought racial classification specific to their own historical and cultural experiences. Only time will tell if this is simply a holding position before their more complete assimilation or the beginning of a new system of racial classification within the United States. Asians and Hispanics have had much more success in residentially integrating within European American communities.[29] Thus, although it appears that racial classification within the United States is in flux, this flux seems to be contained within the boundaries of the dichotomous distinctions of race.

Racial classification is a unique form of social exclusion. The ideas of the "majority and minority," "black and white," are formulations of the collective self and the collective other. These distinctions remain important because of the social differentiation and exclusion; they help to reconfirm social inequality of different populations within the society. To be "black" or a "minority" is not without its own valuation.

The view of race as a reality has dominated most research on race.[30] Thus, "black" and "white" people can be empirically observed in the society.[31] It is rare in the United States for an individual to be judged as an individual member of society; even in the most successful cases, individuals are judged as members of their racial groups. It is this distinguishing character of race in societies that maintains interracial struggle.

Racial isolation and antagonism have stimulated complacency and indifference to racism. The social rejection of blackness has helped maintain a social order in which social opportunities and equality are preferentially offered to some and denied to others on the basis of race. Skin color continues to be a major factor in housing, education, and employment. Individual opportunities are limited by inequality of group opportunities, and African Americans continue to be on the bottom. A program of universal economic reform could potentially benefit everyone; however, history suggests that this help would be race-specific. By not confronting the problem of racial stratification socially and economically, we prolong racial conflict.

Given the clear, although not apparent, class distinctions in America, the dynamic concept of race is appropriate for the social system. The American social system continues to be based on race and class. In a multiracial society conflict results from a legacy of social difference.[32] The assimilationist tradition embodied in *An American Dilemma* stresses the idea that African Americans and other racial groups are below whites socially and morally because of certain values and behavior. The phenotypic characteristics of different groups are viewed as surface manifestations of inner realities, such as values and behavior. For African Americans these deviant values and behavior are thought to have resulted from their endurance of social, political, and economic marginalization. The idea of race has been important in sustaining this view of social difference. Overcoming the shortcomings of this perspective requires a program of research and action that recognizes race as an integral part of American society and seeks to change the society. It is not simply a change in African American values and behavior that is needed. White behavior and values also require modification if we are to move beyond the trap of race relations.

Often we associate individual and group somatic differences with beauty, culture, and intellectual ability. To move beyond the trap of race we must accept the universal contributions of all groups and cultures regardless of if they are black or white. To overcome the hypocrisy of racism we must express this acceptance in our scholarship and behavior.

NOTES

1. Gunnar Myrdal. *An American Dilemma: The Negro Problem and Modern Democracy* (New York: Harper & Row 1962 [1944]), Chap. 3. Myrdal viewed immigrant cultural and physical amalgamation as the solution to blacks' social isolation. However, the contribution of immigrants to the racial composition of the United States is not discussed in a context that is appropriate for the conditions of the latter part of the twentieth century. Myrdal and his colleagues were not aware of the dramatic changes in the immigrant population about to occur at their time of writing in the 1940s. The increase in migrants from Asia and Latin America could not have been foreseen in the context of the 1940s.

2. The confounding of race and immigrant status, or ethnicity, in the study of race relations has its origins in the Chicago School's early, pre-1940s, study of urban conditions within the United States. The Chicago School studied race and class as problems of immigrant assimilation. See Robert E. Park and Ernest W. Burgess. *The City* (Chicago: University of Chicago Press, 1925); Louis Wirth. *The Ghetto* (Chicago: University of Chicago Press, 1928); Franklin Frazier. *The Negro Family in Chicago* (Chicago: University of Chicago Press, 1932).

3. Herman Hoetink. *Caribbean Race Relations: A Study of Two Variants* (London: Oxford University Press, 1962). Also see Oliver C. Cox. *Caste, Class, and Race: A Study in Social Dynamics* (New York: Doubleday, 1948), Chap. 23.

4. Hoetink. *Caribbean Race Relations*, p. 88.

5. See Milton Gorgon. *Human Nature, Class, and Ethnicity* (New York: Oxford University Press, 1978). The major theoretical argument on this issue. Also see Katherine O'Sullivan and William J. Wilson. "Race and Ethnicity." In Neil J. Smelser, ed. *Handbook of Sociology* (New York: Sage, 1988), pp. 224–226, for an excellent summary of the arguments on this issue.

6. Lawrence Bobo and James R. Kluegel. "Opposition to Race-Targeting: Self-Interest, Stratification Ideology, or Racial Attitudes?" *American Sociological Review* 58 (4) (1993): 443–464.

7. Audrey Smedley. *Race in North America: Origin and Evolution of a Worldview* (Boulder: Westview Press, 1993); and Theodore W. Allen. *The Invention of the White Race.* Volume One: *Racial Oppression and Social Control* (New York: Verso, 1994).

8. Frantz Fanon. *Black Skin White Masks.* (New York: Grove Press, 1967 [1952]; Originally published as *Peau Noire, Masques Blancs*); H. Hoetink. *The Two Variants in Caribbean Race Relations: A Contribution to the Sociology of Segmented Societies* (London: Oxford University Press, 1967).

9. Ibid., pp. 120–160.

10. Fanon, pp. 190–191. Also see Edward E. Telles and Edward Murguia. "Phenotypic Discrimination and Income Differences among Mexican Americans." *Social Science Quarterly* 71(4) (1990): 682–696; Keith and Herring. "Skin Tone and Stratification in the Black Community." *American Journal of Sociology* 97(3) (1991): 760–778; Clara E. Rodriguez and Hector Cordero-Guzman. "Placing Race in Context." *Ethnic and Racial Studies* 15(4) (1992): 523–542.

11. Telles and Murguia, and Keith and Herring.

12. The common ancestral ties to Spain and Latin America do not imply an underlying cultural unity among peoples of Hispanic origin. See Frank D. Bean and Marta Tienda. *The Hispanic Population of the United States* (New York: Russell Sage Foundation 1988), Chaps. 1 and 2, for an excellent discussion and summary of the issues surrounding the historical and contemporary problems of classifying the Hispanic population). Mexicans, Puerto Ricans, Cubans, etc. are distinct populations with discernible characteristics. Also see JoAnne Willette et al. "The Demographic and Socioeconomic Characteristics of the Hispanic Population in the United States: 1950–1980." Report to the

Department of Health and Human Services by Development Associates, Inc., and Population Reference Bureau, 1982.

13. In the sixteenth and seventeenth centuries in some colonies the African population outnumbered the European population. See Peter H. Wood. "More Like a Negro Country: Demographic Patterns in Colonial South Carolina, 1700–1740." In Stanley L. Engerman and Eugene D. Genovese, eds. *Race and Slavery in the Western Hemisphere: Quantitative Studies* (Princeton: Princeton University Press, 1975), pp. 131–171.

14. Nancy A. Denton and Douglas S. Massey. "Racial Identity among Caribbean Hispanics." *American Sociological Review* 54(5) (1989): 790–808; Herbert Barringer, Robert W. Gardner, and Michael J. Levin. *Asians and Pacific Islanders in the United States* (New York: Russell Sage Foundation, 1993), pp. 3–8.

15. Rodriguez and Cordero-Guzman. "Placing Race in Context."

16. Yeu Le Espiritu. *Asian American Panethnicity: Bridging Institutions and Identities* (Philadelphia: Temple University Press, 1992), pp. 31–41.

17. See Michael Hoot and Joshua R. Goldstein. "How 4.5 Million Irish Immigrants Became 40 Million Irish Americans: Demographic Americans." *American Sociological Review* 59(1) (1994): 64–82.

18. Denton and Massey.

19. Le Espiritu, pp. 19–52.

20. K. Taeuber and A.F. Taeuber. *Negroes in Cities* (Chicago: Aldine, 1964); E.W. Burgess. "The Growth of the City." In Robert E. Park, Ernest W. Burgess, and R.D. McKenzie, eds. *The City* (Chicago: University of Chicago Press, 1967 [1925]); Robert E. Park. "The City." In Robert E. Park, Ernest W. Burgess, and R.D. McKenzie, eds. *The City* (Chicago: University of Chicago Press, 1967 [1925]).

21. Farley and Allen, pp. 137–145; Douglas S. Massey and Nancy C. Denton. *American Apartheid: Segregation and the Making of the Interclass* (Cambridge: Harvard University Press, 1993).

22. Gilliam Stevens and Linda Owens. "The Ethnic and Linguistic Backgrounds of U.S. Children." Presented at the Annual Meeting of the Southern Demographic Association, 1990.

23. Stanley Lieberson and Mary C. Waters. *From Many Strands: Ethnic and Racial Groups in Contemporary America* (New York: Russell Sage Foundation, 1988), pp. 258–260.

24. Mary C. Waters. "The Social Construction of Race and Ethnicity: Some Examples From Demography." Proceedings from the Albany Conference, American Diversity: A Demographic Challenge for the Twenty-First Century, 1994.

25. M. Belinda Tucker and Claudia Mitchell-Kernan. "New Trends in Black Interracial Marriage: The Social Structural Context." *Journal of Marriage and the Family* 52(1) (1990): 209–218; Peter Blau, Terry C. Blum, and Joseph E. Schwartz. "Heterogeneity and Intermarriage." *American Sociological Review.* 47(1) (1982): 45–62; Sharon M. Lee and Keiko Yamanaka. "Patterns of Asian American Intermarriage and Marital Assimilation." *Journal of Comparative Family Studies* 21(2) (1990): 287–305; Douglas T. Gurak and Joseph P. Fitzpatrick. "Intermarriage among Hispanic Ethnic Groups in New York

City." *American Journal of Sociology* 87(4) (1982): 921–934; Matthijs Kalmijn. "Trends in Black/White Intermarriage." *Social Forces* 72(1) (1993): 119–146.

26. Myrdal, p. 292.

27. Lawrence H. Fuchs. "The Reactions of Black Americans to Immigration." In *Immigration Reconsidered: History, Sociology, and Politics*, (Virginia, ed.: Yans-McLaughlin (1990), pp. 293–314. These fears may be unwarranted. Recent research finds little support for the notion that immigrants have had any significant negative impact on the employment situation of African Americans (Reischauer 1989). Yet immigration may have a significant impact on the fiscal state of local governments. See Eric S. Rothman and Thomas J. Espenshade. "Fiscal Impacts of Immigration to the United States." *Population Index* 58(3) (1992): 381–415. However, these conclusions themselves should be seen as tentative given the limitations of the available data and the questions addressed. This research has focused on wages, earnings, and unemployment, whereas the important impacts may be in labor force participation, working conditions, and internal migration.

28. Rodriguez and Cordero-Guzman. "Placing Race in Context."

29. See Farley and Allen, Table 5.8, p. 145.

30. Cox, pp. 321–352.

31. Franz Boas observed this problem in his 1931 presidential address to the American Association for the Advancement of Science. "When social divisions follow racial lines, as they do among ourselves, the degree of difference between racial forms is an important element in establishing racial groupings and in creating racial conflicts." See Franz Boaz. "Race and Progress." *Science* 74(1931): 5.

32. With almost 50 percent of the prison population being African American and with the majority of the prison population consisting of "minority peoples" the criminal justice system is a clear example of this conflict. The Los Angeles rebellion in April 1992 was multiracial and multiclass. More than anything it reflected the sense of powerlessness many nonwhites feel. The instability caused by such rebellions produces what are known as race problems. It is a race problem because it suggests an adjustment in race relations. As Oliver C. Cox noted in 1948, four years after the publication of *An American Dilemma*, "There is here, then, an irreconcilable antithesis which must inevitably remain a constant source of social unrest. The 'lawlessness of judges' in deciding the law and the 'unlawful enforcement of the law' by policemen are pivotal in the racial system. The social anomaly is inherent" (Cox. *Caste, Class, and Race*, p. 435).

Doris Wilkinson

13

Gender and Social Inequality: The Prevailing Significance of Race

A PARALLEL TO THE NEGRO PROBLEM

In every society there are at least two groups of people besides the Negroes who are characterized by high social visibility expressed in physical appearance, dress, and patterns of behavior, and who have been "suppressed." We refer to women and children. Their present status, as well as their history and their problems in society, reveal striking similarities to those of the Negroes. . . . It will, therefore, give perspective to the Negro problem and prevent faulty interpretations to sketch some of the important similarities between the Negro problem and the women's problem.[1]

IN THE PERCEPTIVE APPENDIX to *An American Dilemma*, Gunnar Myrdal paused to clarify "a parallel to the Negro problem." Concentrating on historical placement, status differentiation, and accompanying socially constructed attributes and behaviors, he interpreted what "marked" Americans of African ancestry in the United States. He observed that their position in the country's racially framed stratification system was analogous to that of free white women since both were under the control of a white male patriarchy. Taking into account the historically racialized social location and treatment of African slaves, without making gender distinctions among them, Myrdal noted that the ironic paternalistic conception of the slave as a "family member ". . . placed him beside women and children. The parallel goes, however, considerably deeper than being only a structural part in the defense ideology built up around slaves. Women (during the era of slavery) lacked a number of rights otherwise belonging to all free white citizens of full age."[2]

Concentrating on white women, Myrdal recognized that at the outset

> ... a tremendous difference existed both in actual status of these different groups and in the tone of sentiment in the respective relations. In the decades before the Civil War, in the conservative and increasingly antiquarian ideology of the American South, woman was elevated as an ornament and looked upon with pride, while the Negro slave became increasingly a chattel and a ward. ... [Yet,] from the very beginning, the fight in America for the liberation of the Negro slaves was, therefore, closely coordinated with the fight for women's emancipation.[3]

This chapter will address aspects of this parallel as it applies to the contemporary racialized social arena in which black–white relations remain significant and polarized. In spite of the diversity ethos and multiculturalism movement engulfing our rapidly changing world, race remains a principal determinant of social organization, privilege, and daily interaction.

THE PARADOXES OF RACE IN A GENDERED SOCIETY

In the latter part of the twentieth century, scholarly work and intellectual discourse are witnessing the transformation of knowledge through the introduction of feminist perspectives and the promulgation of a gender-balanced view of interaction and the structure of society.[4] Multiple emphases emanating from emerging and reconstructed theoretical paradigms—poststructuralism, hermeneutics, aspects of postmodernism—are resulting in a modification of the way in which scholars examine political, economic, and social realities. With literature and the sciences highlighting gendered identities and the conditions of oppression in the diverse experiences of women, inequality in opportunity based on race has received less attention.

Among the multifaceted issues reflecting the correlation between gender and inequality are women's traditional roles, workplace barriers to upward mobility, and the disproportionate male representation in the hierarchies of the corporate culture. In addition, policies are emerging related to the underrepresentation of women in the sciences, "the glass ceiling" restricting their movement into managerial positions, changes in labor force activity. Sexual harassment in the workplace, sexual stereotypes, and family violence are paramount among the issues confronting women.[5]

In our postmodern culture, feminist frameworks have introduced new and different interpretations of the significance of gender. Social class and race also cluster as significant determinants of political and economic inequality. With the political gendering of individuality, self-conceptions, and patterns of interaction, understanding stratification based on racial distinctions and the ensuing racial animosities is minimized. This observation does not negate the legitimate emphases regarding role stereotyping and gender imbalance in the work setting or the placement of women in the system of opportunity.[6]

Current epistemological interest in gendered inequality is accentuated in academic and corporate contexts by white females more often than by African American scholars or even white, male, social and behavioral scientists. This social fact is relevant for interpreting the relationships among status ascription, identity, and political consciousness. If gender were a strategically salient factor in the African American's intergenerationally experienced inferiorization and inequality, attention to this factor would have produced more than minimal positive outcomes for African American women as well as men in all institutional sectors.

Highlighting the salience of gendered inequality in daily interaction and in the structure of society has contributed a new dimension to intellectual dialogue and to scholarly descriptions and interpretations of status arrangements.[7] Examining the importance of gender has similarly enabled a more functional explication of the beliefs and customs that frame our political culture. However, translating the ingrained, systemic, and pervasive influence of race and racism in the country's institutions and ideologies permits greater understanding of the construction and perpetuation of all forms of inequality. Delineating race as the central element in opportunity and in status arrangements permits an explanation of the permanence of an "American Dilemma" within a race-based democracy.[8]

In dissecting the foundation of social and economic disparities, Myrdal highlighted the impact of slavery on the political order, the class structure, and the culture. He framed the setting for contemporary inequities in terms of the contradictions between the "precept of equality of opportunity in the American Creed" and "the norm of personal liberty." Anchored within the matrix of structural inequality, Myrdal interpreted "the major portion of the system of social segregation and discrimination against [Americans of African descent] as a challenge to the American Creed" (p. 574). He considered "a residual amount of idiosyncrasy in purely personal relations which may be upheld by the American liberty norm" (p. 574). It is this sustained shared temperament that has merged with and prescribed race-based inequities in the political and social order.

Moreover, outlining the pervasiveness of racial differentiation, exclusion, and structural isolation in the United States in the mid-twentieth century, Myrdal delineated the one-sided nature of these interlocking customs. Racially dictated discrimination and segregation have always been totally dissimilar from social practices and relations within the purely gendered arena. Detailing the ideological paradox characterizing the unparalleled encounters of African American men and women during the Depression and World War II eras, he observed that they

> are ordinarily never admitted to white churches in the South, but if a strange white man enters a Negro church the visit is received as a great honor (p. 575). Likewise, a white stranger will be received with utmost respect and cordiality in any Negro school, and everything will be done to satisfy his every wish, whereas a Negro under similar circumstances would be pushed off the grounds of a white school. . . . The rules are understood to be for the protection of whites (p. 576). This applies also to social rituals and etiquette. . . . The white man . . . can recognize the Negro on the street . . . or he can ignore him. He can offer his hand to shake, or he can keep it back. . . . It is the white man who chooses between the alternatives as to the character of the contact to be established. . . . Even a Southern white child feels the caste solidarity and learns that he can insult an adult Negro with impunity (p. 677).

Interweaving the philosophy framing the ideology of the American Creed, Myrdal explored the bases of racialized injustice, favoritism, limited opportunities, and disparities in privileges. According to the thesis of *An American Dilemma*, the roots of inequality can be located within the launching of the system of slavery, the embedding of folkways arising from this culturally and legally sanctioned institution, the contriving of Jim Crow laws, and historically reinforcing beliefs that supported the existing stratified arrangements. In addition, the bases of inequality included a ban on intermarriage that linked to a fear of "amalgamation." White upper-class reliance on and "rationalizing of stereotyped beliefs" to preserve their entitlements and lower-class white leverage emanating solely from their racially advantaged status allowed them to pursue inhuman activities such as lynch mobs to maintain the racial hierarchy.

Intermingling gender with race, opportunities for women of African ancestry have always been far more circumscribed than for white women and men. Myrdal recognized the excessive hardship that social discrimination and structural inequality evoked on women. "In 1930, as many as 1,150,000 Negro women earned their living as workers in domestic service and other service industries. . . . The largest group among the female service workers consisted of those employed by private households." Employment options for African American women remained constant during the next decade. The Sixteenth Census of the United States showed that "the employment rates for white females were comparatively uniform all over the country. In most large cities, North as well as South, from one-fifth to one-third of the white women were reported as employed. The rates for Negro women in large southern cities usually ranged from one-third to one-half. In the North, they were less consistent, and frequently much lower. In some cities, like Chicago, Cleveland, Detroit, and Pittsburgh, they were even lower than for white women" (Myrdal, p. 1258). The perplexing standard of differential work chances and occupational distance between women of European and those of African ancestry has been retained throughout the twentieth century.

Events of the early 1940s, in the years just before Myrdal's classic, provide a context for examining the premises of this discussion. In the examples presented as illustrative, the focus centers on the prominence of race and the relative inconsequential impact of gender in the persistence of inequality. Neither gender nor class has been significantly deterministic in the historical patterns of racial exclusion, segregation, and discrimination experienced by African American men and women.

THE STRUCTURE OF RACE RELATIONS IN THE 1940s

When Gunnar Myrdal, a Swedish economist and political activist, wrote *The American Dilemma*, the United States was confronting a new era in its political culture and in its system of stratification. The Depression had ended and World War II was nearing its final phases. It is therefore instructive to reexamine the social thought of a perceptive foreign scholar and his research associates after 50 years. What was observed then about a democratic nation facing a moral paradox over its treatment of former African slaves remains applicable in the waning of the twentieth century. Commenting on the normative and value consequences of the nature of race relations, Myrdal and others highlighted the contradictions.

In 1944, Myrdal, Richard Sterner, and Arnold Rose wrote that "segregation is now becoming so complete that the white Southerner practically never sees a Negro except as his servant and in other standardized and formalized caste situations." Both ecological separation and racial distance were entrenched in the fabric of the nation's beliefs and values and its social class hierarchy. All housing, private and public, was segregated by custom and by law. In fact, the Federal Housing Administration assumed "the policy of segregation used by private institutions, like banks, mortgage companies, building and loan associations, and real estate companies." Myrdal commented on this dilemma: "It is one thing when private tenants, property owners, and financial institutions maintain and extend patterns of racial segregation in housing. It is quite another matter when a federal agency chooses to side with the segregationists."[9] Thus, interracial separation, spatial isolation, and all forms of ecological discrimination were among the myriad of racial restrictions confronting "the American Negro" and the country itself. Nevertheless, the ideological dissonance perceived and translated by Myrdal and his co-researchers as a phenomenon of white America was not a part of the oppressive experiences or the cognitive understanding of the descendants of African slaves. Similarly, gender segregation was obliterated as an issue with equivalent meaning to the structural and cultural segregation and political disenfranchisement of Americans of African descent.

With the contemporary differential interpretation of gender and social inequality, a central focus of current dialogue is on gendered influences and identities. Given this, some brief comments regarding demographic patterns in the country at the time of Myrdal's classic treatise are instructive. As the decade of the 1940s opened, an estimated 13 million Americans of African heritage lived in the United States, representing nearly 10 percent (9.8 percent) of the population. Most of the foreign-born Americans of African descent were from the West Indies.[10] Although the descendants of former slaves and free persons were living in an evolving industrial country founded on democratic principles, their historical conditions, experiences, and life chances were vastly different from those of Euro-American men and women. As Myrdal observed, blacks and whites never encountered each other except in subordinate-superior role relationships.

Furthermore, there were no structural parallels in the placement of white women and slaves or free blacks in the class system nor in the conditions of oppression. More precisely, demographic data for 1940 show that there was a wider racial gap in life expectancy than a gender-specific one. For example, for white females, life expectancy was approximately 66.6 years, for white males, 62.1, for African American females, 54.9, and for African American or nonwhite males, 51.5. These comparative statistics at the time, as today, were empirical indicators of a major consequence of structural inequality based principally on a single ascriptive variable. Within racial categories, significant variations persist in life expectancy. Women of both races then as now have longer life spans than men. Notwithstanding, in any race-gender comparisons, for African American women and men, life expectancy remains unequal. Also, throughout the 1940s, infant and maternal mortality rates were predictably higher for nonwhites, most of whom were African American, than for whites. These disparities were evident in other health areas as well and continue today. Racialized inequality, not gender, is the foundation of these dissimilarities in life chances.

In spite of the organization of racial segregation in the country a half-century ago, race and gender were systemic in the distribution of employment, privileges, and forms of opportunity throughout the North and the South. Data examined on the representation of African American workers among various types of occupations in the United States by region in 1940 vividly reveal the differential occupations and hence unequal economic situation of black men and women vis-à-vis white men and women. Noticeably, a disproportionate number of employed African American women workers were in the service sector. Over one-half of employed black males were in nonfarm labor, with the majority of these in unskilled jobs, service work, or in machine operative positions. In addition, the weight of race and gender in unemployment figures was relatively constant. Throughout the decade, the rate for white males remained less than that for African American males. A wide racial gap also existed for women: white women had much lower unemployment rates than did black women. This racially determined gender inequity characterized the world of work in northern industrial cities, the Midwest, and in the South, where vast disparities in employment opportunities and occupational statuses prevailed.[11]

Juxtaposed with social inequality arising from employment segregation, housing discrimination was also normative—written into custom and law; and schools throughout the land were separate and unequal. Interpreting the nature of this legislated inequality a half-century ago, race emerges as the principal determinant, not gender. Patterns of exclusion and isolation in the life experiences of African American women were the complete opposite of those encountered by Euro-American women. Black and white families lived in racially separate communities in all parts of the country and were segregated by physical and socially constructed barriers. This racial distance occurred even when historical dwelling units and housing patterns dictated their residing on the same street. Myrdal felt that this social reality crystallized the "American Dilemma."

Following the Civil War and throughout the mid-twentieth century, racial customs and laws were interconnected in denying voting privileges and housing and educational opportunities to African American families. Economic class was not a principal component of the definitions of status, benefits, or advantages at any time between the 1940s and 1970s, virtually not since slavery. Neither economic class nor gender affected where Americans of African ancestry would live, work, attend school, or worship. As pointed out earlier, the Federal Housing Administration permitted the deliberate exclusion of "the Negro" from federal housing and even mandated the adoption of restrictive covenants for new housing based solely on race.[12] Converging with this discriminatory act by a federal agency, the FHA did not require that builders sell to African Americans.

Residential separation remains today as culturally normative. It is reinforced by lending institutions as well as by real estate companies, traditional practices, and racial preferences. While the masses of ethnic families in the United States live in distinct and ecologically divided neighborhoods and communities, only the African American remains spatially isolated and virtually restricted to low-income or predominantly black areas. Because of the variability in the amenities that accrue to those in particular residential communities, the salience of race linked to class transcends gender in interpretations of this form of inequality.

Actually, the economic conditions and life chances of African Americans just before and immediately following World War II and the Korean War negated the notion of a quandary in the consciousness of Euro-Americans. Merging with institutionalized, federally supported, and racially based preferential treatment, the system of justice also stood squarely against the descendants of African slaves. Gender was not a basis for the inequities encountered in the administration of justice. Specifically, for capital crimes, the death penalty was applied with greater frequency to blacks than to whites. In the 1990s this tacitly approved practice of the differential allocation of fairness under the law has been relatively unchanged. This is evident through the processes of charging, setting bail, and sentencing to the imposition of the death penalty.[13] Thus, 50 years following *An American Dilemma*, overt racism in the courts has not been eliminated. Any regional variations in police behavior and in judicial outcomes merely show the pervasiveness of a race-based and political culture.

THE PRIMACY OF RACE IN A GENDERED SOCIAL ORDER

The foremost sociodemographic forces underlying experienced inequality in the United States and in many other parts of the world, especially South Africa and England, are race and class. As a consequence, in order to understand status arrangements, the nature of social inequality, and the political culture, these two stratifying factors require explication. For in a racially framed economy that creates nearly permanent disenfranchised and disempowered strata almost independently of the interactive effects of gender and class, dissecting the impact of race alone necessitates thorough scrutiny. Therefore, any discussion of gender and structural differentiation exclusive of race leaves a much greater void in our knowledge base and hence in our comprehension of racialized realities.

Today, gender is recognized as a crucial variable in the construction of life experiences. Nonetheless, it is understandable why sex and gender discrimination were not examined extensively at the time of the unfolding of *An American Dilemma*. The changing status of women and the gendering of the society had not evolved as critical aspects of the dynamic transformation of American social organization and culture. At the same time, sexism and racism have prevailed as ideological forces that affect our values, beliefs, politics, the economy, the health sector, and other institutions. Given our country's political heritage, for the African American, race has always been a far more fundamental basis of placement and interaction than gender. Since Myrdal's analysis, social class has emerged as a highly complex multidimensional variable and somewhat more difficult to extricate from its interdependency with race.[14]

One-half century after *An American Dilemma* and after the dramatic 1954 Supreme Court decision, racial separation continues to produce unequal economic, occupational, residential, and health outcomes for white versus black women and men. One vivid example is illuminated in analyses of variations in labor force participation rates for African American and Euro-American women between 1890 and 1960. This historical interval encompasses post-Reconstruction and the dawning of protest movements of the civil rights era. The period spanned unparalleled changes in the country's political economy from one developed out of slave agricultural production and eventually complete racial separation and exclusion, or Jim Crowism, to an industrial order permeated by slowly evolving quasi-integration.

With rapid industrial growth and the transformation of the economy, structural inequality evolved along sex and racial lines. In the world of work, non-gender-specific placement characterized Americans of African descent. Their restricted occupational outlets gave rise to a "secondary labor market." The original source for this employment differentiation was slavery. Additionally, racism provided the ideological justification for restricting opportunities and stratifying work on the basis of race.

> The institution of slavery in the United States set apart the work and employment privileges of African American males and females from those of European heritage. . . . In the process of equalizing the positions of African American men and women, enslavement embedded in the organization of work a virtually permanent caste-like component up to the mid-twentieth century. By establishing and legally validating rigid separation between the races, the institution generated vastly disparate ranking in the class system. Thus, it was inevitable that the descendants of slaves would inherit this structural pattern."[15]

The complexity of the nation's racially organized class-status hierarchy and patriarchially dominated capitalistic economy, with roots in race, class, and the sexual division of labor, is illustrated in its perpetual structuring of inequality. That is, while political and economic inequities reflect sex differences and gender identities and while these link with social class in the organization of U.S. culture, racial ascription is far more pervasive in its impact, extent, intensity, historical meaning, and durability. Reflecting Myrdal's thinking, the issue of class position does raise perplexing questions. However, the United States is guided in its customs, status hierarchies, beliefs, and normative domain by class domination intertwined with the injurious philosophies of racism and sexism. Whenever race is a part of the mosaic, it outweighs all other potential influences.

RACIAL OPPRESSION IN THE 1990S AND BEYOND

The Supreme Court Decision of 1954 recast the structural paradoxes surrounding education in the United States. Following that historic ruling, the latent puzzles and concealed passions of race began to surface. Gender identity and sexual orientation were not issues at the forefront of the African American's quest for violence reduction, adequate housing, voting rights, schooling, and justice as citizens. Their central emphases were on the elimination of housing discrimination and restrictive covenants, opening the opportunity structure to secure an education and quality schools, being free to enroll in any public college or university, voting privileges, the right to walk the streets without fear of police or other group harassment, the opportunity to serve on juries and to receive justice in the courts, humane treatment, and the chance to hold a job.

Regardless of socioeconomic attainment and gender identity, segregation, discrimination, and restricted access have delimited the life experiences of all African Americans from the founding of the country through most of the twentieth century. As shifts in the economic class hierarchy began to occur in the 1960s, African Americans who had begun to achieve were led to believe that those who were successful or educated were the enemies of the lower classes and all "politically correct thinking" blacks. They were also made to think that Jews were their enemies even though they had helped to build schools, worked on the NAACP and in civil rights organizations, and marched alongside them in the struggle for their freedom and equal protection under the Constitution.[16]

Sex and gender are less potent forces in the lives of African Americans than class or race. Neither of these has declined in significance. When the fabric of the country's political and economic organization is probed impartially and candidly, race emerges as the foundation of inequality for the African American in all phases of life. White men and women in any social class, regardless of educational attainment, level of literacy, skills, ideological orientations, ethnic affiliations, gender, or sexual orientation are aware that our society favors them over all African Americans.

To portray the meaning of this collective sense of identity, racial rank, and shared privileges, the case of a south central university in the 1990s is used to illustrate. It is not atypical of any work setting. In one nonacademic unit of the university, all of the supervisors, secretaries, and mid-level managers are white. Not one has a college degree. The "runners," those who run back and forth across the campus to pick up the mail, are black men with college degrees. When an African American female sought college training, rules were passed stipulating that one could no longer take extensive breaks or enroll for more than one course. This attempt to prohibit

a black female from continuing her education was deliberate and institutionalized racism and was sanctioned at all levels of the division's administrative hierarchy.

Awareness of privilege associated with socially constructed status is a
major dimension of group affiliation and shared behaviors. Independent of
educational achievements and economic class, poor white men and women
know that the entire system treats them preferentially over blacks—the police, the courts, personnel officers, and the daily news media. Coinciding
directly with this is the middle-class white males' and females' complete
awareness that judges, lawyers, health professionals, the Senate, the House,
legislators at local and state levels, college and university administrators of
predominantly white colleges and universities, and doctors, support and
uphold their rights above all Americans of African descent. Being white in
America, regardless of sex or gender identity, means being supported in all
actions over black Americans. This solidified character of the nation's
political culture is merely an interlocking directorate and hierarchy dominated and controlled by men of one race. Myrdal and his associates recognized this phenomenon.

SUMMARY

Appraising Myrdal's status parallels, gender does contribute significantly
to social inequality. However, the United States is racially organized, and
the class structure is racially designed. Racism, along with class oppression
and sexism, pervades the boundaries of the political culture. Throughout
the scope of this country's history and ensuing political economy, the ex-
tensiveness and permanence of race has been sustained. For example, in an
ironic twist of rationality and scientific truths, African American heterosex-
ual women are now being viewed as potentially the most frequent carriers,
perpetrators and victims of the acquired immune deficiency syndrome
(AIDS). This politically contrived racist stereotyping will inevitably affect
the life chances, family life styles and values, the entire future, and the international images of African Americans. The direct link between race and
social inferiorization rather than gendered inequality is evident in this politi-
cization of a worldwide health crisis. For the shift from a disease that was
disproportionately concentrated among men to black female heterosexuals
negates all logic. This deliberate attempt to reconstruct the source and victims of an international pandemic demonstrates the profound influence of
race over gender and class in the United States. Consequently, the notion of
An American Dilemma in the latter part of the twentieth century appears far-
fetched given these surreptitious and purposive constructions. Racial myths

such as these must be addressed directly and immediately just as the matriarchy was challenged so perceptively in the 1970s.[17]

Gender discrimination is a source of structural inequities. It is clearly evidenced with the disproportionate concentration of African American women among poor single mothers. But we live in a social system where race endures as a politically defined attribute and where racism is a paramount ideology along with class domination and economic oppression. The ideology of racism determines and legitimizes as well as reinforces the class-race-gender triangle. Myrdal was too early in his interpretations and descriptions to grasp this fundamental and immutable social reality in the United States.

In assessing the connection between gender, race, and inequality, in addition to ascribing all major diseases to African American men and women, young men are permitted to disseminate and profit from sexist lyrics that defame women. This condoned practice emanates from a racially molded capitalistic economy. While sexually harassing and defamatory "rap" is an obvious route out of the pathos of the colonized black ghetto, the lives and self-esteem of African American women are being damaged. How are African American women to feel in a virulently racist and sexist society that is designating them as carriers of a disease pandemic? How are they to survive in a gendered racist social order where they confront daily humiliation and disrespect and unequal treatment? If a reexamination of *An American Dilemma* does nothing more than expose sexist racism in the use of medical data and outcomes, it will have reinforced the value of Myrdal's classic and documented the moral and economic outcomes of the calculated absence of truth, fairness, and scientific objectivity.

NOTES

1. Gunnar Myrdal. *An American Dilemma: The Negro Problem and Modern Democracy.* (New York: Harper & Brothers, 1944), p. 1073.
2. Ibid.
3. Ibid.
4. D. Wilkinson, M. Baca Zinn, and E. Chow, eds. "Race, Class and Gender." *Gender and Society* 6 (September 1992).
5. P.S. Rothenberg, ed. *Race, Class and Gender in the United States: An Integrated Study*, 2nd ed. (New York: St. Martin's Press, 1992).
6. Ibid.
7. M. Morrissey. *Slave Women in the New World: Gender Stratification in the Caribbean* (Lawrence: University Press of Kansas, 1989).
8. Frances Beale. "Double Jeopardy: To Be Black and Female." In Toni Cade, ed. *The Black Woman: An Anthology* (New York: New American Library, 1970), pp. 190–200. Jacquelyne Jackson. "A Critique of Lerner's Work on Black

Women and Further Thoughts." *Journal of Social and Behavioral Sciences* 21 (Winter 1975): 63–89. Deborah K. King. "Multiple Jeopardies, Multiple Consciousness: The Context of a Black Feminist Ideology." *Signs: Journal of Women in Culture and Society* 14 (1988): 42–72.

9.   Myrdal, pp. 349–350. James E. Blackwell. *The Black Community: Diversity and Unity* (New York: Harper & Row, 1985).

10. Peter M. Bergman and Mort N. Bergman. *The Chronological History of the Negro in America* (New York: Harper & Row, 1969).

11. Doris Wilkinson. "The Segmented Labor Market and African American Women from 1890–1960: A Social History Interpretation." *Race and Ethnic Relations* 6 (1991): 85–104.

12. Blackwell, pp. 151–152.

13. Thomas J. Keil and Gennaro F. Vito. "Race and the Death Penalty in Kentucky Murder Trials: 1976–1991: A Study of Racial Bias as a Factor in Capital Sentencing." Paper presented at the Variations in Capital Punishment panel. Academy of Criminal Justice Science, Chicago, Ill. (March 11, 1994). Raymond Paternoster. "Prosecutorial Discretion in Requesting the Death Penalty: A Case of Victim-Based Racial Discrimination." *Law and Society Review* 18 (1984): 437–478. M. Dwayne Smith. "Patterns of Discrimination in Assessments of the Death Penalty: The Case of Louisiana." *Journal of Criminal Justice* 15 (1987): 279–286.

14. William J. Wilson. *The Declining Significance of Race* (Chicago: University of Chicago Press, 1978).

15. Wilkinson, p. 88. Elizabeth Ross Haynes. "Negroes in Domestic Service in the United States." *Journal of Negro History* 8 (October 1923): 389–421.

16. Doris Wilkinson. "Anti-Semitism and African Americans." *Society* 31 (September/October, 1994): 47–50.

17. Robert Staples. "The Myth of the Black Matriarchy." In Doris Wilkinson and Ronald Taylor, eds. *The Black Male in America* (Chicago: Nelson-Hall, 1977), pp. 174–187.

References

Adams, Carolyn, David Bartlett, David Elesh, Ira Goldstein, Nancy Kleniewski, and William Yancey. 1991. *Philadelphia: Neighborhoods, Division, and Conflict in a Post-Industrial City*. Philadelphia: Temple University Press.

Anderson, James D. 1988. *The Education of Blacks in the South, 1860–1935*. Chapel Hill: University of North Carolina Press.

Ards, Sheila, and Marjorie Lewis. 1992. "Vote Dilution Research: Methods of Analysis." *Trotter Review* 6(2, Fall):29–31.

Asci, Gregory, and Sheldon Danziger. 1990. "Educational Attainment, Industrial Structure, and Male Earnings, 1973–1987." Mimeo, Urban Institute and University of Michigan. November.

Ashenfelter, Orley, and James Heckman. 1976. "Measuring the Effect of an Anti-Discrimination Program." In *Estimating the Labor Market Effects of Social Programs* (pp. 46–84). Edited by Ashenfelter and Blum. Princeton: Princeton University Industrial Relations Section.

Austin, Margery, Michael Fix, and Raymond Struyx. 1991. *Opportunities Denied*. Washington, D.C.: The Urban Institute Press.

Baron, Harold M. 1969. "The Web of Urban Racism." In *Institutional Racism in America* (pp. 134–176). Edited by Louis L. Knowles and Kenneth Prewitt. Englewood Cliffs, N.J.: Prentice-Hall, Inc.

Barringer, Herbert, Robert Gardner, and Michael Levin. 1993. *Asians and Pacific Islanders in the United States*. New York: Russell Sage Foundation.

Berube, Maurice, and Marilyn Gittell, eds. 1969. *Confrontation at Ocean Hill-Brownsville: The New York Strikes of 1968*. New York: Frederick A. Praeger.

Bickford, A., and Douglas Massey. 1991. "Segregation in the Second Ghetto." *Social Forces* 69:1011–1036.

Blackburn, McKinley, David E. Bloom, and Richard B. Freeman. 1990. "The Declining Economic Position of Less Skilled American Men." In *A Future of Lousy Jobs? The Changing Structure of U.S. Wages*. Edited by Gary Burtless. Washington, D.C.: The Brookings Institution.

Blauner, Bob. 1972. *Racial Oppression in America*. New York: Harper & Row.

Blaustein, Albert P., and Robert L. Zangrando, eds. 1968. *Civil Rights and the Black American*. New York: Simon and Schuster.

Bledsoe, Tim. 1991. "From One World, Three: Political Change in Metropolitan Detroit." Working paper. Detroit: Center for Urban Studies, Wayne State University.

Bobo, Lawrence, and James R. Klugel. 1991. "Modern American Prejudices: Stereotypes, Social Distance and Perceptions of Discrimination Towards Blacks, Hispanics and Asians." Paper presented at the annual meeting of the American Sociological Association, Cincinnati. August.

___ 1993. "Opposition to Race-Targeting: Self-Interest, Stratification Ideology, or Racial Attitudes?" *American Sociological Review* 58 (August):443–464.

Bogue, Donald J. 1985. *Population of the United States: Historical Trends and Future Projections*. New York: The Free Press.

Booner-Tompkins, Elaine. 1994. "A Changing Workforce and More Job Training Programs: Their Meaning for African Americans." *CBCF Policy Review* 1:1–9.

Boozer, Michael A., Alan B. Krueger, and Shari Wolkon. 1992. "Race and School Quality Since Brown v. Board of Education." *Brookings Papers: Microeconomics, 1992.*

Borjas, George J., Richard B. Freeman, and Kevin Lang. 1991. "Undocumented Mexican-Born Workers in the United States: How Many and How Permanent?" In *Immigration, Trade, and the Labor Market*. Edited by R. Freeman and J. Abowd. Chicago: University of Chicago Press and NBER.

Borjas, George J., Richard B. Freeman, and Lawrence F. Katz. 1989. "On the Labor Market Effects of Trade and Immigration." Harvard University, Department of Economics, unpublished.

Bound, John, and Richard B. Freeman. 1992. "What Went Wrong? The Erosion of Relative Earnings and Employment Among Young Black Men in the 1980s." *The Quarterly Journal of Economics* CVII(1, February):201–232.

Bound, John, and George Johnson. 1992. "Changes in the Structure of Wages in the 1980's: An Evaluation of Alternative Explanations." *The American Economic Review* 82(3, June):371–392.

Bradbury, Katherine L., Karl E. Case, and Constance R. Dunham. 1989. "Geographic Patterns of Mortgage Lending in Boston: 1982–1987." *New England Economic Review* (September/October):3–30.

Bradford, Calvin, and Gale Cincotta. 1992. "The Legacy, the Promise, and the Unfinished Agenda." In *From Redlining to Reinvestment: Community Responses to Urban Disinvestment* (pp. 228–286). Edited by Gregory D. Squires. Philadelphia: Temple University Press.

Brink, William, and Louis Harris. 1996. "Black and White: A Study of U.S. Racial Attitudes Today." New York: Simon & Schuster.

Brown-Scott, Wendy. 1994. "Race Consciousness in Higher Education: Does 'Sound Educational Policy' Support the Continued Existence of Historically Black Colleges?" *Emory Law Journal* 43(1, Winter):3–81.

Buchanan v. *Warley*. 1917. 245 U.S. 60.

Canot, Robert. 1974. *American Odyssey*. New York: Bantam Books.

Capeci, Dominic J., Jr. 1984. *Race Relations in Wartime Detroit: The Sojourner Truth Housing Controversy of 1942*. Philadelphia: Temple University Press.

Card, David, and Alan B. Krueger. 1992. "School Quality and Black-White Relative Earnings: A Direct Assessment." *The Quarterly Journal of Economics* CVII(1, February):151–200.

Carderelli, Albert P., and Jack McDevitt. 1994. "Crime and Public Safety in Boston: An Overview." In *Boston Update '94: A New Agenda for a New Century*. Edited by Joseph R. Barresi and Joseph S. Slavet. Boston: University of Massachusetts at Boston, McCormack Institute of Public Affairs. April.

Carr, James H., and Isaac F. Megbolugbe. 1993. "The Federal Reserve Bank of Boston Study on Mortgage Lending Revisited." Washington, D.C.: Federal National Mortgage Association, Office of Housing Research, Fannie Mae Working Paper.

Carter, Deborah, and Reginald Wilson. 1993. *Minorities in Higher Education*. Washington, D.C.: American Council on Education.

Carter, Robert L. 1993. "Thirty-Five Years Later: New Perspectives on Brown." In *Race in America: The Struggle for Equality* (pp. 83–96). Edited by Herbert Hill and James E. Jones, Jr. Madison: University of Wisconsin Press.

Chambers, Julius L. 1993. "*Brown* v. *Board of Education*." In *Race in America: The Struggle for Equality* (pp. 184–194). Edited by Herbert Hill and James E. Jones, Jr. Madison: University of Wisconsin Press.

Chicago Commission on Race Relations. 1922. *The Negro in Chicago: A Study of Race Relations and a Race Riot*. Chicago: University of Chicago Press.

Chong, Dennis. 1991. *Collective Action and the Civil Rights Movement*. Chicago: University of Chicago Press.

Clark, William A.V. 1986. "Residential Segregation in American Cities." *Population Research and Policy Review* 5:95–127.

___ 1988. "Understanding Residential Segregation in American Cities: Interpreting the Evidence; Reply to Galster." *Population Research and Policy Review* 7:113–121.

___ 1989. "Residential Segregation in American Cities: Common Ground and Differences in Interpretation." *Population Research and Policy Review* 8:193–197.

___ 1991. "Residential Preferences and Neighborhood Racial Segregation: A Test of the Schelling Segregation Model." *Demography* 28(1):1–19.

Coale, Ansley J., and Norfleet Rives. 1973. "A Statistical Recontruction of the Black Population of the United States 1880–1970: Estimates of the Numbers by Age and Sex, Birth Rates and Total Fertility." *Population Index*.

Coale, Ansley J., and Melvin Zelnik. 1963. *New Estimates of Fertility and Population in the United States*. Princeton: Princeton University Press.

Committee on Civil Rights. 1947. *To Secure These Rights.* Washington, D.C.: U.S. Government Printing Office.

Corrigan v. *Buckley.* 1926. 271 U.S. 323.

Cotton, Jeremiah. 1990. "The Gap at the Top: Relative Occupational Earnings Disadvantage of the Black Male Middle Class." *Review of Black Political Economy* 18(3, Winter):21–38.

Cruse, Harold. 1987. *Plural But Equal: Blacks and Minorities in America's Plural Society.* New York: William Morrow.

Dahl, Robert A. 1957. "The Concept of Power." *Behavioral Science* 2(3, July):201–215.

___ 1993. "Americans Struggle to Cope with a New Political Order That Works in Opaque and Mysterious Ways." *Public Affairs Report* 34(5, September):1–6. Berkeley: University of California Institute of Governmental Studies.

Darity, William A., Jr. 1980. "Illusions of Black Economic Progress." *Review of Black Political Economy* XX(2):153–168.

___ and Samuel L. Myers, Jr. 1980. "Changes in Black-White Income Inequality, 1968–78: A Decade of Progress?" *Review of Black Political Economy* XX(3):355–379.

Davidson, Chandler. 1992. "The Voting Rights Act: A Brief History." In *Controversies in Minority Voting* (pp. i–51). Edited by Bernard Grofman and Chandler Davidson. Washington, D.C.: The Brookings Institution.

Dentler, Robert A. 1991. "School Desegregation since Gunnar Myrdal's *American Dilemma.*" In *The Education of African-Americans* (pp. 27–50). Edited by Charles V. Willie, Antoine M. Garibaldi, and Wornie L. Reed. New York: Auburn House.

___ 1992. "The Los Angeles Riots of Spring 1992: Events, Causes, and Future Policy." *Sociological Practice Review* 3(4):229–244.

Donohue, John H., III, and James Heckman. 1991. "Continuous Versus Episodic Change: The Impact of Civil Rights Policy on the Economic Status of Blacks." *Journal of Economic Literature* XXIX(4, December):1603–1643.

Dossey, John A., Ina V.S. Mullis, Mary M. Lindquist, and Donald L. Chambers. 1988. "The Mathematics Report Card: Are We Measuring Up? Trends and Achievement Based on the 1986 National Assessment." Princeton: National Assessment of Educational Progress at Educational Testing Service.

Drake, St. Clair. 1987. *Black Folk Here and There.* Volume 1. Los Angeles: Center for Afro-American Studies, University of California at Los Angeles.

Eblen, Jack. 1974. "New Estimates of Vital Rates of the United States Black Population During the 19th Century." *Demography* (May).

Edmonds, Patricia. 1991. "FBI Probe of Brutality Is Sought." *Detroit Free Press* (March 13):4A.

Edsall, Thomas B. 1992. "Two Steps Forward, One Step Backlash." *Washington Post National Weekly Edition* (May 11–17):10.

Ellison, Ralph. 1973. "An American Dilemma: A Review." In *The Death of White Sociology* (pp. 81–95). Edited by Joyce A. Ladner. New York: Vintage Books.

Everett, David. 1992. "Confrontation, Negotiation, and Collaboration: Detroit Multibillion Dollar Deal." In *From Redlining to Reinvestment: Community Responses to Urban Disinvestment* (pp. 109–132). Edited by Gregory D. Squires. Philadelphia: Temple University Press.

Farley, Reynolds. 1984. *Blacks and Whites: Narrowing the Gap?* Cambridge: Harvard University Press.

Farley, Reynolds, and Walter Allen. 1987. *The Color Line and the Quality of Life in America*. New York: Russell Sage Foundation.

Farley, Reynolds, and William H. Frey. 1994. "Changes in the Segregation of Whites from Blacks: Small Steps Toward a More Integrated Society." *American Sociological Review* 59(1, February):23–46.

Farley, Reynolds, Howard Schuman, Suzanne Bianchi, Diane Colasanto, and Shirley Hatchett. 1978. "Chocolate City, Vanilla Suburbs: Will the Trend toward Racially Separate Communities Continue?" *Social Science Research* 7:319–344.

Farley, Reynolds, Charlotte Steeh, Maria Krysan, Tara Jackson, and Keith Reeves. 1994. "Stereotypes and Segregation: Neighborhoods in the Detroit Area." *American Journal of Sociology* 100 (3, November):750–780.

___ 1995. "Shifting Challenges: Fifty Years of Economic Change Toward Black-White Earnings Equality." *Daedalus* (Winter).

Ferguson, Ronald F. 1991a. "Paying for Public Education: New Evidence on How and Why Money Matters." *Harvard Journal on Legislation* 28(1, Summer).

___ 1991b. "Racial Patterns in How School and Teacher Quality Affect Achievement and Earnings." *Challenge: A Journal of Research on Black Males* 2(1, May).

___ 1993. "New Evidence on the Growing Value of Skill and Consequences for Racial Disparity and Returns to Schooling." Working Paper No. H-93-10, Weiner Center for Social Policy, John F. Kennedy School of Government, Harvard University.

___ 1994. "How Professionals in Community Based Programs Perceive and Respond to the Needs of Black Male Youth." In *Nurturing Young Black Males*. Edited by Ronald B. Mincy. Washington, D.C.: The Urban Institute Press.

Ferguson, Ronald F., and Randall Filer. 1986. "Do Better Jobs Make Better Workers? Absenteeism from Work Among Inner-City Minority Youth." In *The Black Youth Employment Crisis*. Edited by R. Freeman and H. Holzer. Chicago: University of Chicago Press and NBER.

Ferguson, Ronald F., and Mary S. Jackson. 1994. "Black Male Youth and Drugs: How Racial Prejudice, Parents and Peers Affect Vulnerability." In *Drugs in America*. Edited by Peter J. Venturelli. Boston: Jones and Bartlett.

Fix, Michael, and Raymond J. Struyk, eds. 1993. *Clear and Convincing Evidence*. Washington, D.C.: The Urban Institute Press.

"40 Blacks Now in Congress Can Help Blacks Get Ahead." 1992. *Jet* (November 23):51 ff.

Franklin, John Hope. 1993. *The Color Line: Legacy for the Twenty-First Century*. Columbia: University of Missouri Press.

Franklin, V.P. 1992. *Black Self-Determination: A Cultural History of African American Resistance.* Brooklyn, N.Y.: Lawrence Hill Books.

Frey, William H. 1993. "Race, Class and Poverty across Metro Areas and States: Population Shifts and Migration Dynamics." Research Report No. 93-293. Ann Arbor: Population Studies Center, University of Michigan.

Frey, William H., and Reynolds Farley. 1993. "Latino, Asian, and Black Segregation in Multi-Ethnic Metro Areas: Findings from the 1990 Census." Research Report 93-278. Ann Arbor: University of Michigan, Population Studies Center.

Friedman, L.M. 1967. "Government and Slum Housing: Some General Considerations." *Law and Contemporary Society* 32:357–370.

Fyfe, James. 1981. "Race and Extreme Police-Citizen Violence." In *Race, Crime, and Criminal Justice* (pp. 89–108). Edited by R.L. McNelley and Carl E. Pope. Beverly Hills, Cal.: Sage Publications.

___ 1982. "Blind Justice: Police Shootings in Memphis." *Journal of Criminal Law and Criminology* 73:707–722.

Galster, George. 1986. "More Than Skin Deep: The Effect of Discrimination on the Extent and Pattern of Racial Residential Segregation." In *Housing Desegregation and Federal Policy.* Edited by John Goering. Chapel Hill: University of North Carolina Press.

___ 1988. "Residential Segregation in American Cities: A Contrary Review." *Population Research and Policy Review* 7:93–112.

___ 1990. "Racial Steering by Real Estate Agents: Mechanisms and Motivation." *Review of Black Political Economy* 19:39–63.

___ 1992. "Research on Discrimination in Housing and Mortgage Markets: Assessment and Further Directions." *Housing Policy Debate* 3(2):639–683.

Gatewood, Willard B. 1990. *Aristocrats of Color: The Black Elite—1880–1920.* Bloomington: Indiana University Press.

Giroux, H.A. 1992. *Border Crossings: Cultural Workers and the Politics of Education.* New York: Routledge & Kegan Paul, Ltd.

Gomes, Ralph C., and Linda Faye Williams, eds. 1992. *From Exclusion to Inclusion: The Long Struggle for African-American Political Power.* Westport, Conn.: Greenwood Press.

Good, David L. 1989. *Orvie: The Dictator of Dearborn. The Rise and Reign of Orville L. Hubbard.* Detroit: Wayne State University Press.

Green, Constance McLaughlin. 1967. *The Secret City: A History of Race Relations in the Nation's Capitol.* Princeton: Princeton University Press.

Grofman, Bernard. 1992. "Expert Witness Testimony and the Evolution of Voting Rights Case Law." In *Controversies in Minority Voting* (pp. 197–229). Edited by Bernard Grofman and Chandler Davidson. Washington, D.C.: The Brookings Institution.

Guinier, Lani. 1992. "Voting Rights and Democratic Theory: Where Do We Go from Here?" In *Controversies in Minority Voting* (pp. 283–291). Edited by Bernard Grofman and Chandler Davidson. Washington, D.C.: The Brookings Institution.

Hacker, Andrew. 1992. *Two Nations: Black and White, Separate, Hostile, Unequal.* New York: Ballantine Books.

Hare, Bruce R. 1991. "Toward Effective Desegregated Schools." In *College in Black and White: African American Students in Predominantly White and in Historically Black Public Universities* (pp. 211–224). Edited by W.R. Allen, E.G. Epps, and N.Z. Haniff. Albany: State University of New York Press.

Hechter, Michael. 1974. *Internal Colonialism.* Berkeley: University of California Press.

Hirsch, Arnold R. 1983. *Making the Second Ghetto: Race and Housing in Chicago: 1940–1960.* Chicago: University of Chicago Press.

Hodginson, Harold. 1990. "Policy Analysis" in Report on *A Workforce Diversity Converence: Moving Minorities From Despair to Hope.* Atlanta: Clark Atlanta University and U.S. Department of Labor.

Hollman, Frederick W. 1993. "U.S. Population Estimates by Age, Sex, Race, and Hispanic Origin: 1980 to 1991." U.S. Bureau of the Census, Current Population Reports, P25-1095 Washington, D.C.: U.S. Government Printing Office.

Hughes, Langston. 1993. *The Big Sea.* New York: Hill and Wang. (Originally published in 1940.)

Jackson, Kenneth. 1985. *Crabgrass Frontier: The Suburbanization of the United States.* New York: Oxford University Press.

Jackson, Walter A. 1990. *Gunnar Myrdal and America's Conscience: Social Engineering and Racial Liberalism.* Chapel Hill: University of North Carolina Press.

James, Franklin J., and Steven W. DelCastillo. 1992. "Measuring Job Discrimination: Hopeful Evidence from Recent Audits." *Harvard Journal of African American Public Policy* 1:33–54.

Jaynes, Gerald D., and Robin M. Williams, Jr., eds. 1989. *A Common Destiny: Blacks and American Society.* Washington, D.C.: National Academy Press.

Jencks, Christopher. 1979. *Who Gets Ahead? The Determinants of Economic Success in America.* New York: Basic Books.

Johnson, Charles S. 1943. *Patterns of Negro Segregation.* New York: Harper and Bros.

Jones, Jacqueline. 1980. *Soldiers of Light and Love: Northern Teachers and Georgia Blacks, 1865–1873.* Chapel Hill: University of North Carolina Press.

Juhn, Chinhui, Kevin M. Murphy, and Brooks Pierce. 1991. "Accounting for the Slowdown in Black-White Wage Convergence." In *Workers and Their Wages: Changing Patterns in the United States.* Edited by Marvin H. Kosters. Washington, D.C.: American Enterprise Institute Press.

Katz, Lawrence F., and Kevin M. Murphy. 1992. "Changes in Relative Wages, 1963–1987: Supply and Demand Factors." *The Quarterly Journal of Economics* CVII(1, February):35–78.

Keating, Larry E., Lynn M. Brazen, and Stan F. Fitterman. 1992. "Reluctant Response to Community Pressure in Atlanta." In *From Redlining to Reinvestment: Community Responses to Urban Disinvestment* (pp. 170–193). Edited by Gregory D. Squires. Philadelphia: Temple University Press.

Kellogg, John. 1977. "Negro Urban Clusters in the Postbellum South." *Geographical Review* 67:310–321.

King, Martin Luther, Jr. 1967. *Where Do We Go from Here: Chaos or Community?* Boston: Beacon Press.

Kirschenman, Joleen, and Kathryn M. Neckerman. 1991. "'We'd Love to Hire Them But . . .': The Meaning of Race for Employers." In *The Urban Underclass.* Edited by Christopher Jencks and Paul E. Peterson. Washington, D.C.: The Brookings Institution.

Krueger, Alan B. 1993. "How Computers Have Changed the Wage Structure: Evidence from Microdata, 1984–1989." *The Quarterly Journal of Economics* CVIII (1, February):33–60.

Kusmer, Kenneth L. 1976. *A Ghetto Takes Shape: Black Cleveland, 1870–1930.* Urbana: University of Illinois Press.

Lake, Robert W. 1981. *The New Suburbanites: Race and Housing in the Suburbs.* New Brunswick, N.J.: Center for Urban Policy, Rutgers University.

Lemann, Nicholas. 1991. *The Promised Land: The Great Black Migration and How It Changed America.* New York: Alfred A. Knopf.

Lemelle, Anthony J. 1993. "Review of *From Exclusion to Inclusion: The Long Struggle for African-American Political Power.*" *Contemporary Sociology* 22(1) (January 1993): 63.

Leonard, Jonathan, S. 1984a. "Anti-Discrimination or Reverse Discrimination: The Impact of Changing Demographics, Title VII, and Affirmative Action on Productivity." *Journal of Human Resources* 19(2, Spring):145–172.

___ 1984b. "Employment and Occupational Advance Under Affirmative Action." *Review of Economics and Statistics* 66(3):377–385.

___ 1990. "The Impact of Affirmative Action Regulation and Equal Employment Law on Black Employment." *Journal of Economic Perspectives* 4(4, Fall):47–64.

Levine, David Allan. 1976. *Internal Combustion: The Races in Detroit: 1915–1926.* Westport, Conn.: Greenwood Press.

Levy, Frank, and Richard Murnane. 1992. "U.S. Earnings Levels and Earnings Inequality: A Review of Recent Trends and Proposed Explanations." *Journal of Economic Literature.* XXX(September):1333–1381.

Lewis, David L. 1993. *W.E.B. DuBois: A Biography.* New York: Henry Holt.

Lusane, Clarence. 1992. "A Historic Moment: Black Votes and the 1992 Presidential Race." *Trotter Review* 6(2, Fall):8–10.

Marable, Manning. 1990. "A New Black Politics: We Must Rethink the Concept of Blackness Itself." *The Progressive* (August).

Massey, Douglas S., 1990. "American Apartheid: Segregation and the Making of the Underclass." *American Journal of Sociology* 96:329–57.

Massey, Douglas S. and Nancy A. Denton. 1987. "Trends in the Residential Segregation of Blacks, Hispanics and Asians." *American Sociological Review* 52:802–25.

___ 1993. *American Apartheid: Segregation and the Making of the Underclass.* Cambridge, Mass.: Harvard University Press.

Massey, Walter E. 1992. "Science, Technology and Human Resources: Preparing for the 21st Century" (pp. 157–170). In *The State of Black America 1992.* Edited by Billy J. Tidwell. New York: National Urban League, Inc.

Maxwell, Nan L. 1994. "The Effect on Black-White Wage Differences of Differences in the Quantity and Quality of Education." *Industrial and Labor Relations Review* 47(2, January):249–264.

McDonald, Laughlin. 1990. "The 1982 Amendments of Section 2 and Minority Representation." In *Controversies in Minority Voting* (pp. 66–84). Edited by Bernard Grofman and Chandler Davidson. Washington, D.C.: The Brookings Institution.

McEntire, Davis. 1960. *Residence and Race.* Berkeley: University of California Press.

McNeil, Genna Rae. 1983. *Groundwork: Charles Hamilton Houston and the Struggle for Civil Rights.* Philadelphia: University of Pennsylvania Press.

Metzger, John T. 1992. "The Community Reinvestment Act and Neighborhood Revitalization in Pittsburgh." In *From Redlining to Reinvestment: Community Responses to Urban Disinvestment* (pp. 73–108). Edited by Gregory D. Squires. Philadelphia: Temple University Press.

Milton, Catherine, Jeanne Wahl Halleck, James Lardner, and Gary Abrecht. 1977. *Police Use of Deadly Force.* Washington, D.C.: Police Foundation.

Mincy, Ronald B. 1990. "Preventive Strategies to Assist Young Black Males." Statement before the Congressional Subcommittee on Income, Jobs, and Prices, May 24.

___ 1994. *Nurturing Young Black Males.* Washington, D.C.: The Urban Institute Press.

Mishel, Lawrence, and Ruy A. Teixeira. 1991. "The Myth of the Coming Labor Shortage: Jobs, Skills, and Incomes of America's Workforce 2000." Washington, D.C.: Economic Policy Institute.

Moffitt, Robert, and Peter Gottschalk. 1993. "Trends in the Covariance Structure of Earnings in the United States: 1969–1987." Institute for Research on Poverty Discussion Paper No. 1001-93. Madison: University of Wisconsin.

Morris, Aldon. 1990. *Contemporary Sociology* 19(5):655.

Moss, Philip, and Chris Tilly. 1991. "Why Black Men Are Doing Worse in the Labor Market: A Review of Supply-Side and Demand-Side Explanations." New York: Social Science Research Council.

Mullis, Ina V.S., and Lynn B. Jenkins. 1990. "The Reading Report Card, 1971–1988 Trends from the Nation's Report Card." Princeton: National Assessment of Educational Progress at Educational Testing Service.

Munnell, Alicia H., Lynn E. Browne, James McEneaney, and Geoffrey M.B. Tootell. 1992. "Mortgage Lending in Boston: Interpreting HMDA Data." Working Paper 92-7. Boston: Federal Reserve Bank of Boston. October.

Murnane, Richard J., John B. Willett, and Frank Levy. 1994. "The Growing Importance of Cognitive Skills in Wage Determination." Unpublished paper.

Harvard University, Graduate School of Education (Murnane and Willett) and MIT (Levy).

Murphy, Kevin M., and Finis Welch. 1992. "The Structure of Wages." *The Quarterly Journal of Economics* CVII(1, February):285–326.

Myrdal, Gunnar, with the assistance of Richard Sterner and Arnold Rose. 1944. An *American Dilemma: The Negro Problem and Modern Democracy*. New York and London: Harper & Brothers.

___ 1962. *An American Dilemma: The Negro Problem and Modern Democracy*. Twentieth anniversary edition. New York, Evanston, and London: Harper & Row.

NAACP. 1968. "NAACP Acts in New York School Crisis." *The Crisis* 75(10, December):362–363.

National Advisory Commission on Civil Disorders. 1968. *Report of the National Advisory Commission on Civil Disorders*. New York: Bantam Books.

National Opinion Research Center. Various years. *General Social Surveys*.

Neal, Derek A., and William R. Johnson. 1994. "The Role of Pre-Market Factors in Black-White Wage Differences." Unpublished. University of Chicago (Neal) and University of Virginia (Johnson).

Ogbu, John. 1978. *Minority Education and Caste: The American System in Cross-Cultural Perspective*. New York: Academic Press.

O'Neill, June. 1990. "The Role of Human Capital in Earnings Differences Between Black and White Men." *Journal of Economic Perspectives* 4(4, Fall):25–45.

Orfield, Gary. 1993. "School Desegregation After Two Generations: Race, Schools and Opportunity in Urban Society." In *Race in America: The Struggle for Equality* (pp. 234–262). Edited by Herbert Hill and James E. Jones, Jr. Madison: University of Wisconsin Press.

Pearce, Diana. 1979. "Gatekeepers and Homeseekers: Institutionalized Patterns in Racial Steering." *Social Problems* 26 (February):325–342.

Peltason, Jack. 1961. *Fifty-eight Lonely Men: Southern Judges and School Desegregation*. Chicago: University of Illinois Press.

Pinkney, Alphonso. 1984. *The Myth of Black Progress*. New York: Cambridge University Press.

Plessy v. *Ferguson*. 1896. 163 U.S. 537.

Rabinowitz, Howard N. 1976. *Race Relations in the Urban South: 1865–1890*. New York: Oxford University Press.

Rainwater, Lee. 1970. *Behind Ghetto Walls: Black Family Life in a Federal Slum*. Chicago: Aldine.

Rex, John, and David Mason, eds. 1986. *Theories of Race and Race Relations*. Cambridge: Cambridge University Press.

Ringer, Benjamin B. 1983. *We the People and Others*. New York: Tavistock Institute Press.

Ringer, Benjamin B., and Elinor R. Lawless. 1989. *Race, Ethnicity and Society*. New York: Routledge & Kegan Paul.

Robinson, Gregory, Bashir Ahmed, Prighwis Das Gupta, Karen Woodrow. 1993. "Estimates of Population Coverage in the 1990 United States Census Based on Demographic Analysis." *Journal of the American Statistical Association* (September).

Rodgers, William M., III. 1993a. "Black-White Wage Gaps, 1979–1991: A Distributional Analysis." Unpublished paper. Harvard University. Draft of chapter from dissertation.

Schumann, Howard, Charlotte Steeh, and Lawrence Bobo. 1985. *Racial Attitudes in America: Trends and Interpretations.* Cambridge: Harvard University Press.

Sherman, Lawrence. 1979. "Measuring Homicide by Police Officers." *Journal of Criminal Law and Criminology* 70:546–460.

___ 1980. "Execution Without Trial: Police Homicide and the Constitution." *Vanderbilt Law Review* 33:71–100.

Siegel, Jacob. 1974. "Estimates of Coverage of the Population by Sex, Race, and Age in the 1970 Census." *Demography* (February).

Sigelman, Lee, Susan Welch, Timothy Bledsoe, and Michael Combs. 1994. "The Impact of Police Brutality on Public Attitudes: A Tale of Two Beatings." Unpublished paper.

Smith, James P., and Finis R. Welch. 1986. *Closing the Gap: Forty Years of Economic Progress for Blacks.* Santa Monica, Cal.: The Rand Corporation.

___ 1989. "Black Economic Progress After Myrdal." *Journal of Economic Literature* XXVII(2, June):519–564.

Spear, Allan H. 1967. *Black Chicago: The Making of a Negro Ghetto: 1890–1920.* Chicago: University of Chicago Press.

Squires, Gregory D., Larry Bennett, Kathleen McCourt, and Philip Nyden. 1987. *Chicago: Race, Class, and the Response to Urban Decline.* Philadelphia: Temple University Press.

Steeh, Charlotte. 1993. "Sampling Report from the 1992 Detroit Area Study." Ann Arbor: Detroit Area Study, University of Michigan.

Steele, Calude M. 1992. "Race and Schooling of Black Americans." *The Atlantic Monthly* (November).

Thomas, Richard W. 1992. *Life for Us Is What We Make It: Building Black Community in Detroit: 1915–1945.* Bloomington: Indiana University Press.

Thornton, Russel, and Joan Marsh-Thornton. 1981. "Estimating Prehistoric American Indian Population Size for United States Area: Implication for the Nineteenth Century Population Decline and Nadir." *American Journal of Physical Anthropology.*

Turner, Margery Austin, Raymond L. Stryk, and John Yinger. 1991. *Housing Discrimination Study: Synthesis.* Washington, D.C.: U.S. Department of Housing and Urban Development.

U.S. Bureau of the Census. 1943. *Sixteenth Census of the United States: 1940, Housing.* Volume II, Part 1. Washington, D.C.: U.S. Government Printing Office.

___ 1979. *The Social and Economic Status of the Black Population in the United States: An Historical View, 1790–1978.* Washington, D.C.: U.S. Government Printing Office.

___ 1983. *1980 Census of Population: General Social and Economic Characteristics—United States Summary.* Washington, D.C.: U.S. Government Printing Office.

___ 1989. *Statistical Abstract of the United States: 1989.* 109th Edition. Washington, D.C.: U.S. Government Printing Office.

___ 1991. *The Hispanic Population in the United States: March 1990. Current Population Reports.* Washington, D.C.: U.S. Government Printing Office.

___ 1992. *The Black Population in the United States: March 1991. Current Population Reports*, Series P20-464, September 1992. Washington, D.C.: U.S. Government Printing Office.

___ 1993. *The Black Population in the United States, March 1992.* By Claudette Bennett. Washington, D.C.: Bureau of the Census.

___ 1993. *Census of Population and Housing: 1990.* Public Use Microdata Sample. Washington, D.C.: U.S. Government Printing Office.

___ 1993. *1990 Census of Population: Social and Economic Characteristics—United States.* Washington, D.C.: U.S. Government Printing Office.

___ 1993. *Statistical Abstract of the United States: 1992.* 112th Edition. Washington, D.C.: U.S. Government Printing Office.

U.S. v. *City of Parma.* 1981. 494 F. Supp. 1049.

U.S. Commission on Civil Rights. 1975. *The Voting Rights Act: Ten Years After.* Washington, D.C.: U.S. Government Printing Office.

___ 1986. *The Economic Progress of Black Men in America.* Washington, D.C.: U.S. Government Printing Office.

U.S. Reports. Supreme Court Decisions, 1939–1982.

Vose, Clement E. 1959. *Caucasians Only: The Supreme Court, the NAACP and the Restrictive Covenant Cases.* Berkeley: University of California Press.

Webber, Thomas L. 1978. *Deep Like the Rivers: Education in the Slave Quarter Community, 1831–1865.* New York: W.W. Norton.

Webster, David S., Russell L. Stockard, and James W. Henson. 1981. "Black Student Elite: Enrollment Shifts of High-Achieving, High Socio-Economic Status Black Students from Black to White Colleges During the 1970's." *College and University* (Spring):283–291.

Willette, JoAnne, Robert Haupt, Carl Haub, Leon Bouvier, and Cary Davis. 1982. "The Demographic and Socioeconomic Characteristics of the Hispanic Population in the United States: 1950–1980." Report to the Department of Health and Human Services by Development Associates, Inc. and Population Reference Bureau, Inc. (January 18), Table 1–2.

Willingham, Alex. 1992. "Voting Policy and Voter Participation: The Legacy of the 1980s." *Trotter Review* 6(2, Fall):24–28.

Wilson, William Julius. 1978. *The Declining Significance of Race: Blacks and Changing American Institutions.* Chicago: University of Chicago Press.

___ 1990. "Race-Neutral Policies and the Democratic Coalition." *The American Prospect* 1 (Spring).

Winter, William. 1990. "Luncheon Speech" (pp. 9–11). In *Report on A Workforce Diversity Conference: Moving Minorities From Despair to Hope.* Atlanta: Clark Atlanta University and U.S. Department of Labor.

Yinger, John. 1986. "Measuring Racial Discrimination with Fair Housing Audits: Caught in the Act." *American Economic Review* 76(5, December):881–893.

___ 1991. *Housing Discrimination Study: Incidence and Variation in Discriminatory Behavior.* Washington, D.C.: Department of Housing and Urban Development. Office of Policy Development and Research.

Zunz, Oliver. 1982. *The Changing Face of Inequality: Urbanization, Industrial Development, and Immigrants in Detroit, 1880–1920.* Chicago: University of Chicago Press.

Index

Boldface numbers refer to tables.

315

tional specialization, 60–62. *See also* residential segregation
Houston, Charles Hamilton, 182
Howard University, 4, 5, 16
HUD. *See* Department of Housing and Urban Development
Hughes, Langston, 47
human capital, concept of, 120
Humphrey, Hubert, 14

illiteracy rates, 170, **173–74**. *See also* literacy
immigration, 270–71, 273, 276–83; and the ascension of immigrants, mythology of, 128–29; and assimilation, 180–81, 185, 186, 269, 281–83; and the classification of immigrants as foreign, 270–71, 277–81; and entrepreneurs, 142–43, 159; illegal, 277; impact of, on the labor market, 91, 103, 282–83; legal, by region of last residence, **278**; quotas, 277; and residential segregation, 46. *See also* migration
incarceration, 98, 99–100. *See also* prisons
income. *See* earnings
India, 21
inflation, 123
Ingelstam, Lars, xix
Institute for Future Studies, 20
intelligence, xxiv, 118. *See also* tests
intermarriage, 281–82, 283
IQ tests, 118
Italians, 143
Italy, 21, 47

Jackson, Jesse, 33, 37, 43
Jackson, Walter A., 1–2, 7–8, 10–22
Janowitz, Morris, 160, 161
Japan, 21, 125, 150
Japanese Americans, 13, 143, 146, 150–51, 271. *See also* Asians
Jaynes, David, 25, 30, 38, 41
Jessup, Walter, 10
Jesus Christ, 204
Jewell, Joseph O., xxvi, 169–90
Jews, 13, 42, 128–29, 131; and the black church, 197, 204, 205; and entrepreneurship, 142, 144, 146, 159; and the Nation of Islam, 204; patterns of adjustment

among, 144; and residential segregation, 46, 48, 50–51
Jim Crow laws, xxv, 199, 146, 291, 296; and education, 187; and residential segregation, 46, 50, 54; and the role of the police, 226–27, 229, 237
Johnson, Charles S., xii, 5, 47
Johnson, Lyndon B., 15–17, 30, 92–93; election of, as president, 33; Executive Order 11246, 92, 103; Kerner Commission created by (National Advisory Commission on Civil Disorders), 17, 211–13, 216–22, 225n17; War on Poverty initiated by, 16–17, 201
Johnson Publishing, 156
Johnson v. Zerbst, 249
Jones v. Alfred H. Mayer, 51
Jordan, Vernon, 41
jury selection, 247, 251–54, 261
justice system, 209–68; and caste structure, 227, 229–30, 232–34, 237; and the death penalty, 247, 257–58, 260, 295; and the Kerner Commission, 211 (National Advisory Commission on Civil Disorders), 17, 211–13, 216–22, 225n17; and levels of education, 210, 236, 237; in the 1940s, 209–13. *See also* courts; police

Kennedy, John F., 14–15, 33, 51
Keppel, Frederick, xi–xii, 2–4, 10
Kerner, Otto, 212
Kerner Commission (National Advisory Commission on Civil Disorders), 17, 211–13, 216–22, 225n17
King, Ed, 193
King, Martin Luther, Jr., xix, 15, 39–40; assassination of, 17, 51; on the "cost of change," 35; "I Have a Dream" speech, 14; "Letter from a Birmingham Jail," 198; protests lead by, 29; rise of, Clayton on, 200–201
King, Rodney, 213, 217–18, 224n12, 226
Klineberg, Otto, xii, 5
Kluegel, James, 185, 270
Koreans, 142, 144, 148. *See also* Asians
Korean War, 162, 295
Krueger, A., 81–84, 87
Ku Klux Klan, 29